Dream's End ™

Book 15a in the *ELFQUEST* Reader's Collection

Poughkeepsie
New York

Dream's End

Reprinting **Elfquest: New Blood**
comic book issue numbers 20 through 27

Story by
Barry Blair and Richard Pini

Art by
Art by Barry Blair and Colin Chan

About the ELFQUEST Reader's Collection

The twenty year — and ongoing — saga that is Elfquest has been told in many different comic book titles. The Elfquest Reader's Collection is our attempt to collect all the core stories in book form, so that readers new and old can follow the entire tale from its beginnings on up to the most recent work.

#1 - *Fire and Flight*
#2 - *The Forbidden Grove*
#3 - *Captives of Blue Mountain*
#4 - *Quest's End*
The story of Cutter, chief of the Wolfriders, and his tribe as they confront the perils of their primitive world, encounter new races of elves, and embark on a grand and dangerous quest to unveil the secret of their past.

#5 - *Siege at Blue Mountain*
#6 - *The Secret of Two-Edge*
The adventures of the Wolfriders some years after the end of the first quest, as they face the machinations of a villainess from their past and her enigmatic half-elf, half-troll son.

#7 - *The Cry from Beyond*
#8 - *Kings of the Broken Wheel*
The Wolfriders face their most daunting challenge when one of their number kidnaps Cutter's mate and children into future time, to prevent the accident that first brought the elves to this world.

#8a - *Dreamtime*
The visions of the Wolfriders as they slept for ten thousand years, waiting for the time when Cutter and his family can be united once more.

#9 - *Rogue's Curse*
Tales of Rayek, the magic-user, who carries within him the strangest wyrd imaginable.

#9a - *Wolfrider*
The tale of Cutter's sire Bearclaw, and how he brought two things to the Wolfriders — the enmity of humans and a monstrous tragedy, and a chief's son like no elf the tribe had ever known.

#9b - *Blood of Ten Chiefs*
Stories from the dark and wild past of the Wolfrider tribe and the chiefs that led up to Cutter's time.

#9c - *Kahvi*
The wild tale of the reckless chieftess of the Go-Back tribe, and of an incredible secret hidden in the ancient past.

#10 - *Shards*
#11 - *Legacy*
#11a - *Huntress*
#11b - *Wild Hunt*
#11c - *Shadowstalker*
#12 - *Ascent*
#12a - *Reunion*
Cutter and family are together again, but now a ruthless human warlord threatens the elves' very existence. The Wolfriders must become two tribes — one to fight a terrible war, the other to flee to ensure that the tribe continues. Volume #10 sets the stage; volumes #11, #11a, #11b and #11c follow Cutter's daughter Ember as she leads the Wild Hunt elves into new lands; volumes #12 and #12a take Cutter and his warriors into the flames of battle.

#13 - *The Rebels*
#13a - *Skyward Shadow*
#14 - *Jink!*
#14a - *Mindcoil*
In the far future of the World of Two Moons, human civilization has covered the planet — and the elves have disappeared. Where did they go? Volumes #13 and #13a follows a group of young adventurers as they seek the answer. Volumes #14 and #14a tell the story of a mysterious woman who is more than she seems — for she may be the last surviving descendant of the missing elves.

#15 - *Forevergreen*
#15a - *Dream's End*
#15b - *Phoenix*
Dart, Windkin and their companions follow Cutter's son Suntop out from Sorrow's End, far south to the mysterious rainforest called The Forevergreen. Here, the elves hope to find a new sanctuary for their kind, but they may have stumbled into a fatal trap instead.

#16 - *WaveDancers*
Not all the elves who survived the crash of the Palace of the High Ones made home on the land. Some took to the oceans of the World of Two Moons, where these mer-elves struggle to the present day against both nature and humankind.

#? - *Worldpool*
Tales from the place where the World of Two Moons meets the world of "what if?"

Dream's End

Book 15a in the *ELFQUEST* **Reader's Collection**

Published by Warp Graphics, Inc.
under its Wolfrider Books imprint.

515 Haight Avenue
Poughkeepsie, New York 12603

ISBN 0-936861-65-7
Printed in USA

www.elfquest.com

FOREVERGREEN

PART EIGHT

DRUM BEATS AND VOICES RAISED IN SONG ECHO ACROSS THE STILL WATERS OF THE RIVER KNOWN AS "HIGH ONE'S TEARS."

HUMANS -- OUTCASTS AND REBELS WHO HAVE QUIT THE LOST CITY OF THE HOAN-G'TAY-SHO -- CELEBRATE THEIR NEW-FOUND FRIENDS.

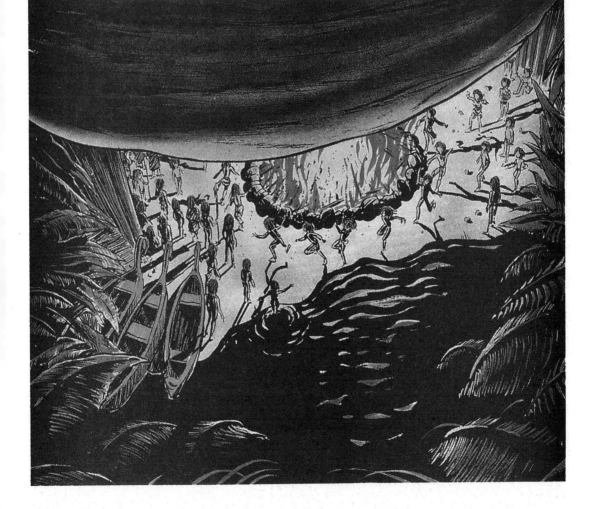

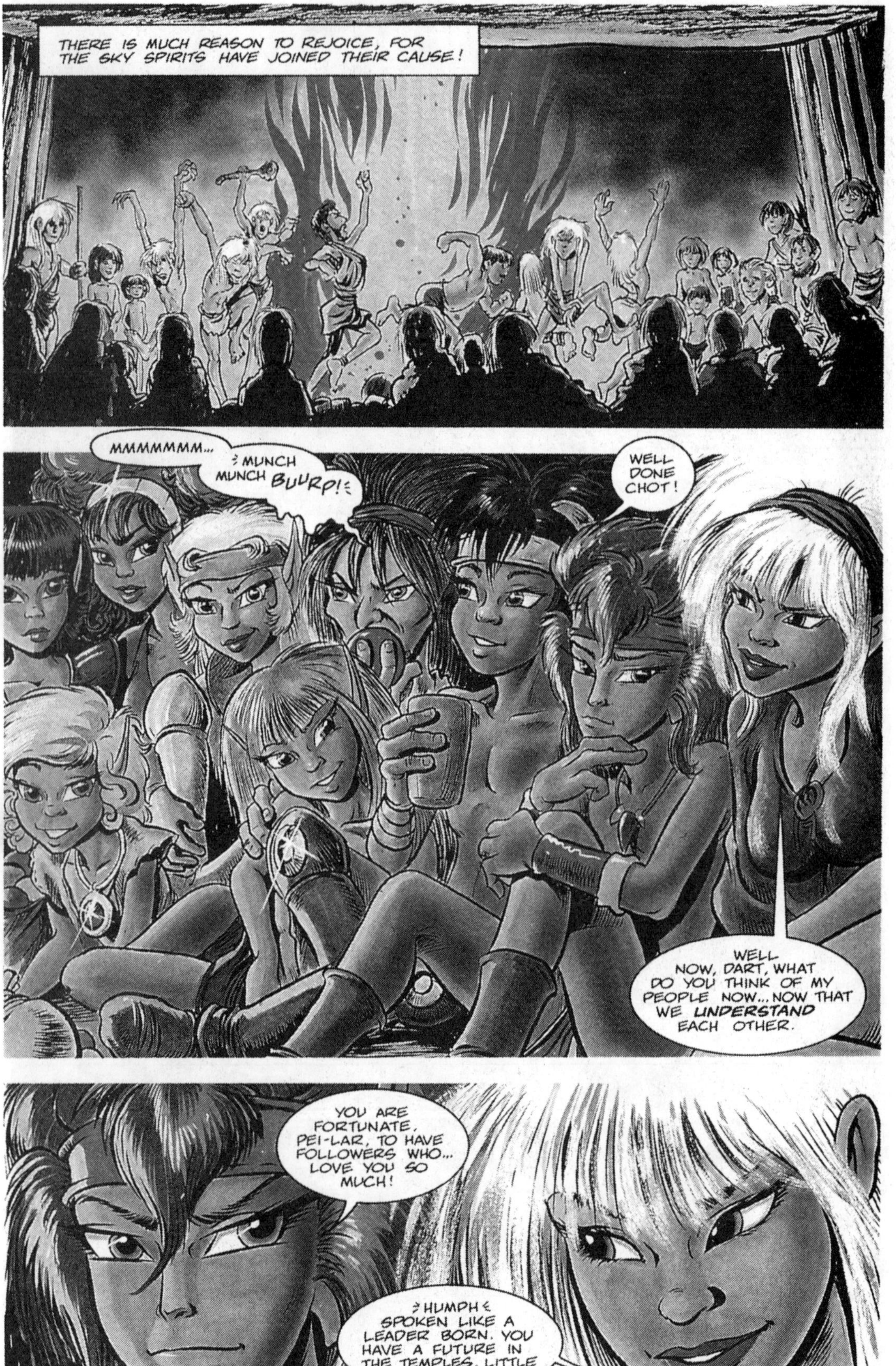
THERE IS MUCH REASON TO REJOICE, FOR THE SKY SPIRITS HAVE JOINED THEIR CAUSE!
MMMMMMM...
MUNCH MUNCH BUURP!
WELL DONE CHOT!
WELL NOW, DART, WHAT DO YOU THINK OF MY PEOPLE NOW... NOW THAT WE UNDERSTAND EACH OTHER.
YOU ARE FORTUNATE, PEI-LAR, TO HAVE FOLLOWERS WHO... LOVE YOU SO MUCH!
HUMPH
SPOKEN LIKE A LEADER BORN. YOU HAVE A FUTURE IN THE TEMPLES, LITTLE SPIRIT!

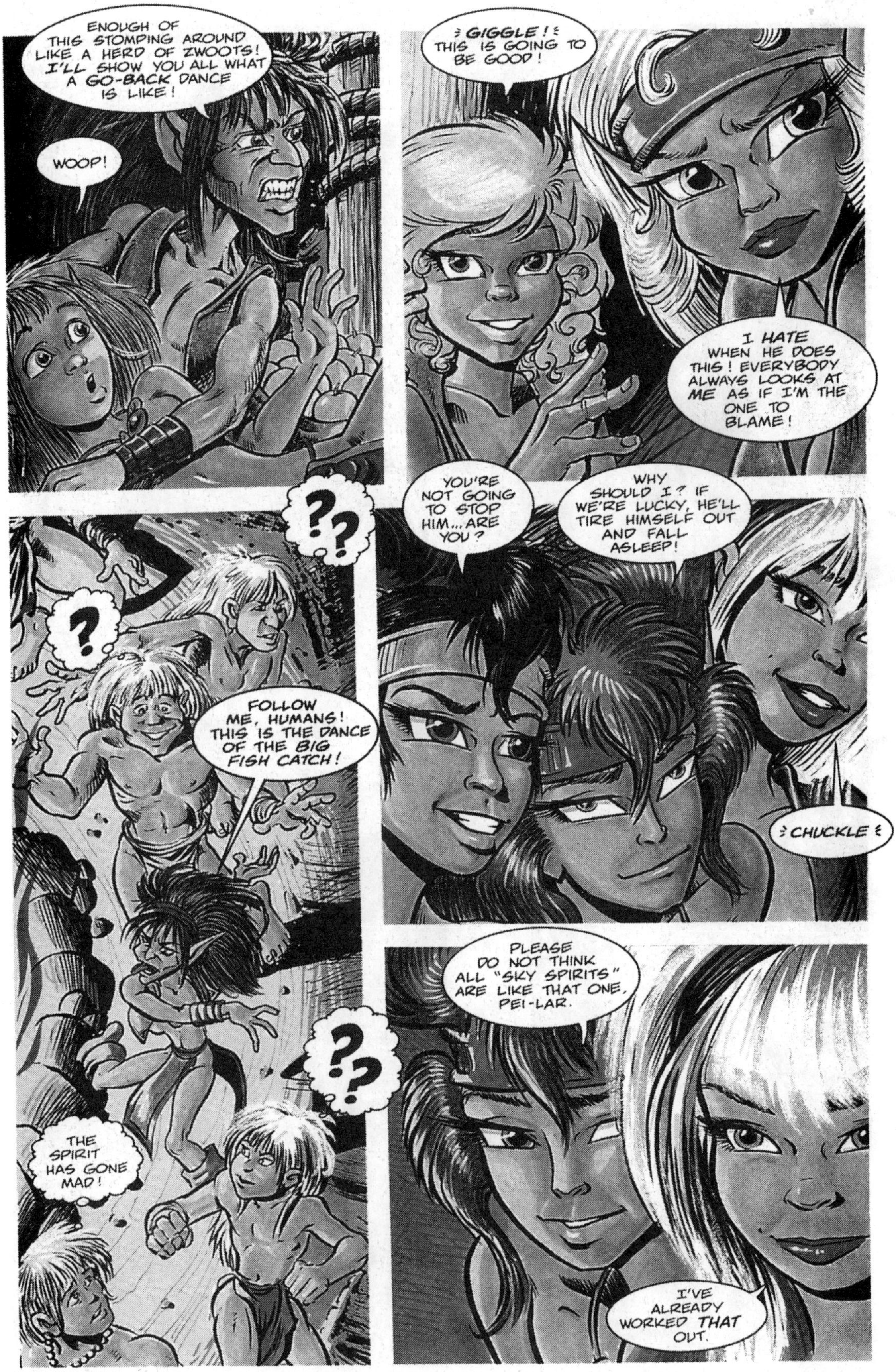
ENOUGH OF THIS STOMPING AROUND LIKE A HERD OF ZWOOTS! I'LL SHOW YOU ALL WHAT A GO-BACK DANCE IS LIKE!
WOOP!
GIGGLE! THIS IS GOING TO BE GOOD!
I HATE WHEN HE DOES THIS! EVERYBODY ALWAYS LOOKS AT ME AS IF I'M THE ONE TO BLAME!
??
?
FOLLOW ME, HUMANS! THIS IS THE DANCE OF THE BIG FISH CATCH!
??
THE SPIRIT HAS GONE MAD!
YOU'RE NOT GOING TO STOP HIM... ARE YOU?
WHY SHOULD I? IF WE'RE LUCKY, HE'LL TIRE HIMSELF OUT AND FALL ASLEEP!
CHUCKLE
PLEASE DO NOT THINK ALL "SKY SPIRITS" ARE LIKE THAT ONE, PEI-LAR.
I'VE ALREADY WORKED THAT OUT.

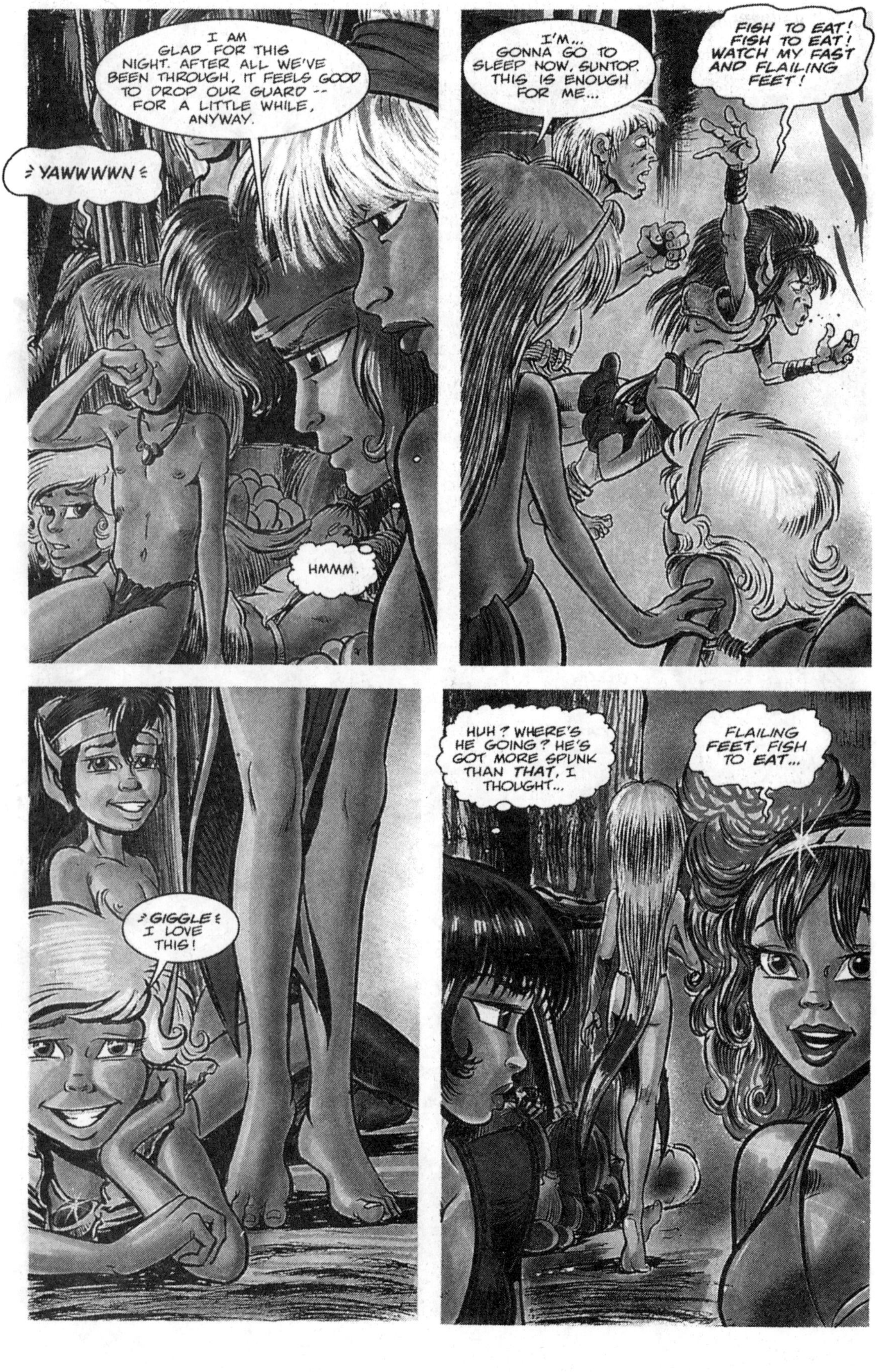
I AM GLAD FOR THIS NIGHT. AFTER ALL WE'VE BEEN THROUGH, IT FEELS GOOD TO DROP OUR GUARD -- FOR A LITTLE WHILE, ANYWAY.
YAWWWWN
HMMM.
I'M... GONNA GO TO SLEEP NOW, SUNTOP. THIS IS ENOUGH FOR ME...
FISH TO EAT! FISH TO EAT! WATCH MY FAST AND FLAILING FEET!
GIGGLE I LOVE THIS!
HUH? WHERE'S HE GOING? HE'S GOT MORE SPUNK THAN THAT, I THOUGHT...
FLAILING FEET, FISH TO EAT...

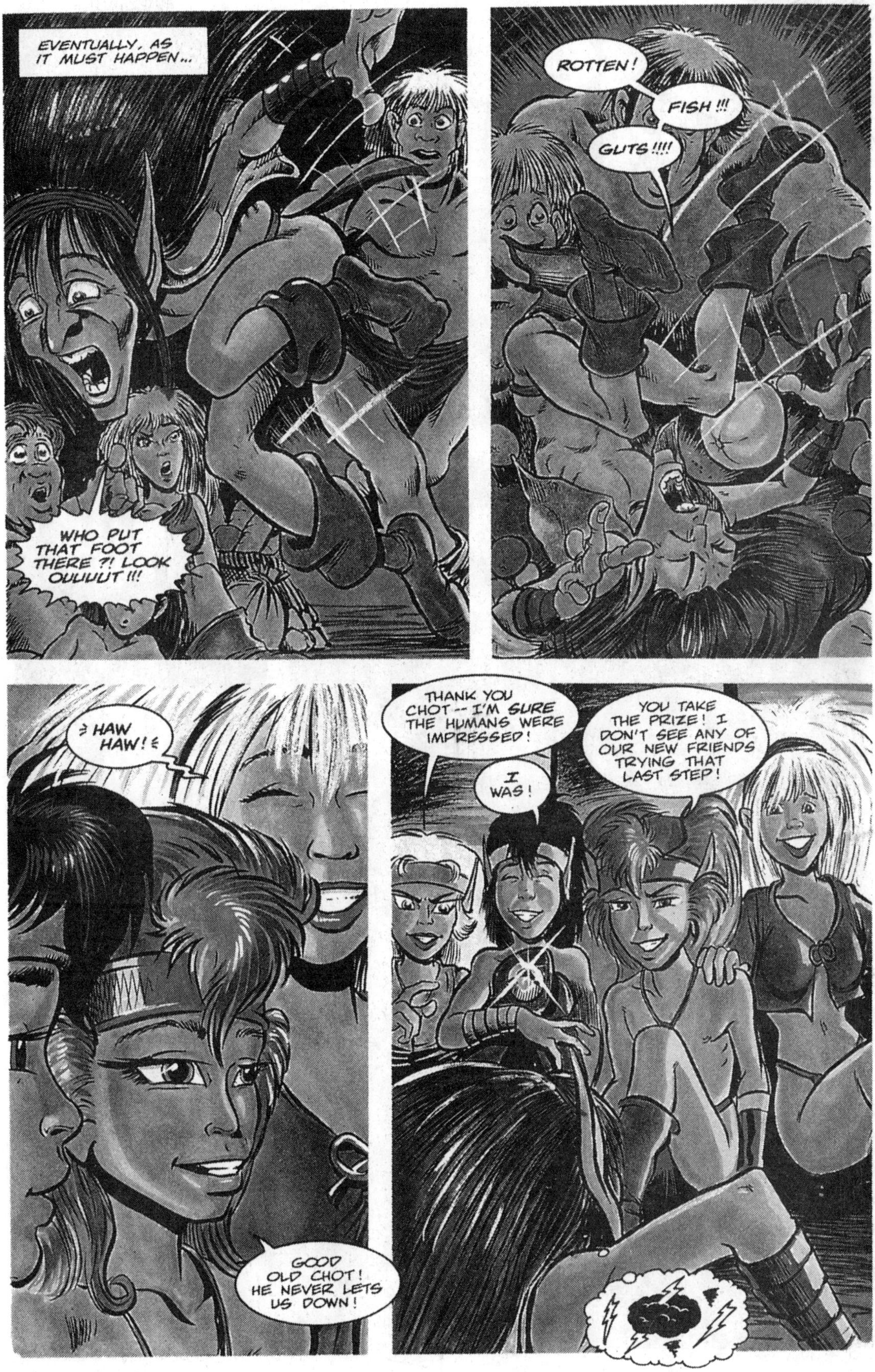
EVENTUALLY, AS IT MUST HAPPEN...
WHO PUT THAT FOOT THERE ?! LOOK OUUUUT !!!
ROTTEN!
FISH !!!
GUTS !!!!
HAW HAW!
GOOD OLD CHOT! HE NEVER LETS US DOWN!
THANK YOU CHOT -- I'M SURE THE HUMANS WERE IMPRESSED!
I WAS!
YOU TAKE THE PRIZE! I DON'T SEE ANY OF OUR NEW FRIENDS TRYING THAT LAST STEP!

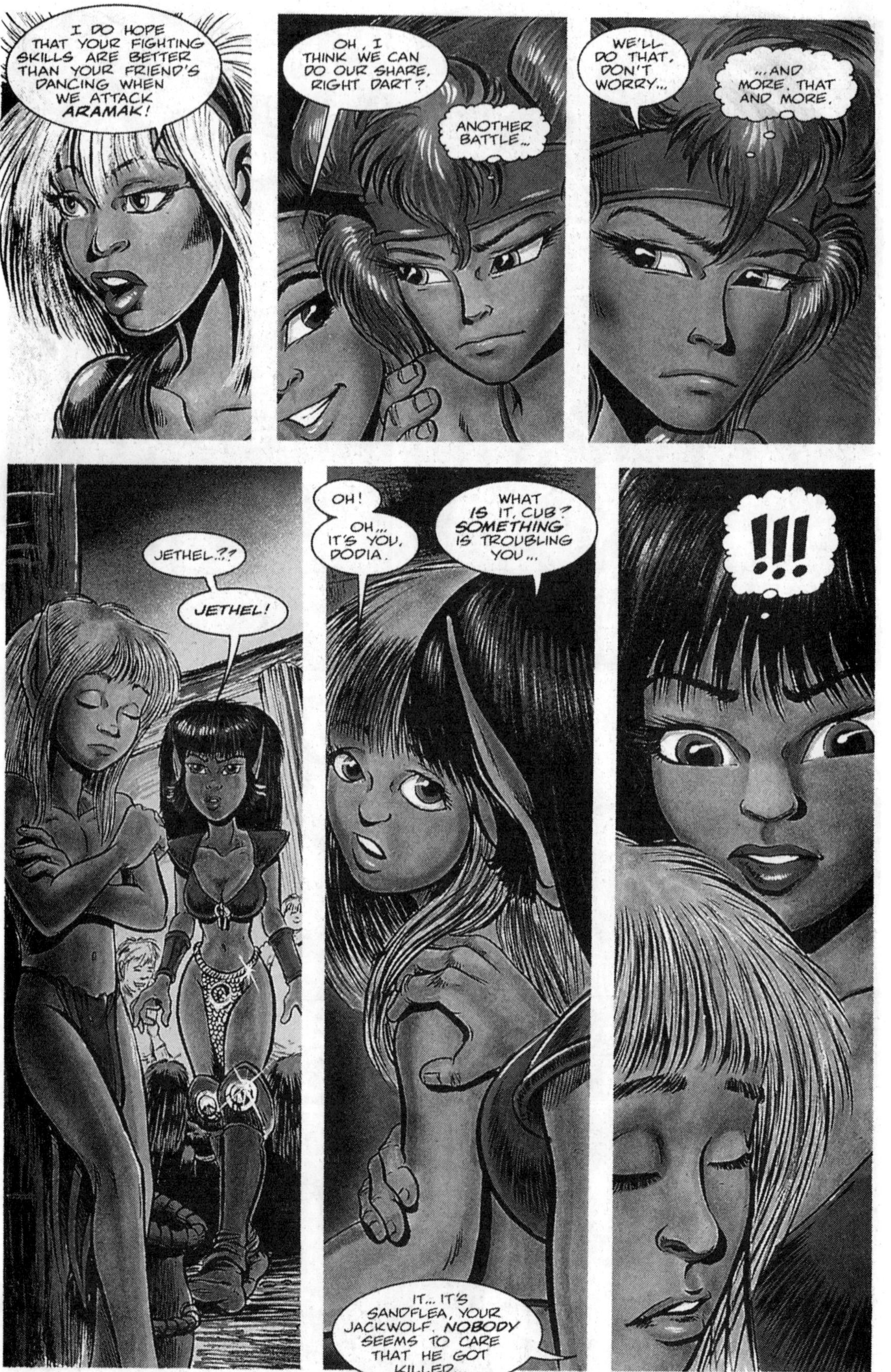
I DO HOPE THAT YOUR FIGHTING SKILLS ARE BETTER THAN YOUR FRIEND'S DANCING WHEN WE ATTACK ARAMAK!
OH, I THINK WE CAN DO OUR SHARE, RIGHT DART?
ANOTHER BATTLE...
WE'LL DO THAT, DON'T WORRY...
...AND MORE. THAT AND MORE.
JETHEL?!?
JETHEL!
OH!
OH... IT'S YOU, DODIA.
WHAT IS IT, CUB? SOMETHING IS TROUBLING YOU...
IT... IT'S SANDFLEA, YOUR JACKWOLF. NOBODY SEEMS TO CARE THAT HE GOT KILLED...
!!!

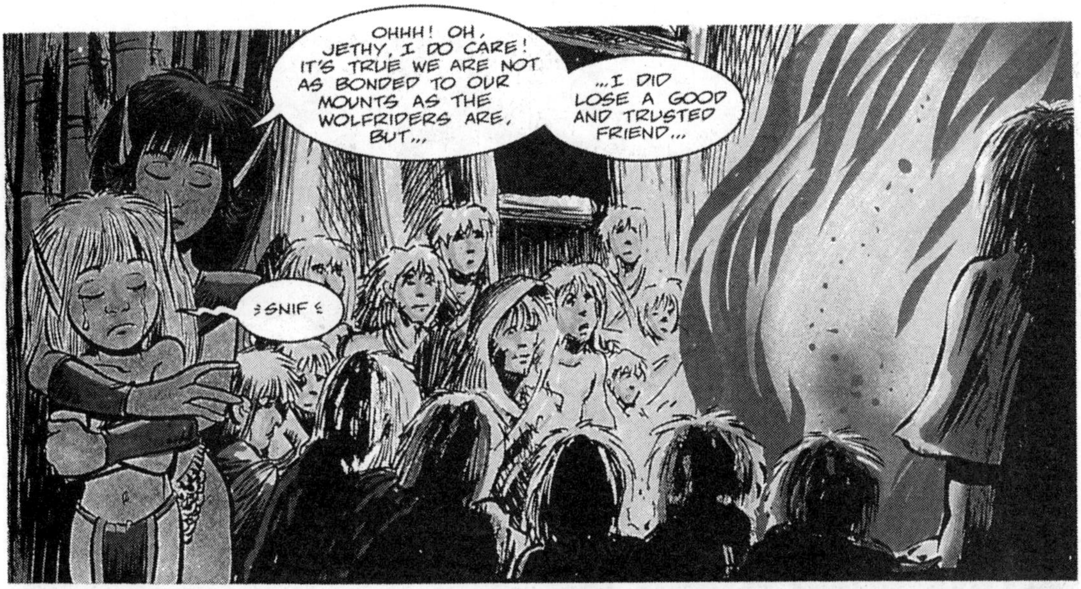
OHHH! OH, JETHY, I DO CARE! IT'S TRUE WE ARE NOT AS BONDED TO OUR MOUNTS AS THE WOLFRIDERS ARE, BUT...
...I DID LOSE A GOOD AND TRUSTED FRIEND...
SNIF

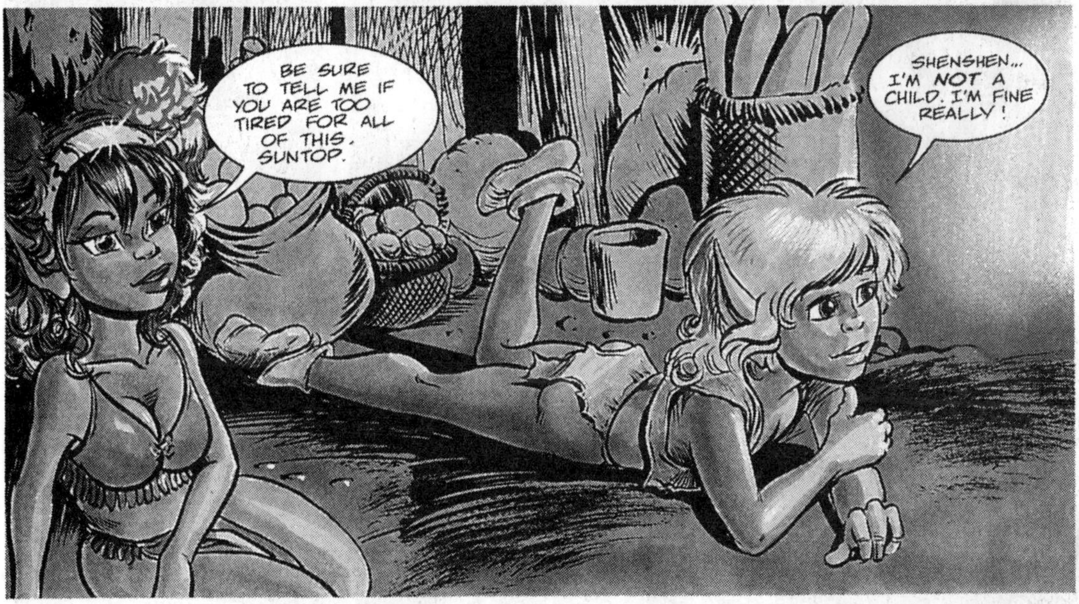
BE SURE TO TELL ME IF YOU ARE TOO TIRED FOR ALL OF THIS, SUNTOP.
SHENSHEN... I'M NOT A CHILD. I'M FINE REALLY!

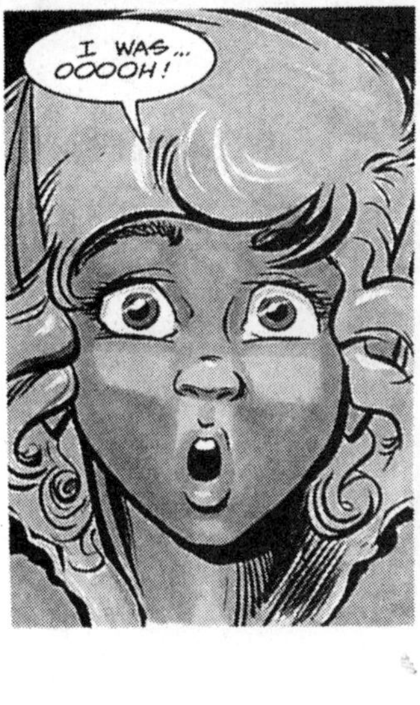
I WAS... OOOOH!

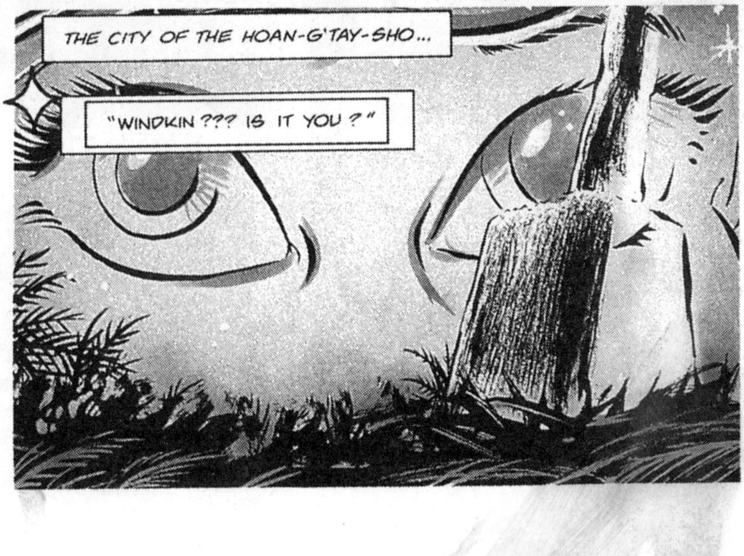
THE CITY OF THE HOAN-G'TAY-SHO...
"WINDKIN ??? IS IT YOU ?"

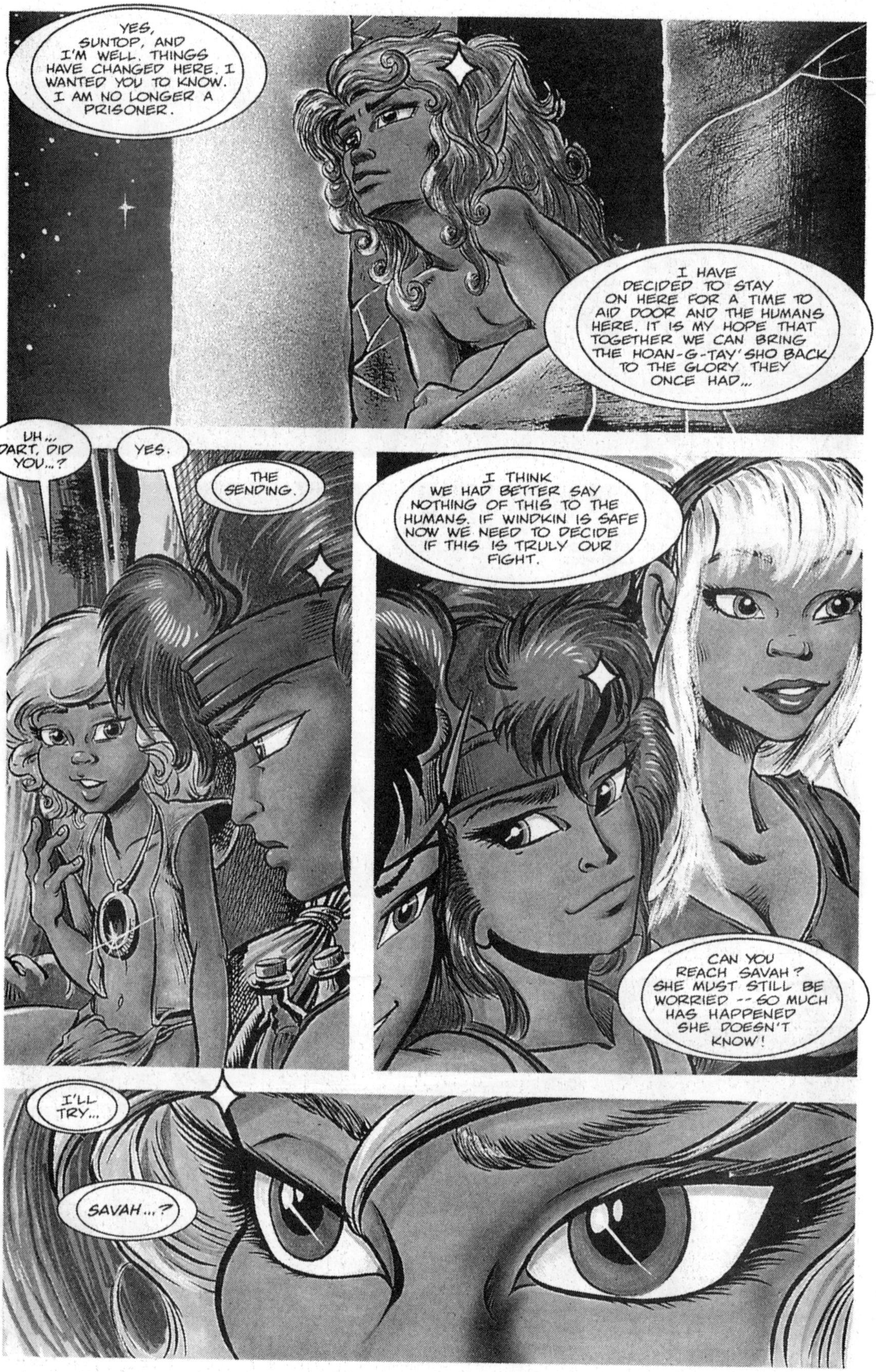
YES, SUNTOP, AND I'M WELL. THINGS HAVE CHANGED HERE. I WANTED YOU TO KNOW. I AM NO LONGER A PRISONER.
I HAVE DECIDED TO STAY ON HERE FOR A TIME TO AID DOOR AND THE HUMANS HERE. IT IS MY HOPE THAT TOGETHER WE CAN BRING THE HOAN-G-TAY'SHO BACK TO THE GLORY THEY ONCE HAD...
UH... DART, DID YOU...?
YES.
THE SENDING.
I THINK WE HAD BETTER SAY NOTHING OF THIS TO THE HUMANS. IF WINDKIN IS SAFE NOW WE NEED TO DECIDE IF THIS IS TRULY OUR FIGHT.
CAN YOU REACH SAVAH? SHE MUST STILL BE WORRIED -- SO MUCH HAS HAPPENED SHE DOESN'T KNOW!
I'LL TRY...
SAVAH...?

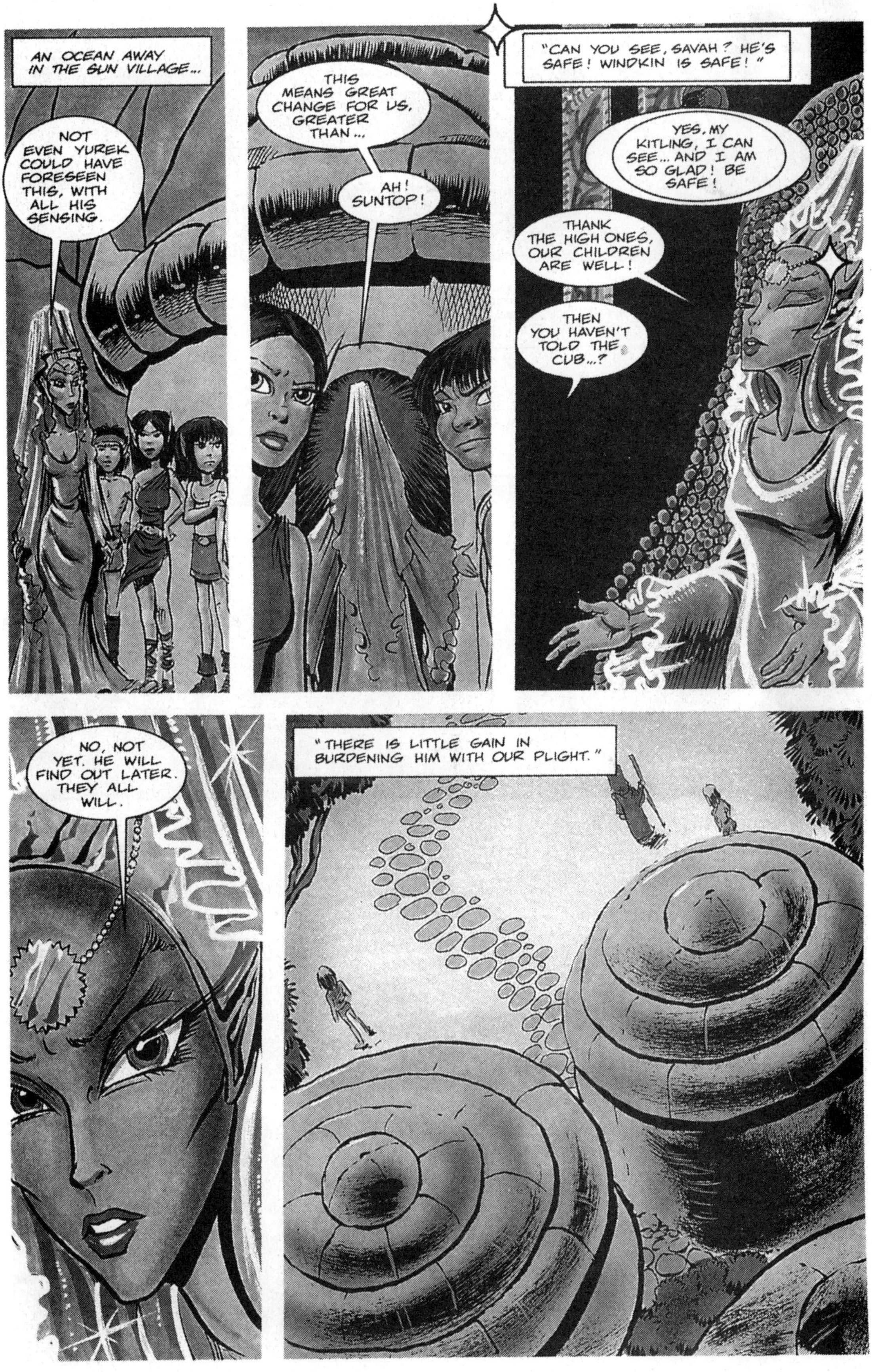
AN OCEAN AWAY IN THE SUN VILLAGE...
NOT EVEN YUREK COULD HAVE FORESEEN THIS, WITH ALL HIS SENSING.
THIS MEANS GREAT CHANGE FOR US, GREATER THAN...
AH! SUNTOP!
"CAN YOU SEE, SAVAH? HE'S SAFE! WINDKIN IS SAFE!"
YES, MY KITLING, I CAN SEE... AND I AM SO GLAD! BE SAFE!
THANK THE HIGH ONES, OUR CHILDREN ARE WELL!
THEN YOU HAVEN'T TOLD THE CUB...?
NO, NOT YET. HE WILL FIND OUT LATER. THEY ALL WILL.
"THERE IS LITTLE GAIN IN BURDENING HIM WITH OUR PLIGHT."

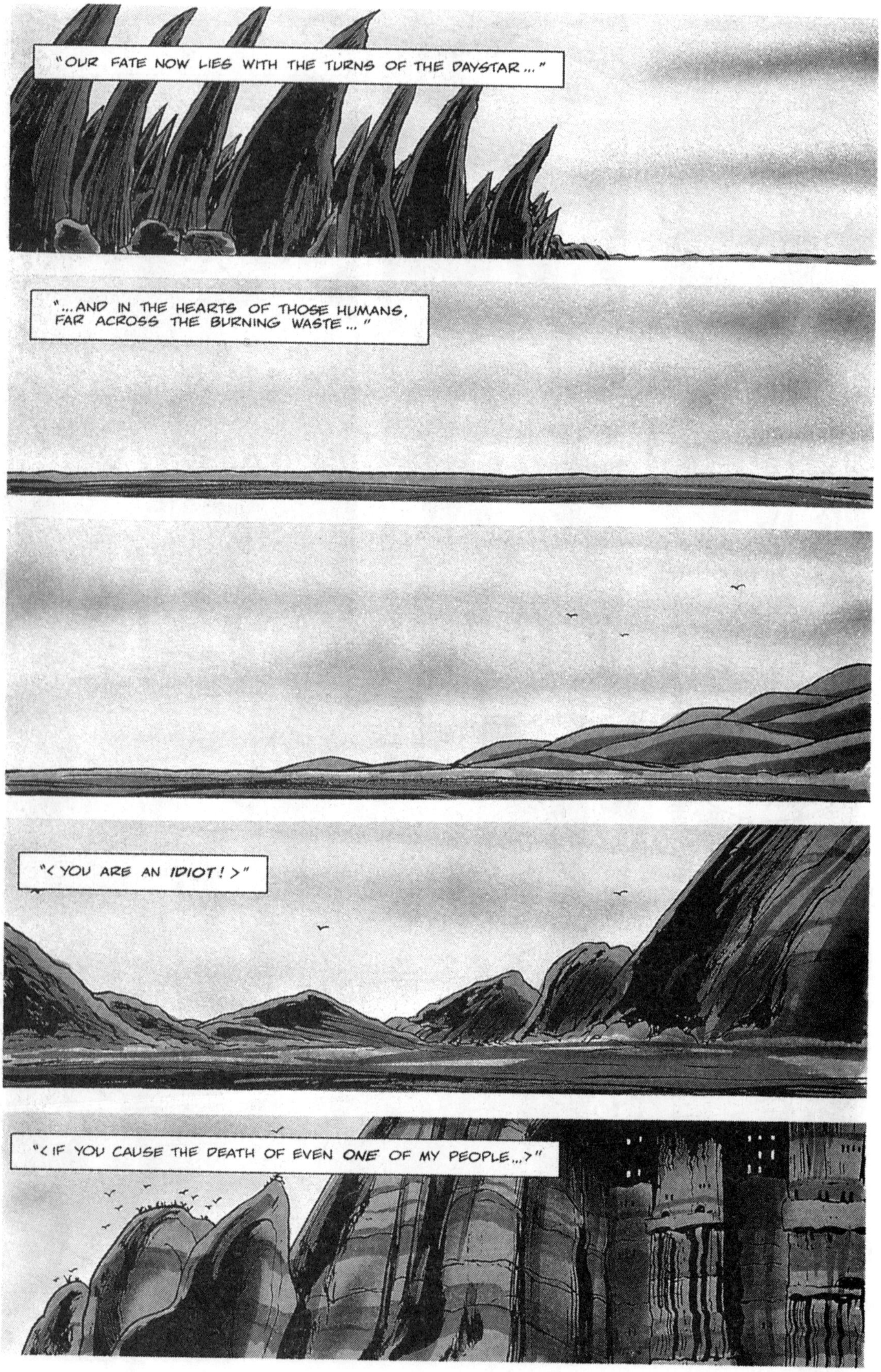
"OUR FATE NOW LIES WITH THE TURNS OF THE DAYSTAR..."
"...AND IN THE HEARTS OF THOSE HUMANS, FAR ACROSS THE BURNING WASTE..."
"< YOU ARE AN IDIOT! >"
"< IF YOU CAUSE THE DEATH OF EVEN ONE OF MY PEOPLE...>"

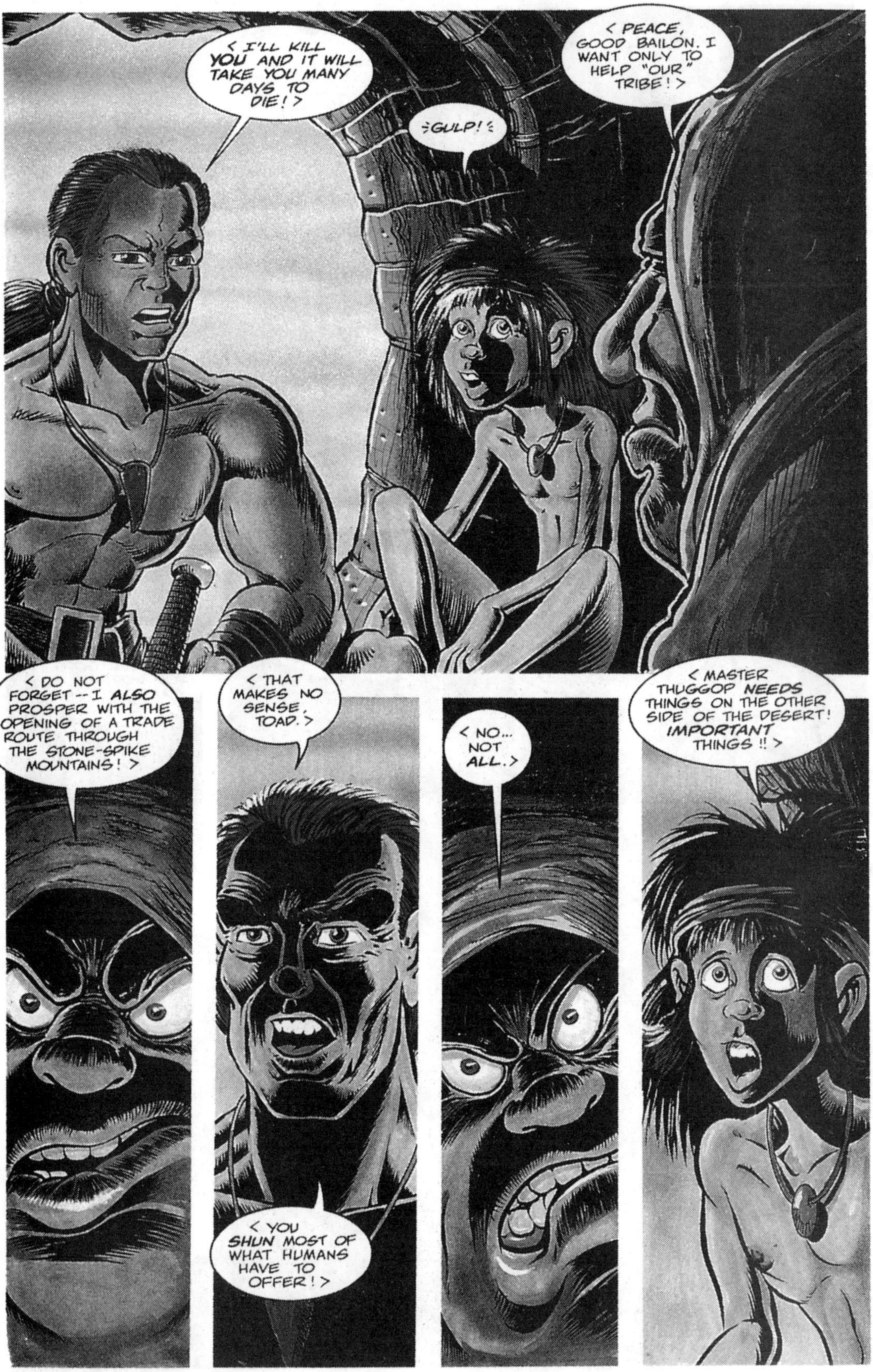
< I'LL KILL YOU AND IT WILL TAKE YOU MANY DAYS TO DIE! >
GULP!
< PEACE, GOOD BAILON. I WANT ONLY TO HELP "OUR" TRIBE! >
< DO NOT FORGET -- I ALSO PROSPER WITH THE OPENING OF A TRADE ROUTE THROUGH THE STONE-SPIKE MOUNTAINS! >
< THAT MAKES NO SENSE, TOAD. >
< YOU SHUN MOST OF WHAT HUMANS HAVE TO OFFER! >
< NO... NOT ALL. >
< MASTER THUGGOP NEEDS THINGS ON THE OTHER SIDE OF THE DESERT! IMPORTANT THINGS !! >

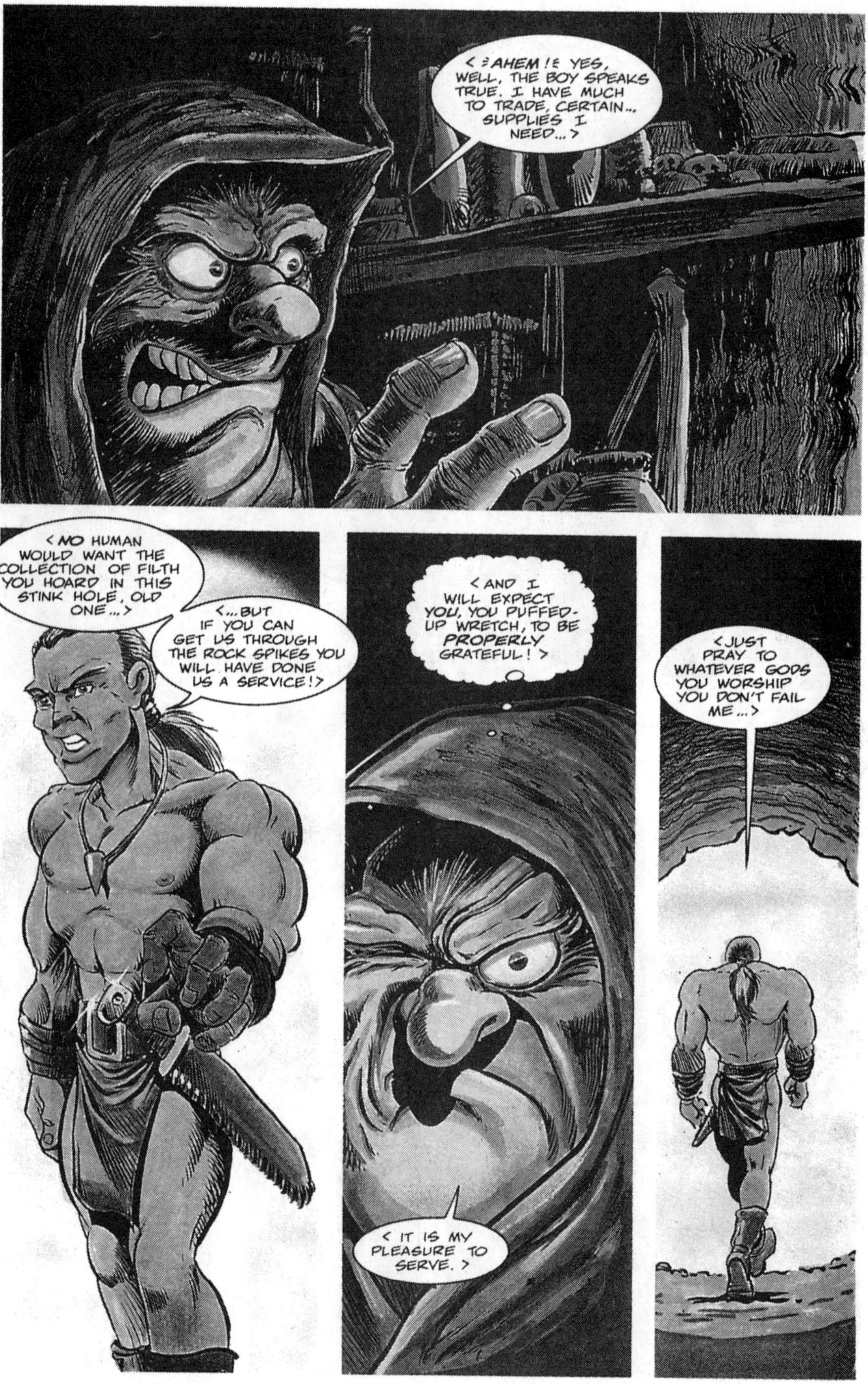
< AHEM! YES, WELL, THE BOY SPEAKS TRUE. I HAVE MUCH TO TRADE, CERTAIN... SUPPLIES I NEED... >
< NO HUMAN WOULD WANT THE COLLECTION OF FILTH YOU HOARD IN THIS STINK HOLE, OLD ONE... >
< ...BUT IF YOU CAN GET US THROUGH THE ROCK SPIKES YOU WILL HAVE DONE US A SERVICE! >
< AND I WILL EXPECT YOU, YOU PUFFED-UP WRETCH, TO BE PROPERLY GRATEFUL! >
< IT IS MY PLEASURE TO SERVE. >
< JUST PRAY TO WHATEVER GODS YOU WORSHIP YOU DON'T FAIL ME... >

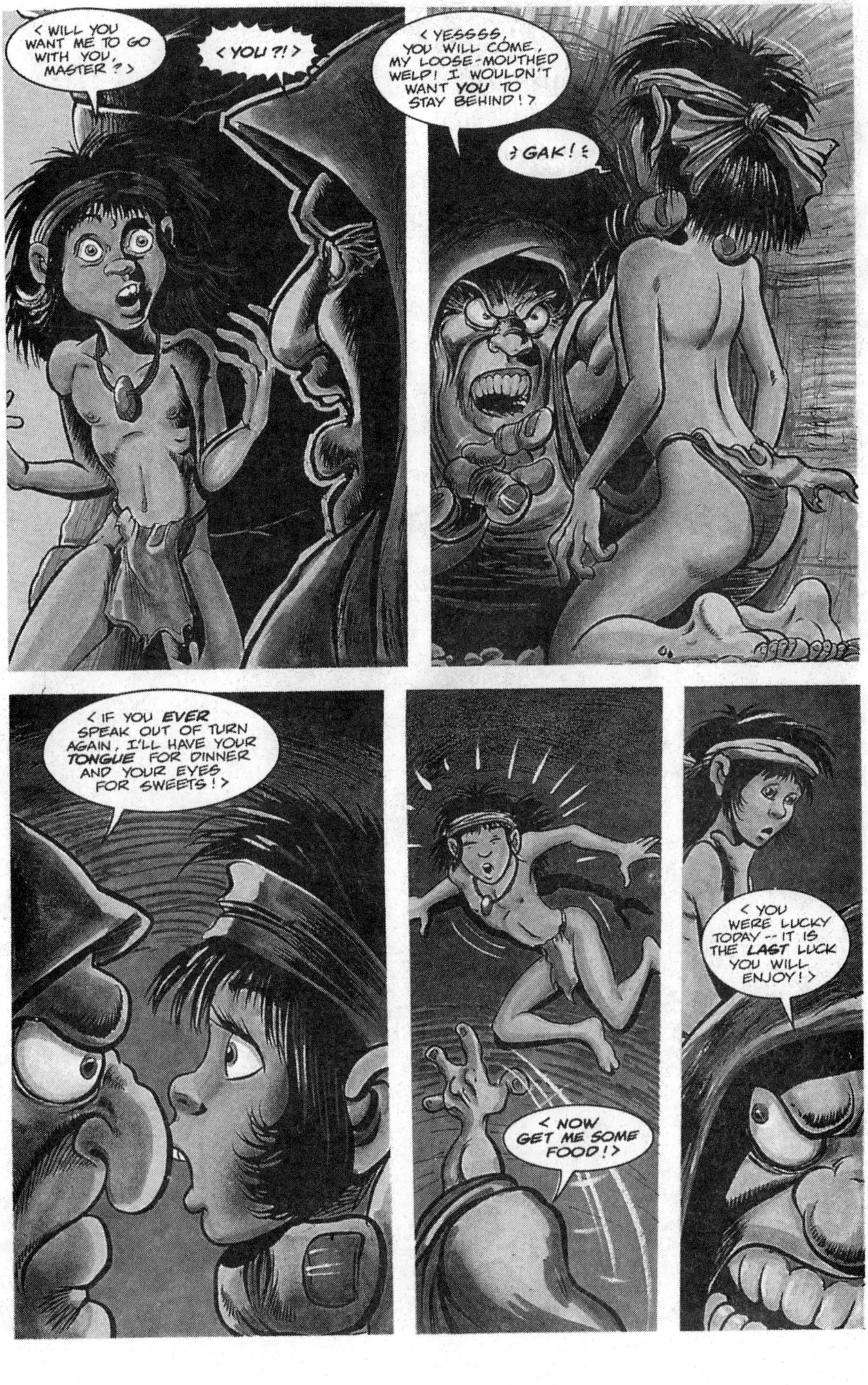
< WILL YOU WANT ME TO GO WITH YOU, MASTER ?>
< YOU ?! >
< YESSSS, YOU WILL COME, MY LOOSE-MOUTHED WELP! I WOULDN'T WANT YOU TO STAY BEHIND! >
GAK!
< IF YOU EVER SPEAK OUT OF TURN AGAIN, I'LL HAVE YOUR TONGUE FOR DINNER AND YOUR EYES FOR SWEETS! >
< NOW GET ME SOME FOOD! >
< YOU WERE LUCKY TODAY -- IT IS THE LAST LUCK YOU WILL ENJOY! >

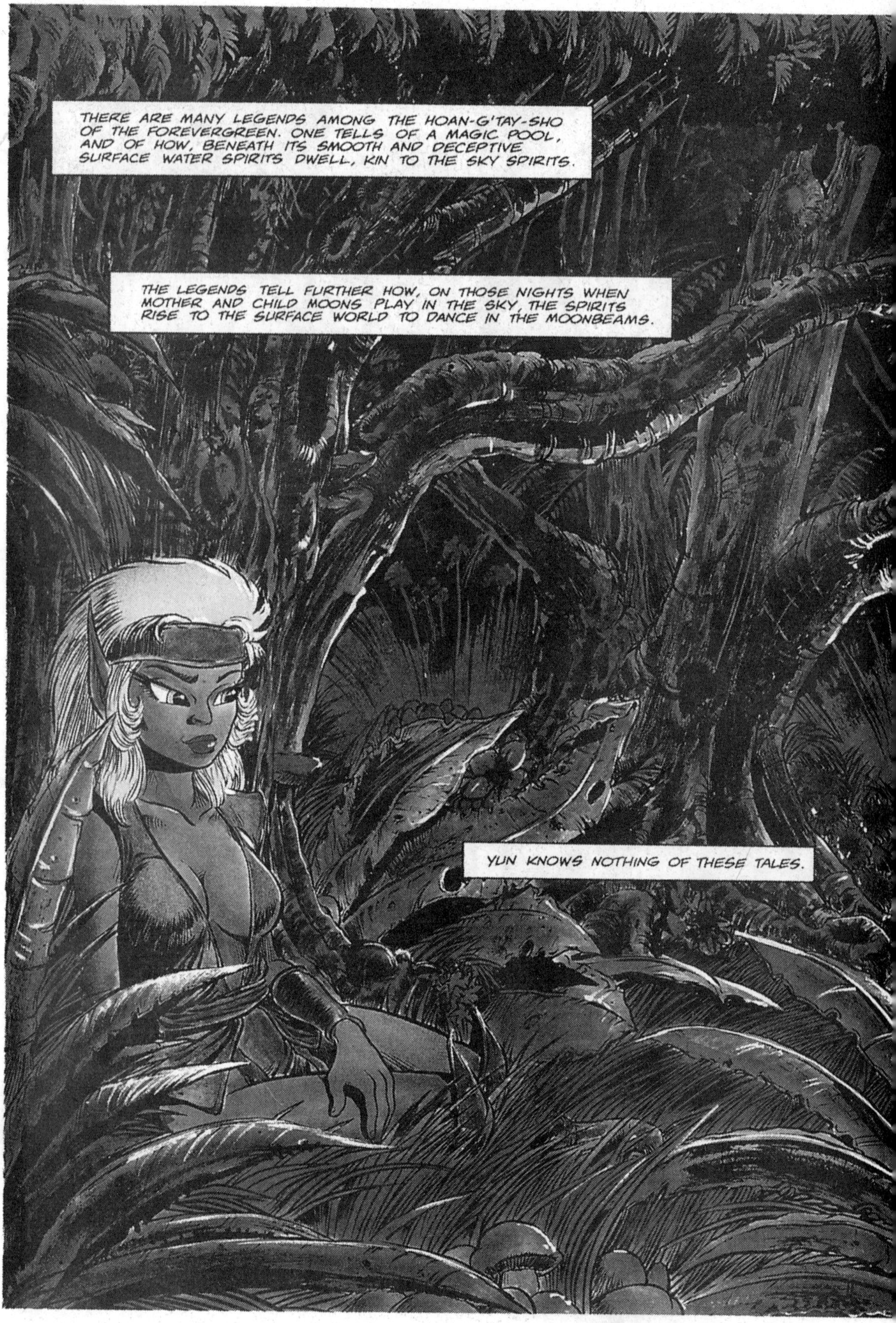
THERE ARE MANY LEGENDS AMONG THE HOAN-G'TAY-SHO OF THE FOREVERGREEN. ONE TELLS OF A MAGIC POOL, AND OF HOW, BENEATH ITS SMOOTH AND DECEPTIVE SURFACE WATER SPIRITS DWELL, KIN TO THE SKY SPIRITS.
THE LEGENDS TELL FURTHER HOW, ON THOSE NIGHTS WHEN MOTHER AND CHILD MOONS PLAY IN THE SKY, THE SPIRITS RISE TO THE SURFACE WORLD TO DANCE IN THE MOONBEAMS.
YUN KNOWS NOTHING OF THESE TALES.

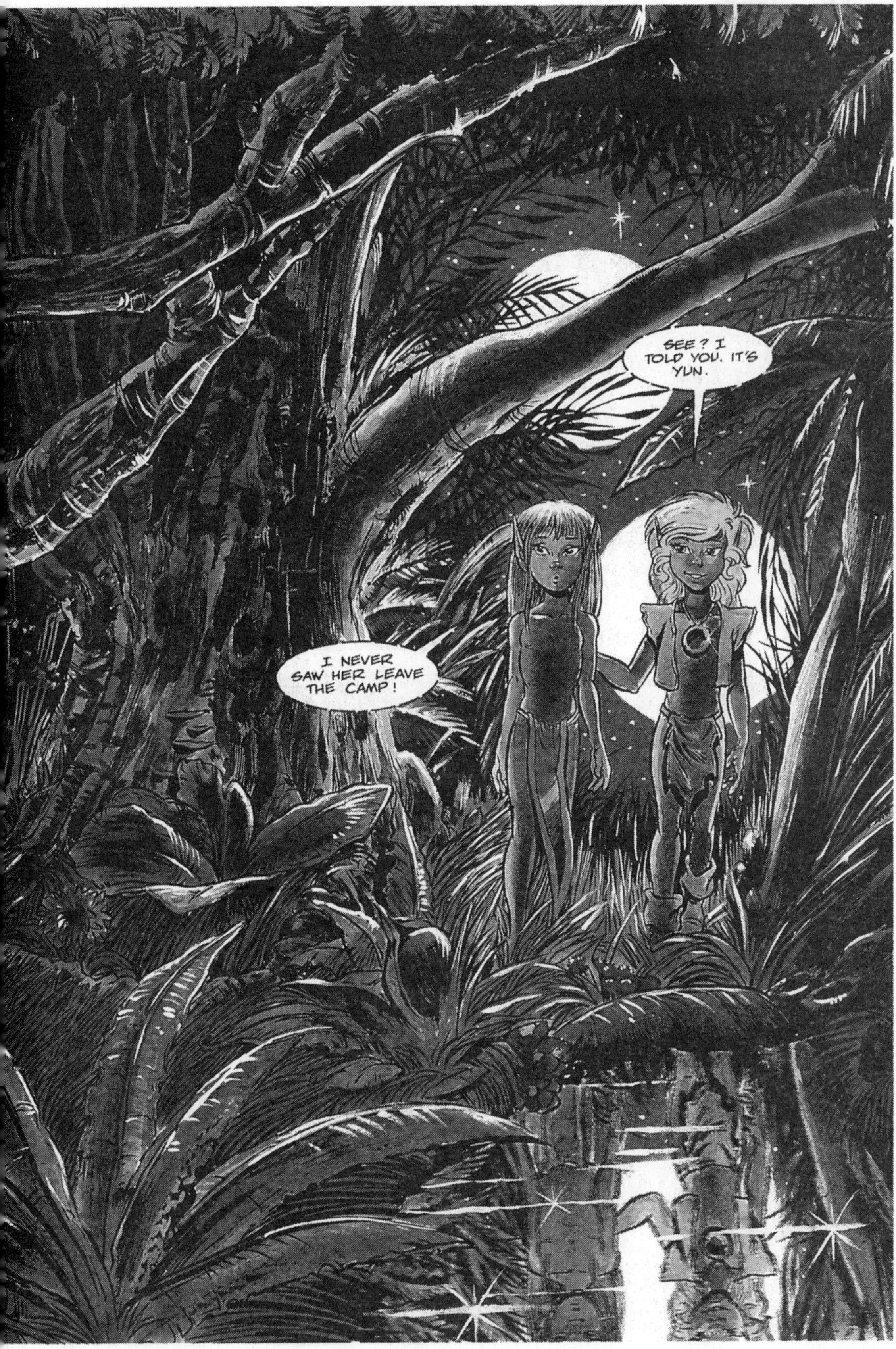
SEE? I TOLD YOU. IT'S YUN.
I NEVER SAW HER LEAVE THE CAMP!

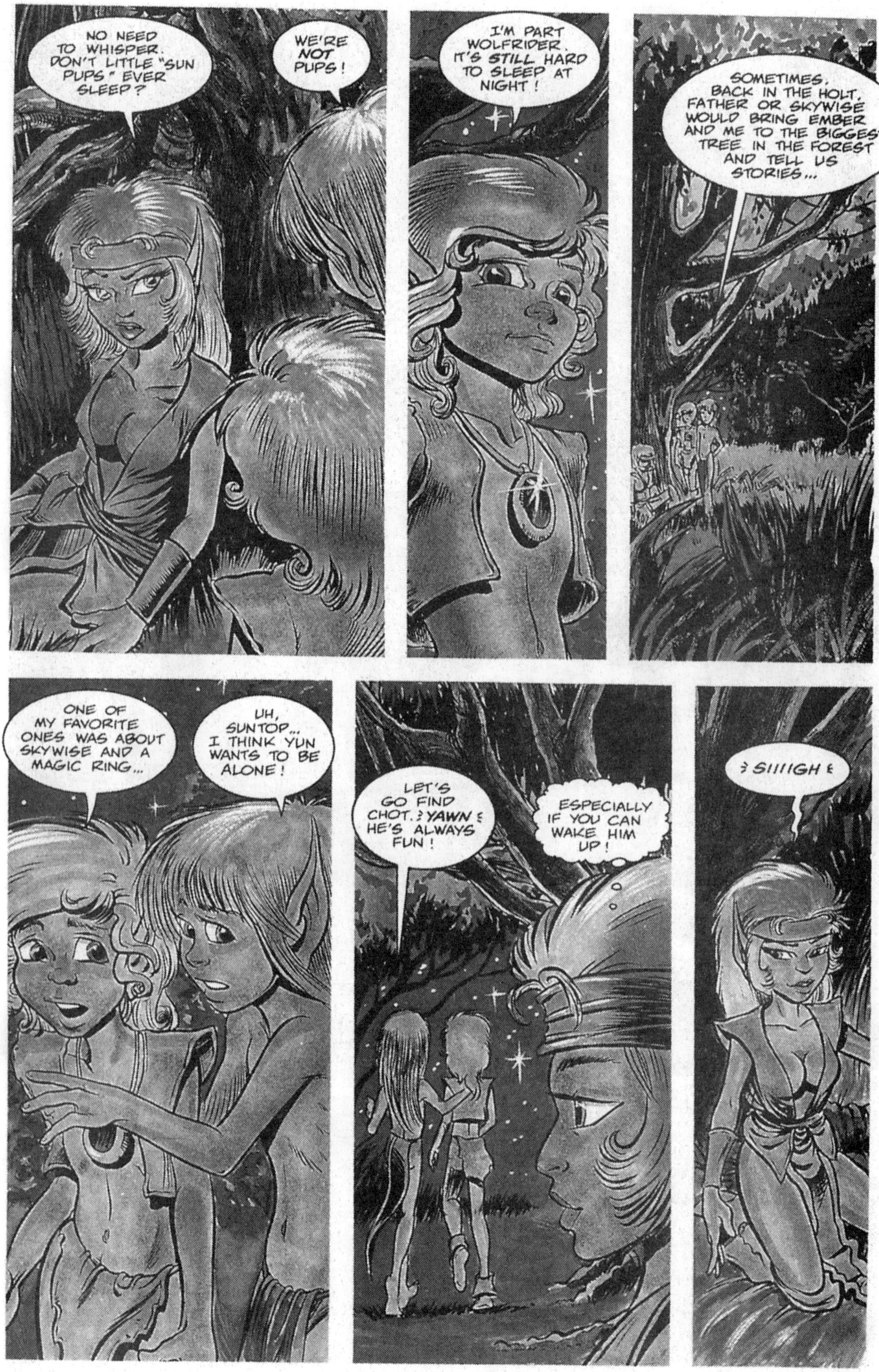
NO NEED TO WHISPER. DON'T LITTLE "SUN PUPS" EVER SLEEP?
WE'RE NOT PUPS!
I'M PART WOLFRIDER. IT'S STILL HARD TO SLEEP AT NIGHT!
SOMETIMES, BACK IN THE HOLT, FATHER OR SKYWISE WOULD BRING EMBER AND ME TO THE BIGGEST TREE IN THE FOREST AND TELL US STORIES...
ONE OF MY FAVORITE ONES WAS ABOUT SKYWISE AND A MAGIC RING...
UH, SUNTOP... I THINK YUN WANTS TO BE ALONE!
LET'S GO FIND CHOT. ≥YAWN≤ HE'S ALWAYS FUN!
ESPECIALLY IF YOU CAN WAKE HIM UP!
≥SIIIIGH≤

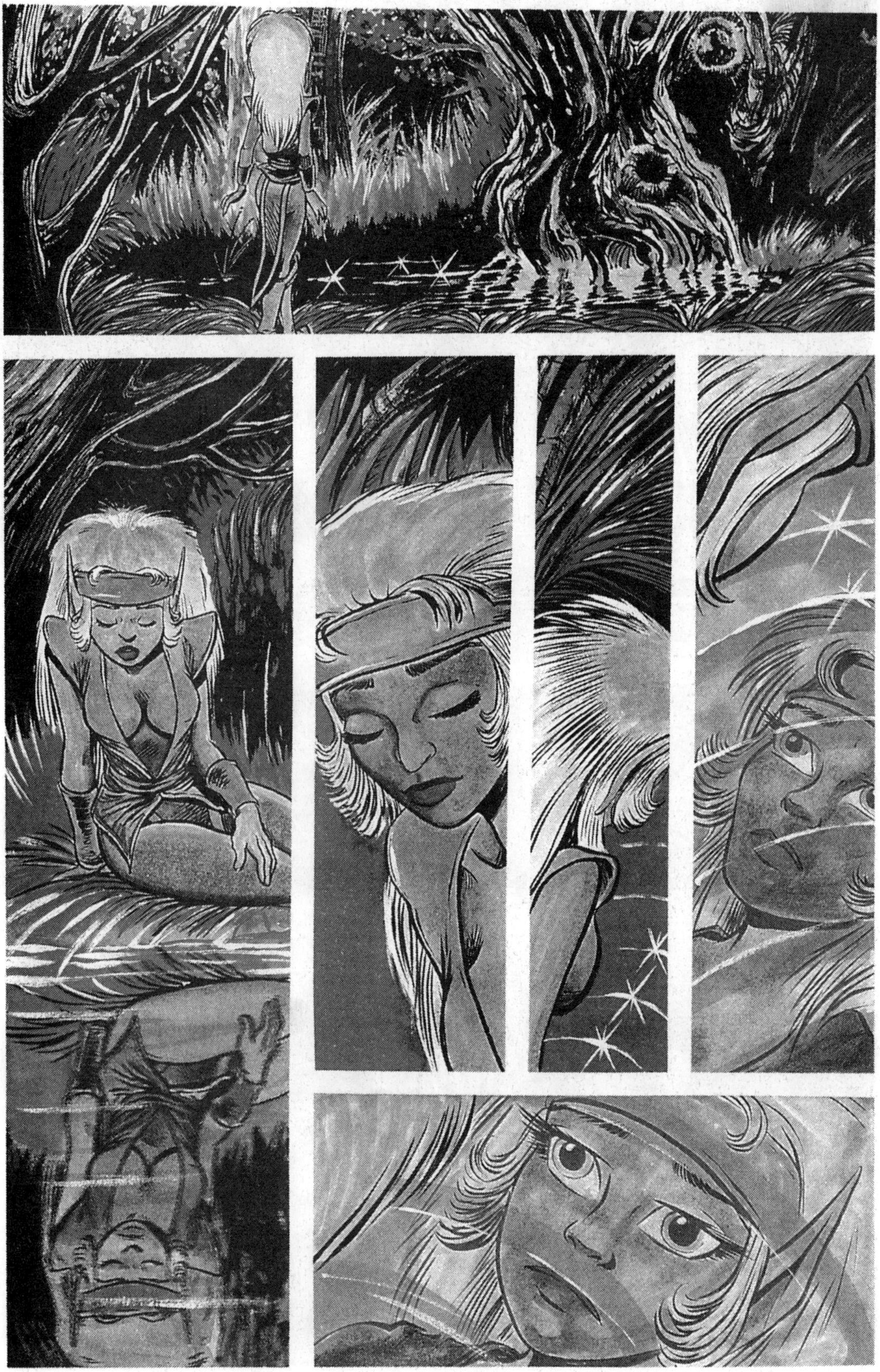

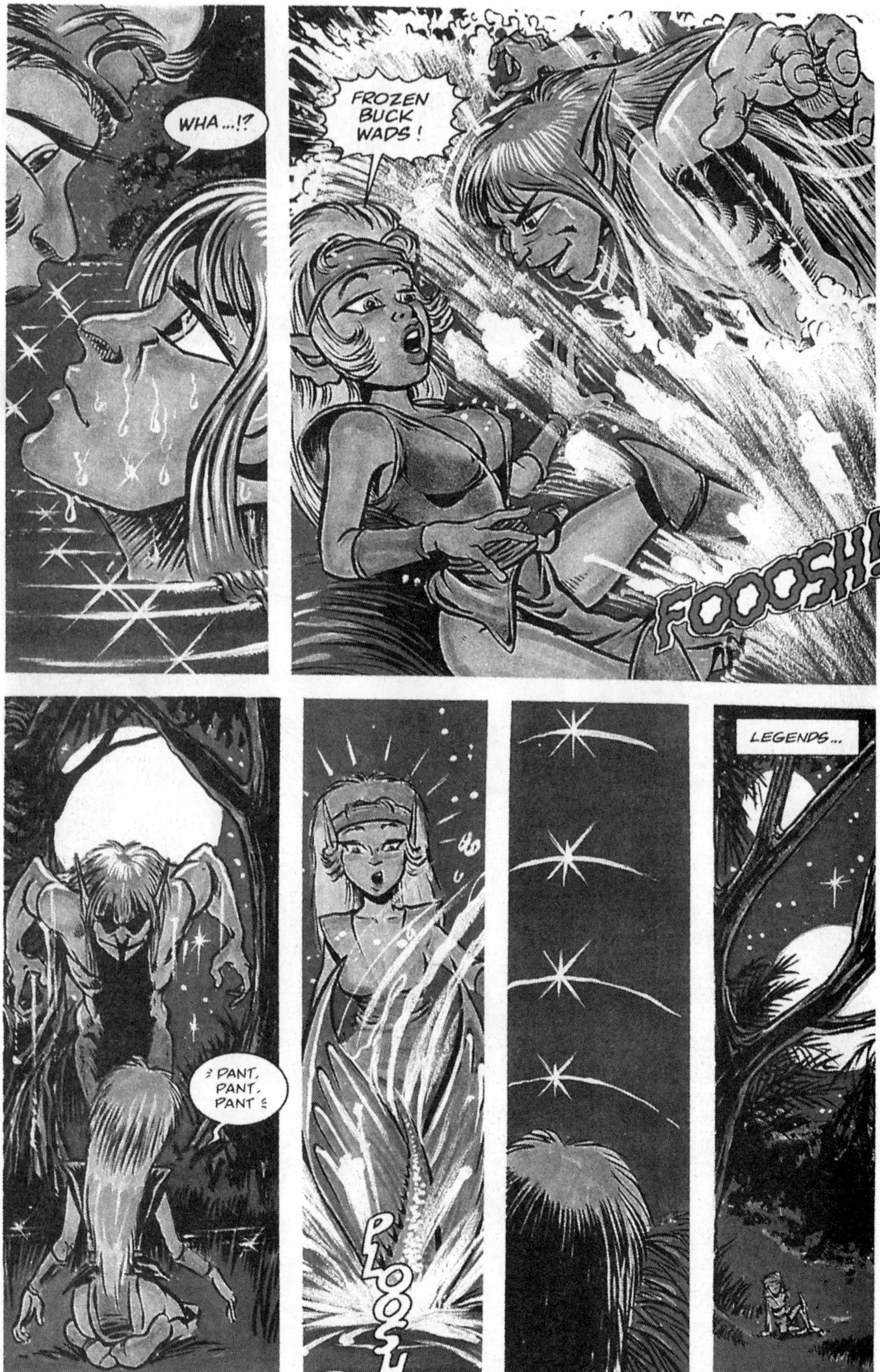
WHA...!?
FROZEN BUCK WADS!
FOOOSH!
PANT, PANT, PANT
PLOOSH
LEGENDS...

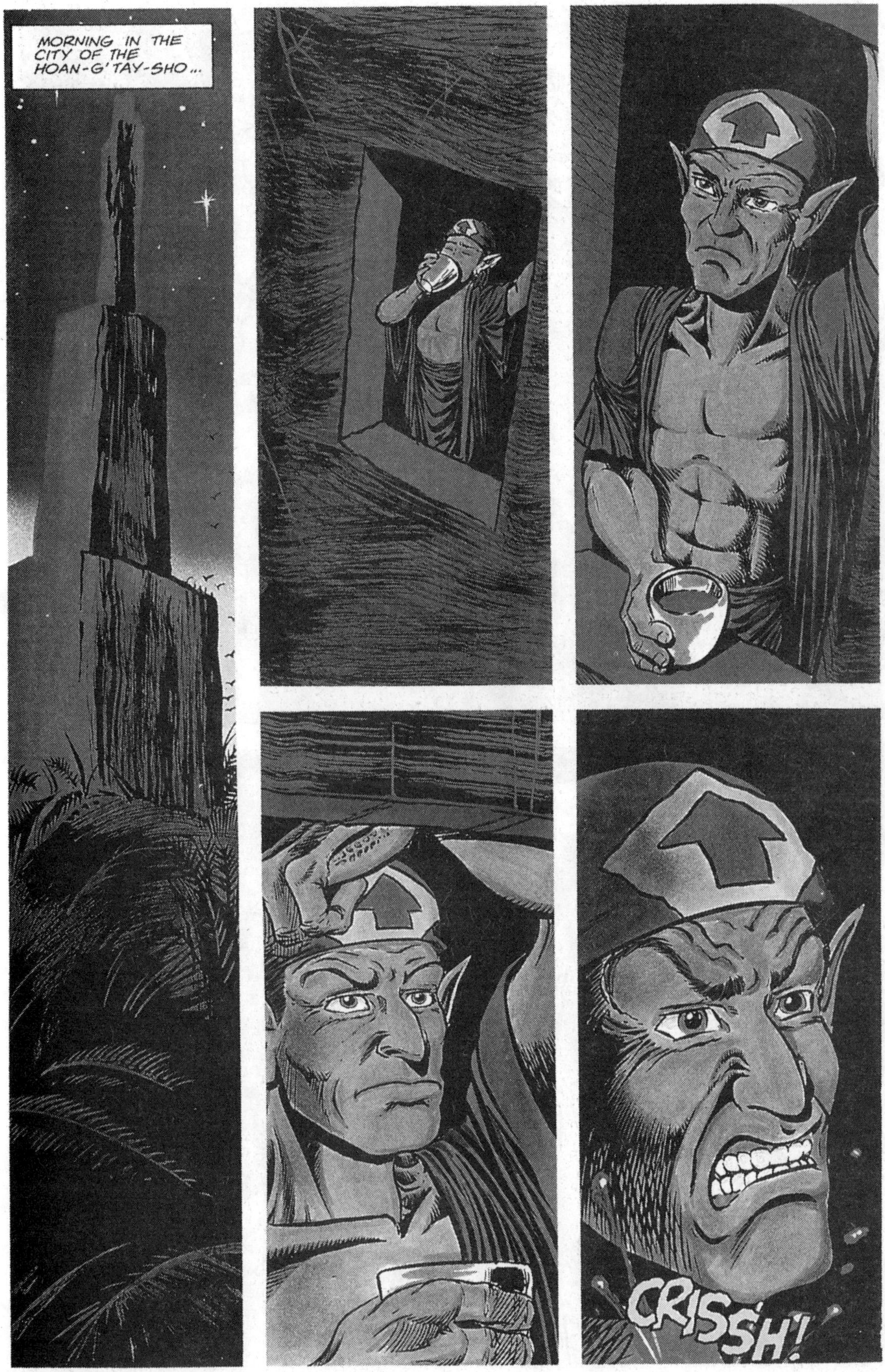
MORNING IN THE CITY OF THE HOAN-G'TAY-SHO...
CRISSH!

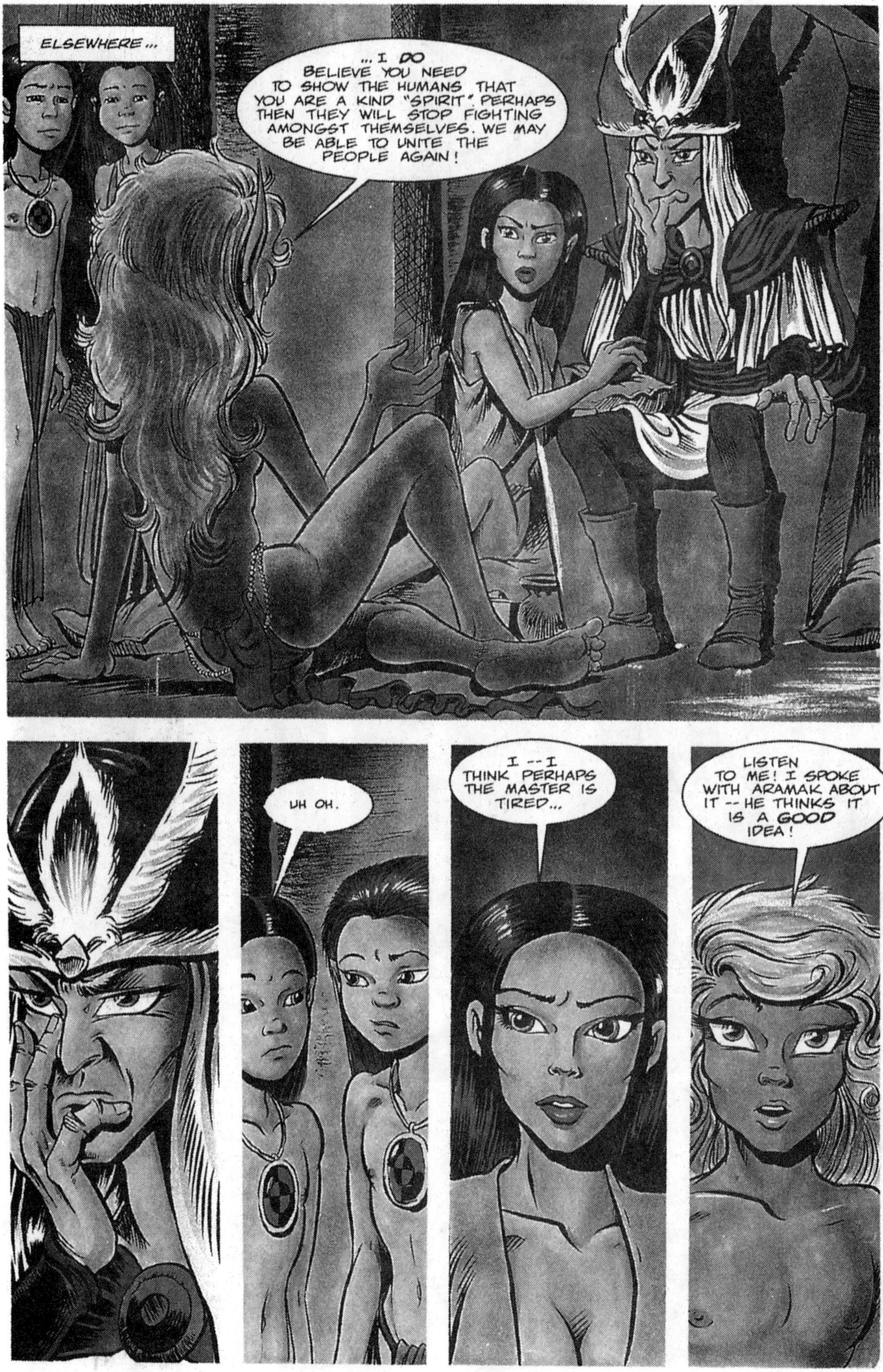
ELSEWHERE...
...I DO BELIEVE YOU NEED TO SHOW THE HUMANS THAT YOU ARE A KIND "SPIRIT". PERHAPS THEN THEY WILL STOP FIGHTING AMONGST THEMSELVES. WE MAY BE ABLE TO UNITE THE PEOPLE AGAIN!
UH OH.
I --I THINK PERHAPS THE MASTER IS TIRED...
LISTEN TO ME! I SPOKE WITH ARAMAK ABOUT IT -- HE THINKS IT IS A GOOD IDEA!

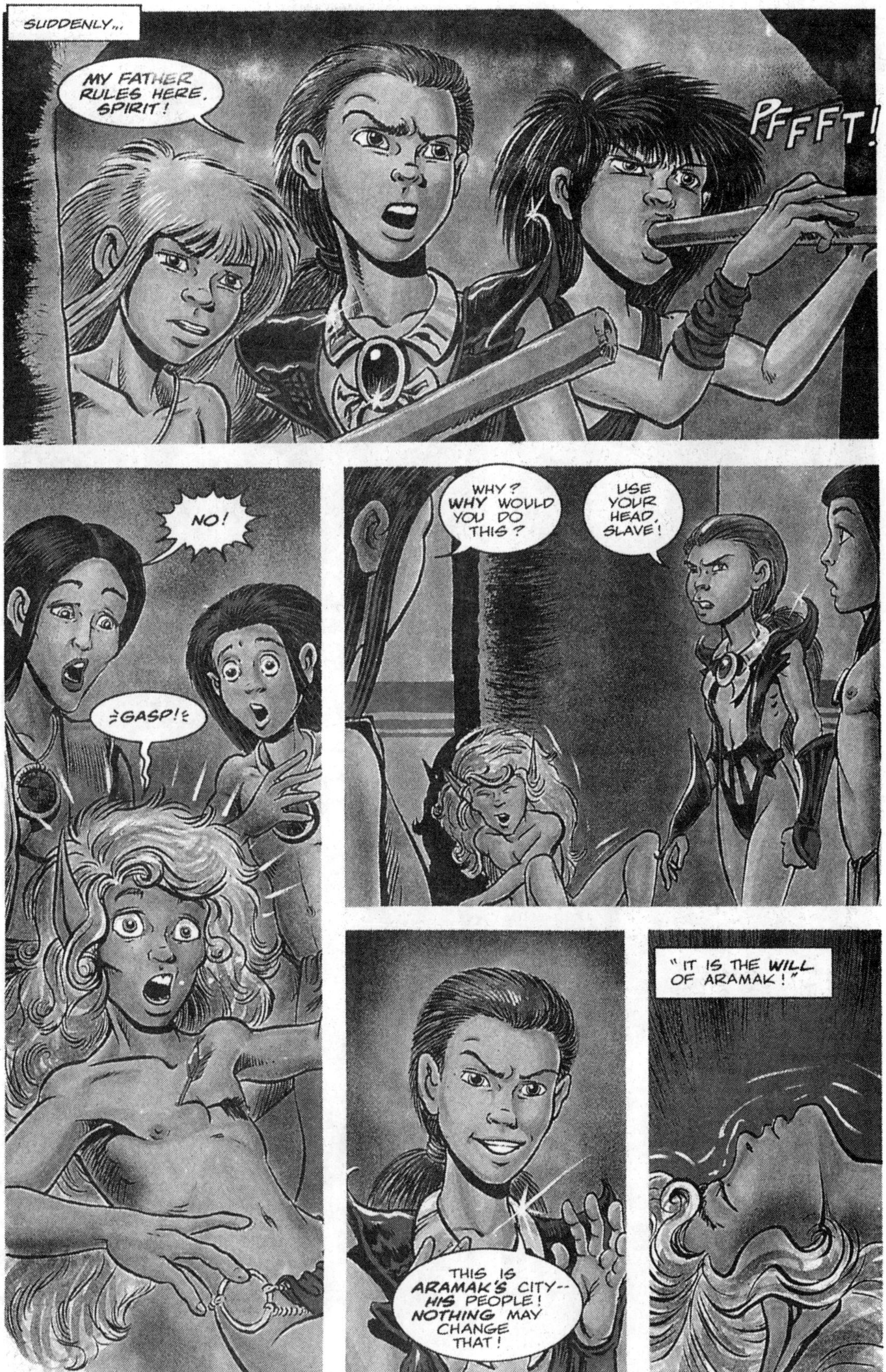
SUDDENLY...
MY FATHER RULES HERE, SPIRIT!
PFFFT!
NO!
GASP!
WHY? WHY WOULD YOU DO THIS?
USE YOUR HEAD, SLAVE!
THIS IS ARAMAK'S CITY-- HIS PEOPLE! NOTHING MAY CHANGE THAT!
"IT IS THE WILL OF ARAMAK!"

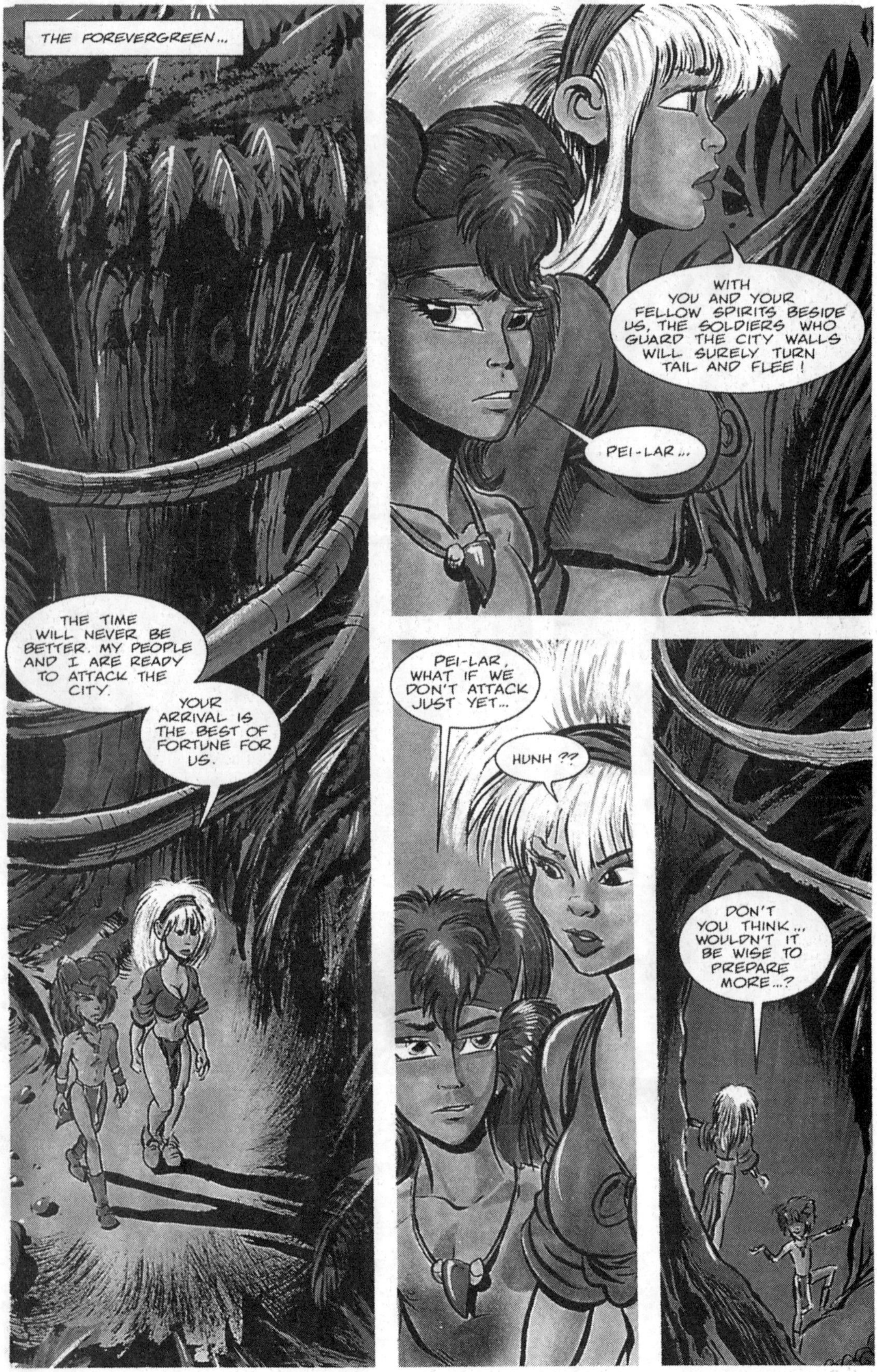
THE FOREVERGREEN...
THE TIME WILL NEVER BE BETTER. MY PEOPLE AND I ARE READY TO ATTACK THE CITY.
YOUR ARRIVAL IS THE BEST OF FORTUNE FOR US.
WITH YOU AND YOUR FELLOW SPIRITS BESIDE US, THE SOLDIERS WHO GUARD THE CITY WALLS WILL SURELY TURN TAIL AND FLEE!
PEI-LAR...
PEI-LAR, WHAT IF WE DON'T ATTACK JUST YET...
HUNH ??
DON'T YOU THINK... WOULDN'T IT BE WISE TO PREPARE MORE...?

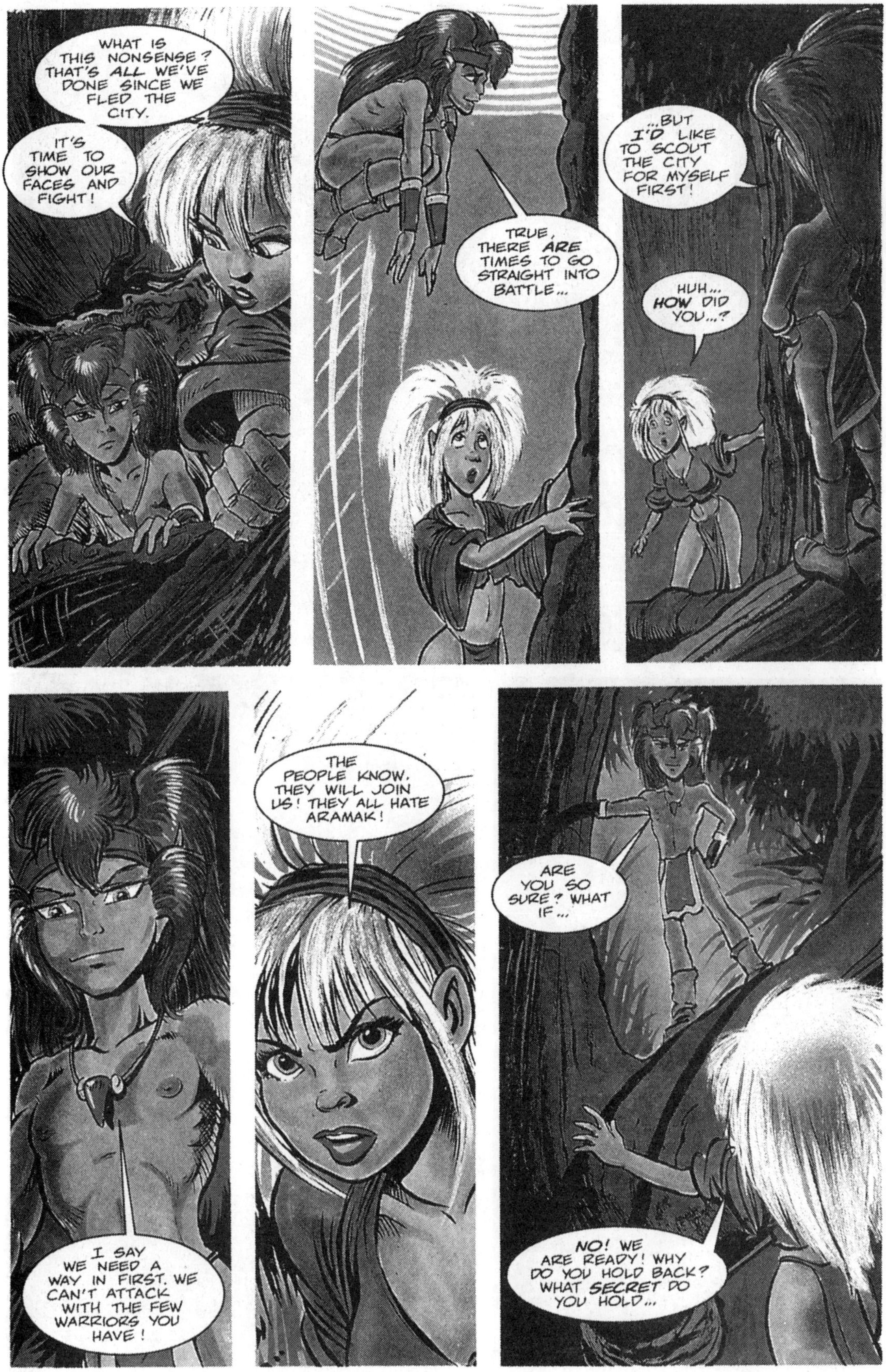
WHAT IS THIS NONSENSE? THAT'S ALL WE'VE DONE SINCE WE FLED THE CITY.
IT'S TIME TO SHOW OUR FACES AND FIGHT!
TRUE, THERE ARE TIMES TO GO STRAIGHT INTO BATTLE...
...BUT I'D LIKE TO SCOUT THE CITY FOR MYSELF FIRST!
HUH... HOW DID YOU...?
I SAY WE NEED A WAY IN FIRST. WE CAN'T ATTACK WITH THE FEW WARRIORS YOU HAVE!
THE PEOPLE KNOW. THEY WILL JOIN US! THEY ALL HATE ARAMAK!
ARE YOU SO SURE? WHAT IF...
NO! WE ARE READY! WHY DO YOU HOLD BACK? WHAT SECRET DO YOU HOLD...

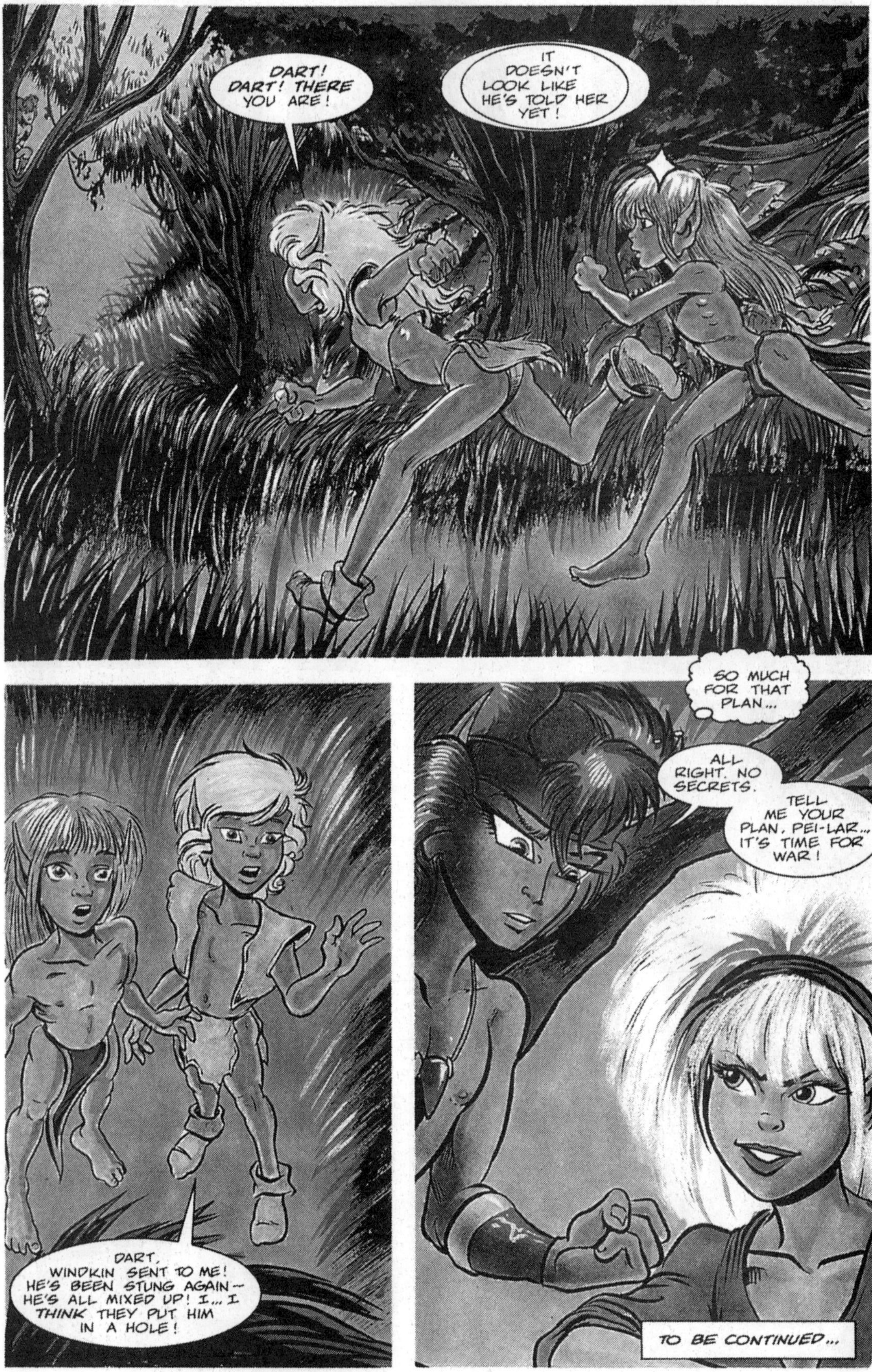
DART! DART! THERE YOU ARE!
IT DOESN'T LOOK LIKE HE'S TOLD HER YET!
DART, WINDKIN SENT TO ME! HE'S BEEN STUNG AGAIN-- HE'S ALL MIXED UP! I... I THINK THEY PUT HIM IN A HOLE!
SO MUCH FOR THAT PLAN...
ALL RIGHT. NO SECRETS.
TELL ME YOUR PLAN, PEI-LAR... IT'S TIME FOR WAR!
TO BE CONTINUED...

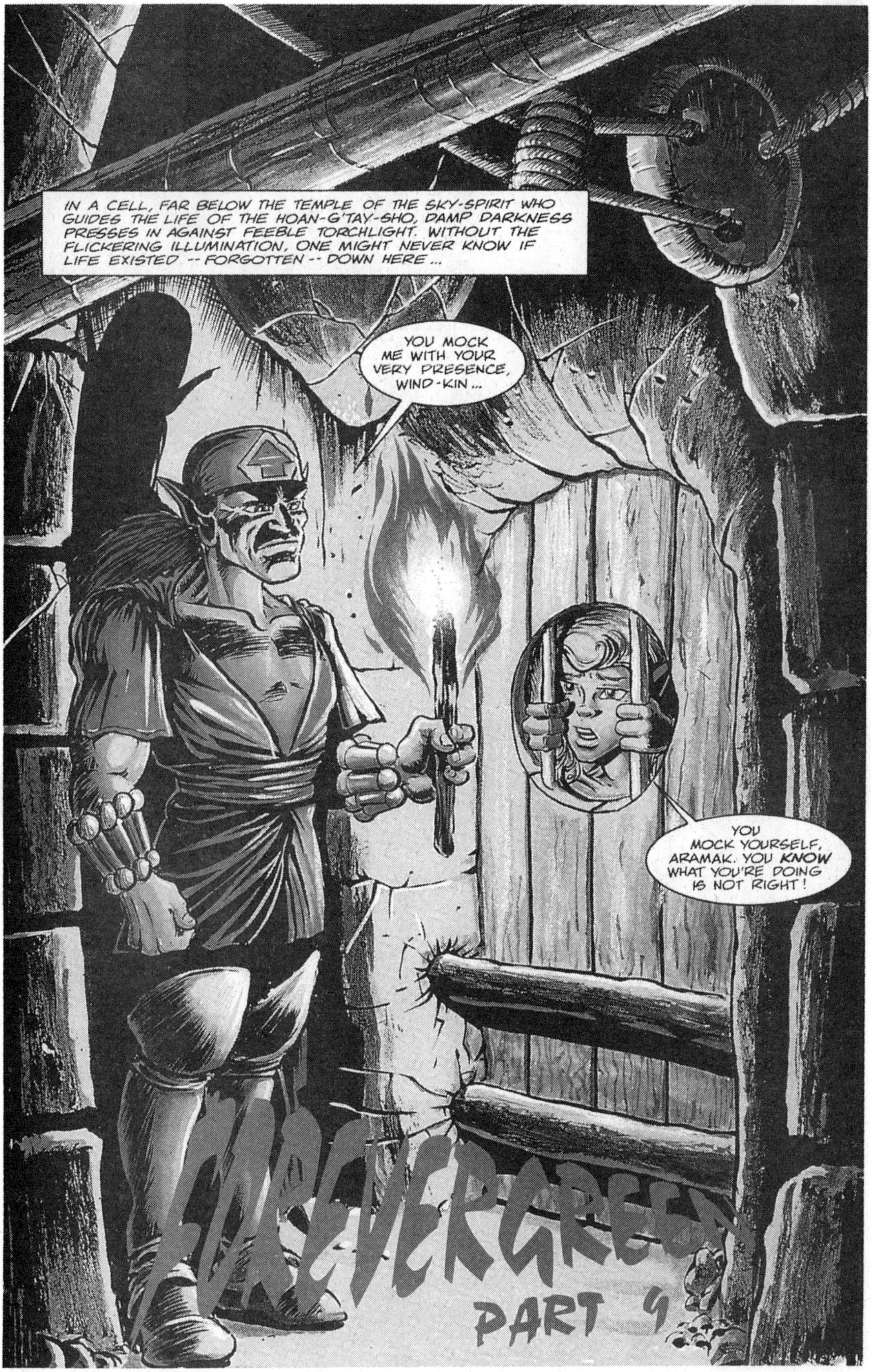
IN A CELL, FAR BELOW THE TEMPLE OF THE SKY-SPIRIT WHO GUIDES THE LIFE OF THE HOAN-G'TAY-SHO, DAMP DARKNESS PRESSES IN AGAINST FEEBLE TORCHLIGHT. WITHOUT THE FLICKERING ILLUMINATION, ONE MIGHT NEVER KNOW IF LIFE EXISTED -- FORGOTTEN -- DOWN HERE...
YOU MOCK ME WITH YOUR VERY PRESENCE, WIND-KIN...
YOU MOCK YOURSELF, ARAMAK. YOU KNOW WHAT YOU'RE DOING IS NOT RIGHT!
FOREVERGREEN
PART 9

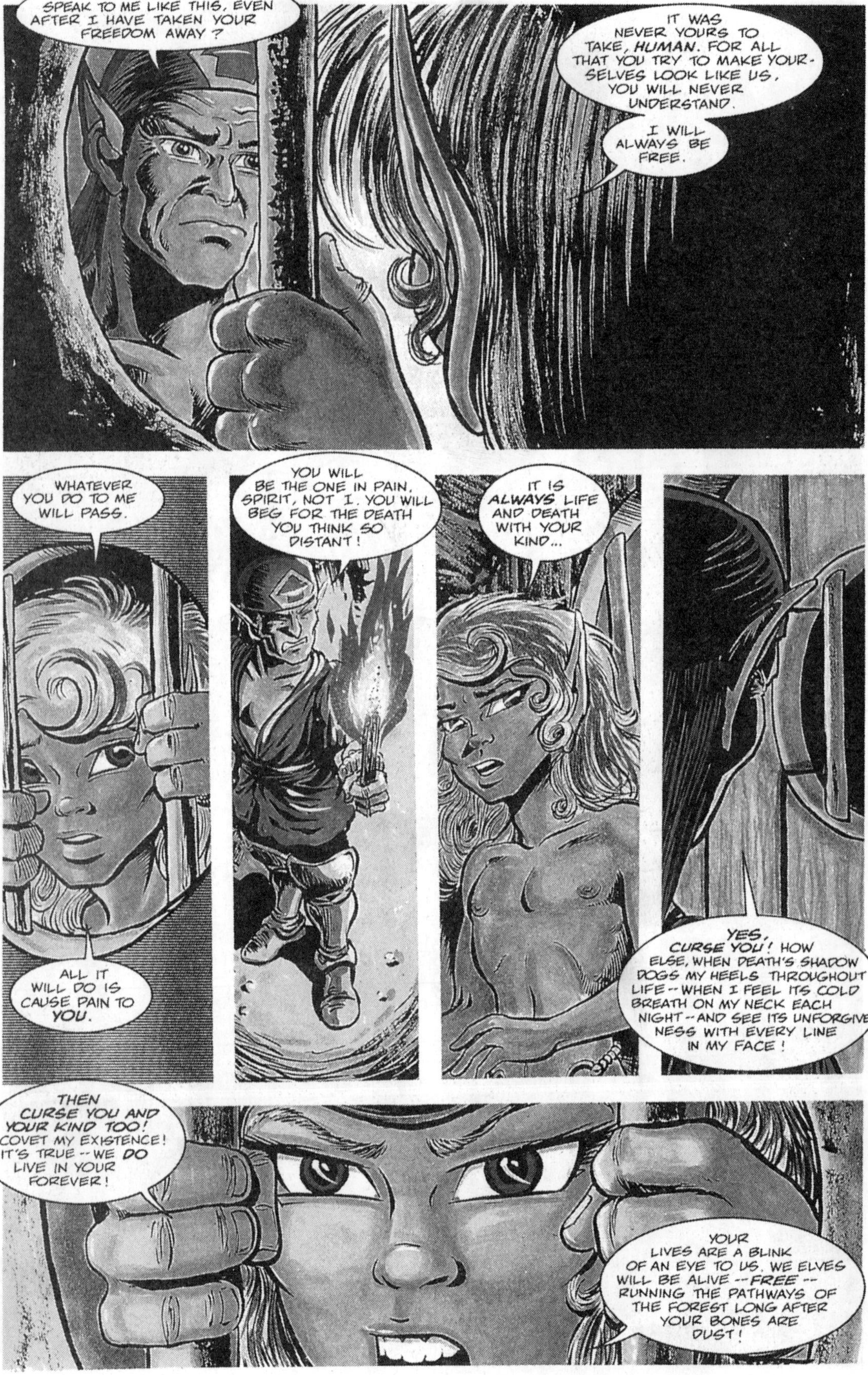

YOU STILL DARE TO SPEAK TO ME LIKE THIS, EVEN AFTER I HAVE TAKEN YOUR FREEDOM AWAY?
IT WAS NEVER YOURS TO TAKE, HUMAN. FOR ALL THAT YOU TRY TO MAKE YOURSELVES LOOK LIKE US, YOU WILL NEVER UNDERSTAND.
I WILL ALWAYS BE FREE.
WHATEVER YOU DO TO ME WILL PASS.
ALL IT WILL DO IS CAUSE PAIN TO YOU.
YOU WILL BE THE ONE IN PAIN, SPIRIT, NOT I. YOU WILL BEG FOR THE DEATH YOU THINK SO DISTANT!
IT IS ALWAYS LIFE AND DEATH WITH YOUR KIND...
YES, CURSE YOU! HOW ELSE, WHEN DEATH'S SHADOW DOGS MY HEELS THROUGHOUT LIFE -- WHEN I FEEL ITS COLD BREATH ON MY NECK EACH NIGHT -- AND SEE ITS UNFORGIVENESS WITH EVERY LINE IN MY FACE!
THEN CURSE YOU AND YOUR KIND TOO! COVET MY EXISTENCE! IT'S TRUE -- WE DO LIVE IN YOUR FOREVER!
YOUR LIVES ARE A BLINK OF AN EYE TO US. WE ELVES WILL BE ALIVE -- FREE -- RUNNING THE PATHWAYS OF THE FOREST LONG AFTER YOUR BONES ARE DUST!

AND THAT'S WHY I HATE YOU, WINDRIDER!

YOUR HATE IS *JEALOUSY*, AND IT IS A *HUMAN* SICKNESS!

SO, THEN! BUT *YOU'LL* NOT WITNESS IT ANY LONGER. I'M DONE WITH YOU AND YOUR FILTHY BEAUTY!

YOU WILL STAY HERE IN THE DARK AND ROT!

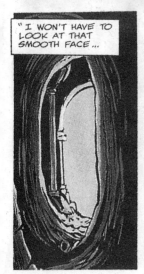

"I WON'T HAVE TO LOOK AT THAT SMOOTH FACE...

"...AND SEE MY OWN, SO LONG AGO!"

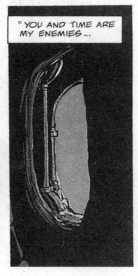

"YOU AND TIME ARE MY ENEMIES...

"...AND I WILL NOT LOOK AT YOU AGAIN!"

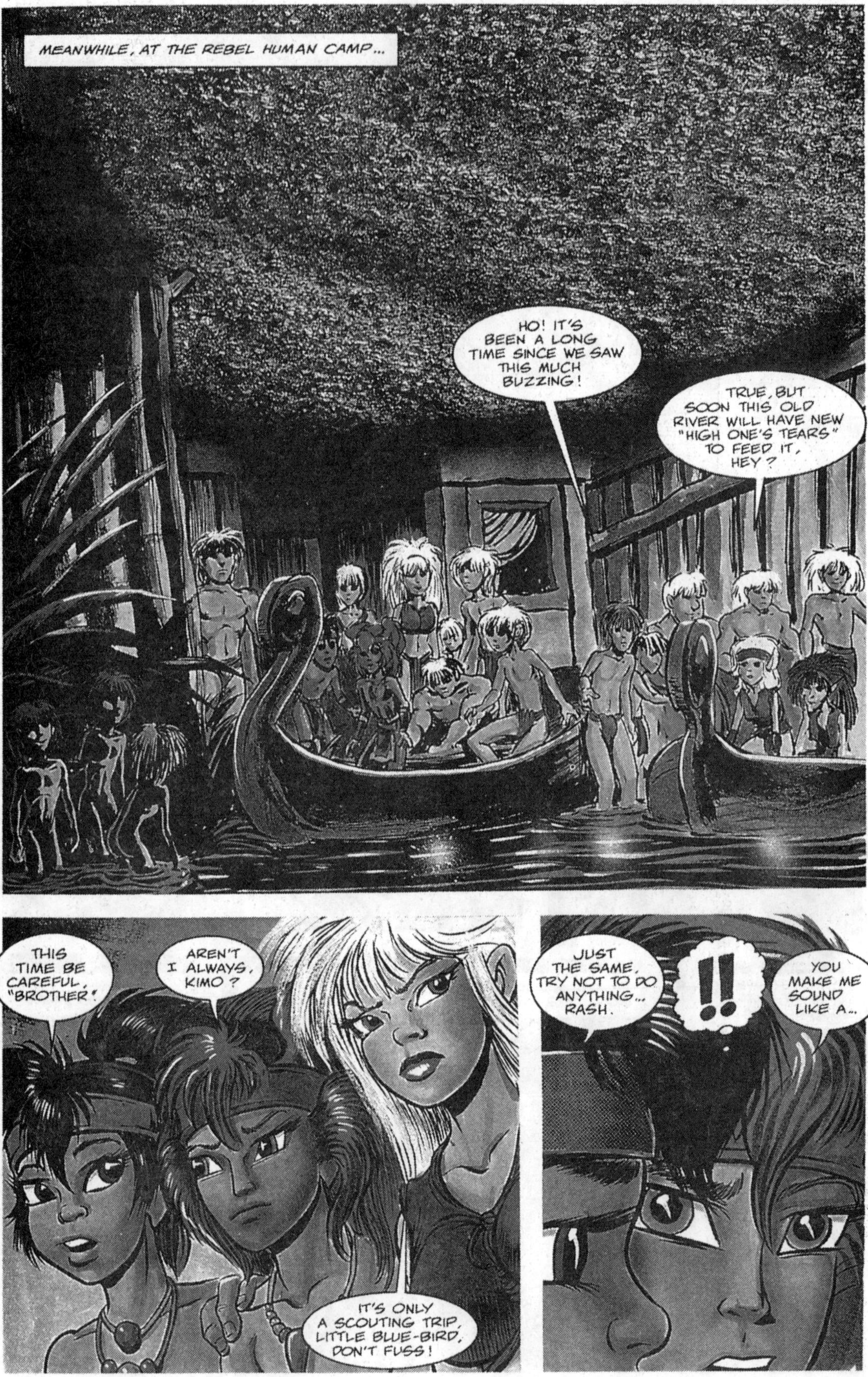
MEANWHILE, AT THE REBEL HUMAN CAMP...
HO! IT'S BEEN A LONG TIME SINCE WE SAW THIS MUCH BUZZING!
TRUE, BUT SOON THIS OLD RIVER WILL HAVE NEW "HIGH ONE'S TEARS" TO FEED IT, HEY?
THIS TIME BE CAREFUL, "BROTHER".
AREN'T I ALWAYS, KIMO?
IT'S ONLY A SCOUTING TRIP, LITTLE BLUE-BIRD, DON'T FUSS!
JUST THE SAME, TRY NOT TO DO ANYTHING... RASH.
!!
YOU MAKE ME SOUND LIKE A...

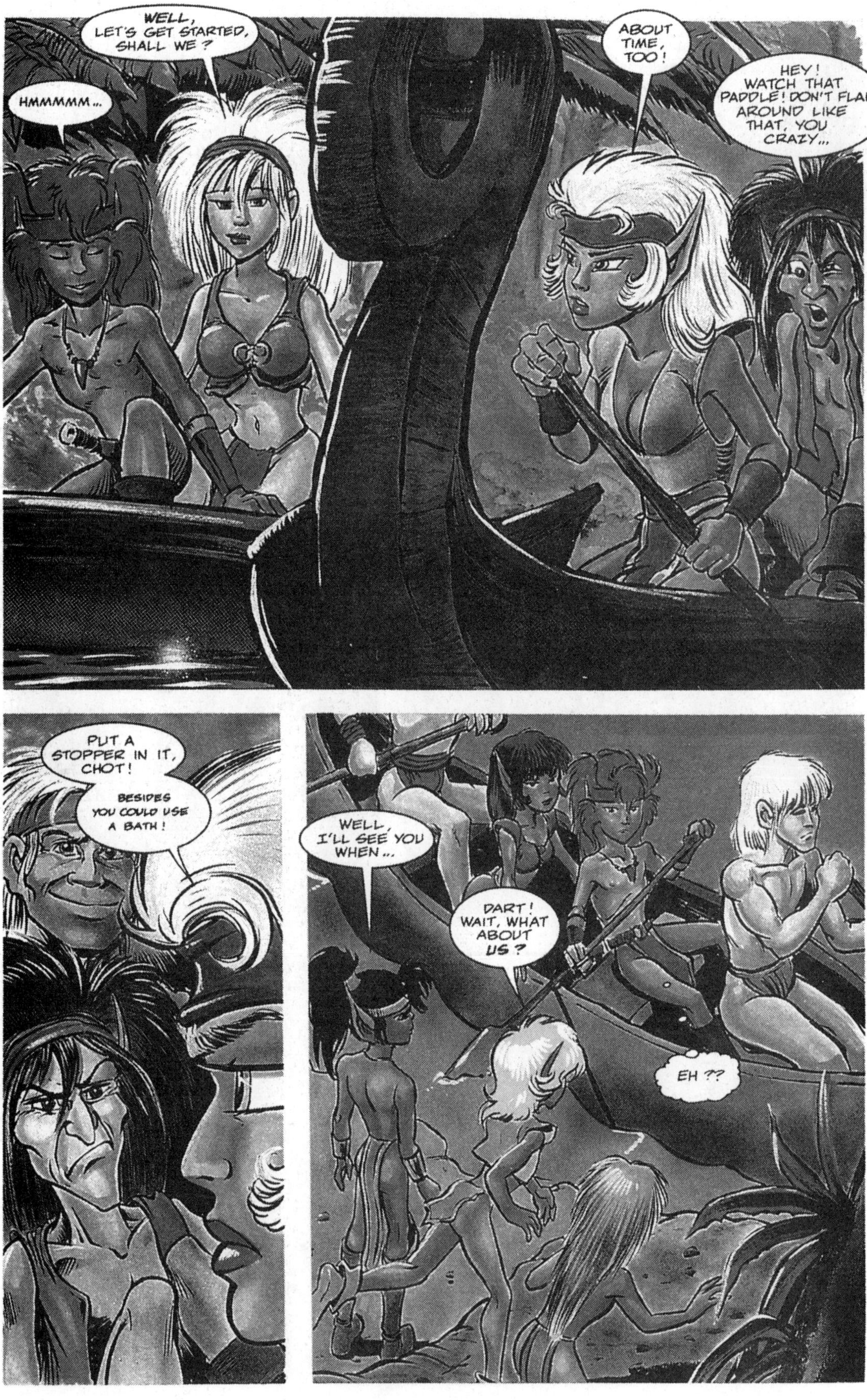
HMMMMM...
WELL, LET'S GET STARTED, SHALL WE?
ABOUT TIME, TOO!
HEY! WATCH THAT PADDLE! DON'T FLAIL AROUND LIKE THAT, YOU CRAZY...
PUT A STOPPER IN IT, CHOT!
BESIDES YOU COULD USE A BATH!
WELL, I'LL SEE YOU WHEN...
DART! WAIT, WHAT ABOUT US?
EH??

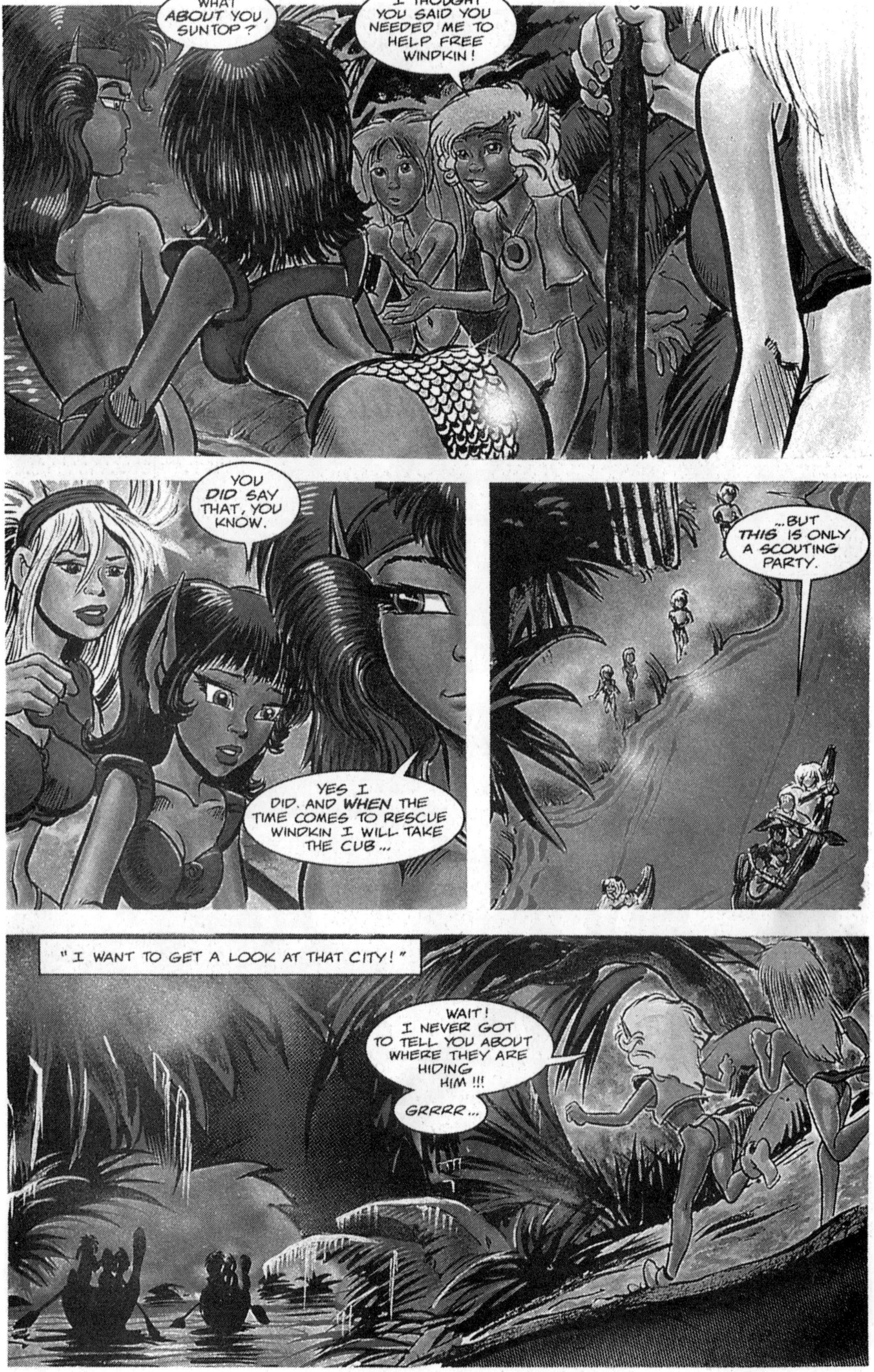
WHAT ABOUT YOU, SUNTOP?
I THOUGHT YOU SAID YOU NEEDED ME TO HELP FREE WINDKIN!
YOU DID SAY THAT, YOU KNOW.
YES I DID. AND WHEN THE TIME COMES TO RESCUE WINDKIN I WILL TAKE THE CUB...
...BUT THIS IS ONLY A SCOUTING PARTY.
"I WANT TO GET A LOOK AT THAT CITY!"
WAIT! I NEVER GOT TO TELL YOU ABOUT WHERE THEY ARE HIDING HIM!!!
GRRRR...

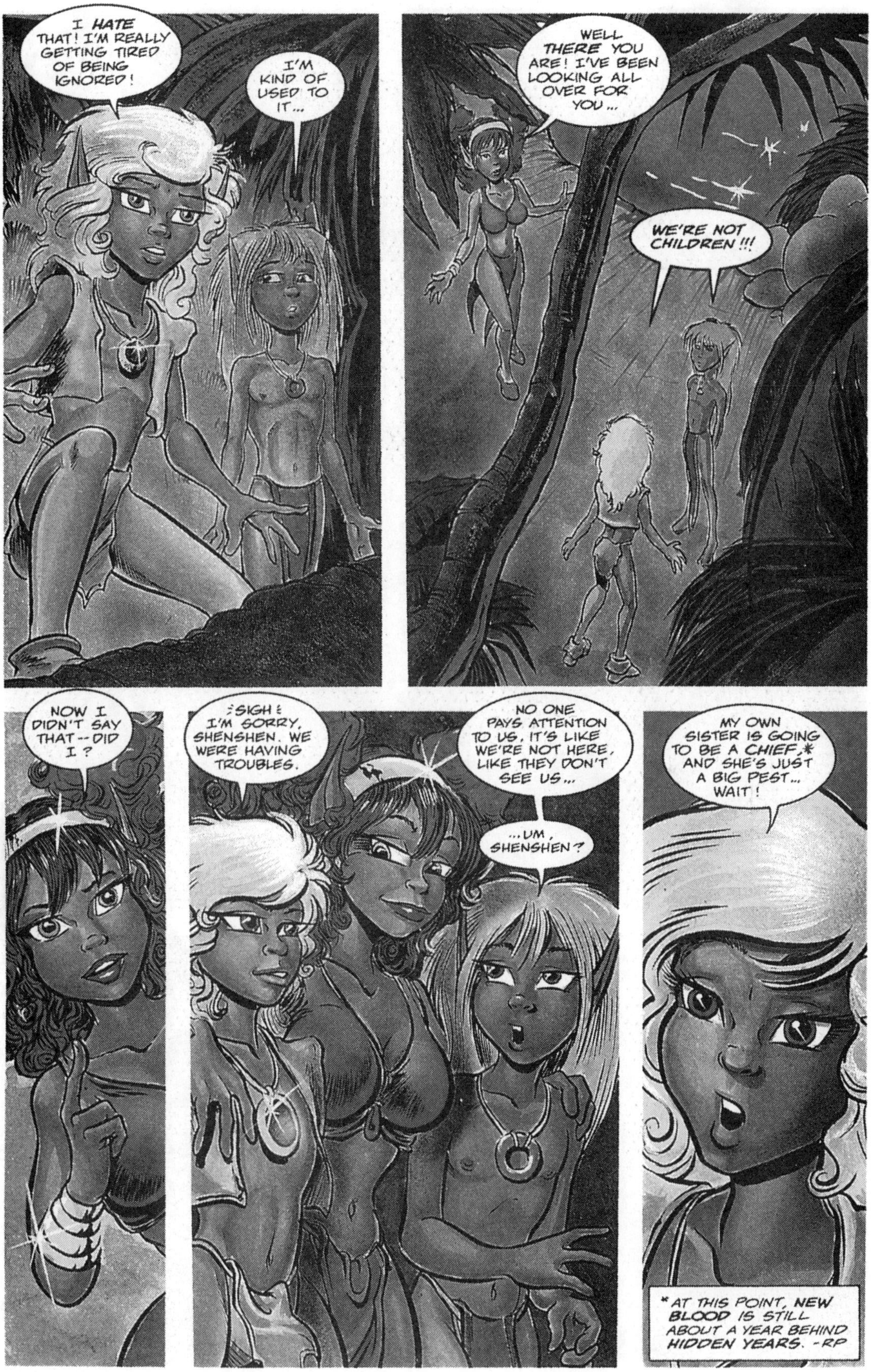
I HATE THAT! I'M REALLY GETTING TIRED OF BEING IGNORED!
I'M KIND OF USED TO IT...
WELL THERE YOU ARE! I'VE BEEN LOOKING ALL OVER FOR YOU...
WE'RE NOT CHILDREN!!!
NOW I DIDN'T SAY THAT--DID I?
:SIGH: I'M SORRY, SHENSHEN. WE WERE HAVING TROUBLES.
NO ONE PAYS ATTENTION TO US. IT'S LIKE WE'RE NOT HERE, LIKE THEY DON'T SEE US...
...UM, SHENSHEN?
MY OWN SISTER IS GOING TO BE A CHIEF,* AND SHE'S JUST A BIG PEST... WAIT!
*AT THIS POINT, NEW BLOOD IS STILL ABOUT A YEAR BEHIND HIDDEN YEARS. -RP

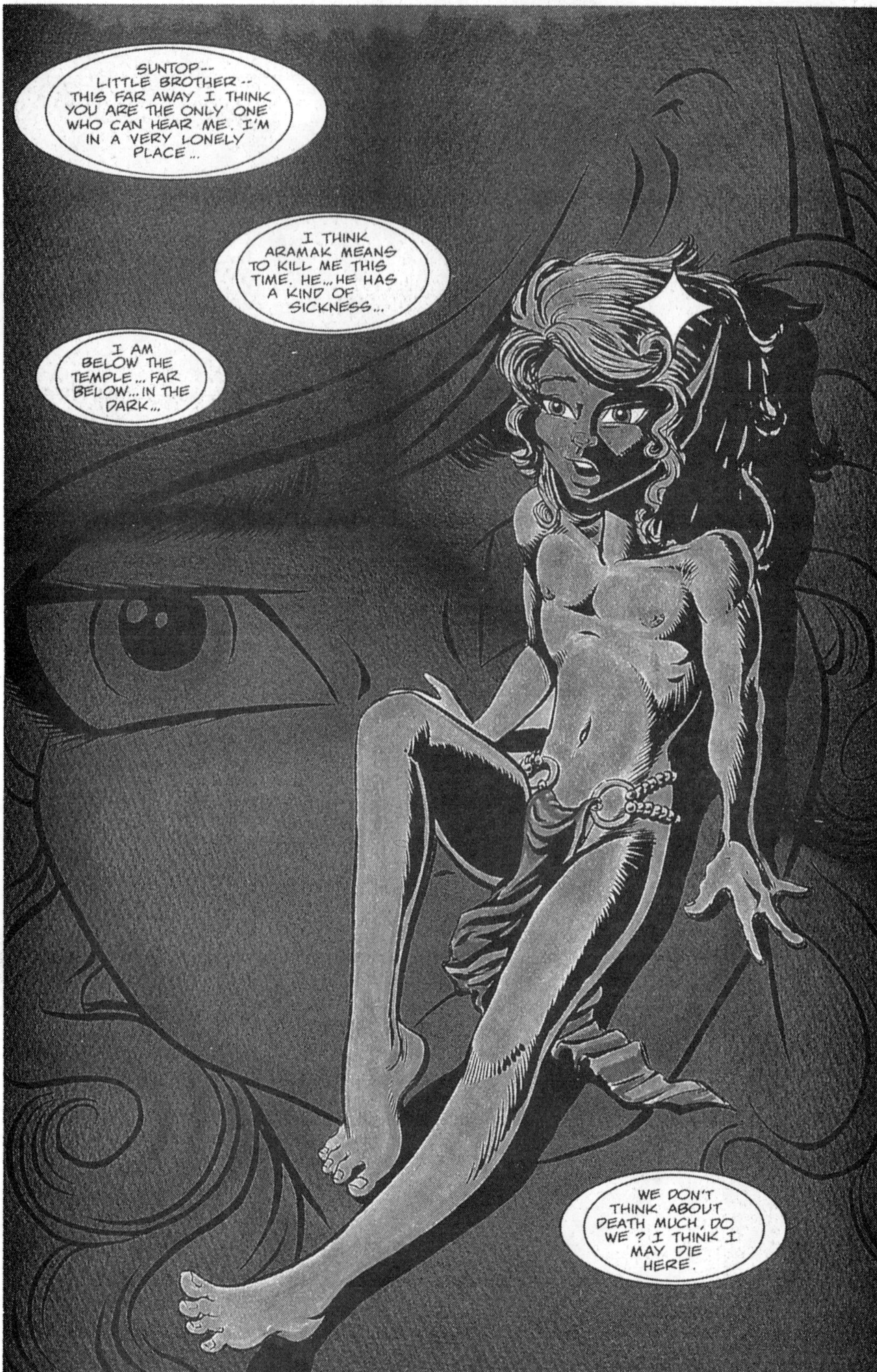
SUNTOP-- LITTLE BROTHER-- THIS FAR AWAY I THINK YOU ARE THE ONLY ONE WHO CAN HEAR ME. I'M IN A VERY LONELY PLACE...
I THINK ARAMAK MEANS TO KILL ME THIS TIME. HE...HE HAS A KIND OF SICKNESS...
I AM BELOW THE TEMPLE... FAR BELOW...IN THE DARK...
WE DON'T THINK ABOUT DEATH MUCH, DO WE? I THINK I MAY DIE HERE.

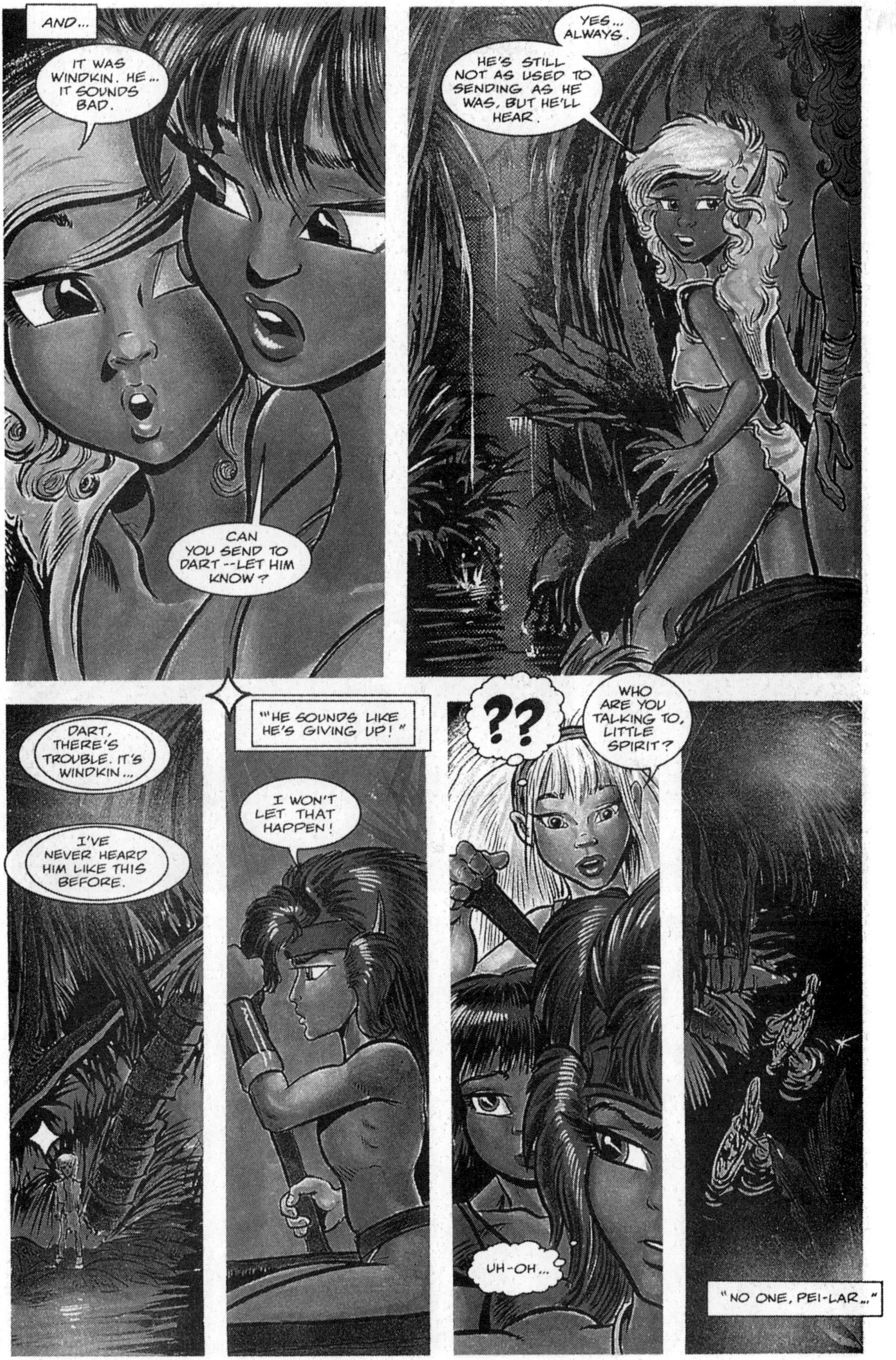
AND...
IT WAS WINDKIN. HE... IT SOUNDS BAD.
CAN YOU SEND TO DART--LET HIM KNOW?
YES... ALWAYS.
HE'S STILL NOT AS USED TO SENDING AS HE WAS, BUT HE'LL HEAR.
DART, THERE'S TROUBLE. IT'S WINDKIN...
I'VE NEVER HEARD HIM LIKE THIS BEFORE.
"HE SOUNDS LIKE HE'S GIVING UP!"
I WON'T LET THAT HAPPEN!
??
WHO ARE YOU TALKING TO, LITTLE SPIRIT?
UH-OH...
"NO ONE, PEI-LAR..."

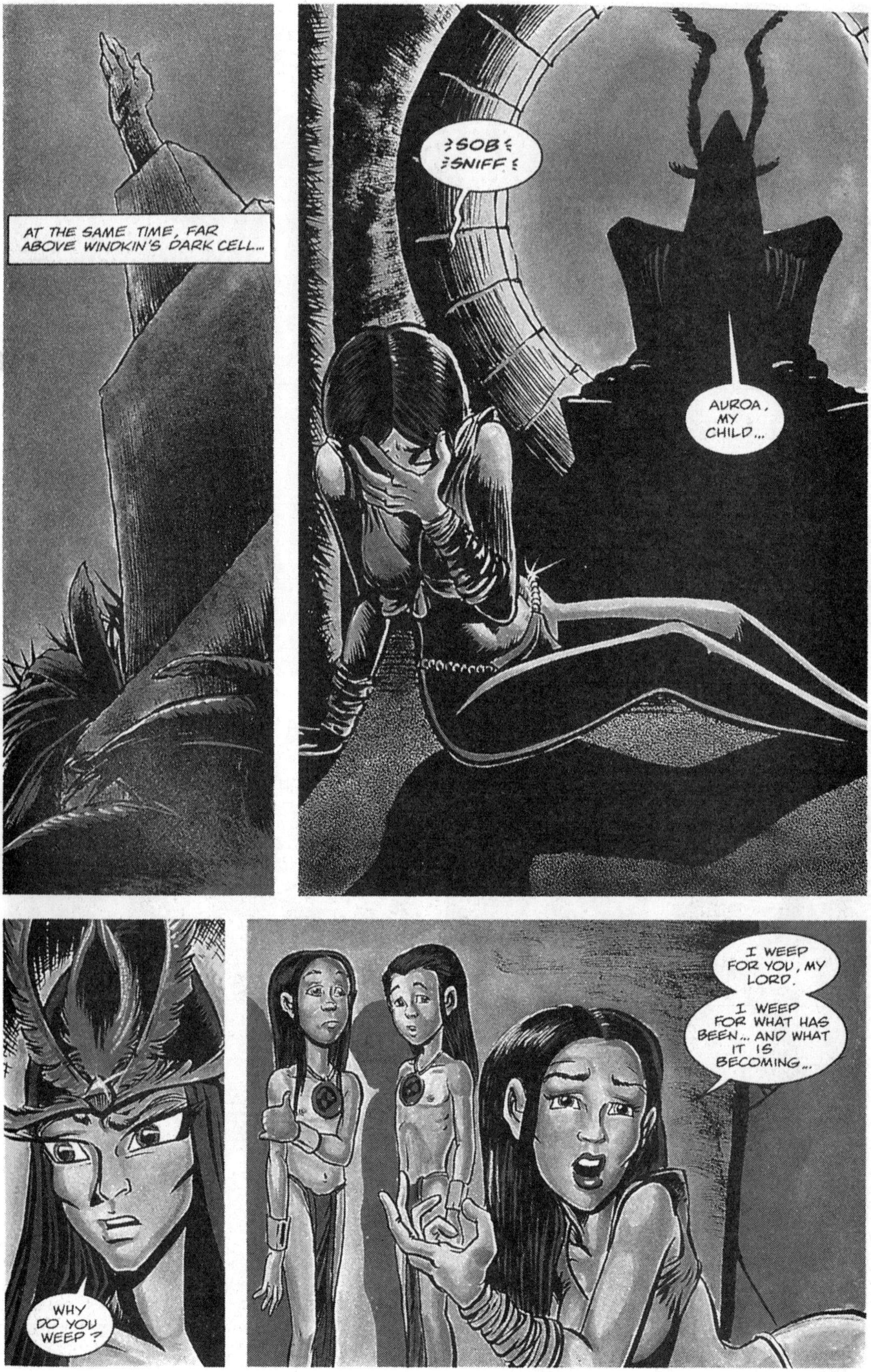
AT THE SAME TIME, FAR ABOVE WINDKIN'S DARK CELL...
SOB SNIFF
AUROA, MY CHILD...
WHY DO YOU WEEP?
I WEEP FOR YOU, MY LORD.
I WEEP FOR WHAT HAS BEEN... AND WHAT IT IS BECOMING...

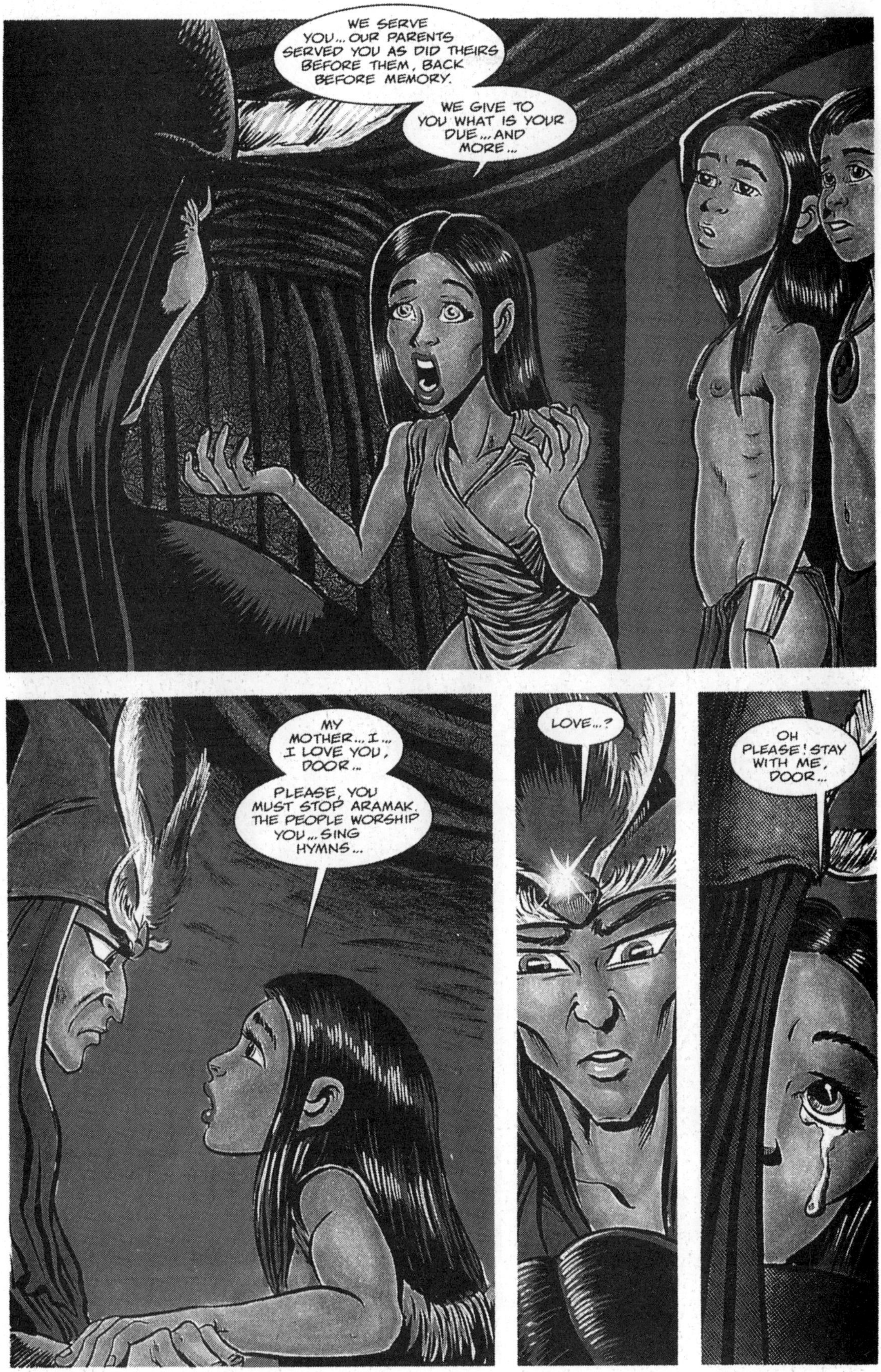
WE SERVE YOU... OUR PARENTS SERVED YOU AS DID THEIRS BEFORE THEM, BACK BEFORE MEMORY.
WE GIVE TO YOU WHAT IS YOUR DUE... AND MORE...
MY MOTHER... I... I LOVE YOU, DOOR...
PLEASE, YOU MUST STOP ARAMAK. THE PEOPLE WORSHIP YOU... SING HYMNS...
LOVE...?
OH PLEASE! STAY WITH ME, DOOR...

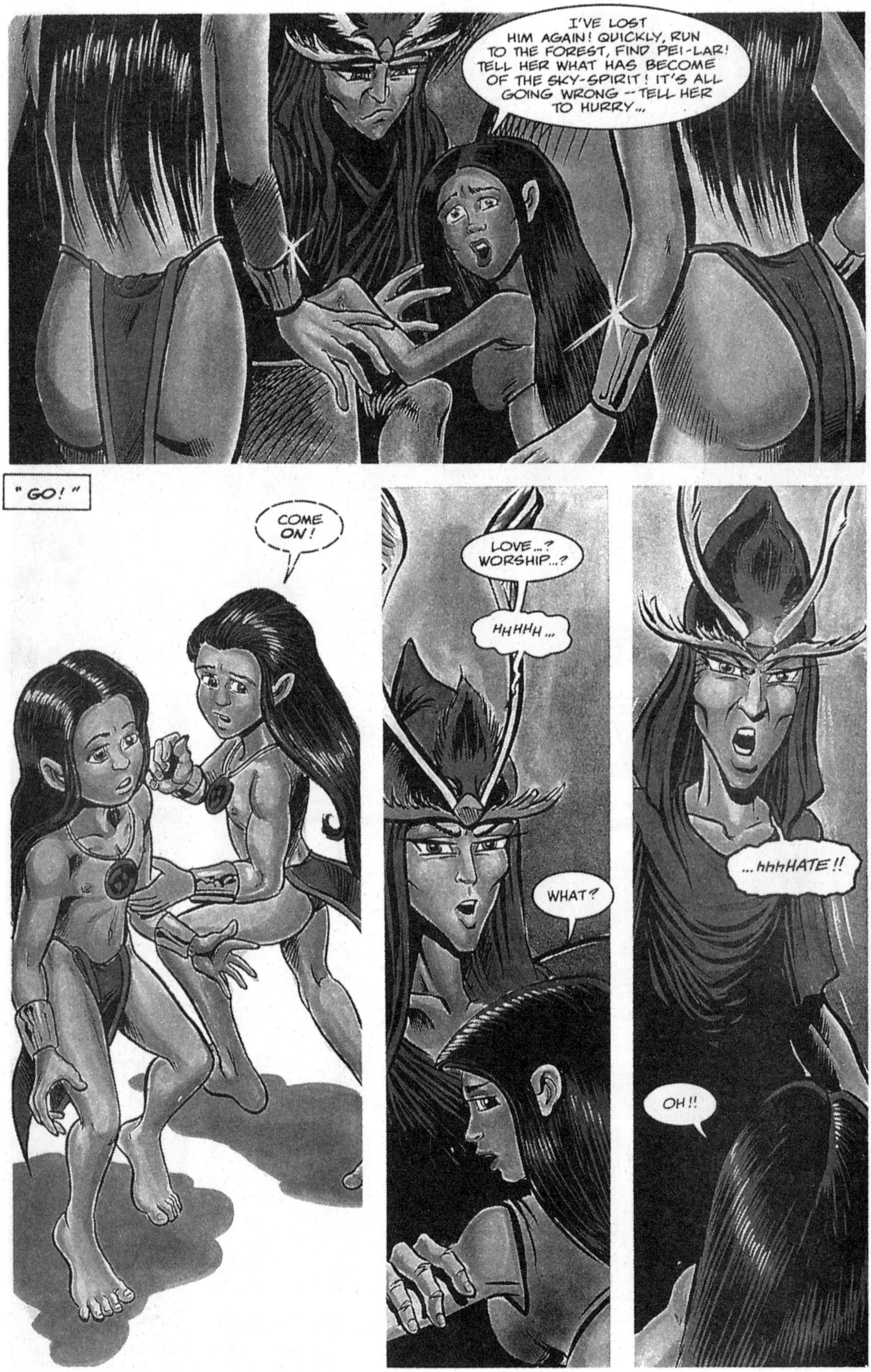
I'VE LOST HIM AGAIN! QUICKLY, RUN TO THE FOREST, FIND PEI-LAR! TELL HER WHAT HAS BECOME OF THE SKY-SPIRIT! IT'S ALL GOING WRONG -- TELL HER TO HURRY...
"GO!"
COME ON!
LOVE...? WORSHIP...?
HHHHH...
WHAT?
...hhhHATE!!
OH!!

NO! NO ONE LEAVES UNTIL I BID!
I AM THE SKY SPIRIT. I AM THE FIRST, THE ATTAINED ONE.
I AM ALL THAT REMAINS OF THE BLACK SNAKE!

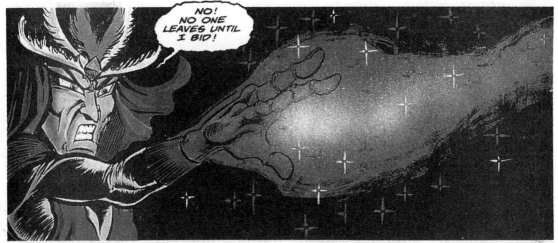

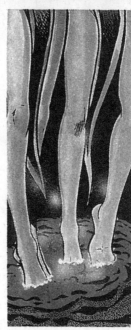

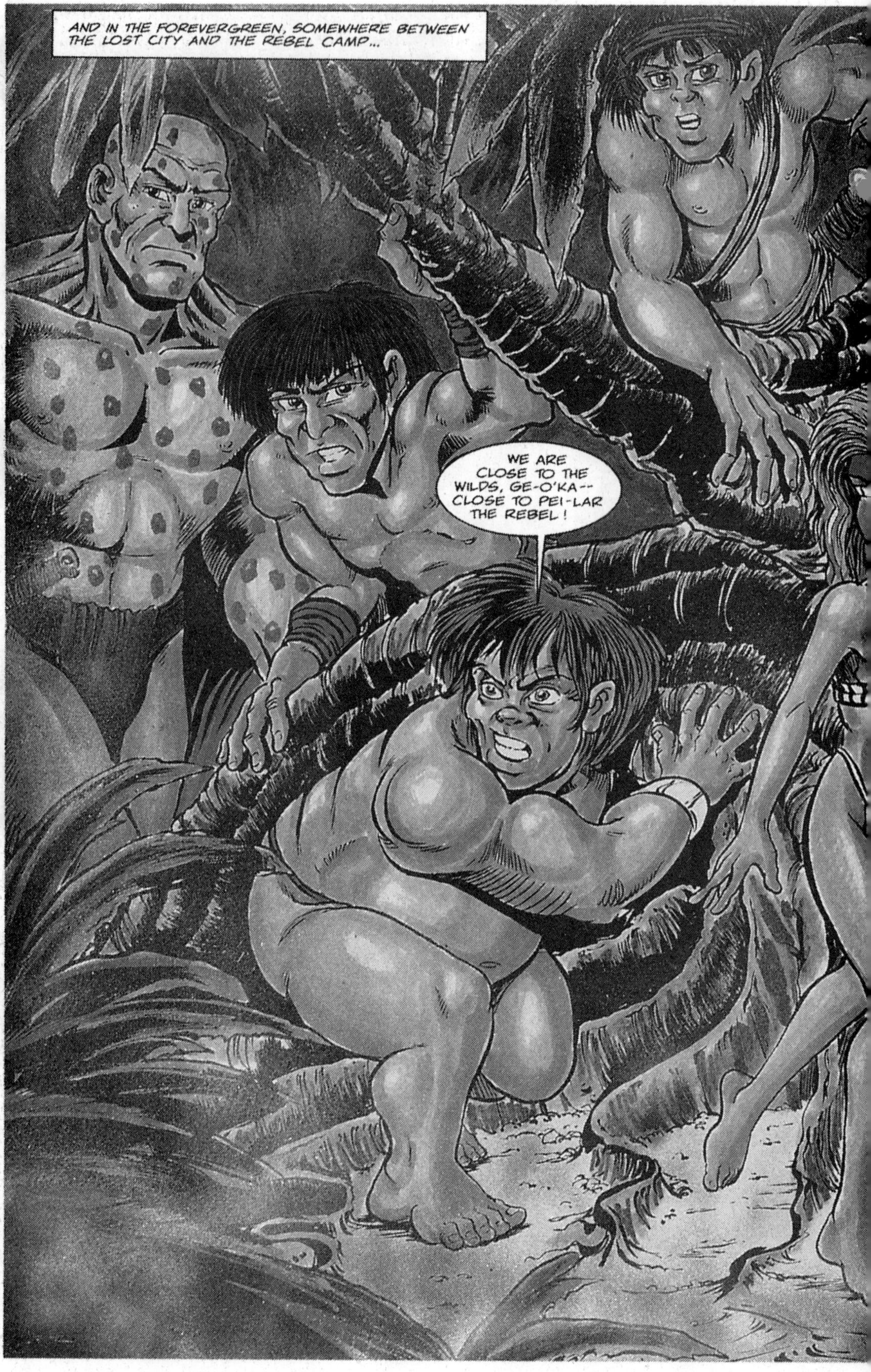
AND IN THE FOREVERGREEN, SOMEWHERE BETWEEN THE LOST CITY AND THE REBEL CAMP...
WE ARE CLOSE TO THE WILDS, GE-O'KA-- CLOSE TO PEI-LAR THE REBEL!

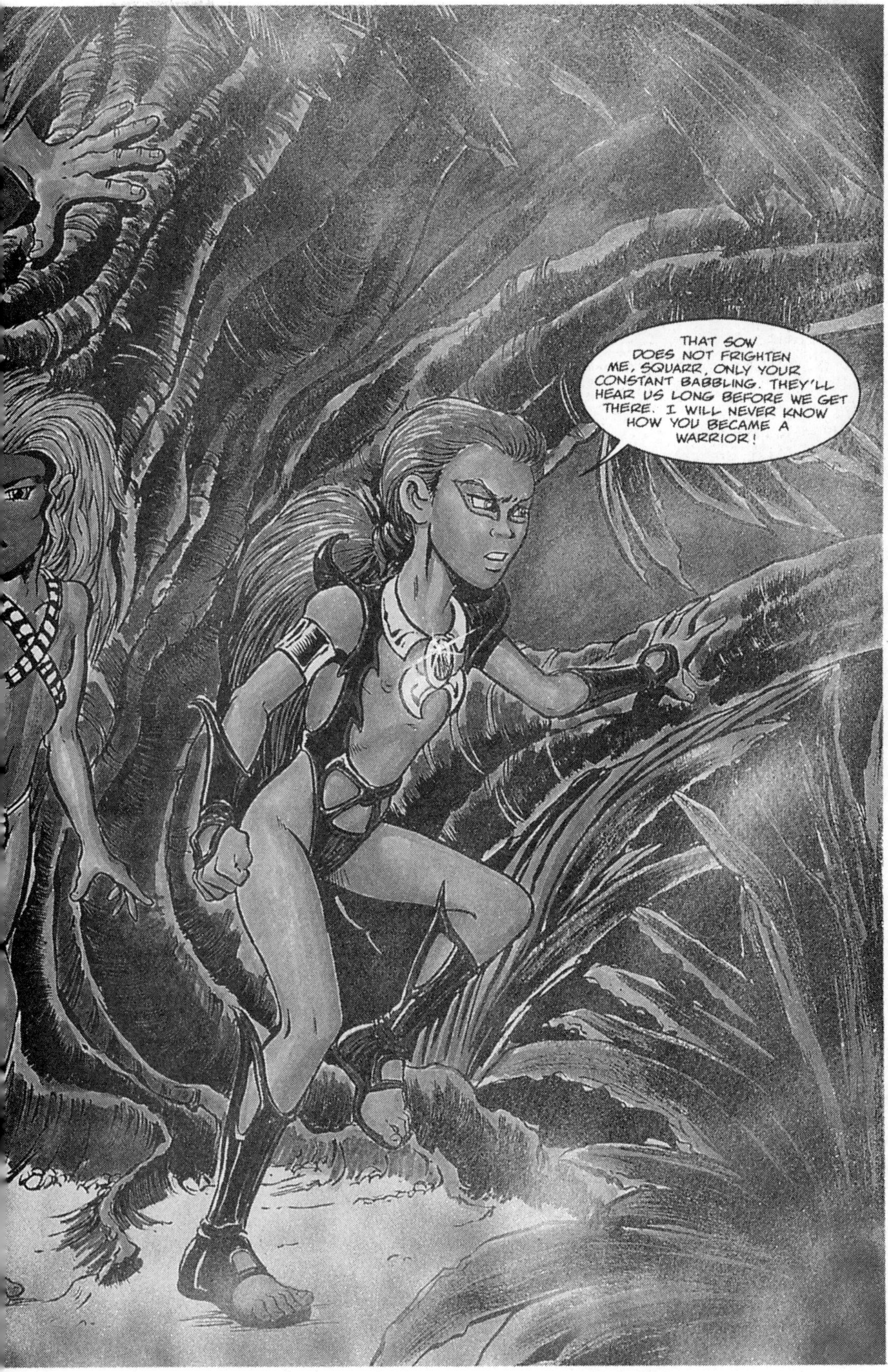
THAT SOW DOES NOT FRIGHTEN ME, SQUARR, ONLY YOUR CONSTANT BABBLING. THEY'LL HEAR US LONG BEFORE WE GET THERE. I WILL NEVER KNOW HOW YOU BECAME A WARRIOR!

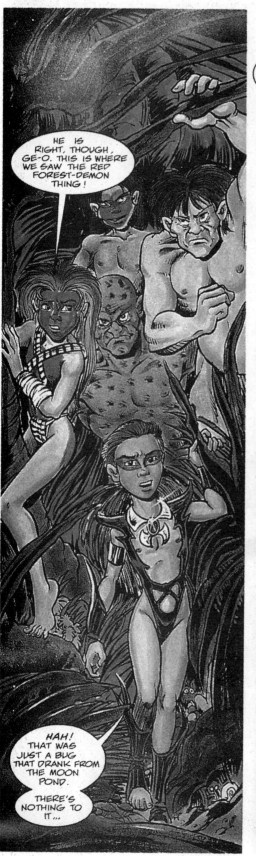

HE IS RIGHT, THOUGH, GE-O. THIS IS WHERE WE SAW THE RED FOREST-DEMON THING!

HAH! THAT WAS JUST A BUG THAT DRANK FROM THE MOON POND.

THERE'S NOTHING TO IT...

EVEN SO, THERE ARE STRANGE THINGS IN THESE WOODS.

DOES YOUR MOTHER STILL TELL YOU THOSE TALES WHEN SHE TUCKS YOU IN AT NIGHT, AHN-LAI?

≶CHUCKLE≶

≶SNICKER≶

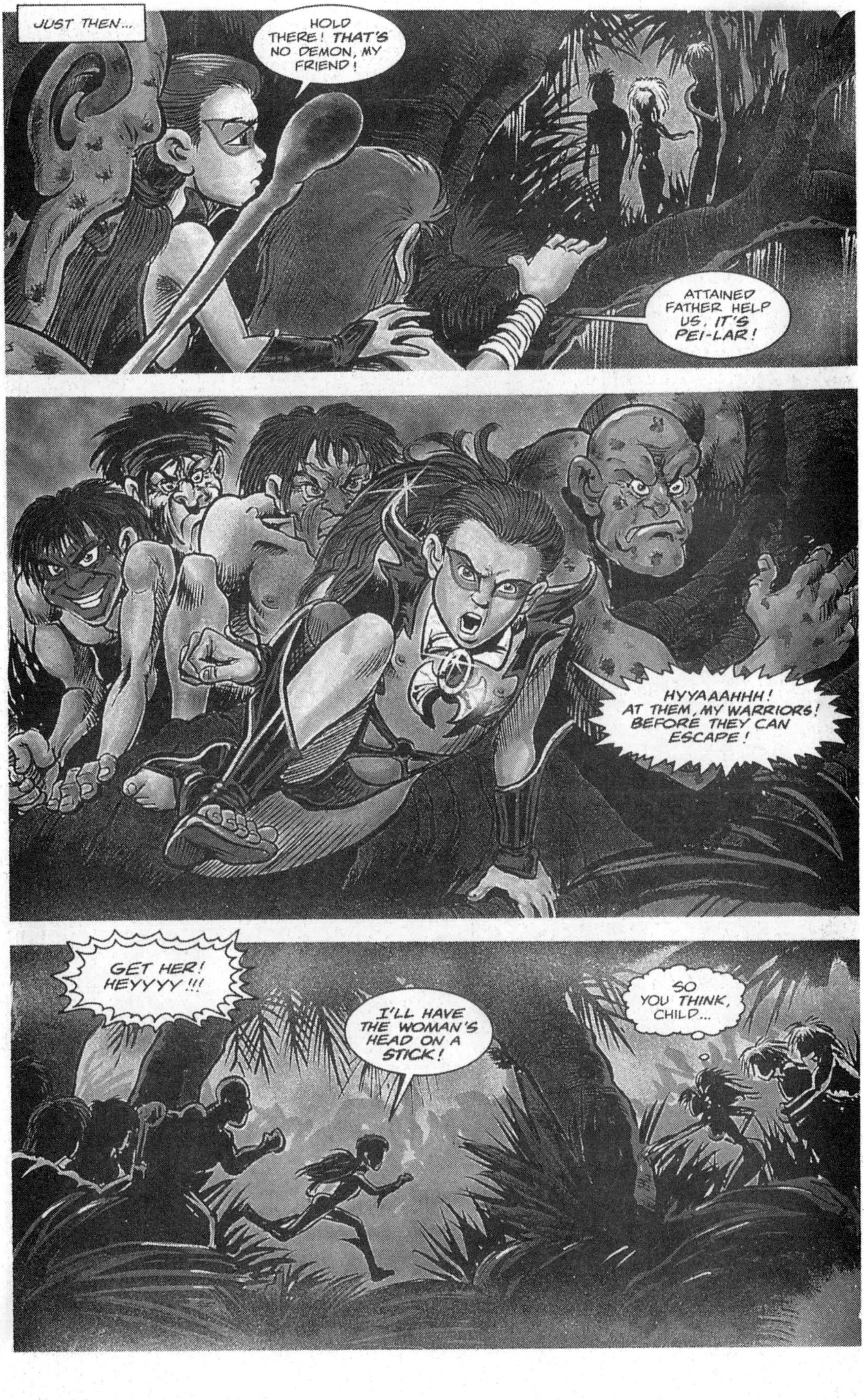
JUST THEN...
HOLD THERE! THAT'S NO DEMON, MY FRIEND!
ATTAINED FATHER HELP US. IT'S PEI-LAR!
HYYAAAHHH! AT THEM, MY WARRIORS! BEFORE THEY CAN ESCAPE!
GET HER! HEYYYY!!!
I'LL HAVE THE WOMAN'S HEAD ON A STICK!
SO YOU THINK, CHILD...

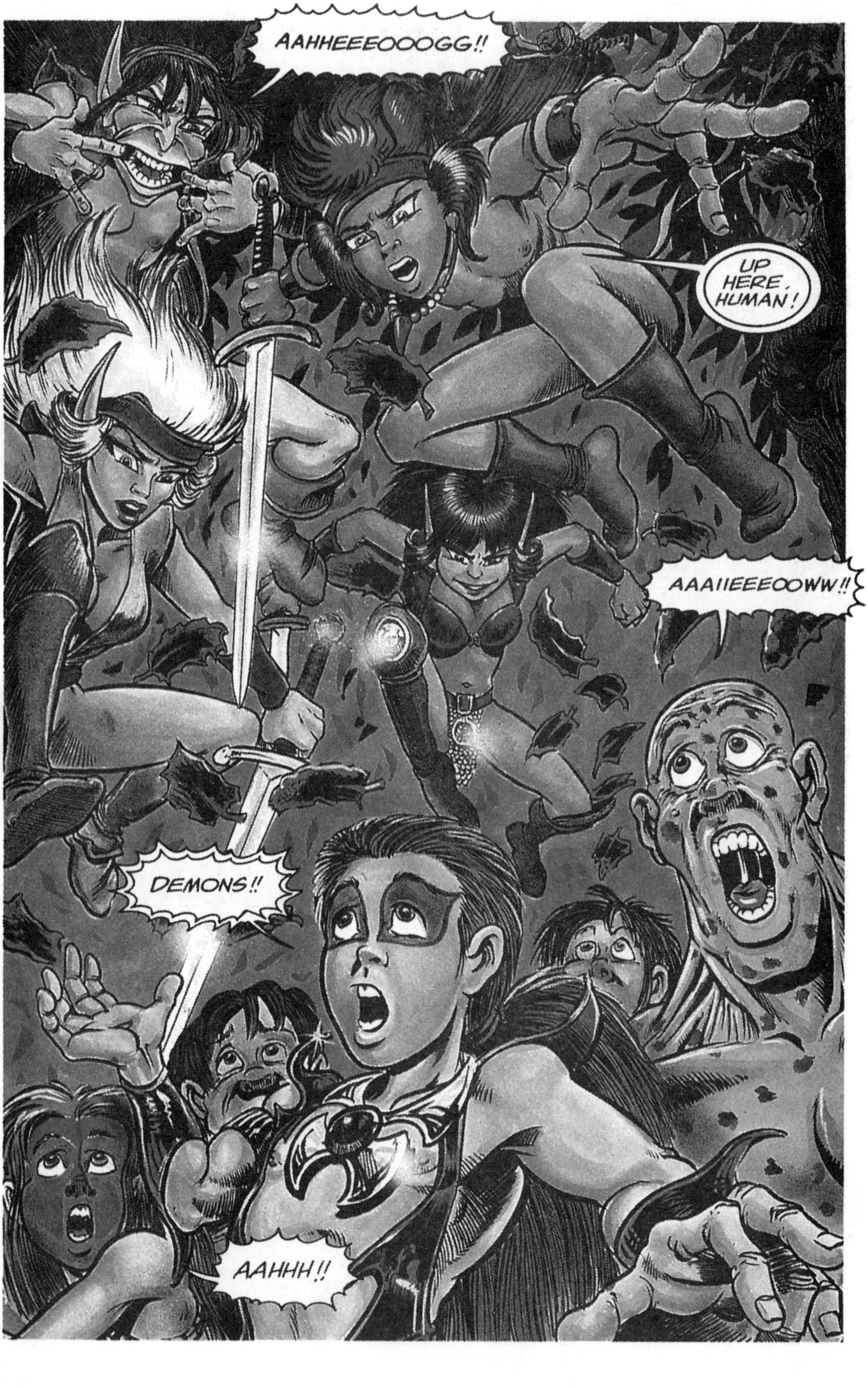
AAHHEEEOOOGG!!
UP HERE, HUMAN!
AAAIIEEEOOWW!!
DEMONS!!
AAHHH!!

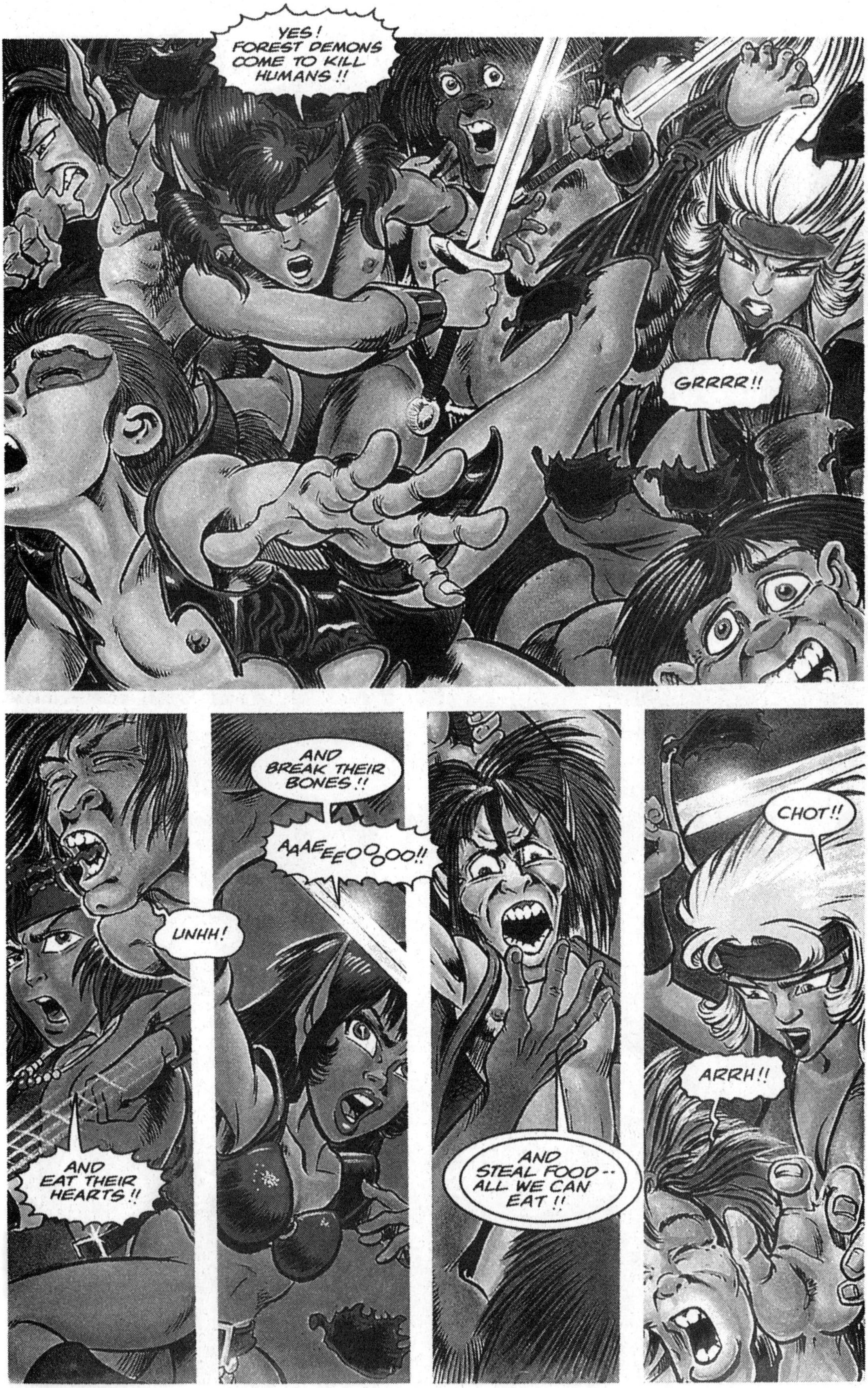
YES! FOREST DEMONS COME TO KILL HUMANS!!
GRRRR!!
AND BREAK THEIR BONES!!
AAAEEEOOOOO!!
UNHH!
AND EAT THEIR HEARTS!!
AND STEAL FOOD-- ALL WE CAN EAT!!
CHOT!!
ARRH!!

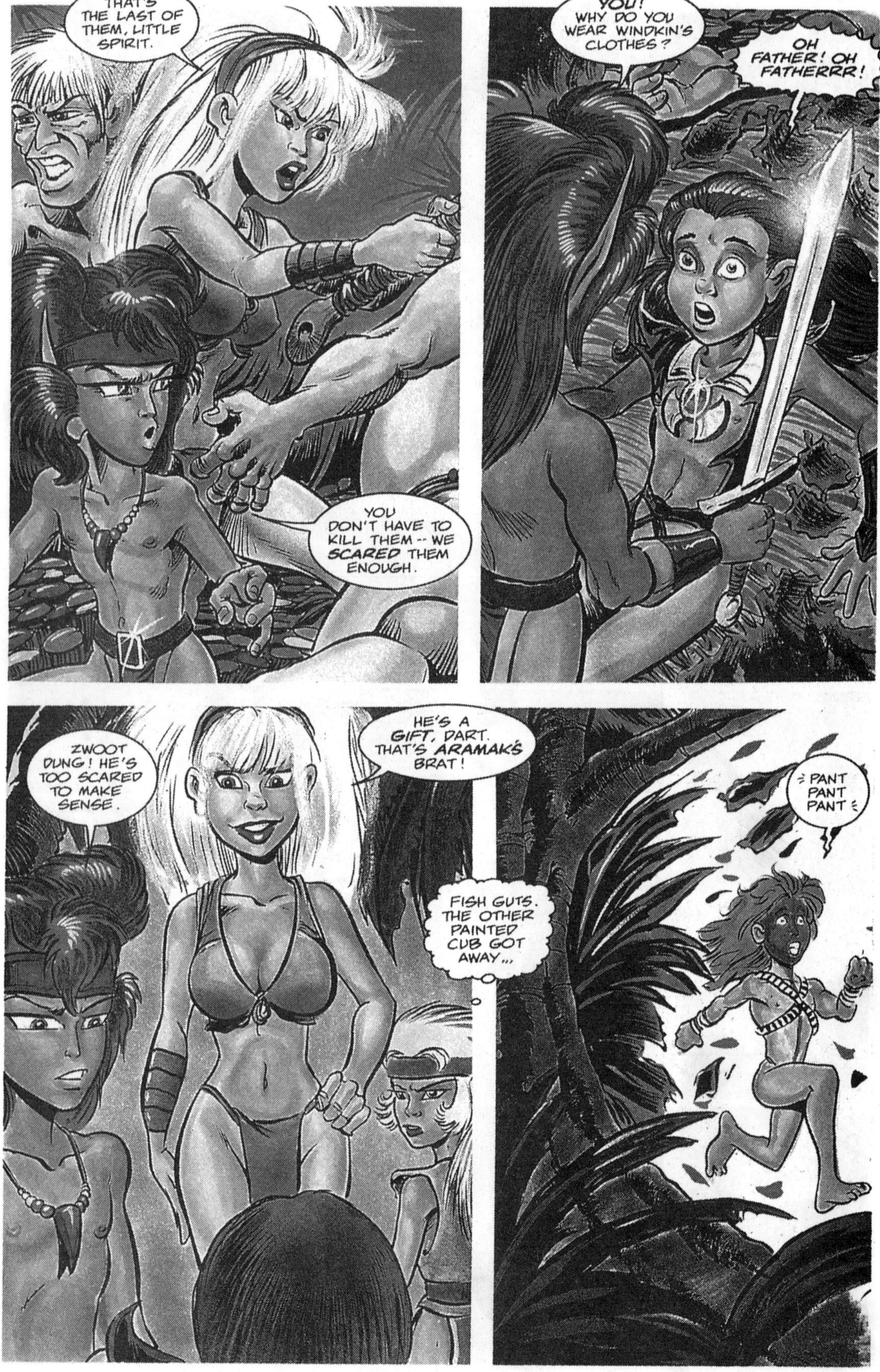
THAT'S THE LAST OF THEM, LITTLE SPIRIT.
YOU DON'T HAVE TO KILL THEM -- WE SCARED THEM ENOUGH.
YOU! WHY DO YOU WEAR WINDKIN'S CLOTHES?
OH FATHER! OH FATHERRR!
ZWOOT DUNG! HE'S TOO SCARED TO MAKE SENSE.
HE'S A GIFT, DART. THAT'S ARAMAK'S BRAT!
FISH GUTS. THE OTHER PAINTED CUB GOT AWAY...
PANT PANT PANT

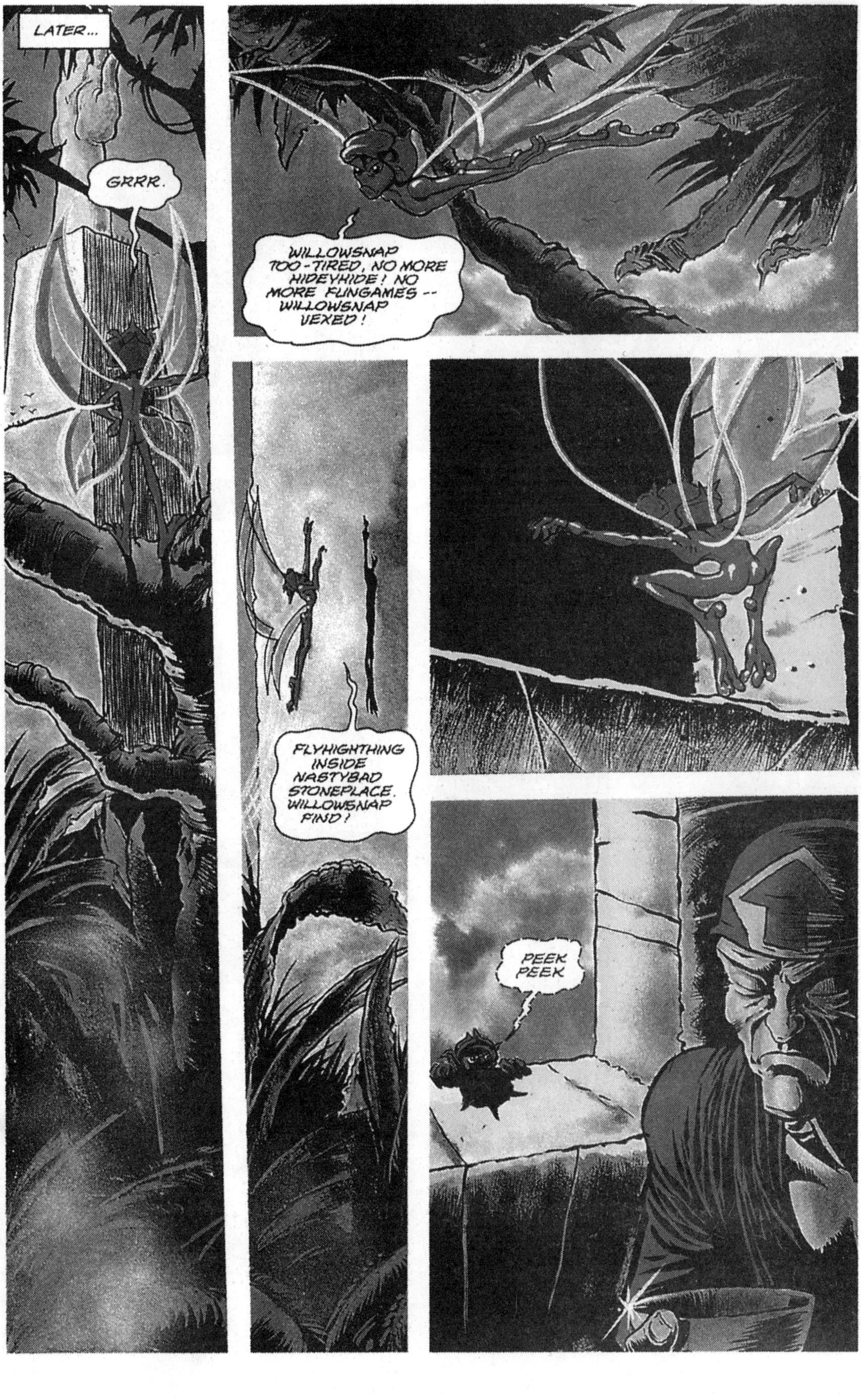
LATER...
GRRR.
WILLOWSNAP TOO-TIRED, NO MORE HIDEYHIDE! NO MORE FUNGAMES -- WILLOWSNAP VEXED!
FLYHIGHTHING INSIDE NASTYBAD STONEPLACE. WILLOWSNAP FIND!
PEEK PEEK

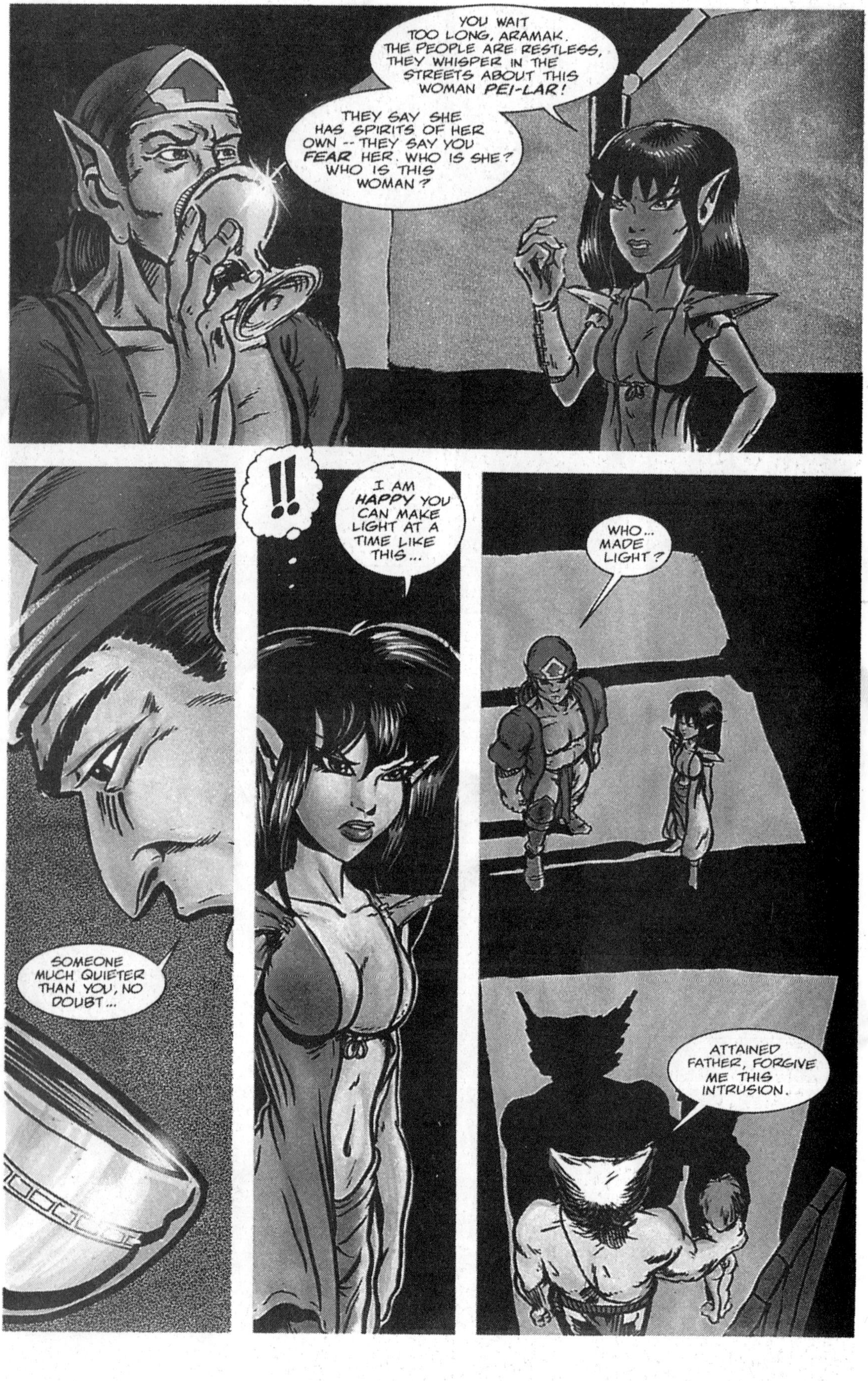
YOU WAIT TOO LONG, ARAMAK. THE PEOPLE ARE RESTLESS, THEY WHISPER IN THE STREETS ABOUT THIS WOMAN PEI-LAR!
THEY SAY SHE HAS SPIRITS OF HER OWN -- THEY SAY YOU FEAR HER. WHO IS SHE? WHO IS THIS WOMAN?
!!
I AM HAPPY YOU CAN MAKE LIGHT AT A TIME LIKE THIS...
SOMEONE MUCH QUIETER THAN YOU, NO DOUBT...
WHO... MADE LIGHT?
ATTAINED FATHER, FORGIVE ME THIS INTRUSION.

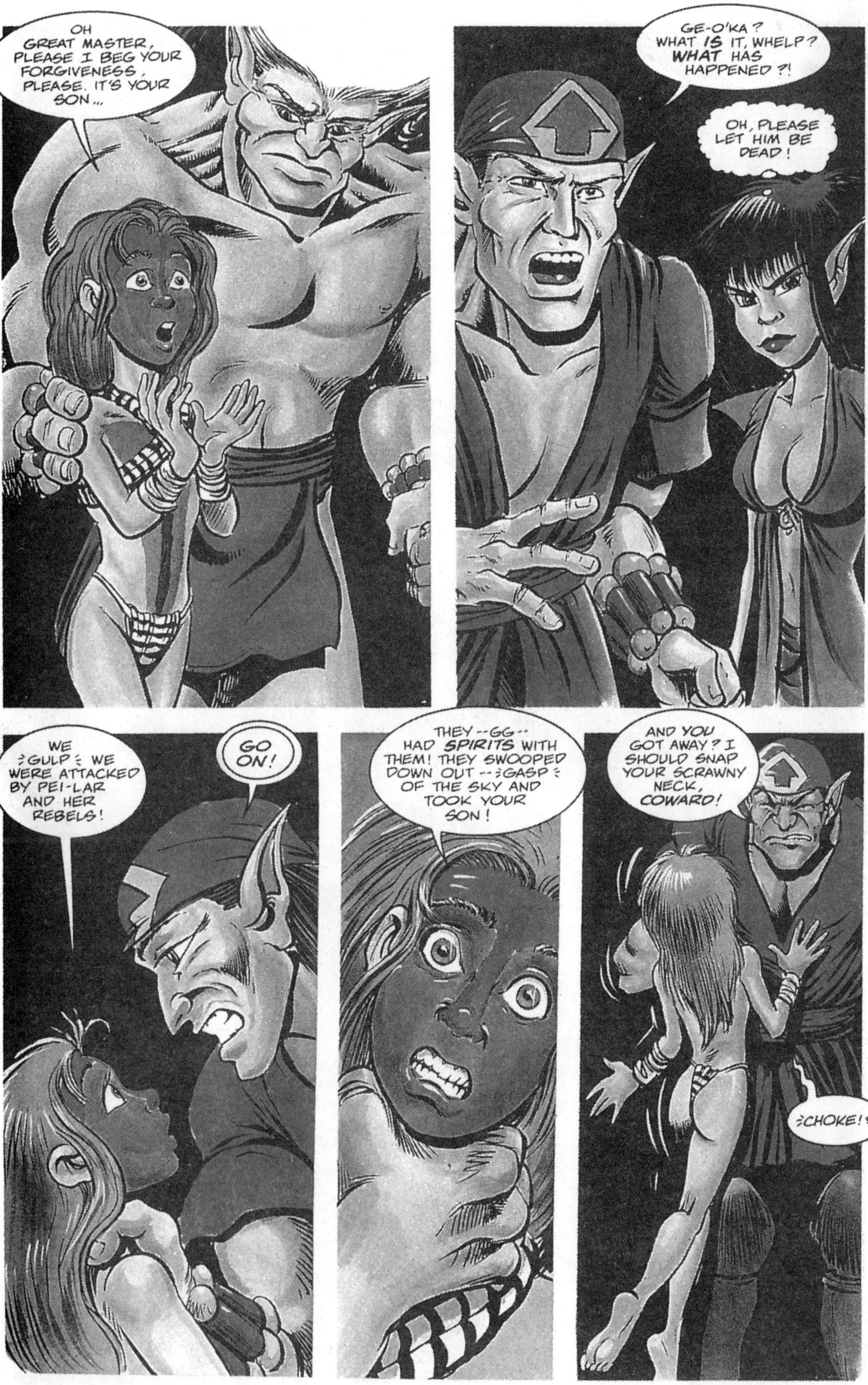

OH GREAT MASTER, PLEASE I BEG YOUR FORGIVENESS, PLEASE. IT'S YOUR SON...
GE-O'KA? WHAT IS IT, WHELP? WHAT HAS HAPPENED?!
OH, PLEASE LET HIM BE DEAD!
WE ~GULP~ WE WERE ATTACKED BY PEI-LAR AND HER REBELS!
GO ON!
THEY --GG-- HAD SPIRITS WITH THEM! THEY SWOOPED DOWN OUT --~GASP~ OF THE SKY AND TOOK YOUR SON!
AND YOU GOT AWAY? I SHOULD SNAP YOUR SCRAWNY NECK, COWARD!
~CHOKE!~

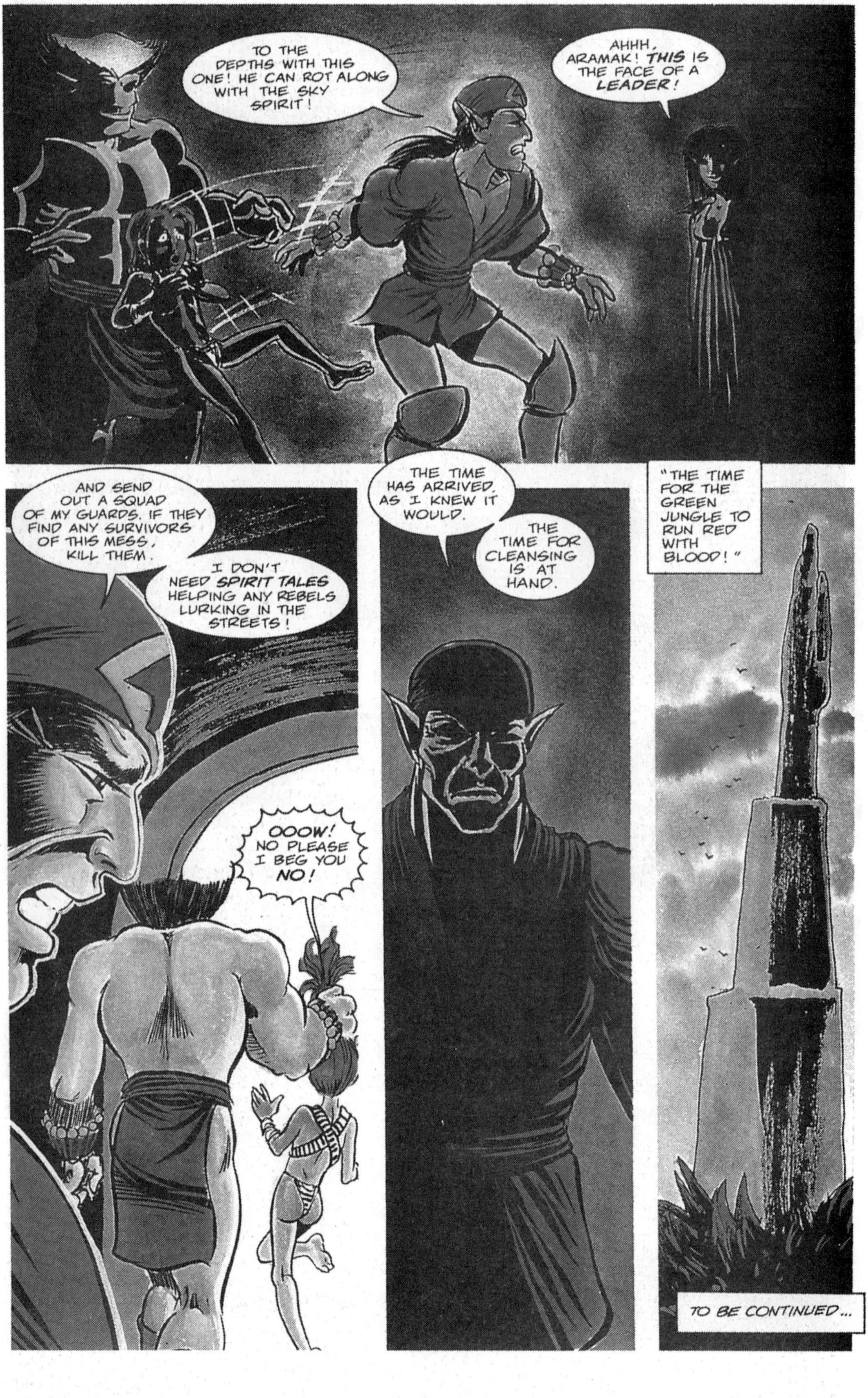
TO THE DEPTHS WITH THIS ONE! HE CAN ROT ALONG WITH THE SKY SPIRIT!
AHHH, ARAMAK! THIS IS THE FACE OF A LEADER!
AND SEND OUT A SQUAD OF MY GUARDS. IF THEY FIND ANY SURVIVORS OF THIS MESS, KILL THEM.
I DON'T NEED SPIRIT TALES HELPING ANY REBELS LURKING IN THE STREETS!
OOOW! NO PLEASE I BEG YOU NO!
THE TIME HAS ARRIVED, AS I KNEW IT WOULD.
THE TIME FOR CLEANSING IS AT HAND.
"THE TIME FOR THE GREEN JUNGLE TO RUN RED WITH BLOOD!"
TO BE CONTINUED...

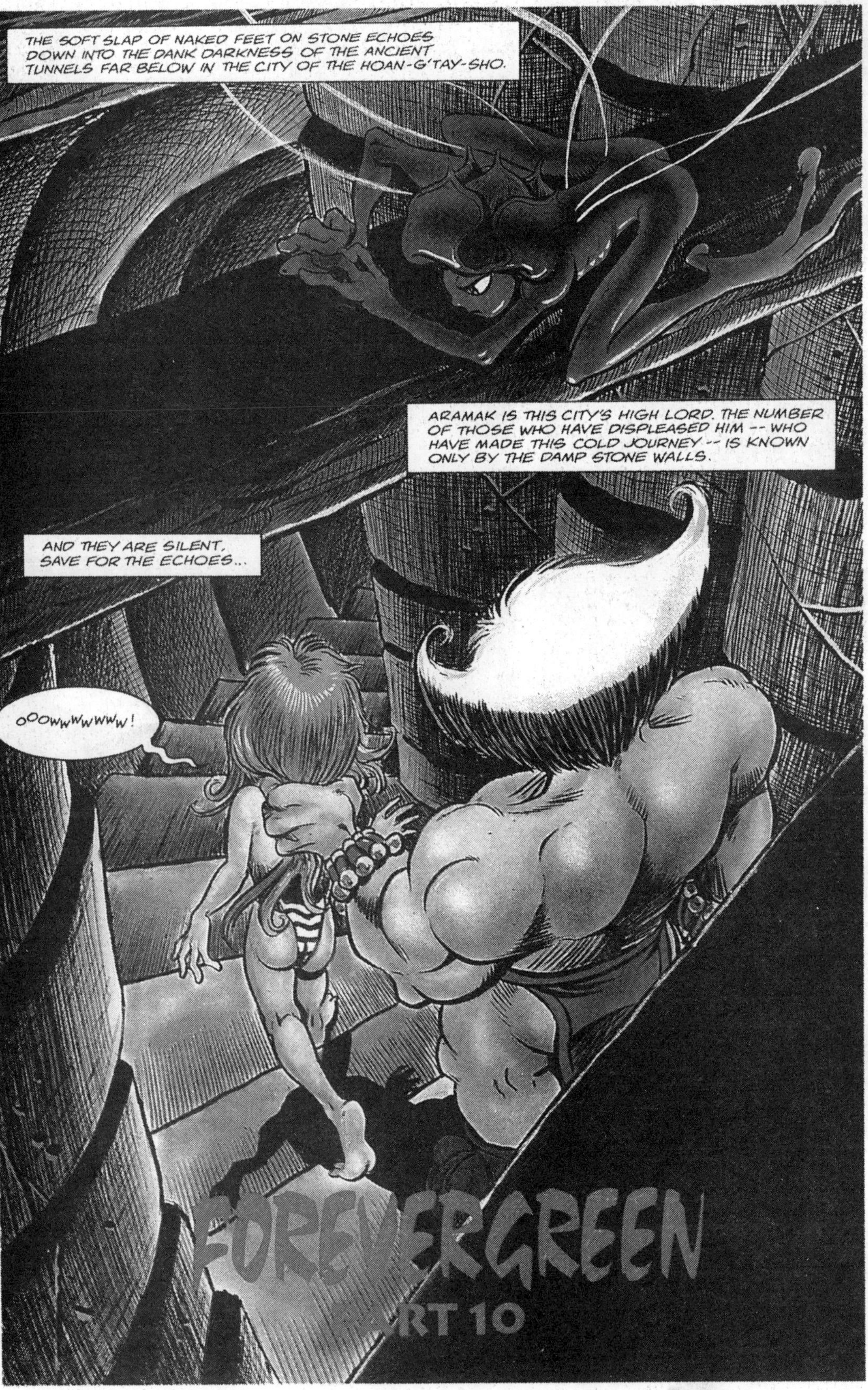
THE SOFT SLAP OF NAKED FEET ON STONE ECHOES DOWN INTO THE DANK DARKNESS OF THE ANCIENT TUNNELS FAR BELOW IN THE CITY OF THE HOAN-G'TAY-SHO.
ARAMAK IS THIS CITY'S HIGH LORD. THE NUMBER OF THOSE WHO HAVE DISPLEASED HIM -- WHO HAVE MADE THIS COLD JOURNEY -- IS KNOWN ONLY BY THE DAMP STONE WALLS.
AND THEY ARE SILENT, SAVE FOR THE ECHOES...
OOOWWWWWWW!
FOREVERGREEN

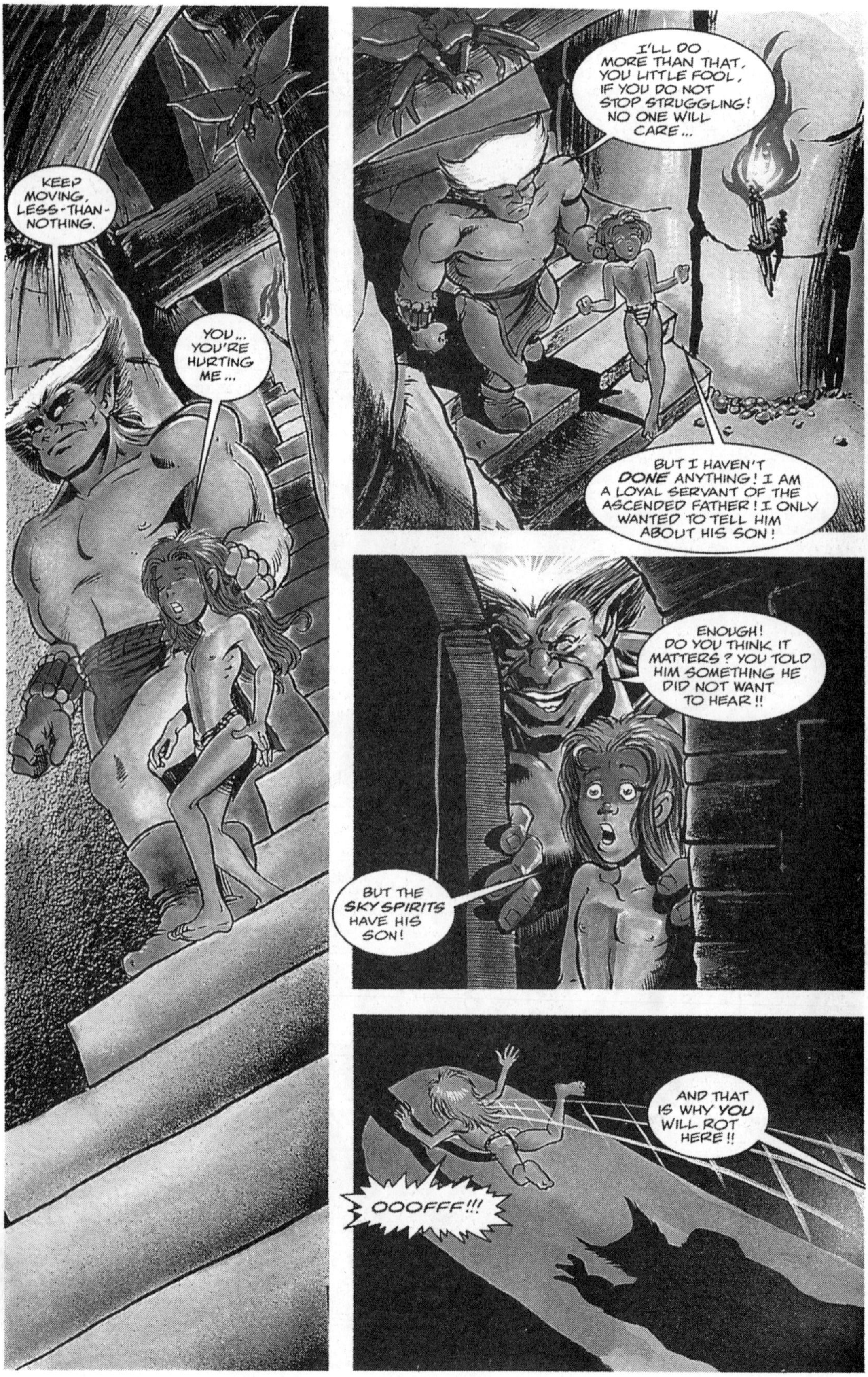
KEEP MOVING, LESS-THAN-NOTHING.
YOU... YOU'RE HURTING ME...
I'LL DO MORE THAN THAT, YOU LITTLE FOOL, IF YOU DO NOT STOP STRUGGLING! NO ONE WILL CARE...
BUT I HAVEN'T DONE ANYTHING! I AM A LOYAL SERVANT OF THE ASCENDED FATHER! I ONLY WANTED TO TELL HIM ABOUT HIS SON!
ENOUGH! DO YOU THINK IT MATTERS? YOU TOLD HIM SOMETHING HE DID NOT WANT TO HEAR!!
BUT THE SKY SPIRITS HAVE HIS SON!
AND THAT IS WHY YOU WILL ROT HERE!!
OOOFFF!!!

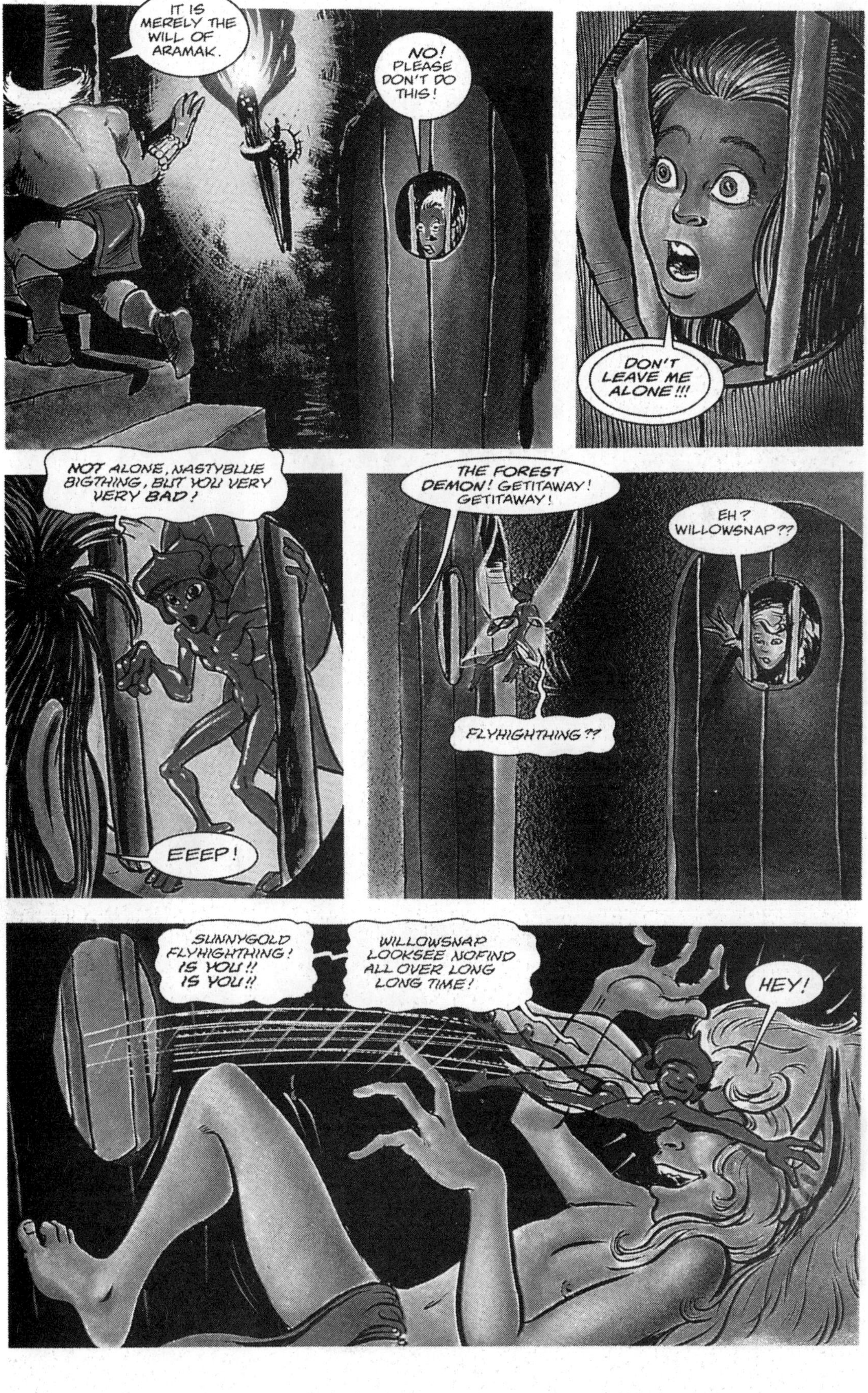
IT IS MERELY THE WILL OF ARAMAK.
NO! PLEASE DON'T DO THIS!
DON'T LEAVE ME ALONE!!!
NOT ALONE, NASTYBLUE BIGTHING, BUT YOU VERY VERY BAD!
EEEP!
THE FOREST DEMON! GETITAWAY! GETITAWAY!
EH? WILLOWSNAP??
FLYHIGHTHING??
SUNNYGOLD FLYHIGHTHING! IS YOU!! IS YOU!!
WILLOWSNAP LOOKSEE NOFIND ALL OVER LONG LONG TIME!
HEY!

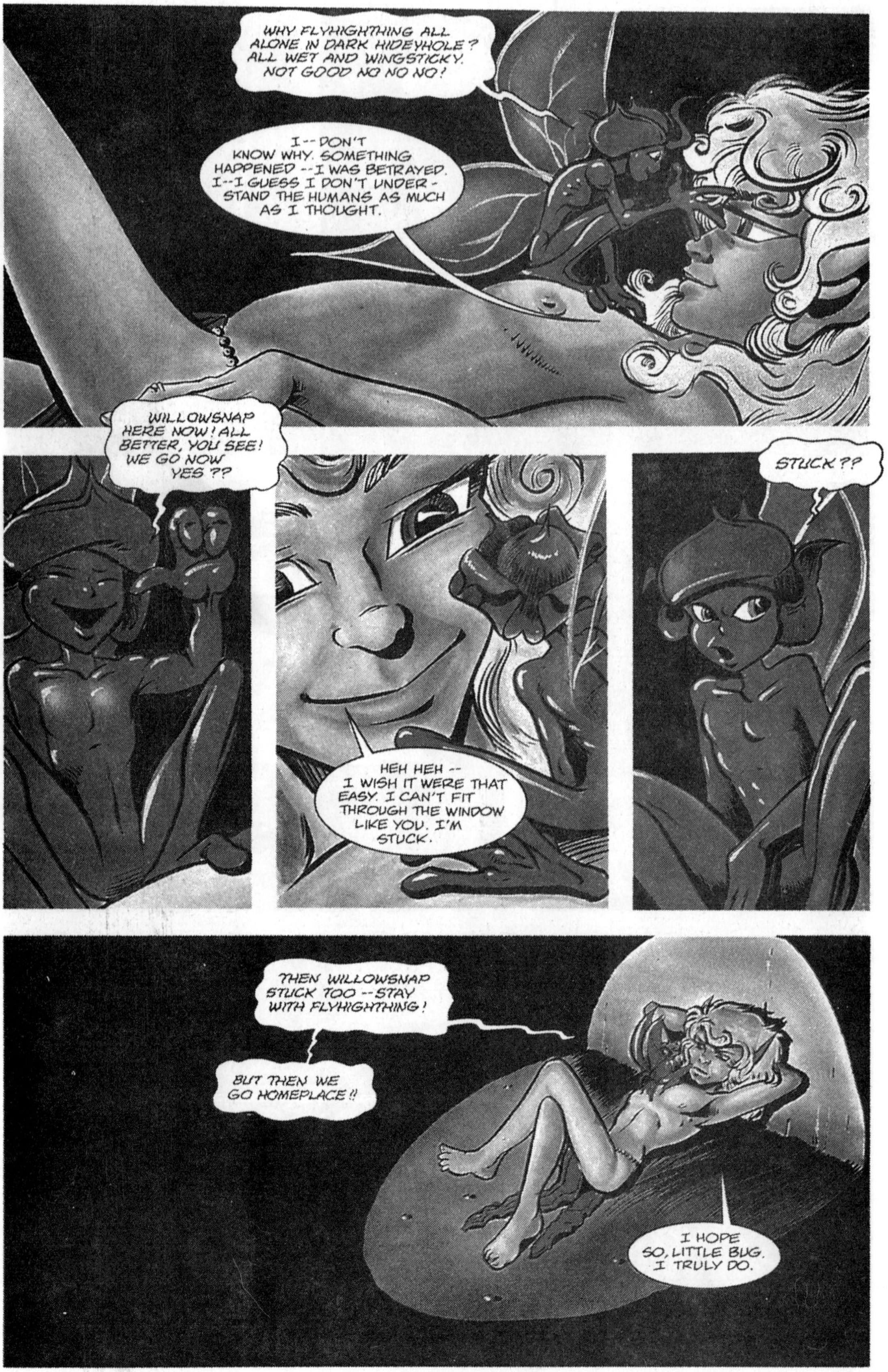
WHY FLYHIGHTHING ALL ALONE IN DARK HIDEYHOLE? ALL WET AND WINGSTICKY. NOT GOOD NO NO NO!
I--DON'T KNOW WHY. SOMETHING HAPPENED--I WAS BETRAYED. I--I GUESS I DON'T UNDERSTAND THE HUMANS AS MUCH AS I THOUGHT.
WILLOWSNAP HERE NOW! ALL BETTER, YOU SEE! WE GO NOW YES??
HEH HEH -- I WISH IT WERE THAT EASY. I CAN'T FIT THROUGH THE WINDOW LIKE YOU. I'M STUCK.
STUCK??
THEN WILLOWSNAP STUCK TOO--STAY WITH FLYHIGHTHING!
BUT THEN WE GO HOMEPLACE!!
I HOPE SO, LITTLE BUG. I TRULY DO.

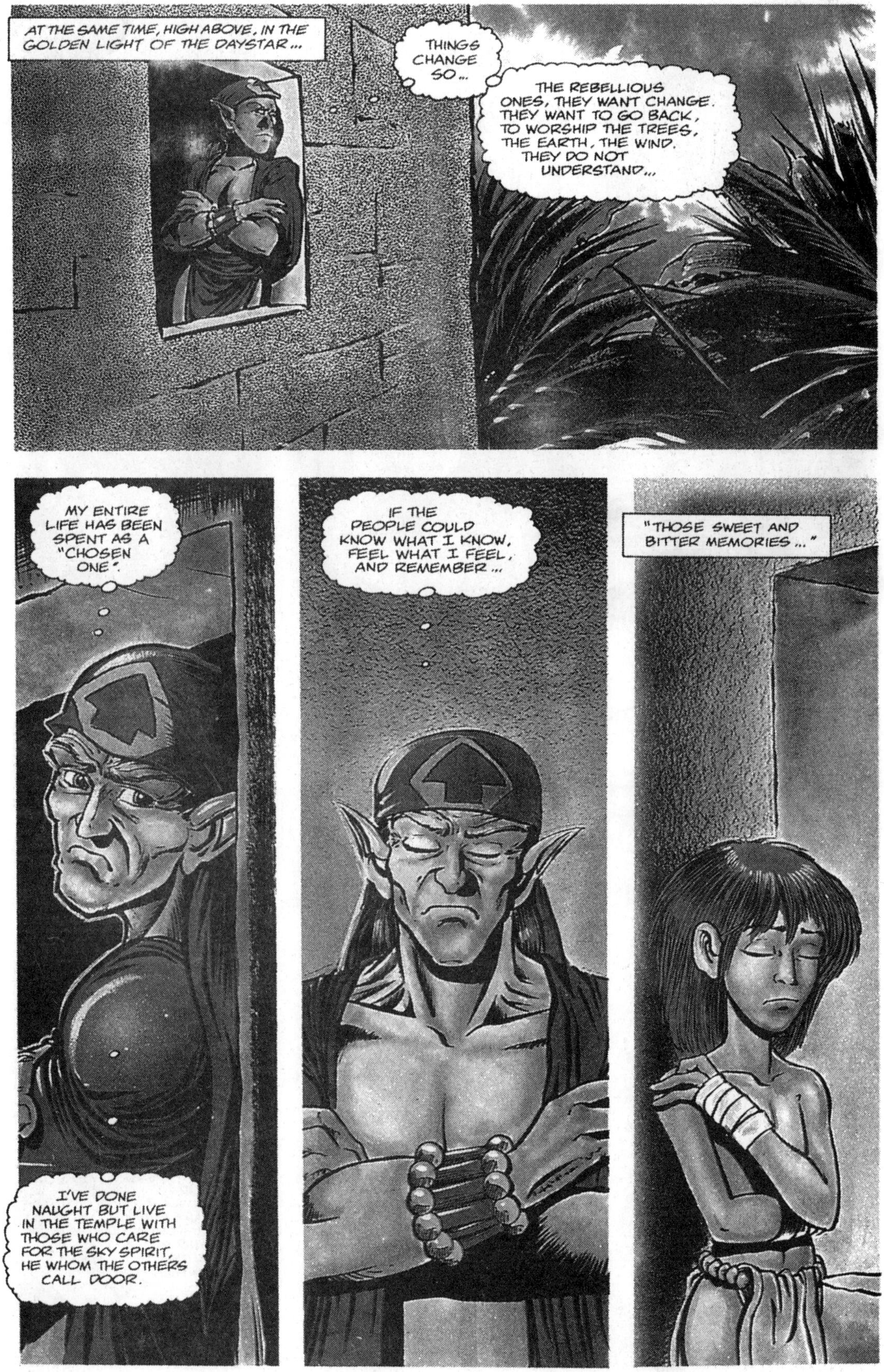
AT THE SAME TIME, HIGH ABOVE, IN THE GOLDEN LIGHT OF THE DAYSTAR...
THINGS CHANGE SO...
THE REBELLIOUS ONES, THEY WANT CHANGE. THEY WANT TO GO BACK, TO WORSHIP THE TREES, THE EARTH, THE WIND. THEY DO NOT UNDERSTAND...
MY ENTIRE LIFE HAS BEEN SPENT AS A "CHOSEN ONE".
I'VE DONE NAUGHT BUT LIVE IN THE TEMPLE WITH THOSE WHO CARE FOR THE SKY SPIRIT, HE WHOM THE OTHERS CALL DOOR.
IF THE PEOPLE COULD KNOW WHAT I KNOW, FEEL WHAT I FEEL, AND REMEMBER...
"THOSE SWEET AND BITTER MEMORIES..."

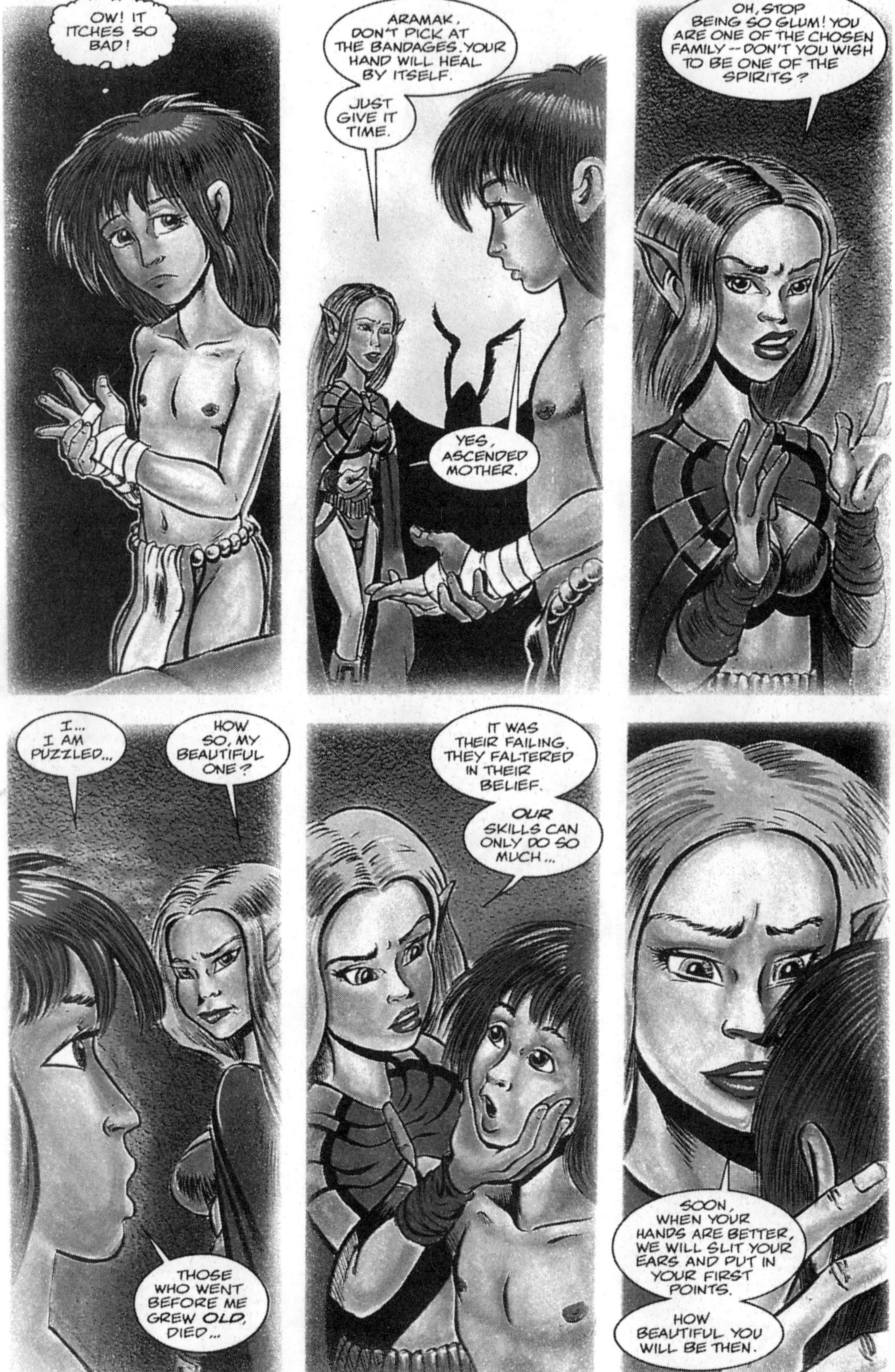

OW! IT ITCHES SO BAD!
ARAMAK, DON'T PICK AT THE BANDAGES. YOUR HAND WILL HEAL BY ITSELF.
JUST GIVE IT TIME.
YES, ASCENDED MOTHER.
OH, STOP BEING SO GLUM! YOU ARE ONE OF THE CHOSEN FAMILY -- DON'T YOU WISH TO BE ONE OF THE SPIRITS?
I... I AM PUZZLED...
HOW SO, MY BEAUTIFUL ONE?
THOSE WHO WENT BEFORE ME GREW OLD, DIED...
IT WAS THEIR FAILING. THEY FALTERED IN THEIR BELIEF.
OUR SKILLS CAN ONLY DO SO MUCH...
SOON, WHEN YOUR HANDS ARE BETTER, WE WILL SLIT YOUR EARS AND PUT IN YOUR FIRST POINTS.
HOW BEAUTIFUL YOU WILL BE THEN.

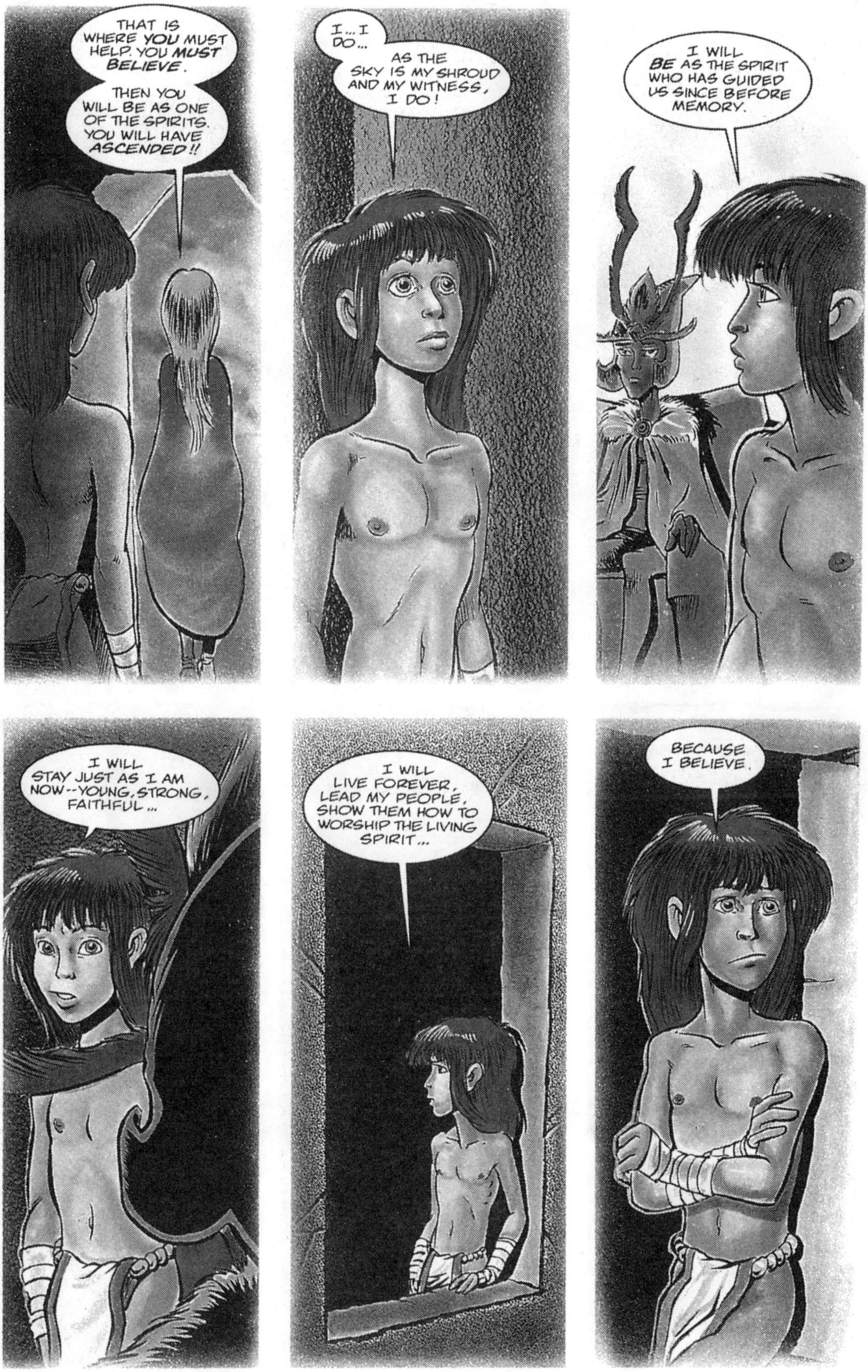
THAT IS WHERE YOU MUST HELP. YOU MUST BELIEVE.
THEN YOU WILL BE AS ONE OF THE SPIRITS. YOU WILL HAVE ASCENDED!!
I... I DO...
AS THE SKY IS MY SHROUD AND MY WITNESS, I DO!
I WILL BE AS THE SPIRIT WHO HAS GUIDED US SINCE BEFORE MEMORY.
I WILL STAY JUST AS I AM NOW--YOUNG, STRONG, FAITHFUL...
I WILL LIVE FOREVER, LEAD MY PEOPLE, SHOW THEM HOW TO WORSHIP THE LIVING SPIRIT...
BECAUSE I BELIEVE.

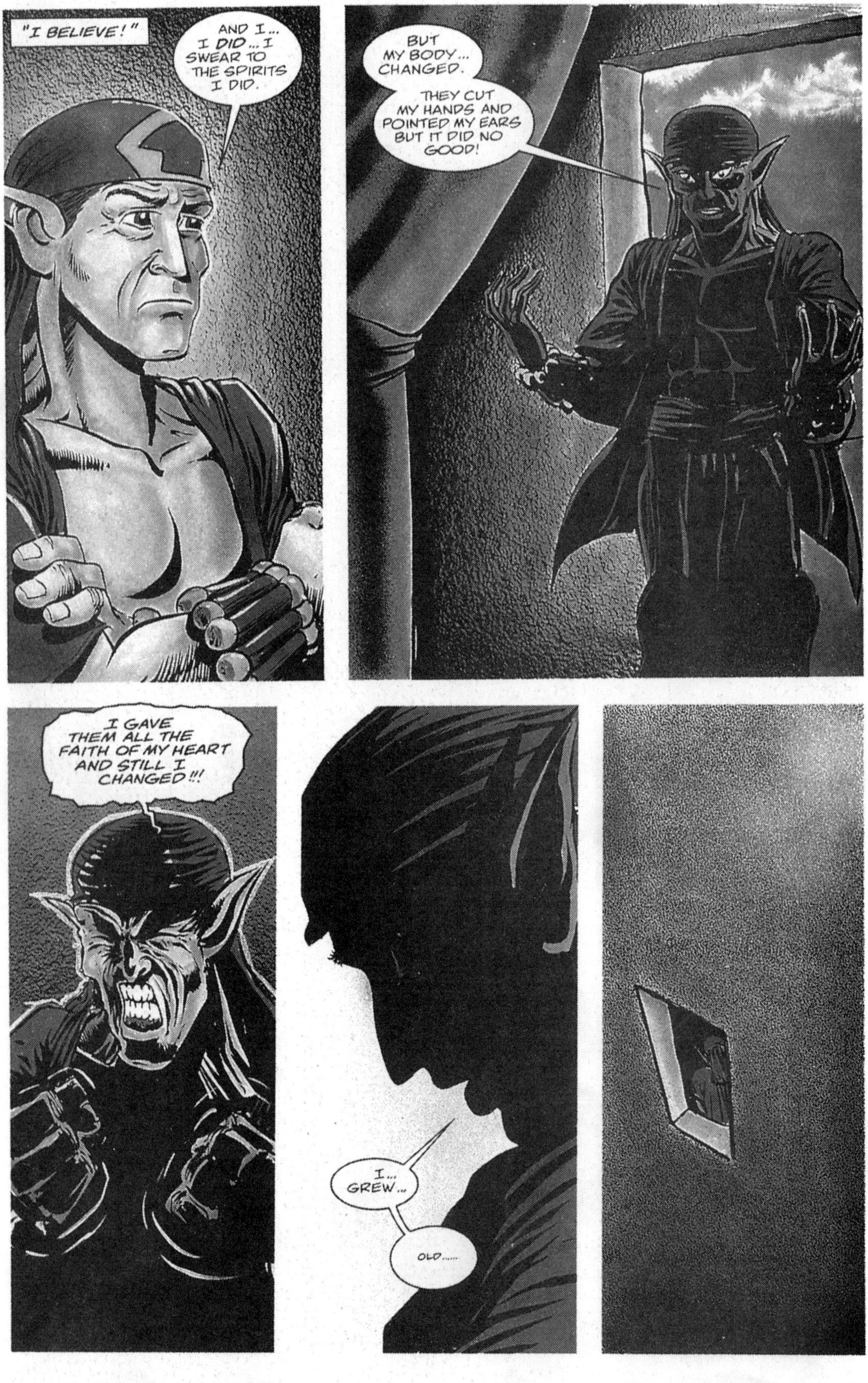
"I BELIEVE!"
AND I... I DID... I SWEAR TO THE SPIRITS I DID.
BUT MY BODY... CHANGED.
THEY CUT MY HANDS AND POINTED MY EARS BUT IT DID NO GOOD!
I GAVE THEM ALL THE FAITH OF MY HEART AND STILL I CHANGED!!!
I... GREW...
OLD......

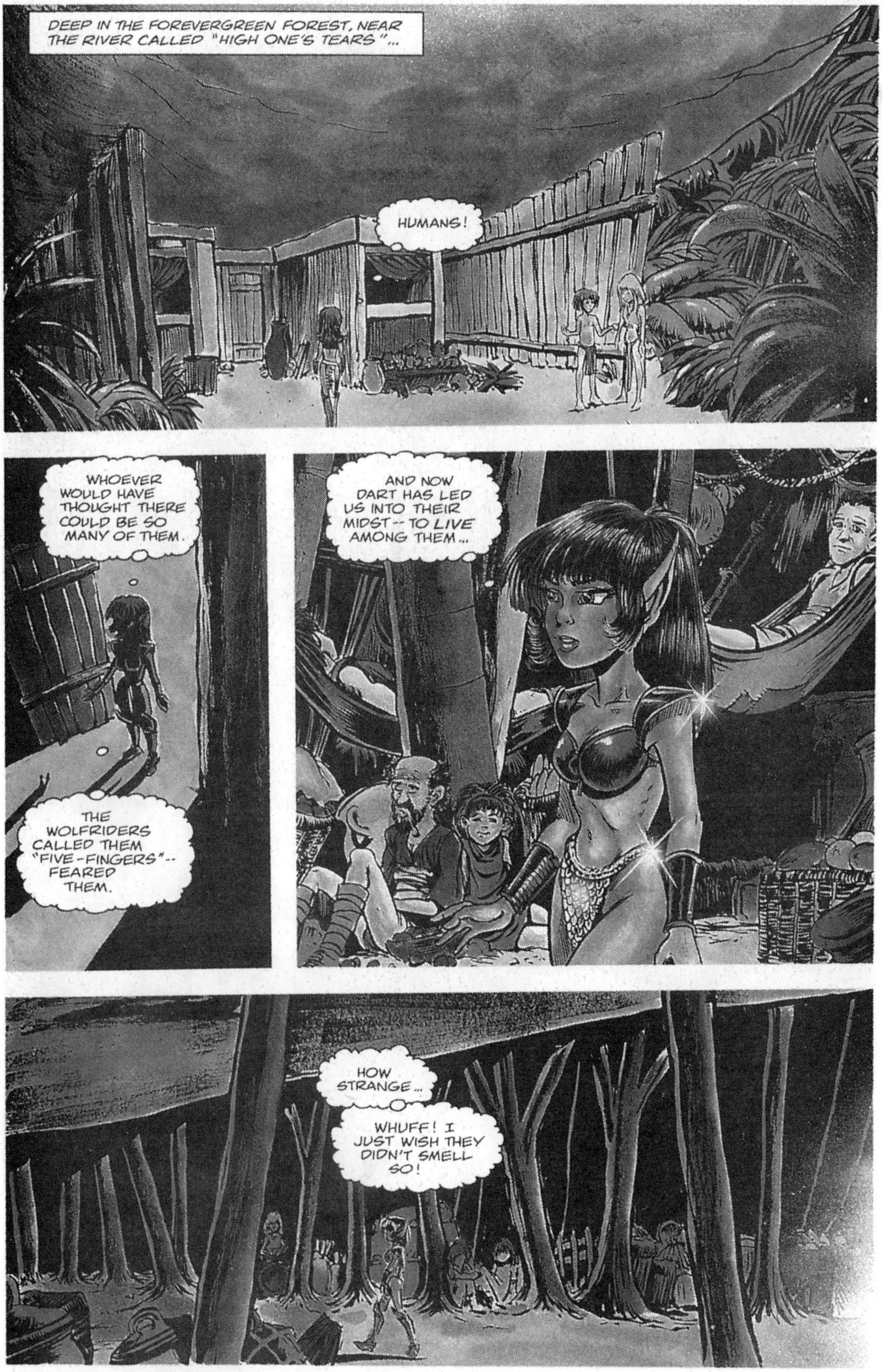
DEEP IN THE FOREVERGREEN FOREST, NEAR THE RIVER CALLED "HIGH ONE'S TEARS"...
HUMANS!
WHOEVER WOULD HAVE THOUGHT THERE COULD BE SO MANY OF THEM.
THE WOLFRIDERS CALLED THEM "FIVE-FINGERS"-- FEARED THEM.
AND NOW DART HAS LED US INTO THEIR MIDST--TO LIVE AMONG THEM...
HOW STRANGE...
WHUFF! I JUST WISH THEY DIDN'T SMELL SO!

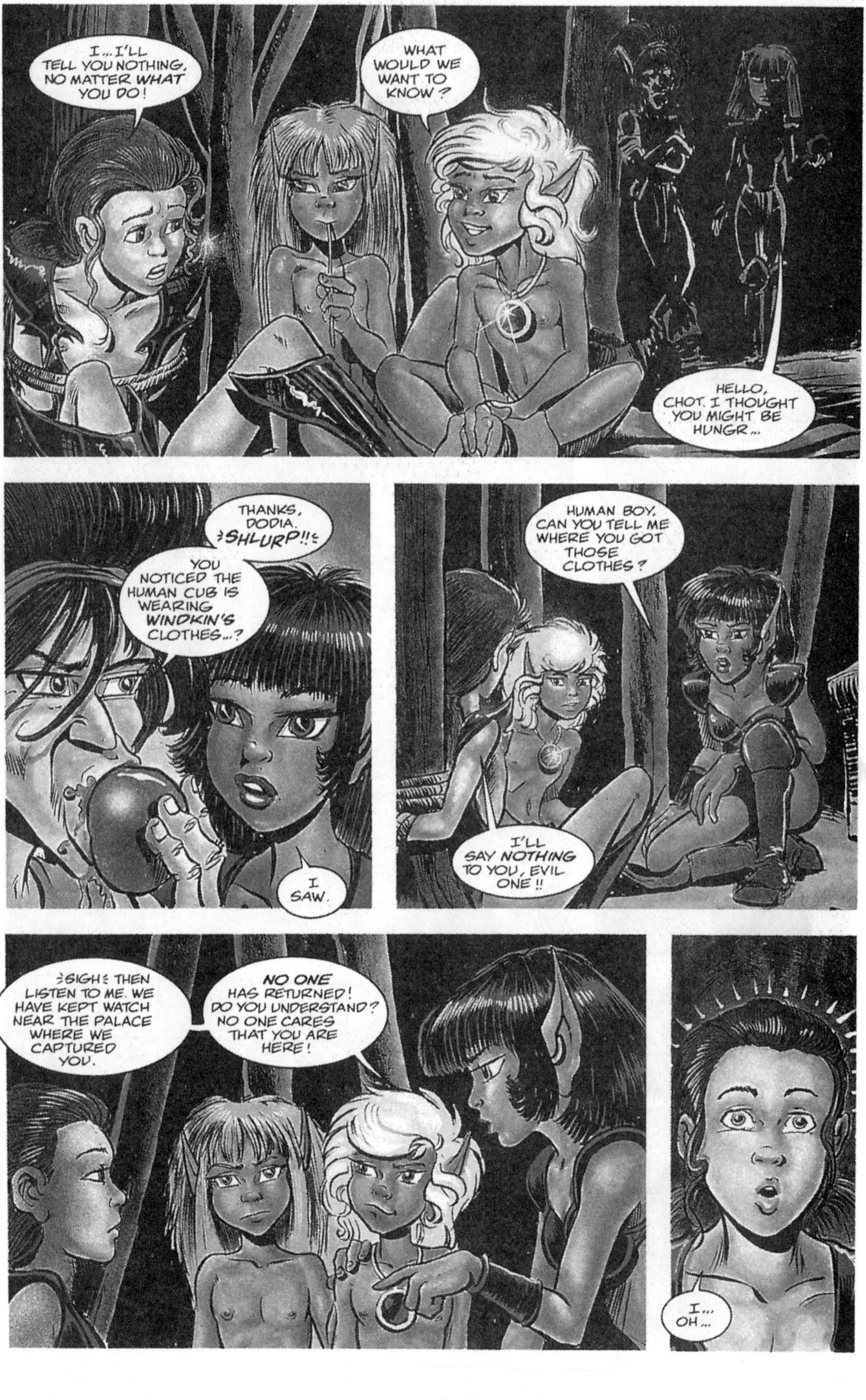

I... I'LL TELL YOU NOTHING, NO MATTER WHAT YOU DO!
WHAT WOULD WE WANT TO KNOW?
HELLO, CHOT. I THOUGHT YOU MIGHT BE HUNGR...
THANKS, DODIA.
SHLURP!!
YOU NOTICED THE HUMAN CUB IS WEARING WINDKIN'S CLOTHES...?
I SAW.
HUMAN BOY, CAN YOU TELL ME WHERE YOU GOT THOSE CLOTHES?
I'LL SAY NOTHING TO YOU, EVIL ONE!!
SIGH THEN LISTEN TO ME. WE HAVE KEPT WATCH NEAR THE PALACE WHERE WE CAPTURED YOU.
NO ONE HAS RETURNED! DO YOU UNDERSTAND? NO ONE CARES THAT YOU ARE HERE!
I... OH...

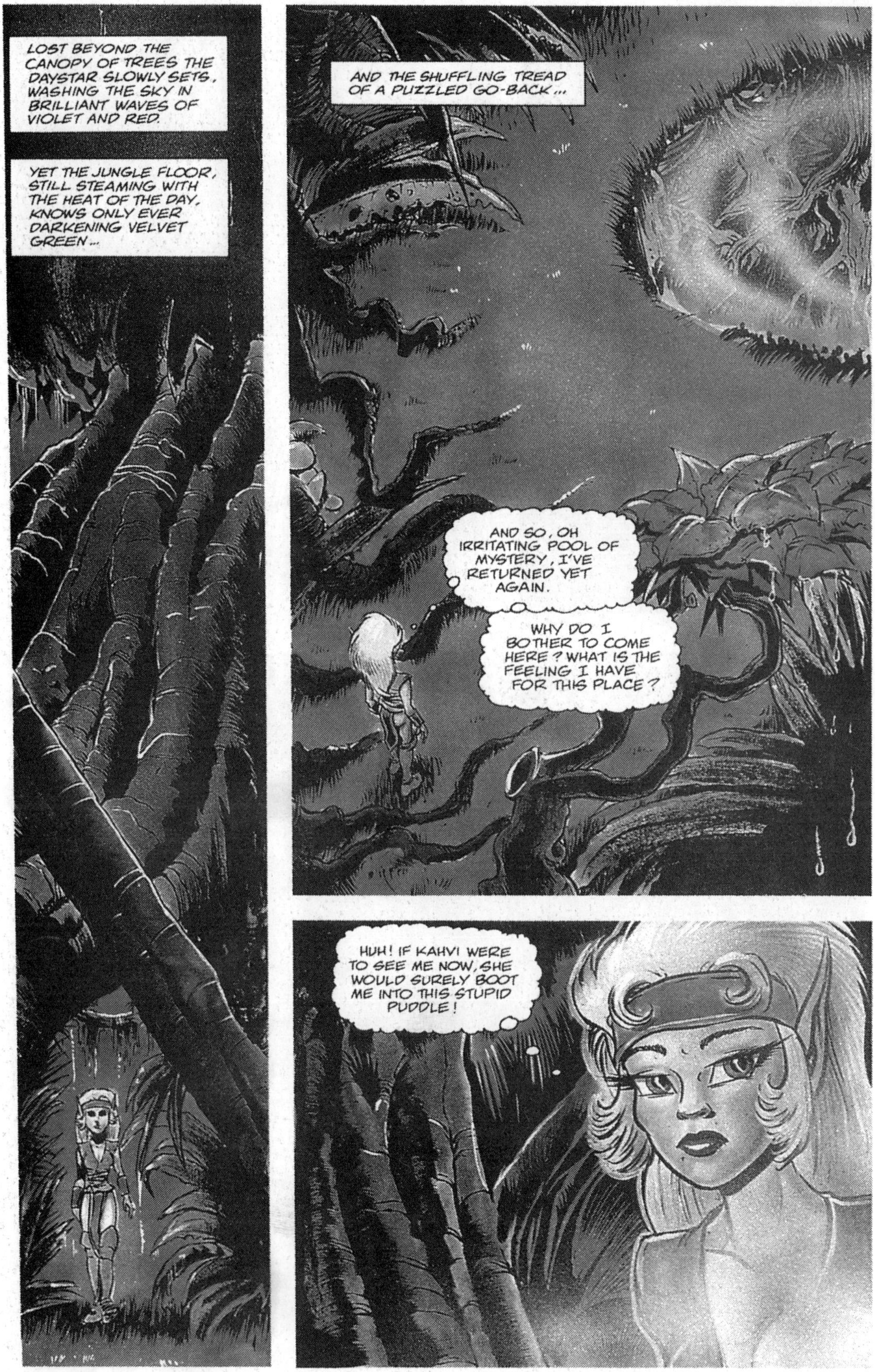
LOST BEYOND THE CANOPY OF TREES THE DAYSTAR SLOWLY SETS, WASHING THE SKY IN BRILLIANT WAVES OF VIOLET AND RED.
YET THE JUNGLE FLOOR, STILL STEAMING WITH THE HEAT OF THE DAY, KNOWS ONLY EVER DARKENING VELVET GREEN...
AND THE SHUFFLING TREAD OF A PUZZLED GO-BACK...
AND SO, OH IRRITATING POOL OF MYSTERY, I'VE RETURNED YET AGAIN.
WHY DO I BOTHER TO COME HERE? WHAT IS THE FEELING I HAVE FOR THIS PLACE?
HUH! IF KAHVI WERE TO SEE ME NOW, SHE WOULD SURELY BOOT ME INTO THIS STUPID PUDDLE!

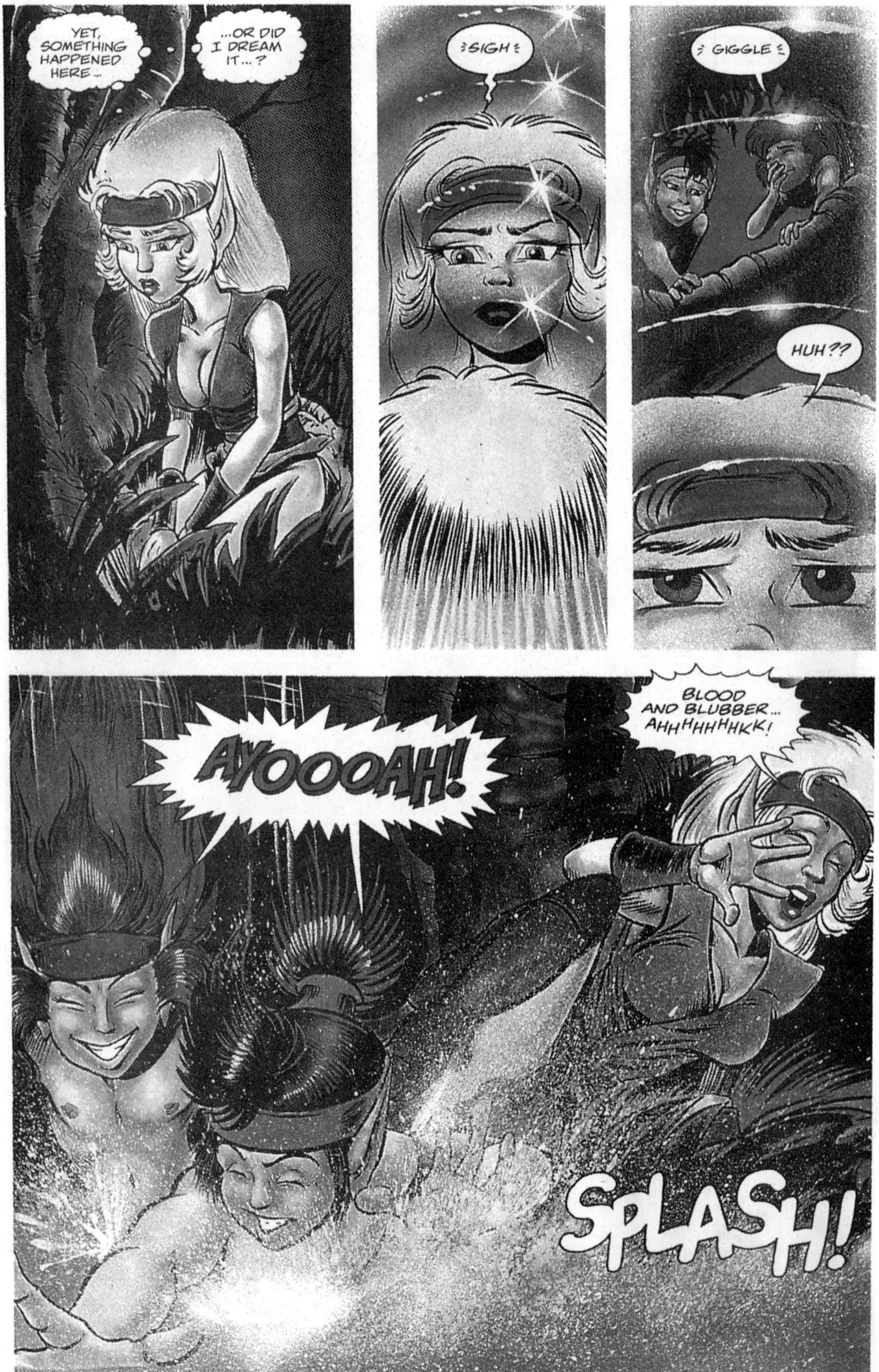
YET, SOMETHING HAPPENED HERE...
...OR DID I DREAM IT...?
SIGH
GIGGLE
HUH??
AYOOOAH!
BLOOD AND BLUBBER... AHHHHHHHKK!
SPLASH!

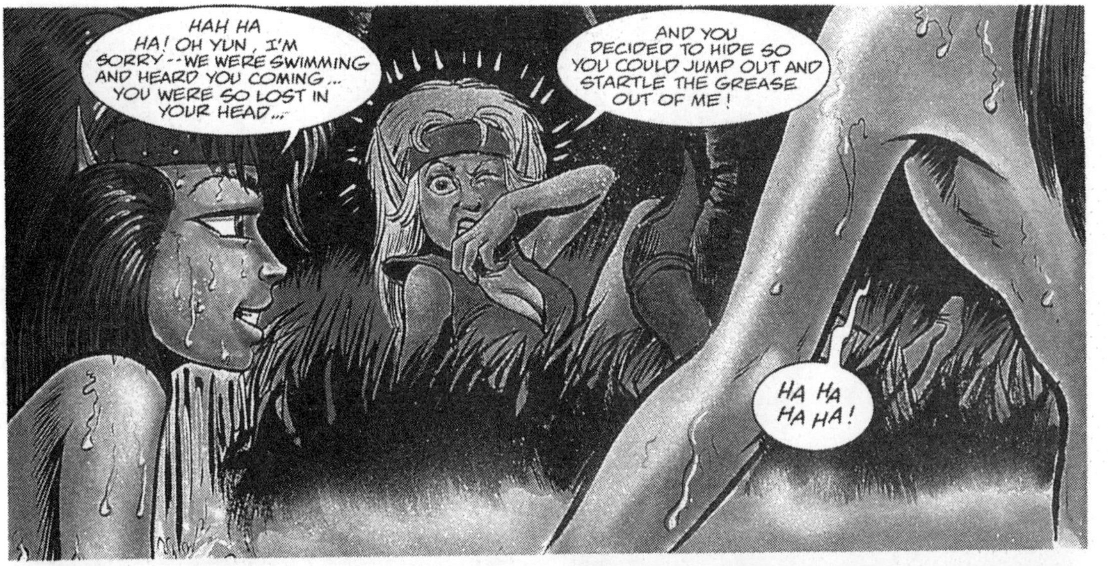
HAH HA HA! OH YUN, I'M SORRY--WE WERE SWIMMING AND HEARD YOU COMING... YOU WERE SO LOST IN YOUR HEAD...
AND YOU DECIDED TO HIDE SO YOU COULD JUMP OUT AND STARTLE THE GREASE OUT OF ME!
HA HA HA HA!

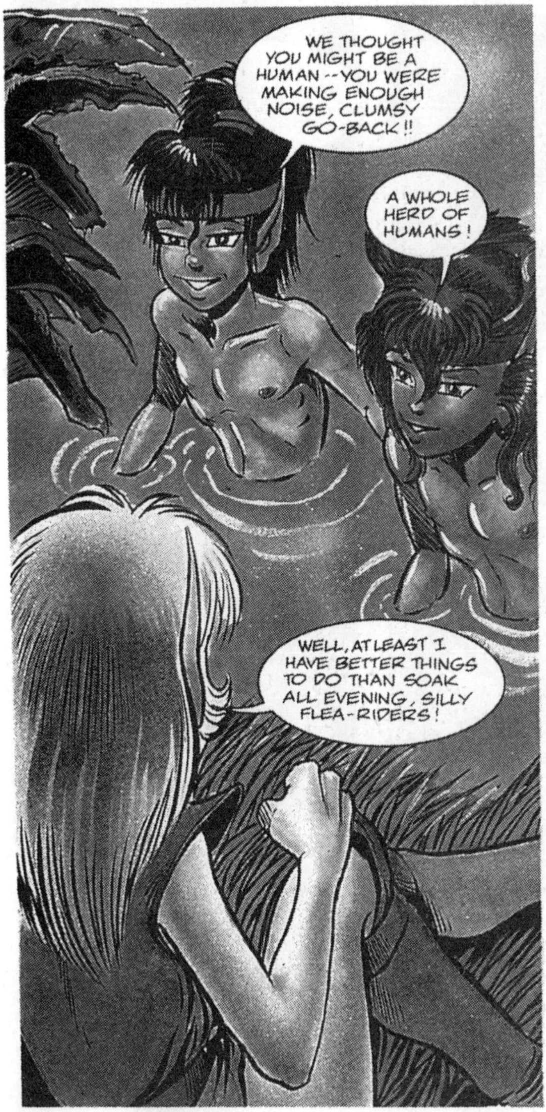
WE THOUGHT YOU MIGHT BE A HUMAN--YOU WERE MAKING ENOUGH NOISE, CLUMSY GO-BACK!!
A WHOLE HERD OF HUMANS!
WELL, AT LEAST I HAVE BETTER THINGS TO DO THAN SOAK ALL EVENING, SILLY FLEA-RIDERS!

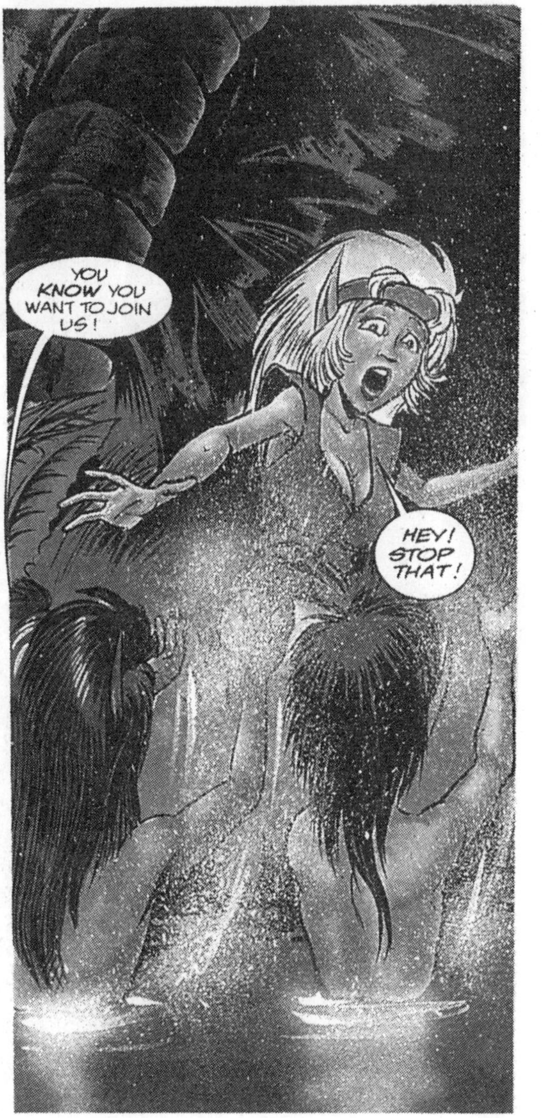
YOU KNOW YOU WANT TO JOIN US!
HEY! STOP THAT!

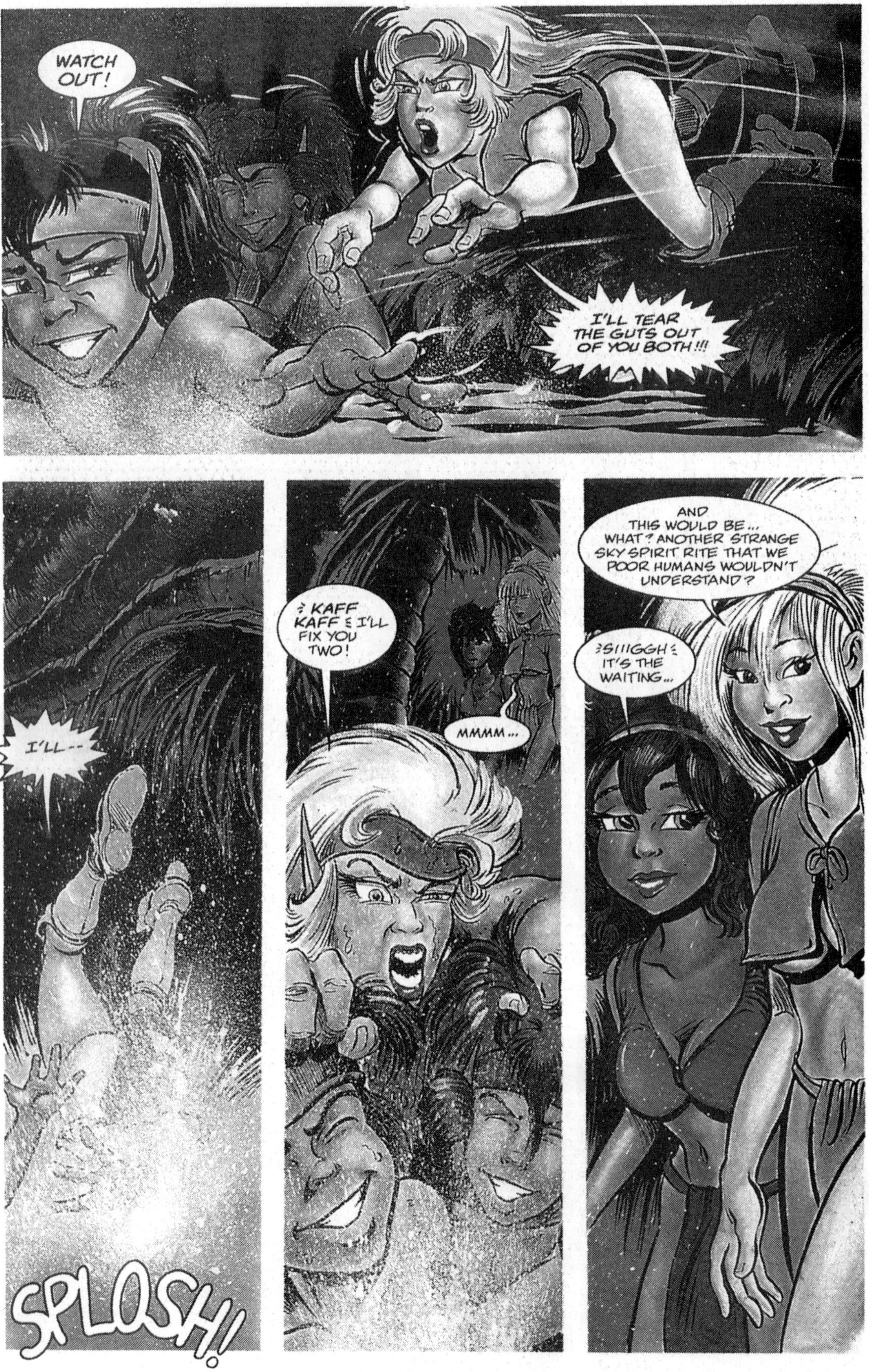
WATCH OUT!
I'LL TEAR THE GUTS OUT OF YOU BOTH!!!
I'LL--
SPLOSH!
KAFF KAFF I'LL FIX YOU TWO!
MMMM...
AND THIS WOULD BE... WHAT? ANOTHER STRANGE SKY SPIRIT RITE THAT WE POOR HUMANS WOULDN'T UNDERSTAND?
SIIIGGH IT'S THE WAITING...

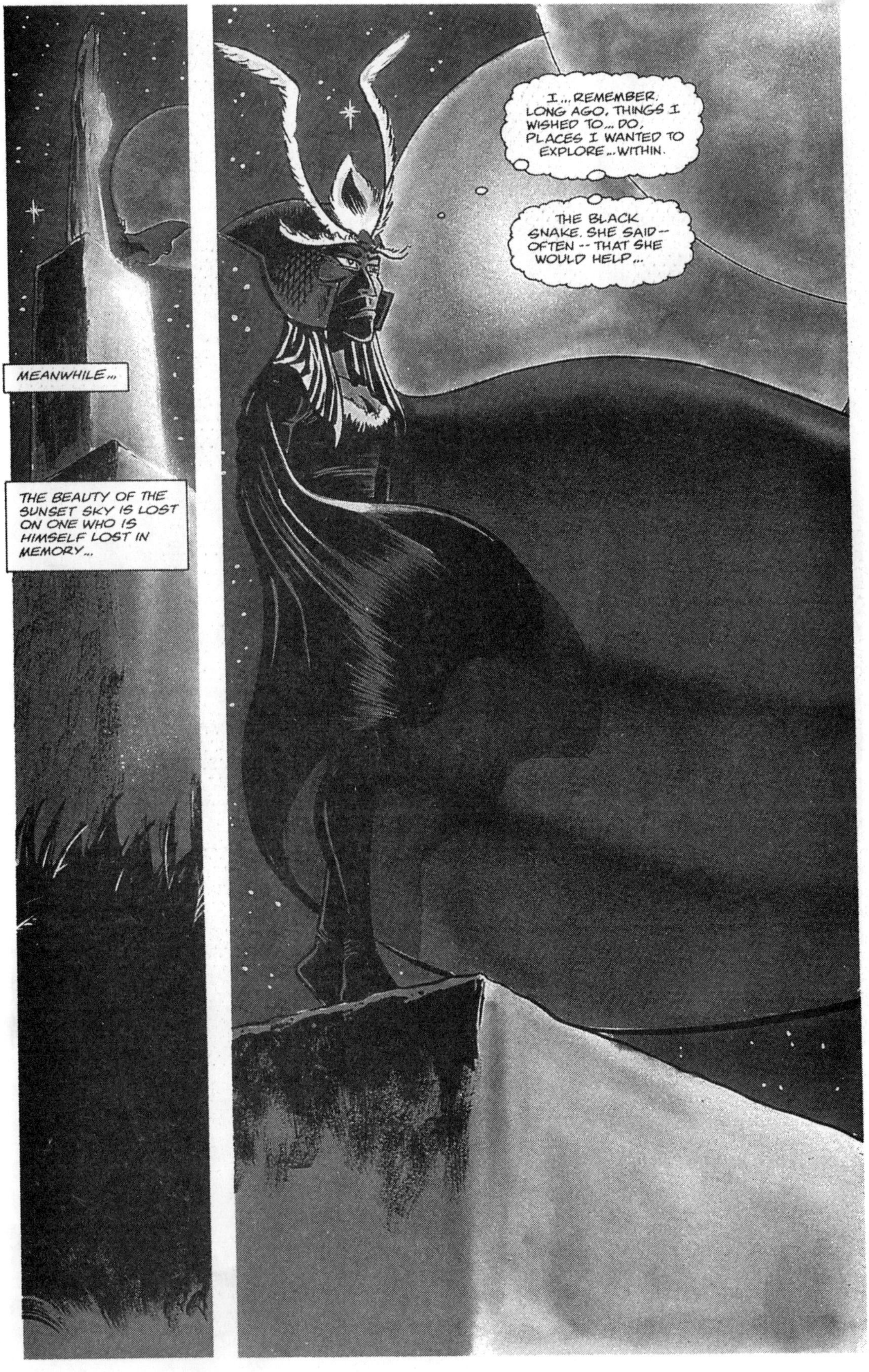
MEANWHILE...
THE BEAUTY OF THE SUNSET SKY IS LOST ON ONE WHO IS HIMSELF LOST IN MEMORY...
I... REMEMBER. LONG AGO. THINGS I WISHED TO... DO, PLACES I WANTED TO EXPLORE... WITHIN.
THE BLACK SNAKE. SHE SAID-- OFTEN -- THAT SHE WOULD HELP...

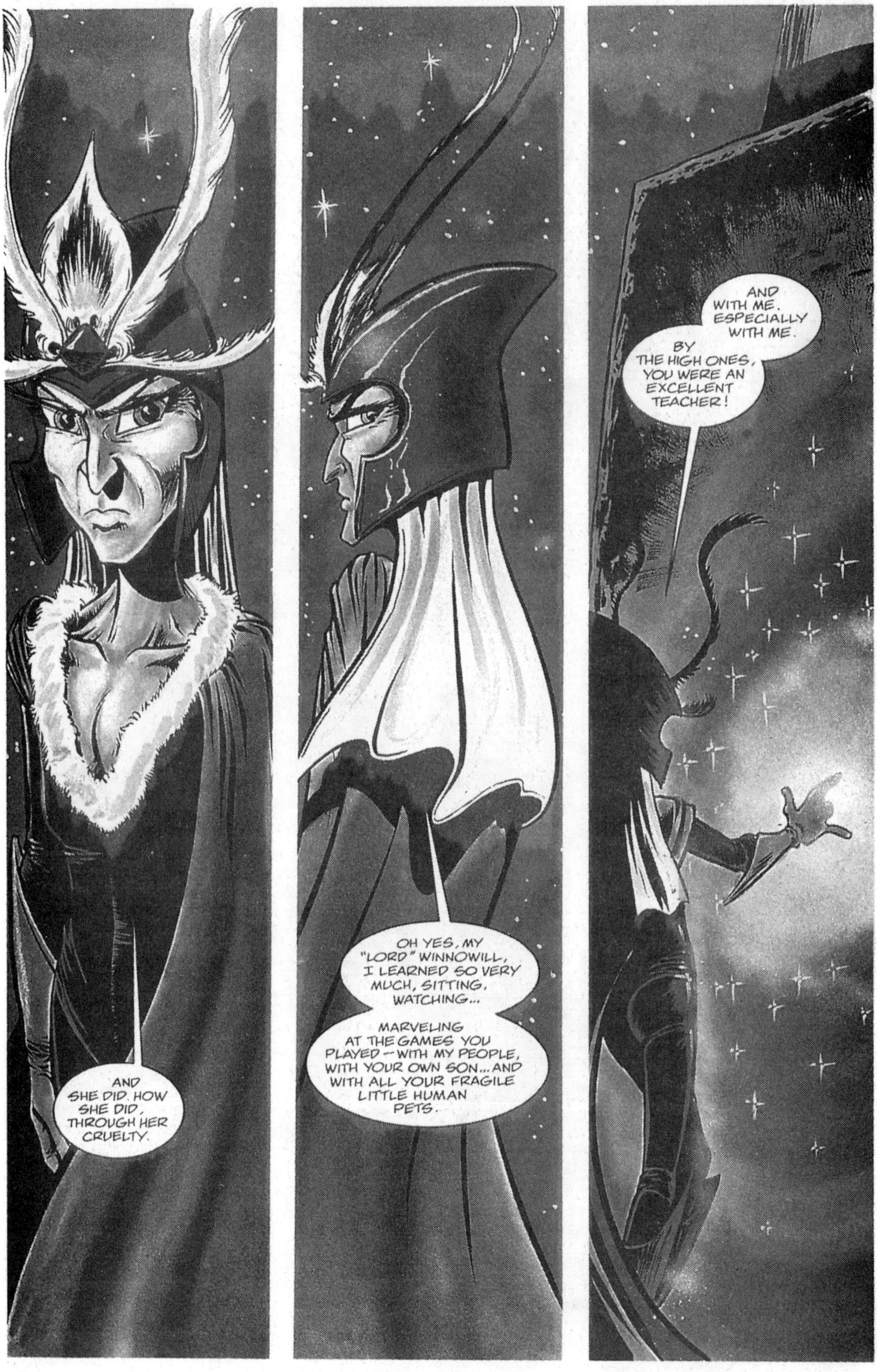
AND SHE DID. HOW SHE DID, THROUGH HER CRUELTY.
OH YES, MY "LORD" WINNOWILL, I LEARNED SO VERY MUCH, SITTING, WATCHING...
MARVELING AT THE GAMES YOU PLAYED -- WITH MY PEOPLE, WITH YOUR OWN SON... AND WITH ALL YOUR FRAGILE LITTLE HUMAN PETS.
AND WITH ME. ESPECIALLY WITH ME.
BY THE HIGH ONES, YOU WERE AN EXCELLENT TEACHER!

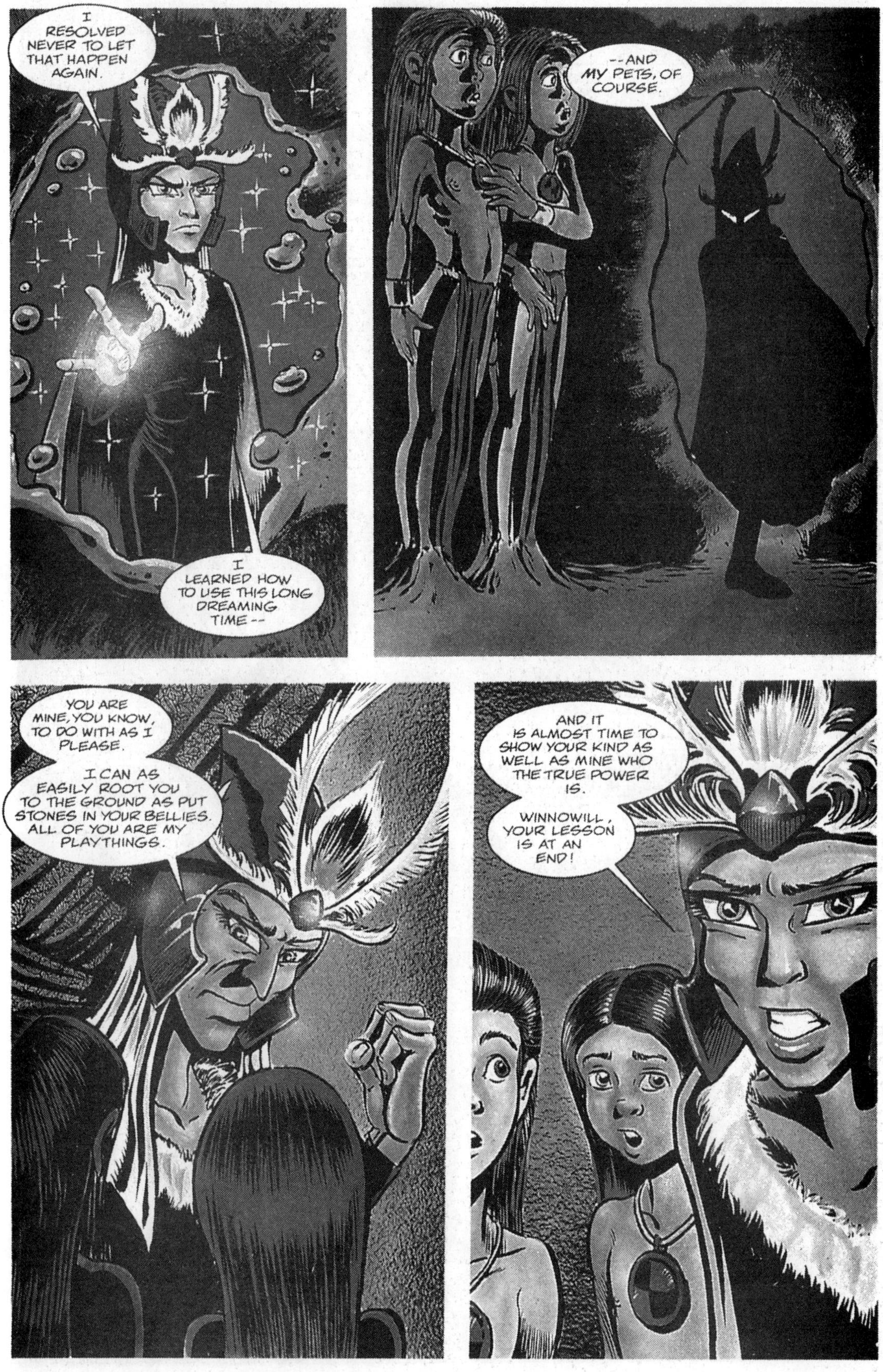
I RESOLVED NEVER TO LET THAT HAPPEN AGAIN.
I LEARNED HOW TO USE THIS LONG DREAMING TIME --
--AND MY PETS, OF COURSE.
YOU ARE MINE, YOU KNOW, TO DO WITH AS I PLEASE.
I CAN AS EASILY ROOT YOU TO THE GROUND AS PUT STONES IN YOUR BELLIES. ALL OF YOU ARE MY PLAYTHINGS.
AND IT IS ALMOST TIME TO SHOW YOUR KIND AS WELL AS MINE WHO THE TRUE POWER IS.
WINNOWILL, YOUR LESSON IS AT AN END!

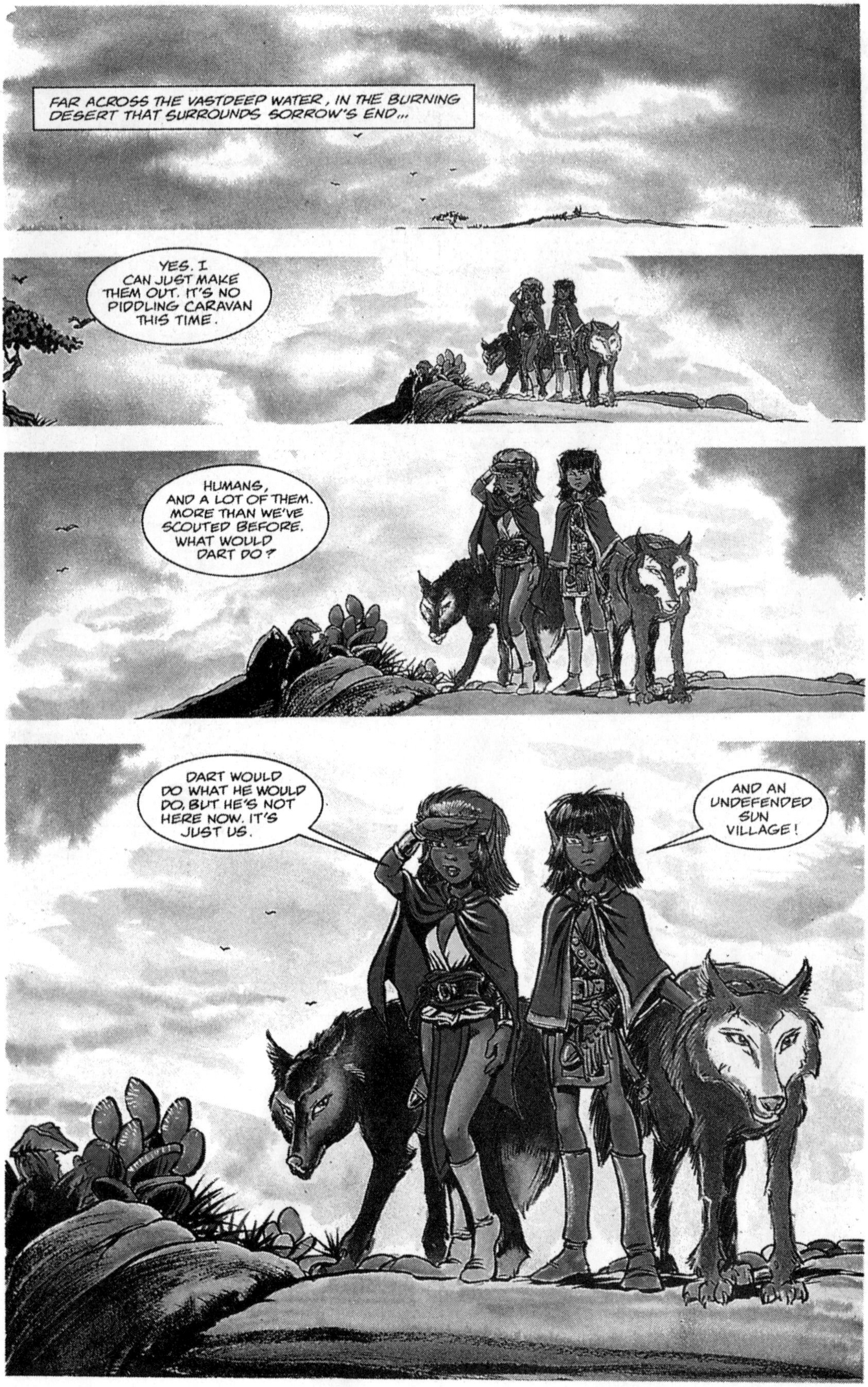
FAR ACROSS THE VASTDEEP WATER, IN THE BURNING DESERT THAT SURROUNDS SORROW'S END...
YES. I CAN JUST MAKE THEM OUT. IT'S NO PIDDLING CARAVAN THIS TIME.
HUMANS, AND A LOT OF THEM. MORE THAN WE'VE SCOUTED BEFORE. WHAT WOULD DART DO?
DART WOULD DO WHAT HE WOULD DO, BUT HE'S NOT HERE NOW. IT'S JUST US.
AND AN UNDEFENDED SUN VILLAGE!

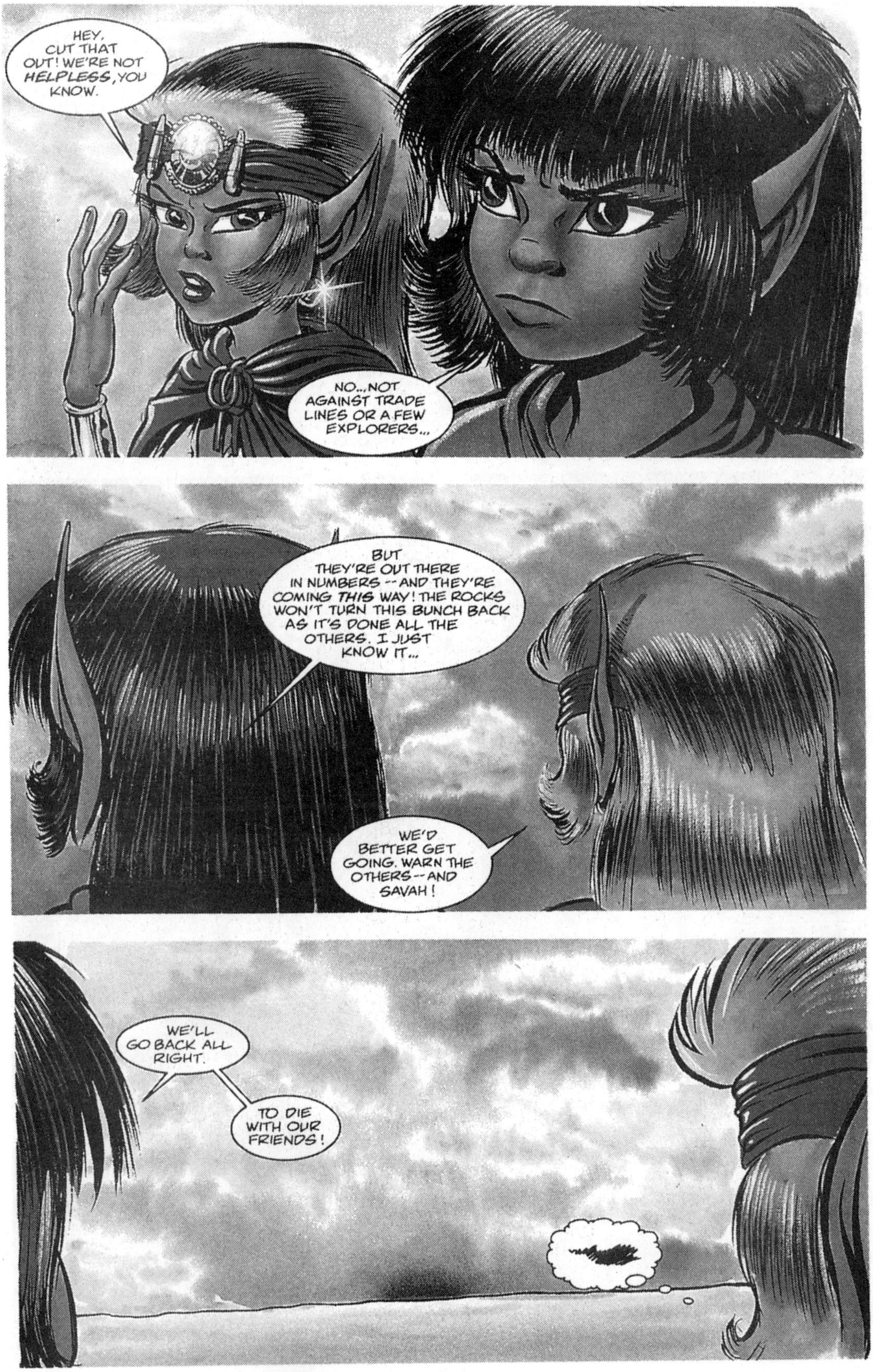
HEY, CUT THAT OUT! WE'RE NOT HELPLESS, YOU KNOW.
NO...NOT AGAINST TRADE LINES OR A FEW EXPLORERS...
BUT THEY'RE OUT THERE IN NUMBERS -- AND THEY'RE COMING THIS WAY! THE ROCKS WON'T TURN THIS BUNCH BACK AS IT'S DONE ALL THE OTHERS. I JUST KNOW IT...
WE'D BETTER GET GOING. WARN THE OTHERS -- AND SAVAH!
WE'LL GO BACK ALL RIGHT.
TO DIE WITH OUR FRIENDS!

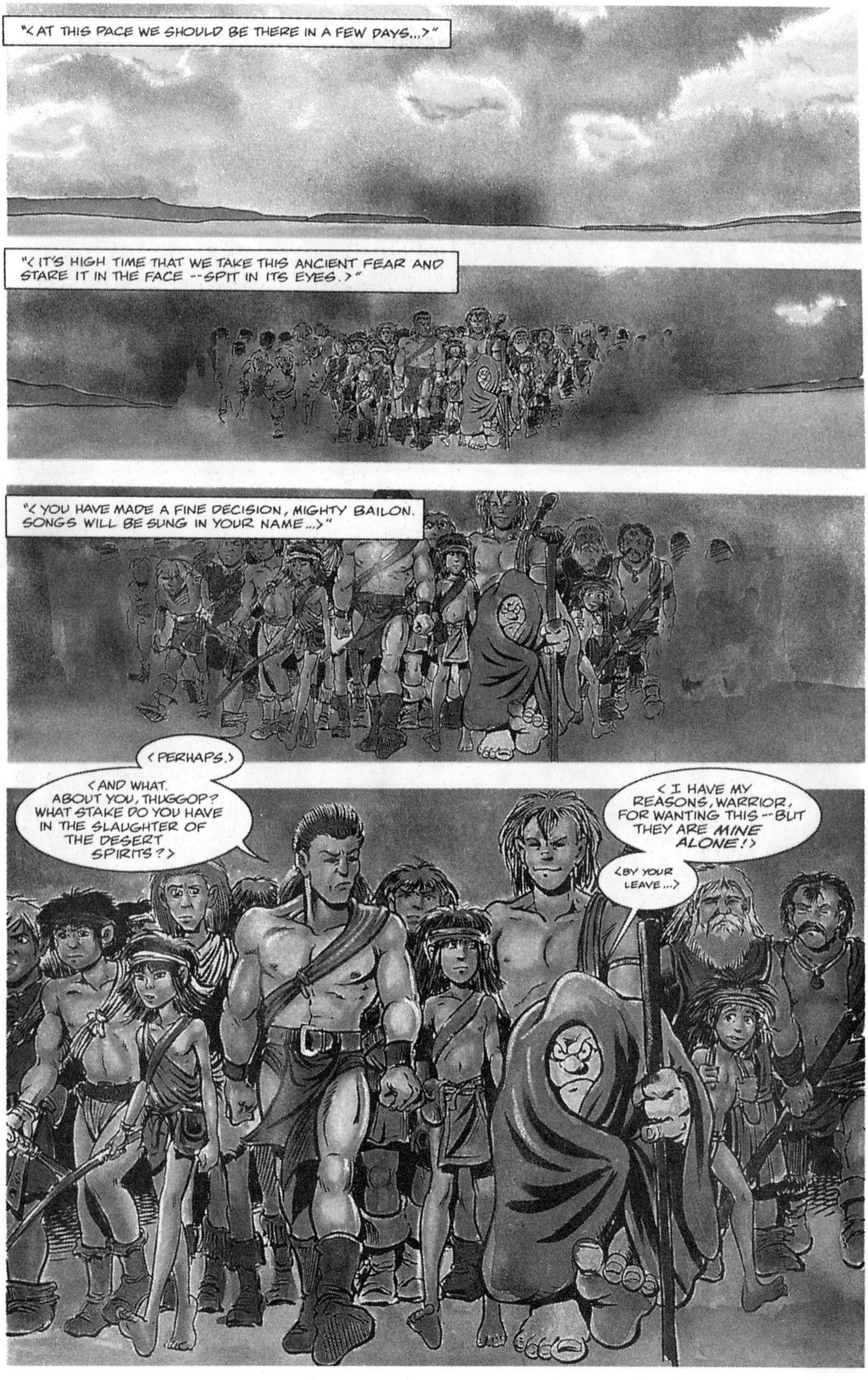
"< AT THIS PACE WE SHOULD BE THERE IN A FEW DAYS...>"
"< IT'S HIGH TIME THAT WE TAKE THIS ANCIENT FEAR AND STARE IT IN THE FACE --SPIT IN ITS EYES.>"
"< YOU HAVE MADE A FINE DECISION, MIGHTY BAILON. SONGS WILL BE SUNG IN YOUR NAME...>"
< PERHAPS.>
< AND WHAT. ABOUT YOU, THUGGOP? WHAT STAKE DO YOU HAVE IN THE SLAUGHTER OF THE DESERT SPIRITS?>
< I HAVE MY REASONS, WARRIOR, FOR WANTING THIS --BUT THEY ARE *MINE ALONE!*>
<BY YOUR LEAVE...>

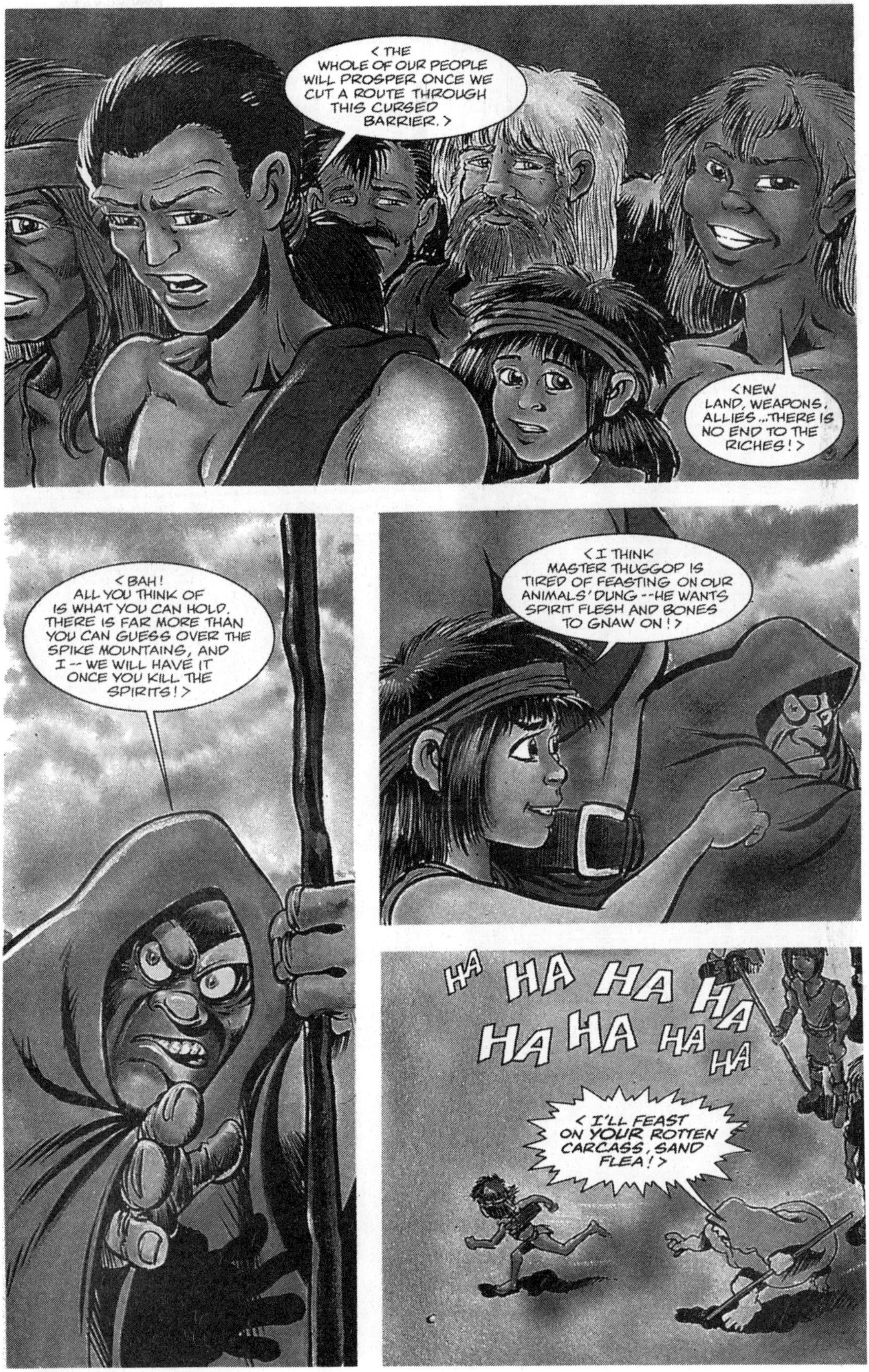
< THE WHOLE OF OUR PEOPLE WILL PROSPER ONCE WE CUT A ROUTE THROUGH THIS CURSED BARRIER. >
< NEW LAND, WEAPONS, ALLIES... THERE IS NO END TO THE RICHES! >
< BAH! ALL YOU THINK OF IS WHAT YOU CAN HOLD. THERE IS FAR MORE THAN YOU CAN GUESS OVER THE SPIKE MOUNTAINS, AND I -- WE WILL HAVE IT ONCE YOU KILL THE SPIRITS! >
< I THINK MASTER THUGGOP IS TIRED OF FEASTING ON OUR ANIMALS' DUNG -- HE WANTS SPIRIT FLESH AND BONES TO GNAW ON! >
HA HA HA HA HA HA HA HA HA
< I'LL FEAST ON YOUR ROTTEN CARCASS, SAND FLEA! >

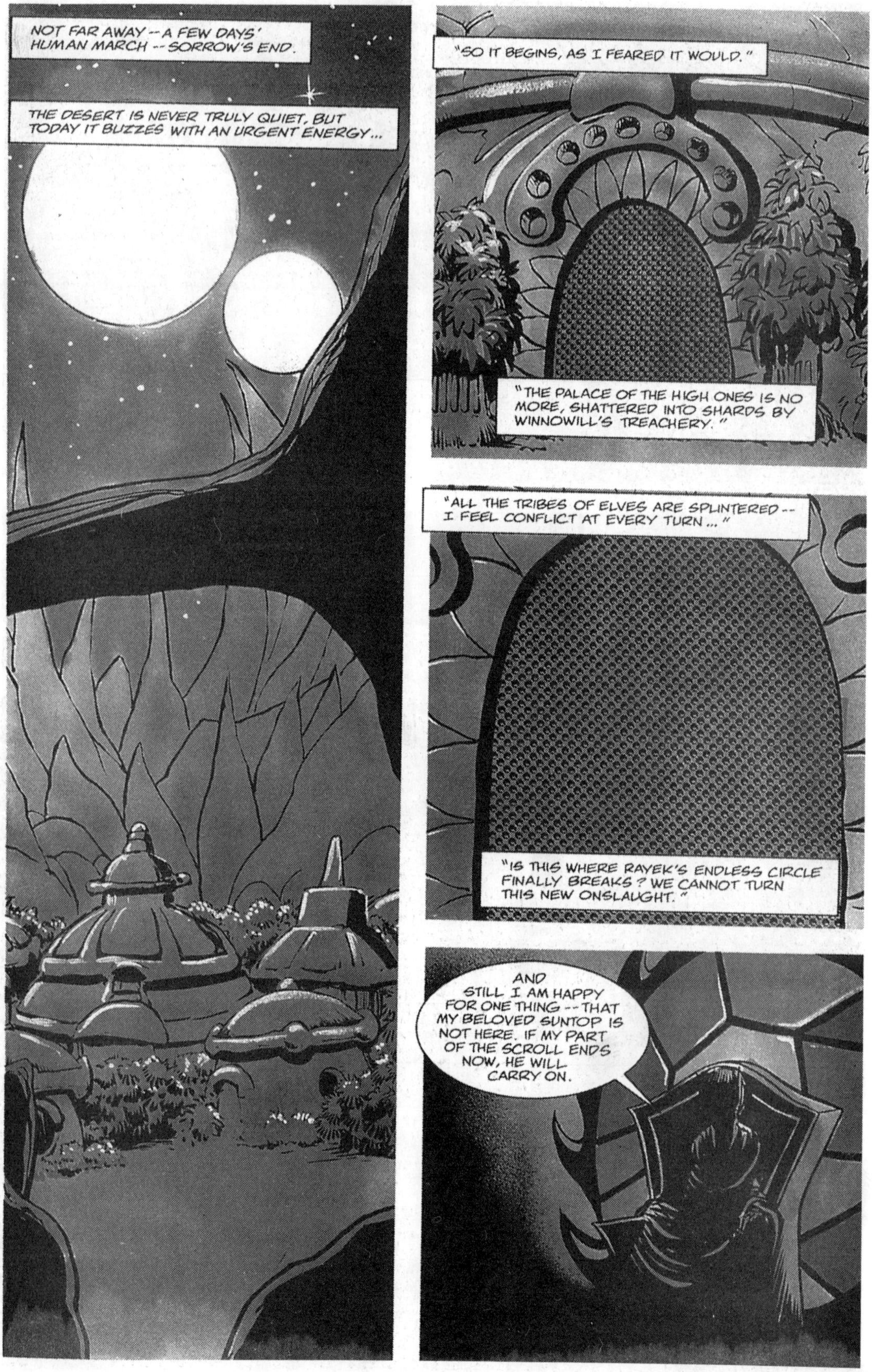
NOT FAR AWAY -- A FEW DAYS' HUMAN MARCH -- SORROW'S END.
THE DESERT IS NEVER TRULY QUIET, BUT TODAY IT BUZZES WITH AN URGENT ENERGY...
"SO IT BEGINS, AS I FEARED IT WOULD."
"THE PALACE OF THE HIGH ONES IS NO MORE, SHATTERED INTO SHARDS BY WINNOWILL'S TREACHERY."
"ALL THE TRIBES OF ELVES ARE SPLINTERED -- I FEEL CONFLICT AT EVERY TURN..."
"IS THIS WHERE RAYEK'S ENDLESS CIRCLE FINALLY BREAKS? WE CANNOT TURN THIS NEW ONSLAUGHT."
AND STILL I AM HAPPY FOR ONE THING -- THAT MY BELOVED SUNTOP IS NOT HERE. IF MY PART OF THE SCROLL ENDS NOW, HE WILL CARRY ON.

SO MUCH IS YET TO BE. THIS WORLD, ABODE TO SO MANY MINDS AND HEARTS, CONTAINS THE SEEDS OF SO MUCH BEAUTY, SO MUCH FULFILLMENT.

HOW TEMPTED I AM TO SEND TO MY KITLING AND TELL HIM OF ALL THAT TIME –YET–TO– COME HOLDS.

AND YET I CANNOT... *MUST NOT.* HE IS TOO GOOD AT WHAT I HAVE TAUGHT HIM ...

HE WOULD SEE IN THE FUTURE I REVEAL, THE PRESENT I CANNOT HIDE FROM HIM ...

AND I WOULD SPARE HIM THAT GRIEF, AT LEAST FOR A TIME.

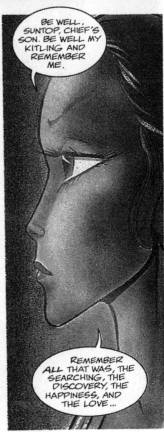

BE WELL, SUNTOP, CHIEF'S SON. BE WELL MY KITLING AND REMEMBER ME.

REMEMBER ALL THAT WAS, THE SEARCHING, THE DISCOVERY, THE HAPPINESS, AND THE LOVE ...

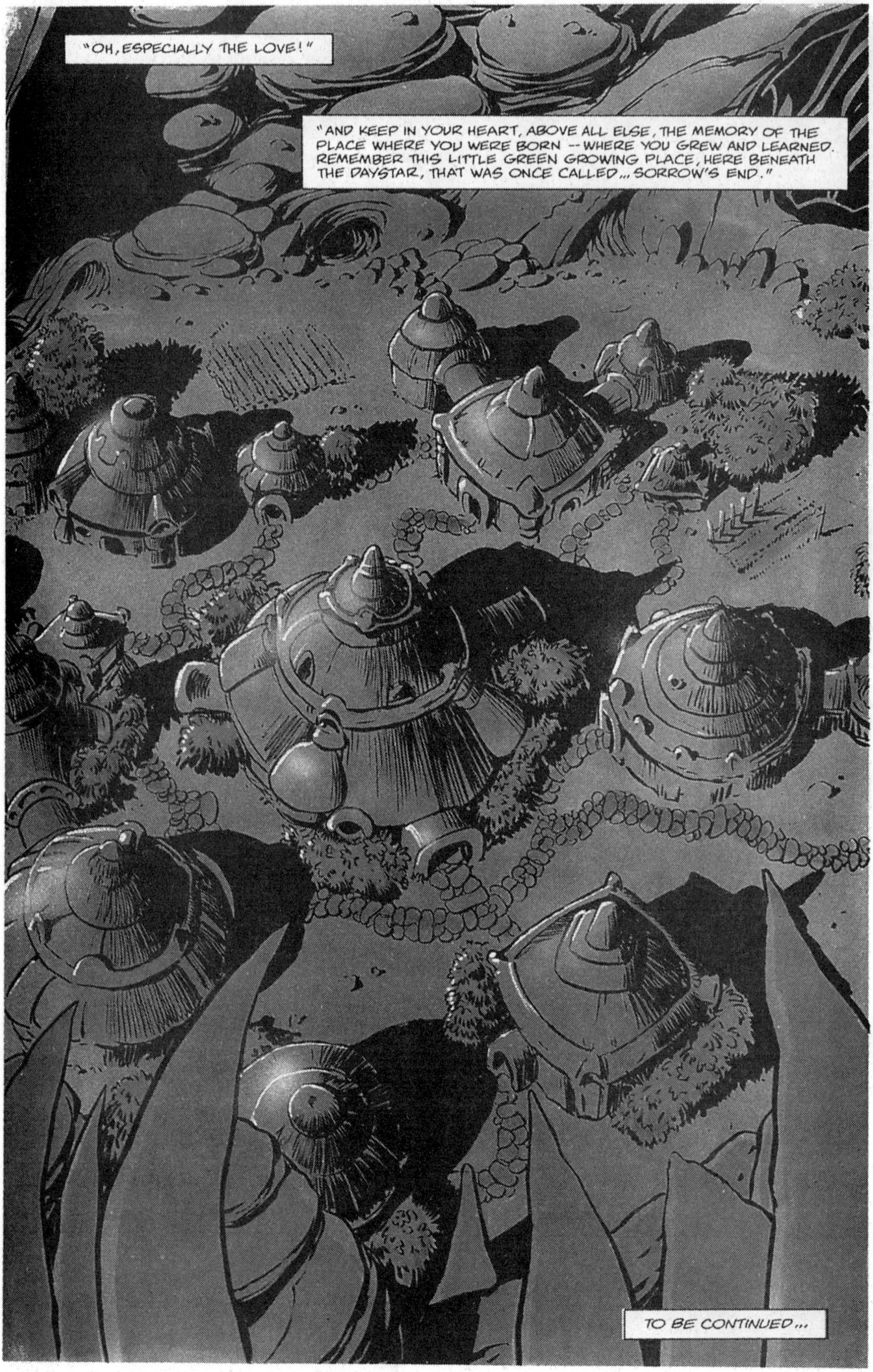
"OH, ESPECIALLY THE LOVE!"
"AND KEEP IN YOUR HEART, ABOVE ALL ELSE, THE MEMORY OF THE PLACE WHERE YOU WERE BORN -- WHERE YOU GREW AND LEARNED. REMEMBER THIS LITTLE GREEN GROWING PLACE, HERE BENEATH THE DAYSTAR, THAT WAS ONCE CALLED... SORROW'S END."
TO BE CONTINUED...

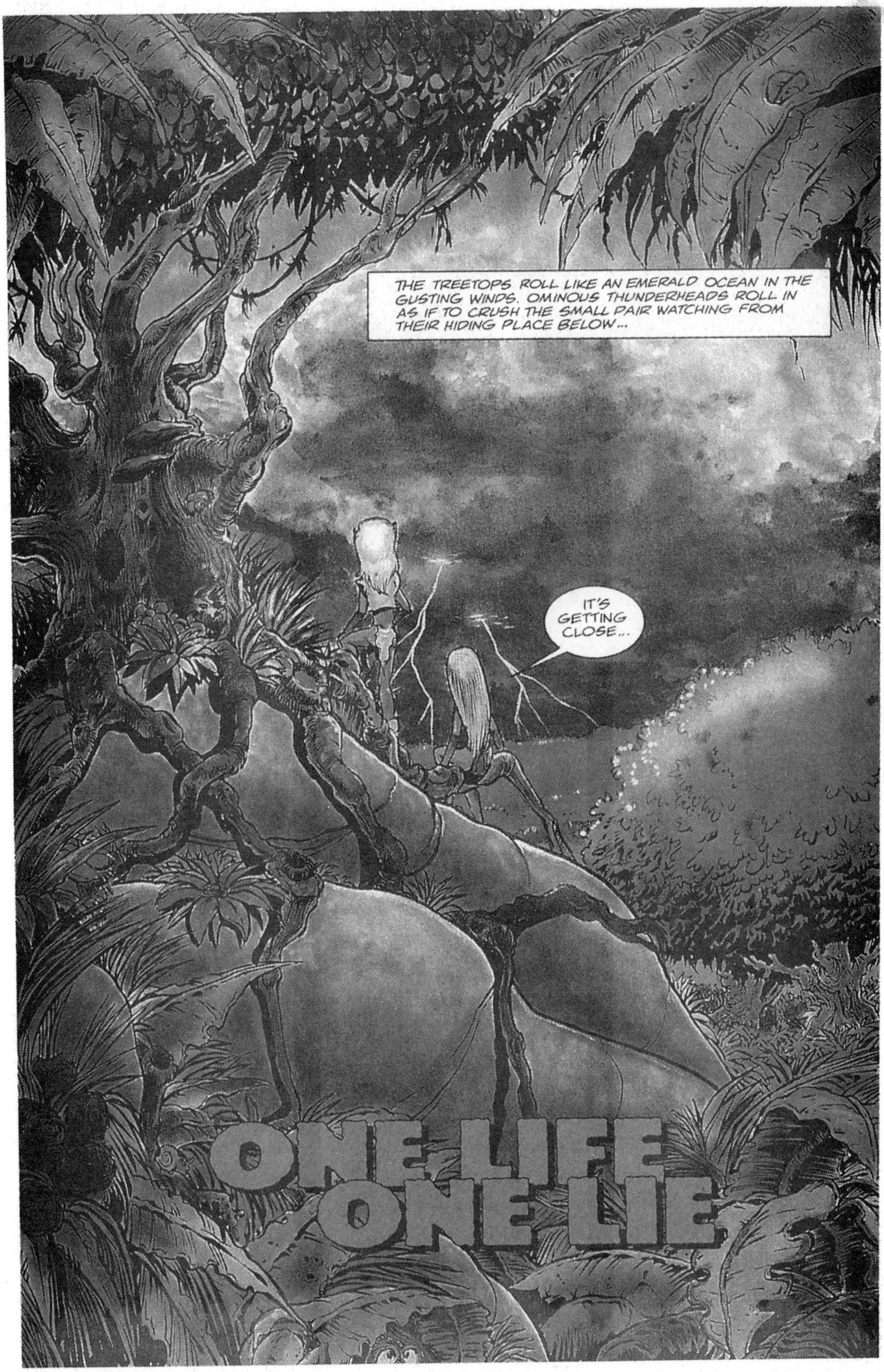
THE TREETOPS ROLL LIKE AN EMERALD OCEAN IN THE GUSTING WINDS. OMINOUS THUNDERHEADS ROLL IN AS IF TO CRUSH THE SMALL PAIR WATCHING FROM THEIR HIDING PLACE BELOW...
IT'S GETTING CLOSE...
ONE LIFE ONE LIE

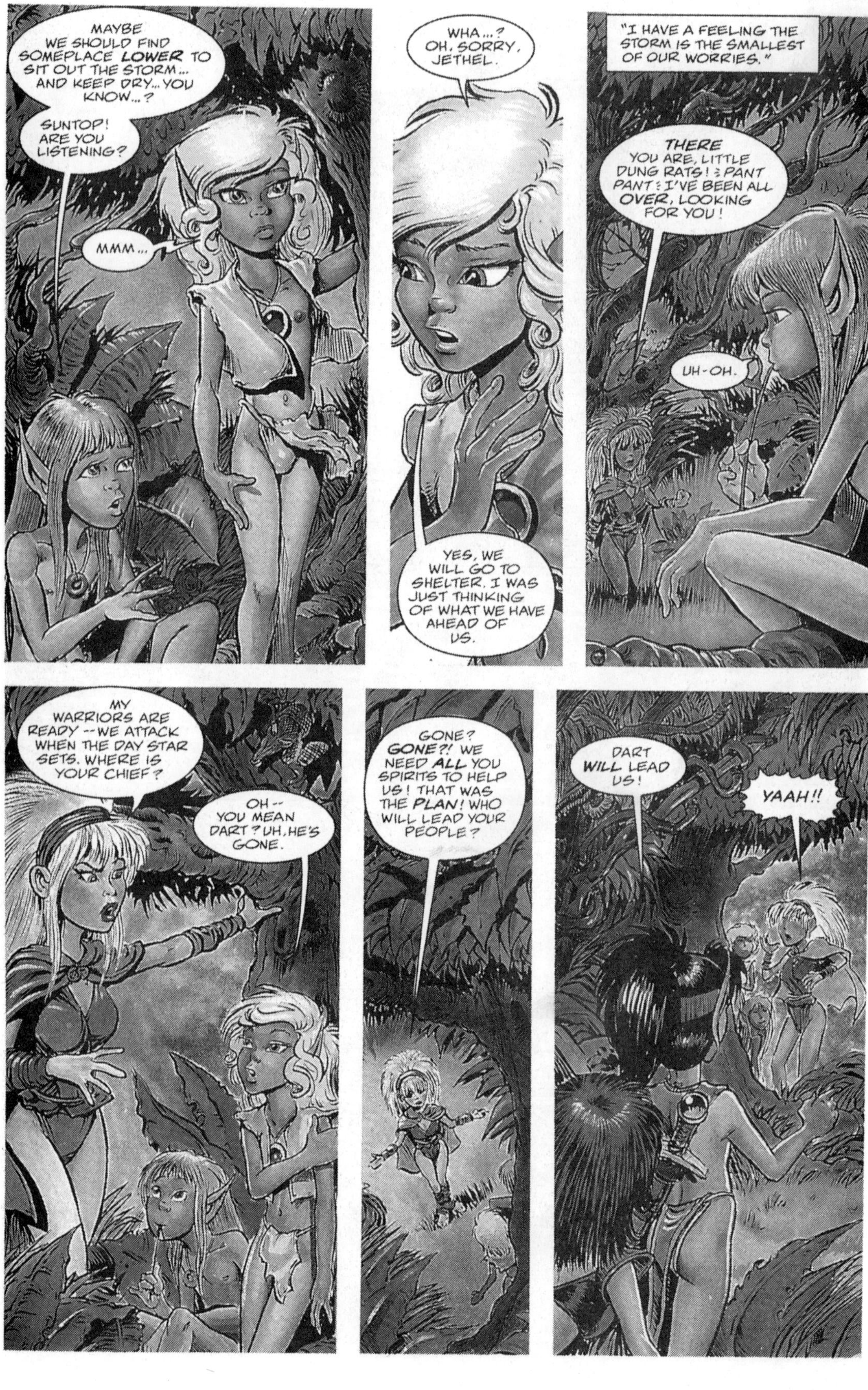
MAYBE WE SHOULD FIND SOMEPLACE LOWER TO SIT OUT THE STORM... AND KEEP DRY... YOU KNOW...?
SUNTOP! ARE YOU LISTENING?
MMM...
WHA...? OH. SORRY, JETHEL.
YES, WE WILL GO TO SHELTER. I WAS JUST THINKING OF WHAT WE HAVE AHEAD OF US.
"I HAVE A FEELING THE STORM IS THE SMALLEST OF OUR WORRIES."
THERE YOU ARE, LITTLE DUNG RATS! ≷PANT PANT≶ I'VE BEEN ALL OVER, LOOKING FOR YOU!
UH-OH.
MY WARRIORS ARE READY -- WE ATTACK WHEN THE DAY STAR SETS. WHERE IS YOUR CHIEF?
OH -- YOU MEAN DART? UH, HE'S GONE.
GONE? GONE?! WE NEED ALL YOU SPIRITS TO HELP US! THAT WAS THE PLAN! WHO WILL LEAD YOUR PEOPLE?
DART WILL LEAD US!
YAAH!!

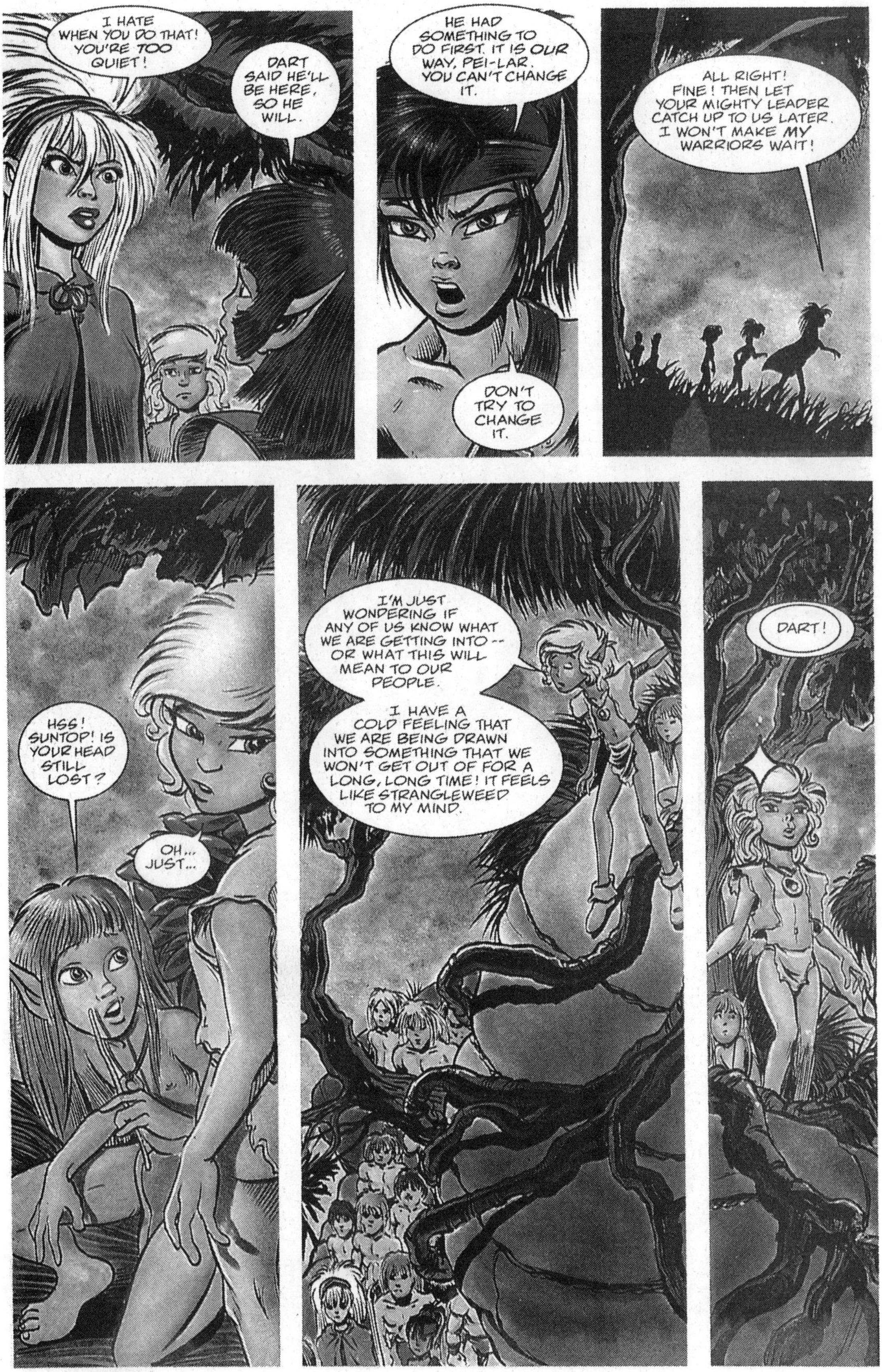
I HATE WHEN YOU DO THAT! YOU'RE TOO QUIET!
DART SAID HE'LL BE HERE, SO HE WILL.
HE HAD SOMETHING TO DO FIRST. IT IS OUR WAY, PEI-LAR. YOU CAN'T CHANGE IT.
DON'T TRY TO CHANGE IT.
ALL RIGHT! FINE! THEN LET YOUR MIGHTY LEADER CATCH UP TO US LATER. I WON'T MAKE MY WARRIORS WAIT!
HSS! SUNTOP! IS YOUR HEAD STILL LOST?
OH... JUST...
I'M JUST WONDERING IF ANY OF US KNOW WHAT WE ARE GETTING INTO-- OR WHAT THIS WILL MEAN TO OUR PEOPLE.
I HAVE A COLD FEELING THAT WE ARE BEING DRAWN INTO SOMETHING THAT WE WON'T GET OUT OF FOR A LONG, LONG TIME! IT FEELS LIKE STRANGLEWEED TO MY MIND.
DART!

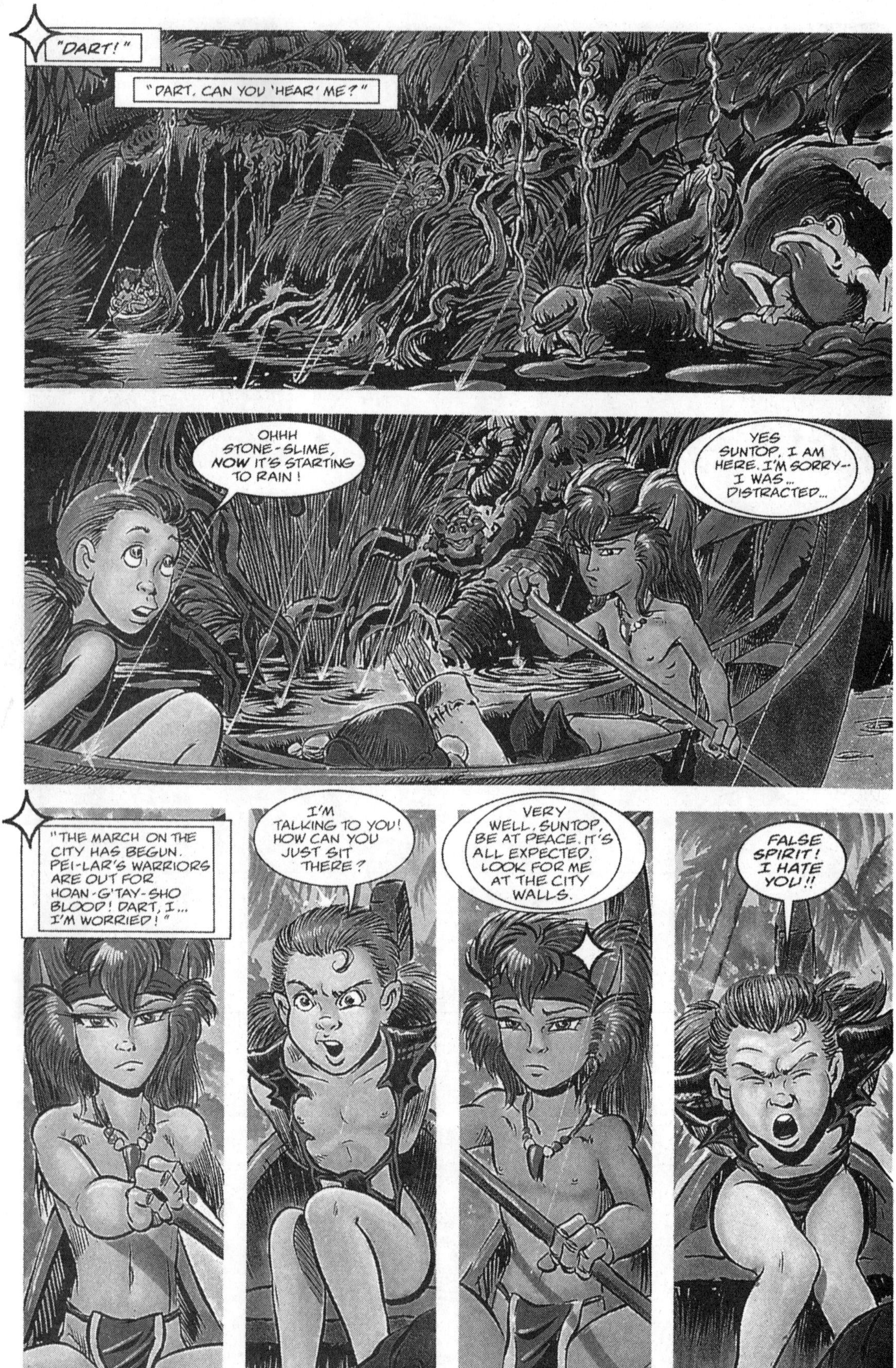
"DART!"
"DART, CAN YOU 'HEAR' ME?"
OHHH STONE-SLIME, NOW IT'S STARTING TO RAIN!
YES SUNTOP, I AM HERE. I'M SORRY-- I WAS... DISTRACTED...
"THE MARCH ON THE CITY HAS BEGUN. PEI-LAR'S WARRIORS ARE OUT FOR HOAN-G'TAY-SHO BLOOD! DART, I... I'M WORRIED!"
I'M TALKING TO YOU! HOW CAN YOU JUST SIT THERE?
VERY WELL, SUNTOP, BE AT PEACE. IT'S ALL EXPECTED. LOOK FOR ME AT THE CITY WALLS.
FALSE SPIRIT! I HATE YOU!!

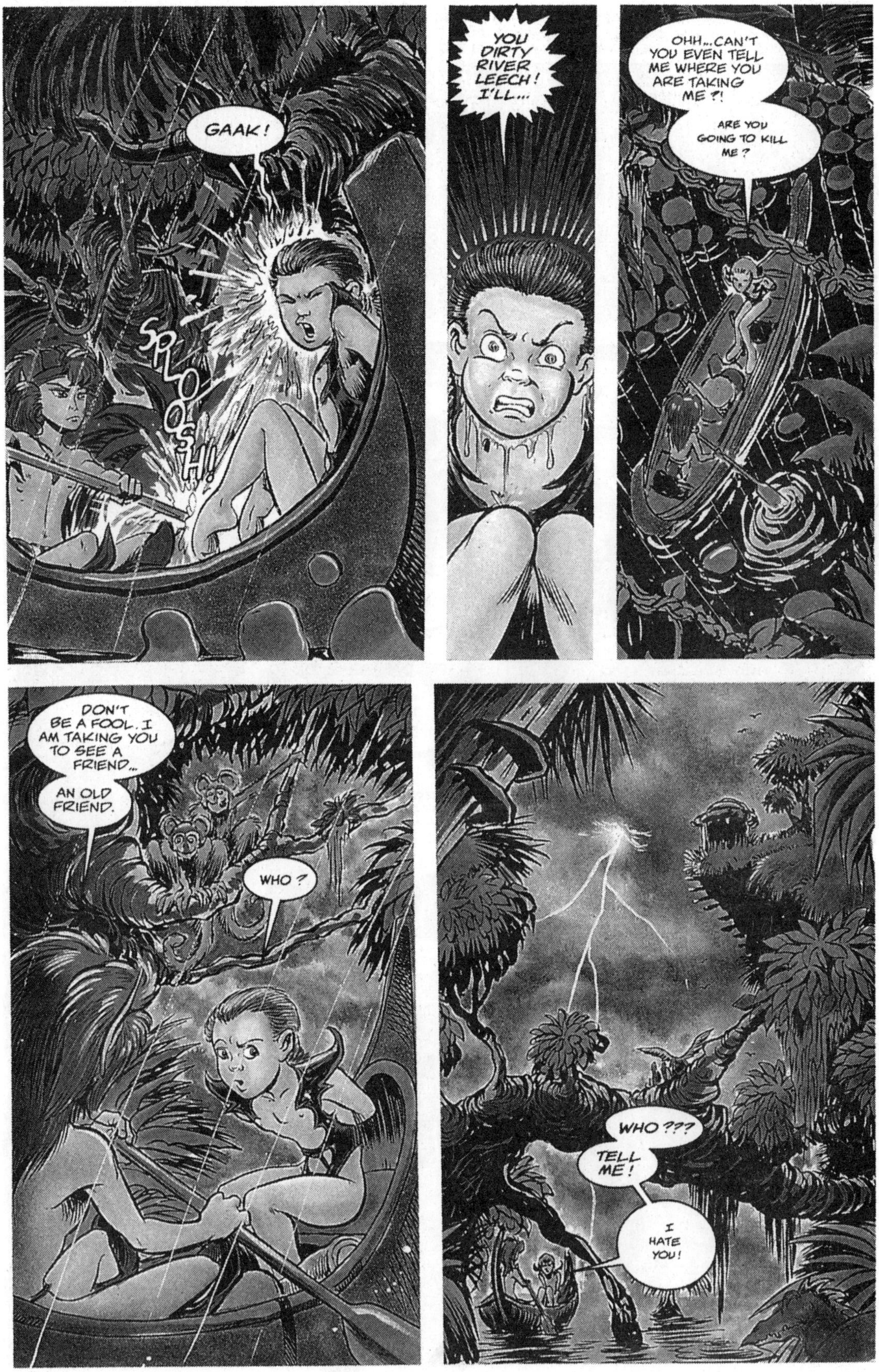
GAAK!
SPLOOSH!
YOU DIRTY RIVER LEECH! I'LL...
OHH...CAN'T YOU EVEN TELL ME WHERE YOU ARE TAKING ME?!
ARE YOU GOING TO KILL ME?
DON'T BE A FOOL. I AM TAKING YOU TO SEE A FRIEND...
AN OLD FRIEND.
WHO?
WHO???
TELL ME!
I HATE YOU!

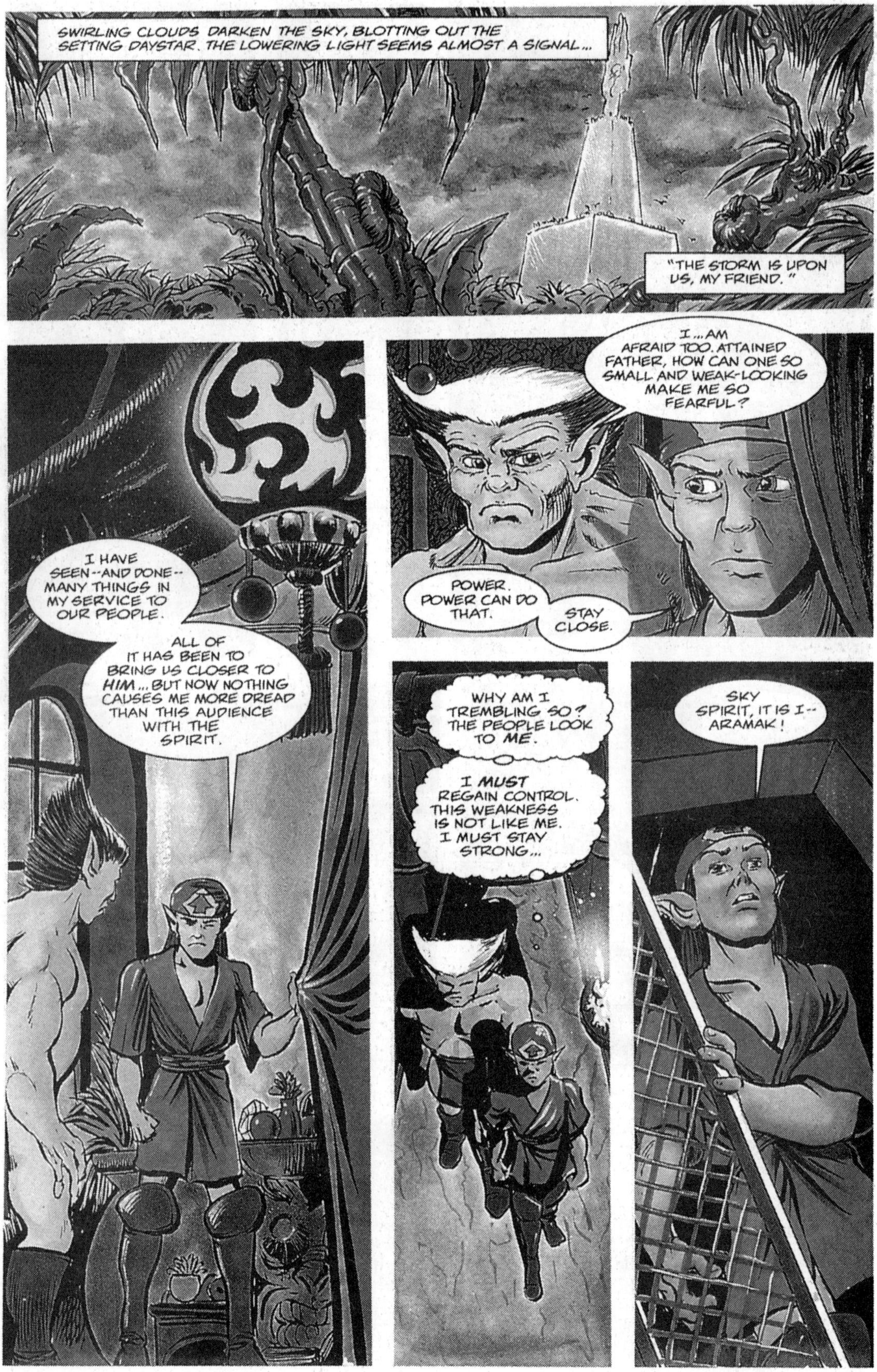
SWIRLING CLOUDS DARKEN THE SKY, BLOTTING OUT THE SETTING DAYSTAR. THE LOWERING LIGHT SEEMS ALMOST A SIGNAL...
"THE STORM IS UPON US, MY FRIEND."
I HAVE SEEN--AND DONE--MANY THINGS IN MY SERVICE TO OUR PEOPLE.
ALL OF IT HAS BEEN TO BRING US CLOSER TO HIM... BUT NOW NOTHING CAUSES ME MORE DREAD THAN THIS AUDIENCE WITH THE SPIRIT.
I...AM AFRAID TOO. ATTAINED FATHER, HOW CAN ONE SO SMALL AND WEAK-LOOKING MAKE ME SO FEARFUL?
POWER. POWER CAN DO THAT.
STAY CLOSE.
WHY AM I TREMBLING SO? THE PEOPLE LOOK TO ME.
I MUST REGAIN CONTROL. THIS WEAKNESS IS NOT LIKE ME. I MUST STAY STRONG...
SKY SPIRIT, IT IS I-- ARAMAK!

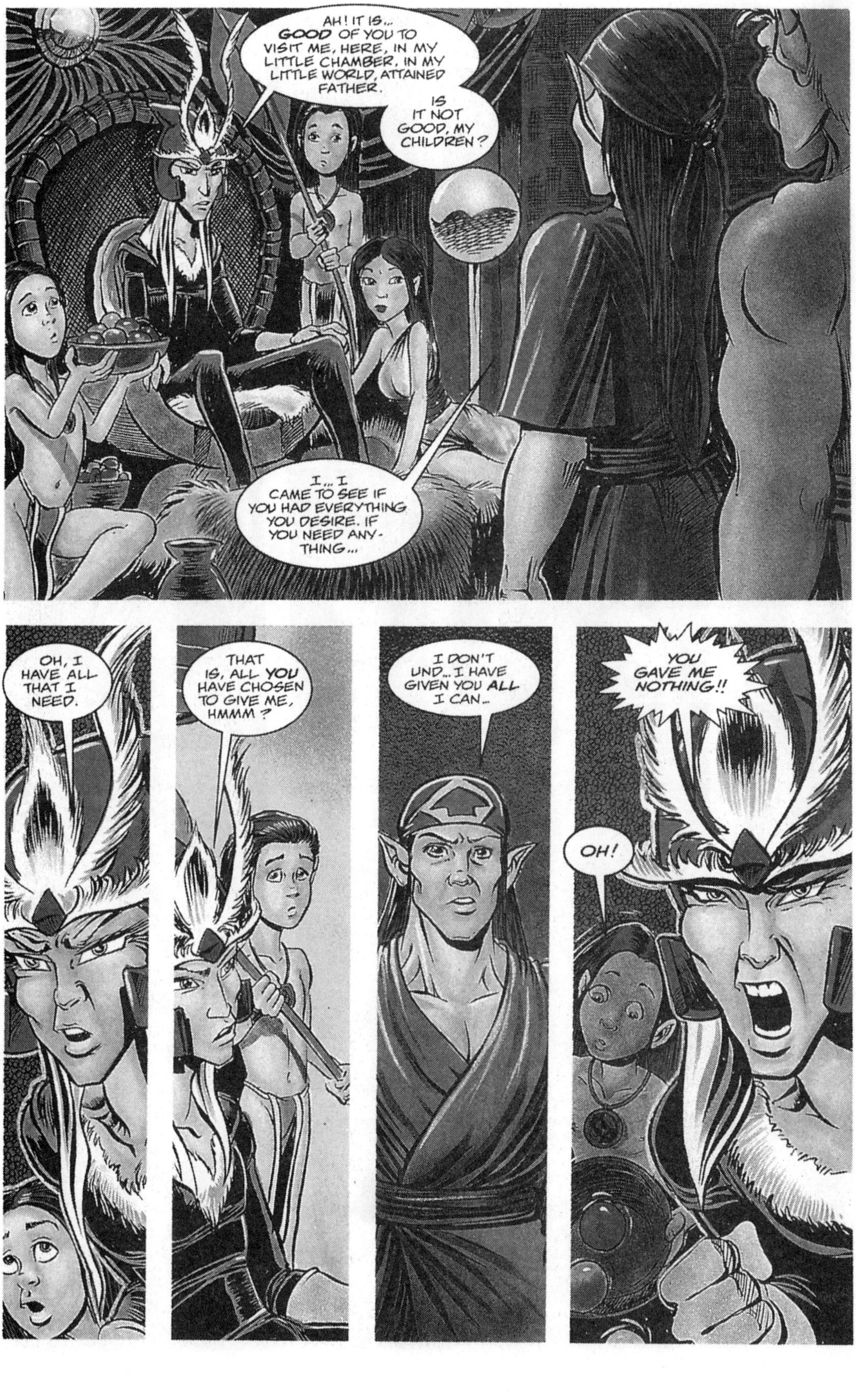
AH! IT IS... **GOOD** OF YOU TO VISIT ME, HERE, IN MY LITTLE CHAMBER, IN MY LITTLE WORLD, ATTAINED FATHER.
IS IT NOT GOOD, MY CHILDREN?
I... I CAME TO SEE IF YOU HAD EVERYTHING YOU DESIRE. IF YOU NEED ANY-THING...
OH, I HAVE ALL THAT I NEED.
THAT IS, ALL **YOU** HAVE CHOSEN TO GIVE ME, HMMM?
I DON'T UND... I HAVE GIVEN YOU **ALL** I CAN...
YOU GAVE ME NOTHING!!
OH!

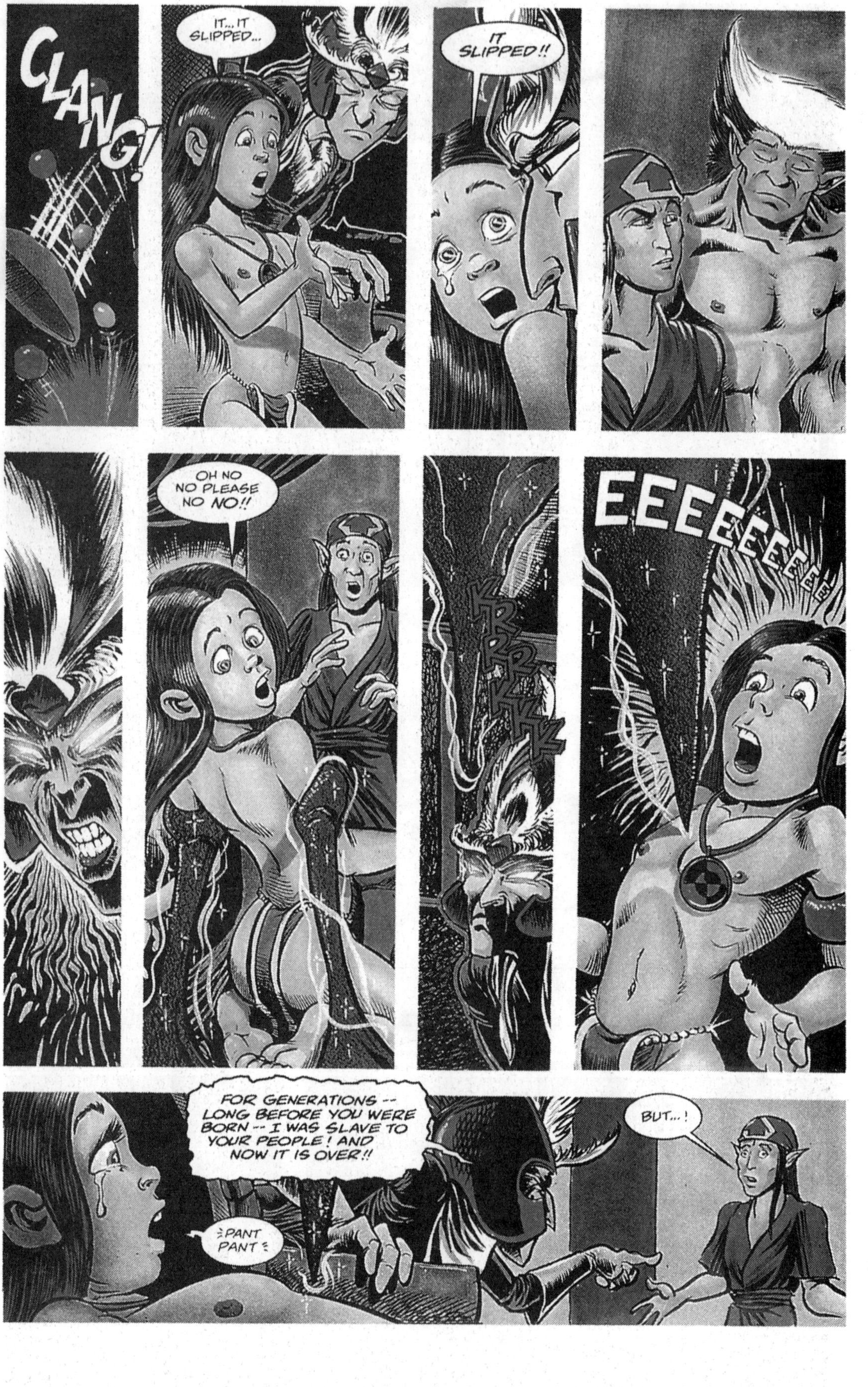
CLANG!
IT... IT SLIPPED...
IT SLIPPED!!
OH NO NO PLEASE NO NO!!
EEEEEEEE
FOR GENERATIONS -- LONG BEFORE YOU WERE BORN -- I WAS SLAVE TO YOUR PEOPLE! AND NOW IT IS OVER!!
PANT PANT
BUT...!

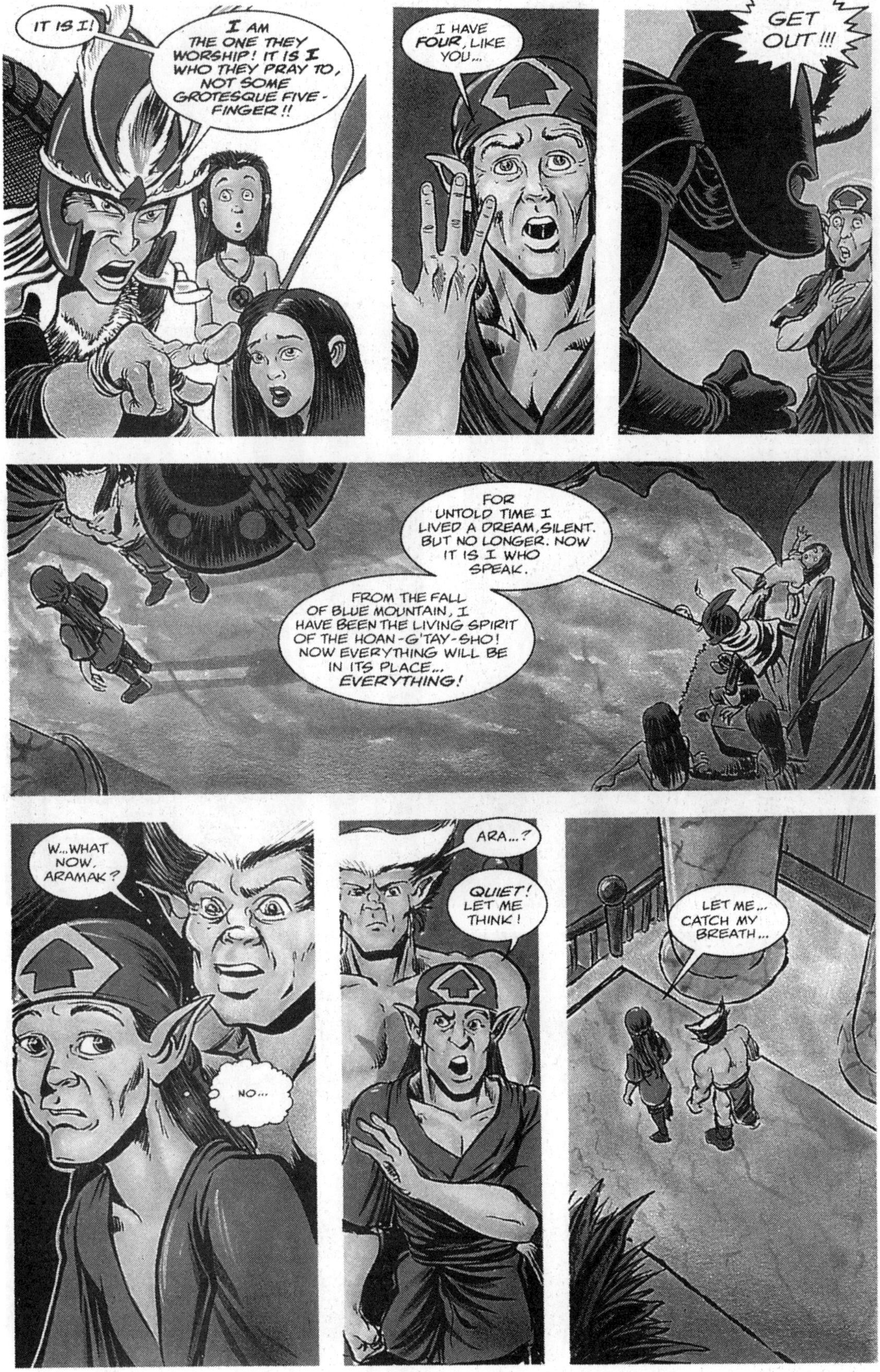
IT IS I!
I AM THE ONE THEY WORSHIP! IT IS I WHO THEY PRAY TO, NOT SOME GROTESQUE FIVE-FINGER!!
I HAVE FOUR, LIKE YOU...
GET OUT!!!
FOR UNTOLD TIME I LIVED A DREAM, SILENT. BUT NO LONGER. NOW IT IS I WHO SPEAK.
FROM THE FALL OF BLUE MOUNTAIN, I HAVE BEEN THE LIVING SPIRIT OF THE HOAN-G'TAY-SHO! NOW EVERYTHING WILL BE IN ITS PLACE... EVERYTHING!
W...WHAT NOW, ARAMAK?
NO...
ARA...?
QUIET! LET ME THINK!
LET ME... CATCH MY BREATH...

THE GUTTERING TORCHES, DEEP IN THE DUNGEONS BELOW THE CITY, MAKE A SOUND ALMOST AS IF SOME GREAT BEAST WERE BREATHING. THE LOW NOISE MASKS THE FURTIVE WHISPERS IN THE DARK.

"TRY AGAIN, WILLOWSNAP..."

WILLOWSNAP IS TRYING AND TRYING AND TRYING!

JUST DO IT AGAIN, LITTLE FRIEND, ONLY SLOWLY... VERY SLOWLY.

SHTHUPP

NOW WHA WIWWOWTHAP THOO?

HOLD STILL.

...EASY...

JUST A LITTLE PULL...

LOOKIE?

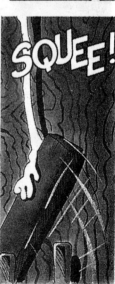

SQUEE!

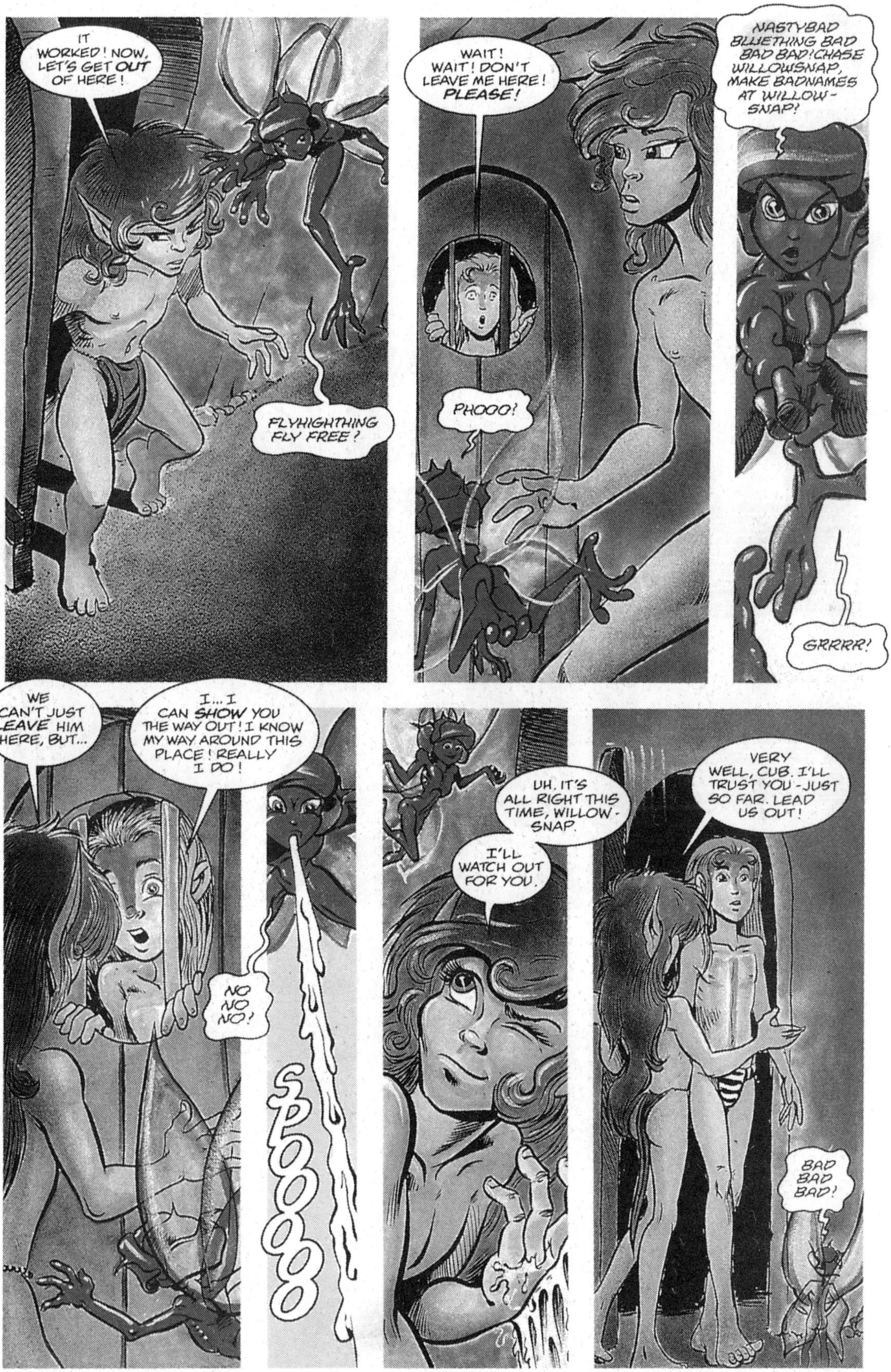
IT WORKED! NOW, LET'S GET OUT OF HERE!
FLYHIGHTHING FLY FREE?
WAIT! WAIT! DON'T LEAVE ME HERE! PLEASE!
PHOOO!
NASTYBAD BLUETHING BAD BAD BAD! CHASE WILLOWSNAP, MAKE BADNAMES AT WILLOW-SNAP!
GRRRR!
WE CAN'T JUST LEAVE HIM HERE, BUT...
I... I CAN SHOW YOU THE WAY OUT! I KNOW MY WAY AROUND THIS PLACE! REALLY I DO!
NO NO NO!
SPOOOOO
UH. IT'S ALL RIGHT THIS TIME, WILLOW-SNAP.
I'LL WATCH OUT FOR YOU.
VERY WELL, CUB. I'LL TRUST YOU - JUST SO FAR. LEAD US OUT!
BAD BAD BAD!

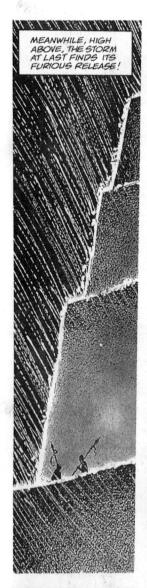

MEANWHILE, HIGH ABOVE, THE STORM AT LAST FINDS ITS FURIOUS RELEASE!

WHAT A WRETCHED NIGHT! I WISH I WAS IN BED RIGHT NOW!

IF YOU HADN'T SAID THOSE THINGS TO ARAMAK'S WOMAN, YOU WOULD BE. I ONLY WISH I...WAIT!

OH NO!!

"SOUND THE ALARM! CALL THE ATTAINED FATHER!!"

WHAT IS IT? WHO DARES, ON SUCH A FOUL NIGHT?

THE OUTCASTS! THE UNBELIEVERS ARE HERE!!

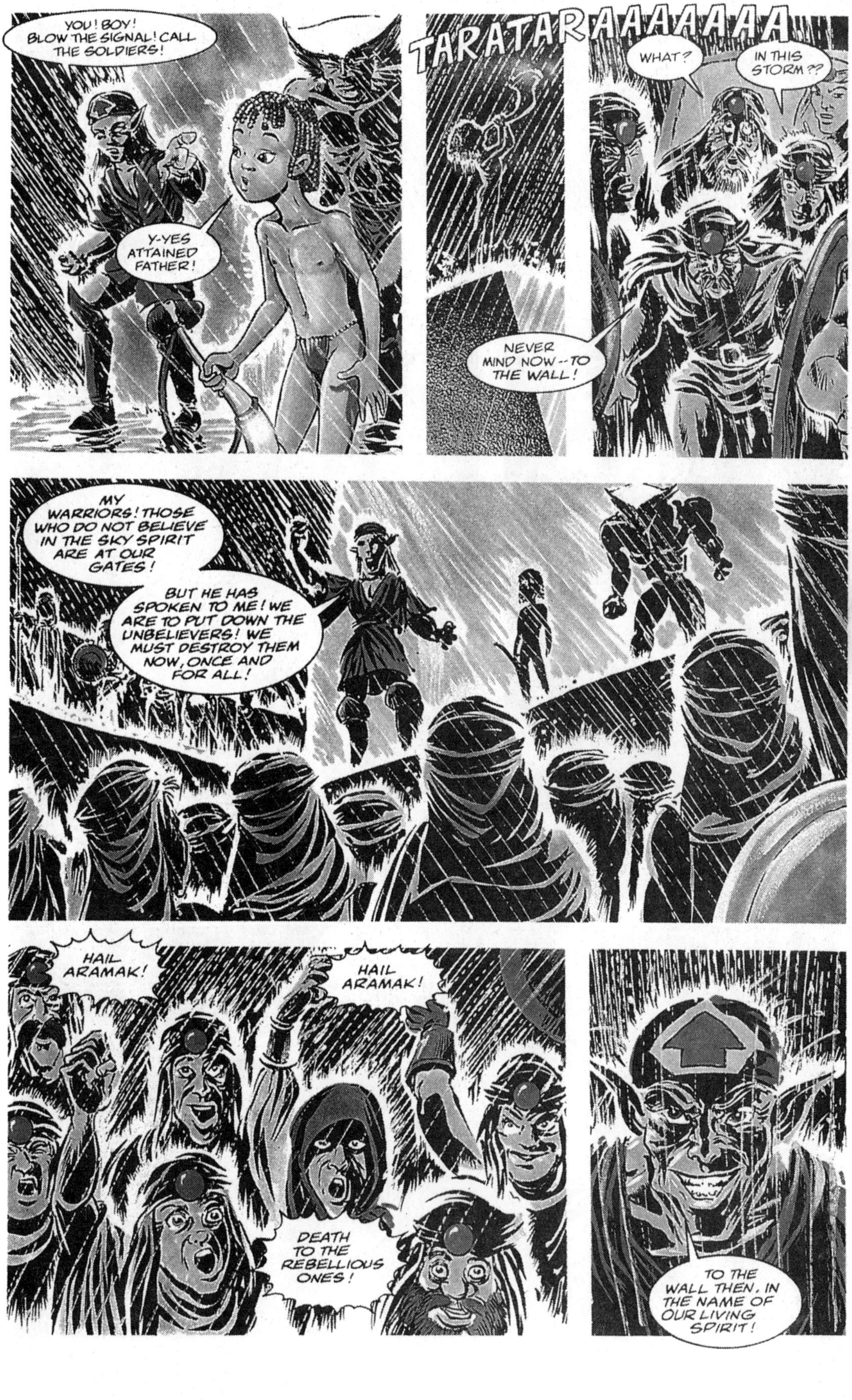
YOU! BOY! BLOW THE SIGNAL! CALL THE SOLDIERS!
Y-YES ATTAINED FATHER!
TARATARAAAAAAA
WHAT?
IN THIS STORM??
NEVER MIND NOW--TO THE WALL!
MY WARRIORS! THOSE WHO DO NOT BELIEVE IN THE SKY SPIRIT ARE AT OUR GATES!
BUT HE HAS SPOKEN TO ME! WE ARE TO PUT DOWN THE UNBELIEVERS! WE MUST DESTROY THEM NOW, ONCE AND FOR ALL!
HAIL ARAMAK!
HAIL ARAMAK!
DEATH TO THE REBELLIOUS ONES!
TO THE WALL THEN, IN THE NAME OF OUR LIVING SPIRIT!

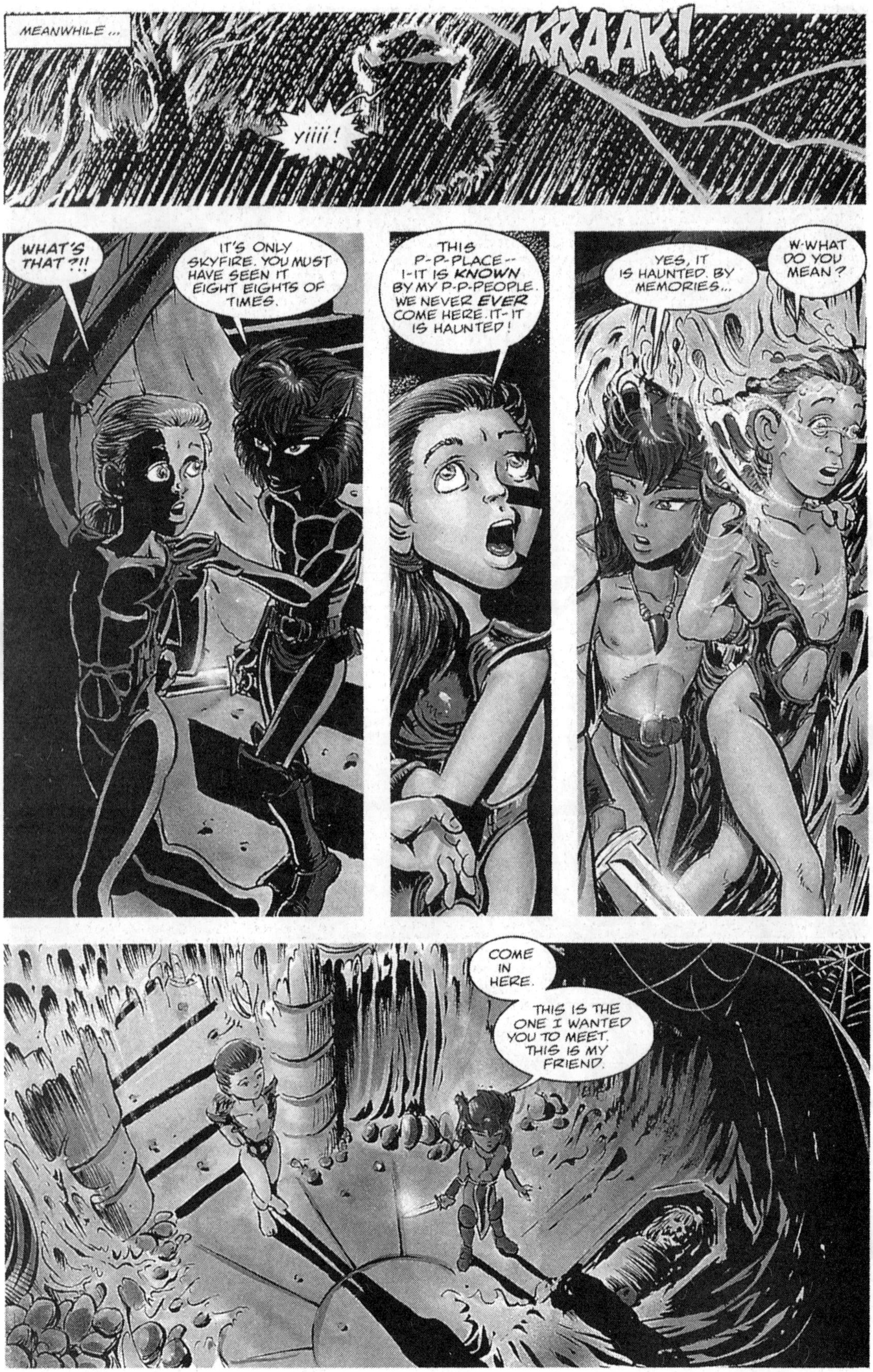

MEANWHILE ...
KRAAK!
yiiii!
WHAT'S THAT?!!
IT'S ONLY SKYFIRE. YOU MUST HAVE SEEN IT EIGHT EIGHTS OF TIMES.
THIS P-P-PLACE-- I-IT IS KNOWN BY MY P-P-PEOPLE. WE NEVER EVER COME HERE. IT-IT IS HAUNTED!
YES, IT IS HAUNTED. BY MEMORIES...
W-WHAT DO YOU MEAN?
COME IN HERE.
THIS IS THE ONE I WANTED YOU TO MEET. THIS IS MY FRIEND.

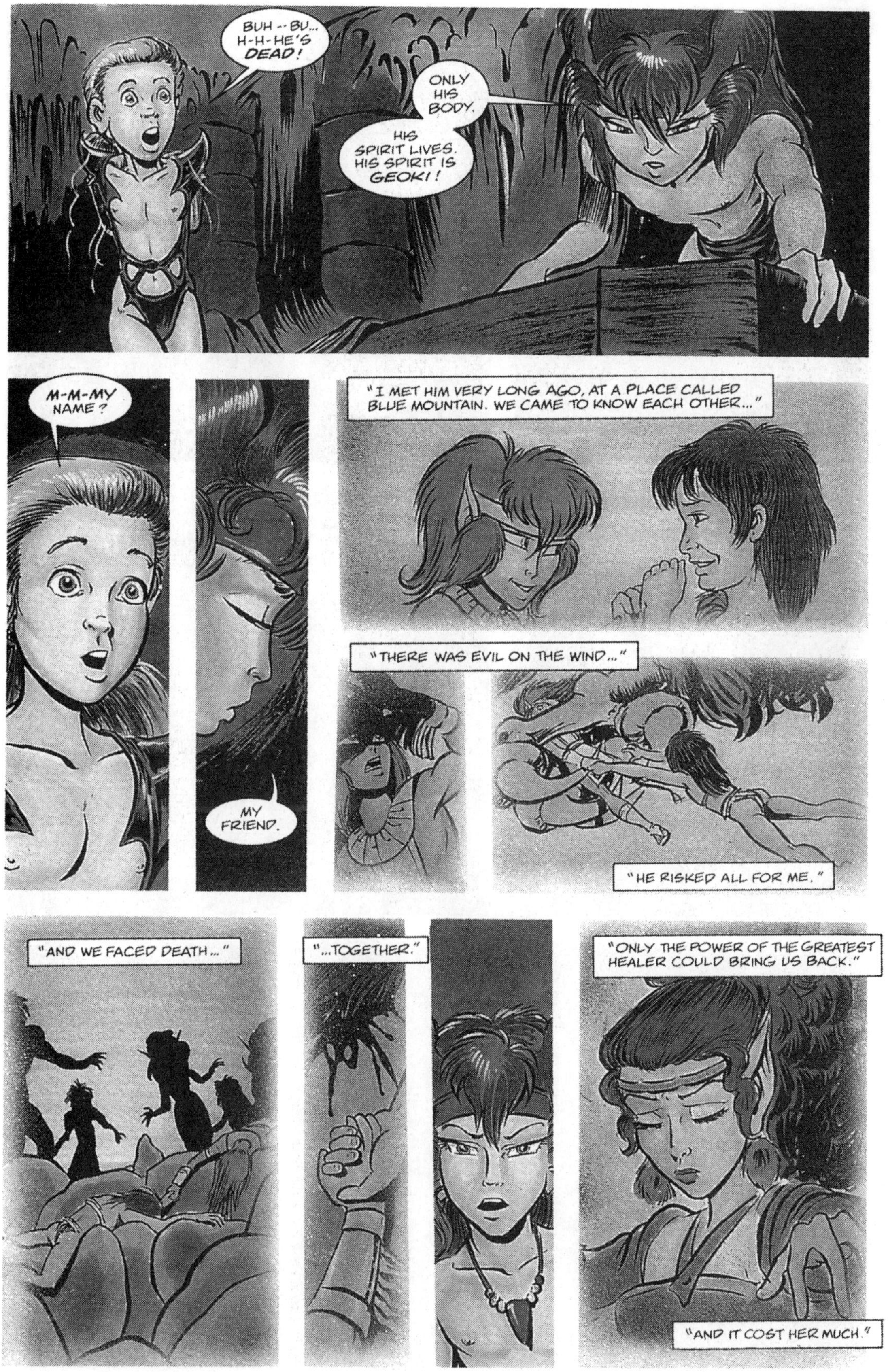

BUH -- BU... H-H-HE'S DEAD!
ONLY HIS BODY.
HIS SPIRIT LIVES. HIS SPIRIT IS GEOKI!
M-M-MY NAME?
MY FRIEND.
"I MET HIM VERY LONG AGO, AT A PLACE CALLED BLUE MOUNTAIN. WE CAME TO KNOW EACH OTHER..."
"THERE WAS EVIL ON THE WIND..."
"HE RISKED ALL FOR ME."
"AND WE FACED DEATH..."
"...TOGETHER."
"ONLY THE POWER OF THE GREATEST HEALER COULD BRING US BACK."
"AND IT COST HER MUCH."

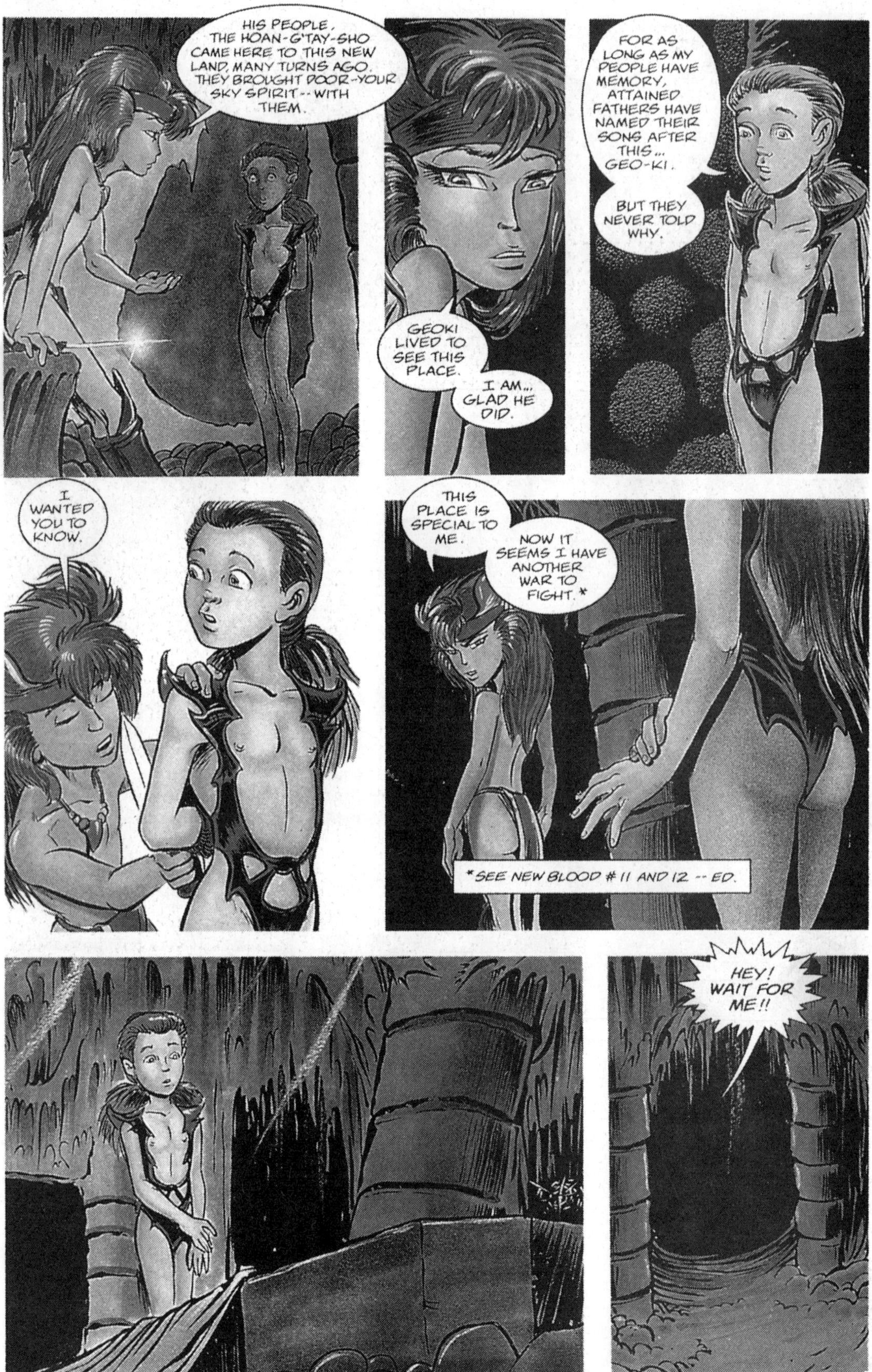
HIS PEOPLE, THE HOAN-G'TAY-SHO CAME HERE TO THIS NEW LAND, MANY TURNS AGO. THEY BROUGHT DOOR-YOUR SKY SPIRIT--WITH THEM.
GEOKI LIVED TO SEE THIS PLACE.
I AM... GLAD HE DID.
FOR AS LONG AS MY PEOPLE HAVE MEMORY, ATTAINED FATHERS HAVE NAMED THEIR SONGS AFTER THIS... GEO-KI.
BUT THEY NEVER TOLD WHY.
I WANTED YOU TO KNOW.
THIS PLACE IS SPECIAL TO ME.
NOW IT SEEMS I HAVE ANOTHER WAR TO FIGHT.*
*SEE NEW BLOOD #11 AND 12 -- ED.
HEY! WAIT FOR ME!!

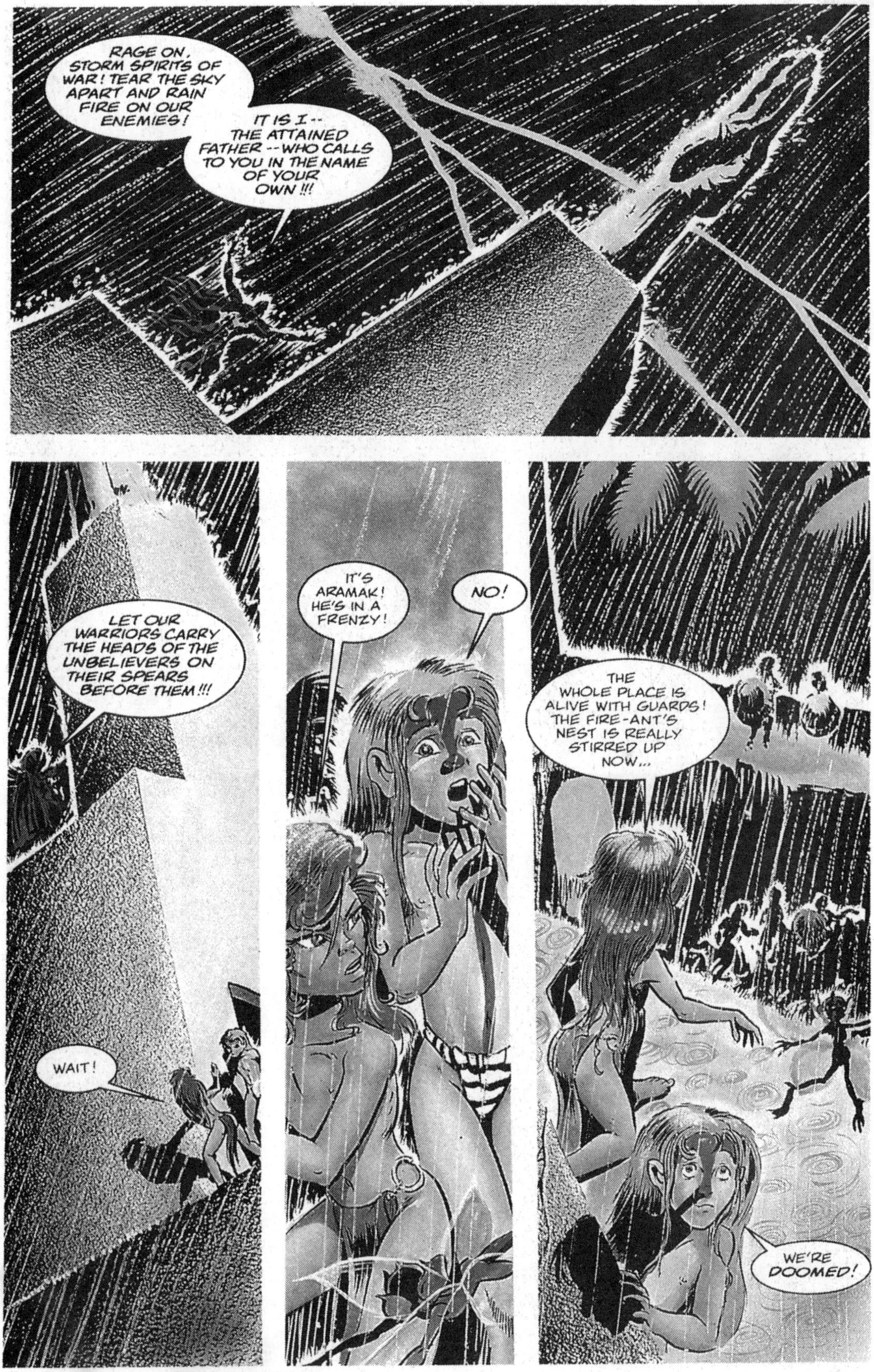
RAGE ON, STORM SPIRITS OF WAR! TEAR THE SKY APART AND RAIN FIRE ON OUR ENEMIES!
IT IS I -- THE ATTAINED FATHER -- WHO CALLS TO YOU IN THE NAME OF YOUR OWN!!!
LET OUR WARRIORS CARRY THE HEADS OF THE UNBELIEVERS ON THEIR SPEARS BEFORE THEM!!!
WAIT!
IT'S ARAMAK! HE'S IN A FRENZY!
NO!
THE WHOLE PLACE IS ALIVE WITH GUARDS! THE FIRE-ANT'S NEST IS REALLY STIRRED UP NOW...
WE'RE DOOMED!

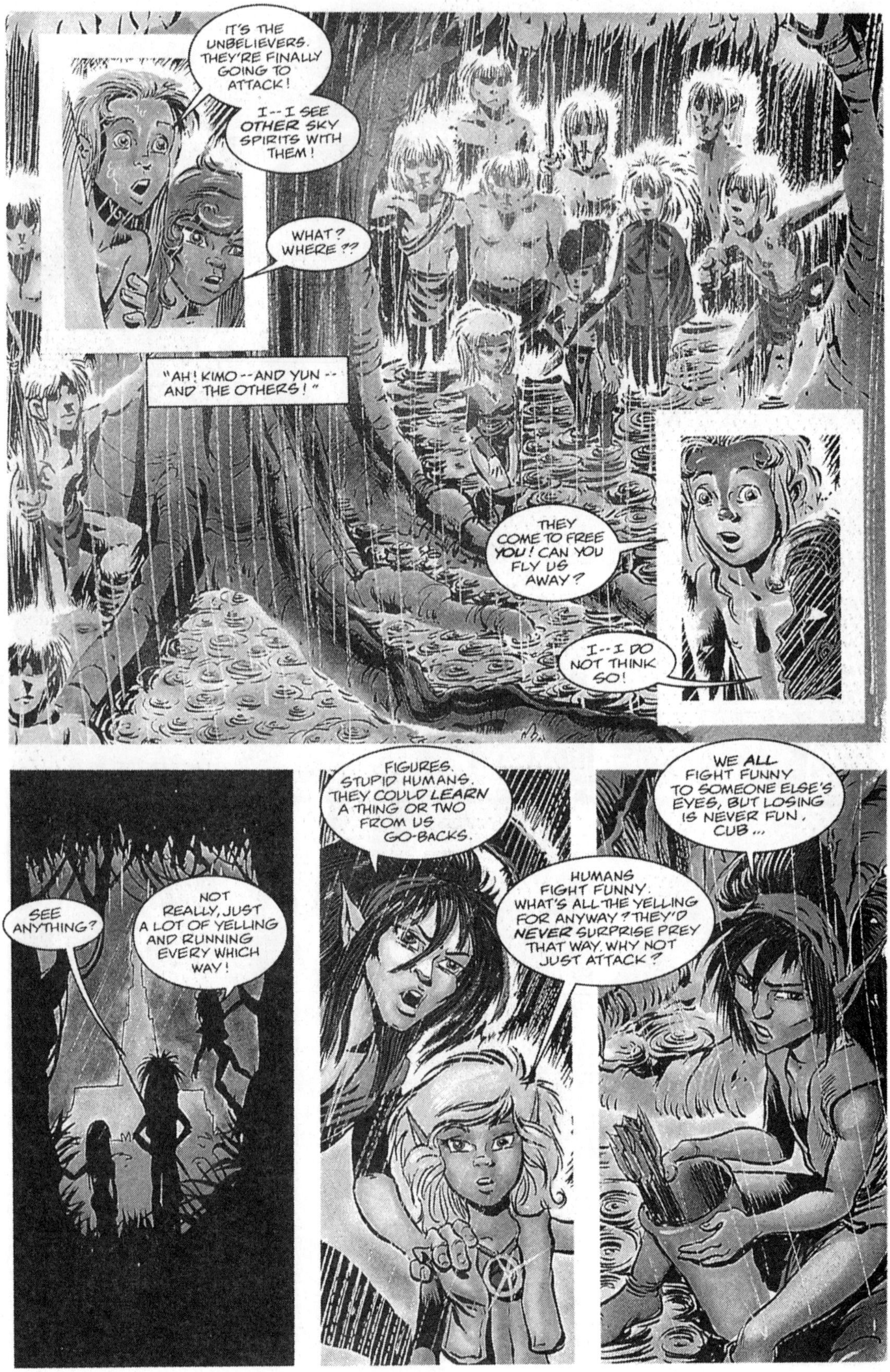
IT'S THE UNBELIEVERS. THEY'RE FINALLY GOING TO ATTACK!
I-- I SEE OTHER SKY SPIRITS WITH THEM!
WHAT? WHERE??
"AH! KIMO --AND YUN -- AND THE OTHERS!"
THEY COME TO FREE YOU! CAN YOU FLY US AWAY?
I-- I DO NOT THINK SO!
SEE ANYTHING?
NOT REALLY, JUST A LOT OF YELLING AND RUNNING EVERY WHICH WAY!
FIGURES. STUPID HUMANS. THEY COULD LEARN A THING OR TWO FROM US GO-BACKS.
HUMANS FIGHT FUNNY. WHAT'S ALL THE YELLING FOR ANYWAY? THEY'D NEVER SURPRISE PREY THAT WAY. WHY NOT JUST ATTACK?
WE ALL FIGHT FUNNY TO SOMEONE ELSE'S EYES, BUT LOSING IS NEVER FUN, CUB...

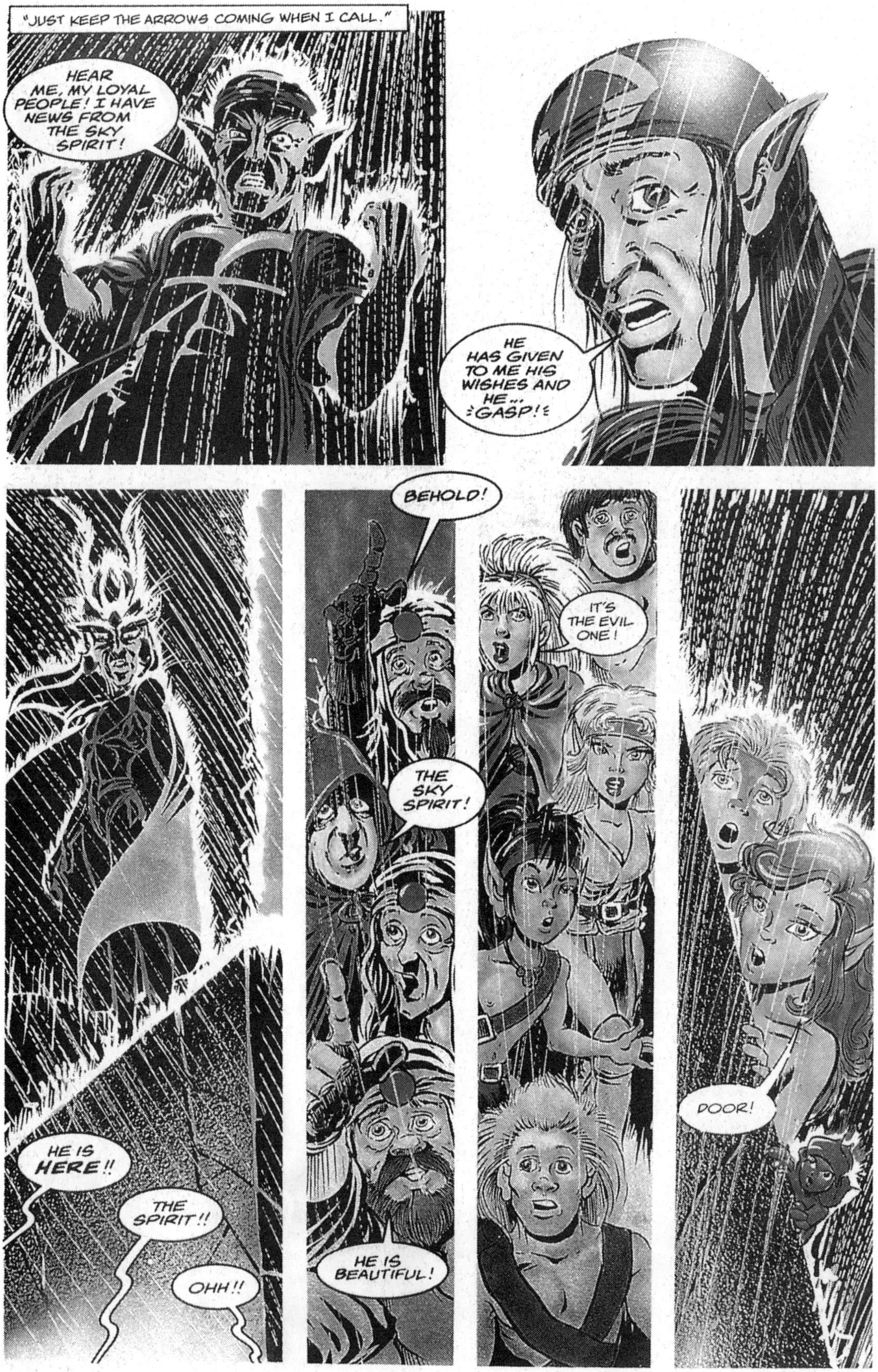
"JUST KEEP THE ARROWS COMING WHEN I CALL."
HEAR ME, MY LOYAL PEOPLE! I HAVE NEWS FROM THE SKY SPIRIT!
HE HAS GIVEN TO ME HIS WISHES AND HE... GASP!
HE IS HERE!!
THE SPIRIT!!
OHH!!
BEHOLD!
THE SKY SPIRIT!
HE IS BEAUTIFUL!
IT'S THE EVIL ONE!
DOOR!

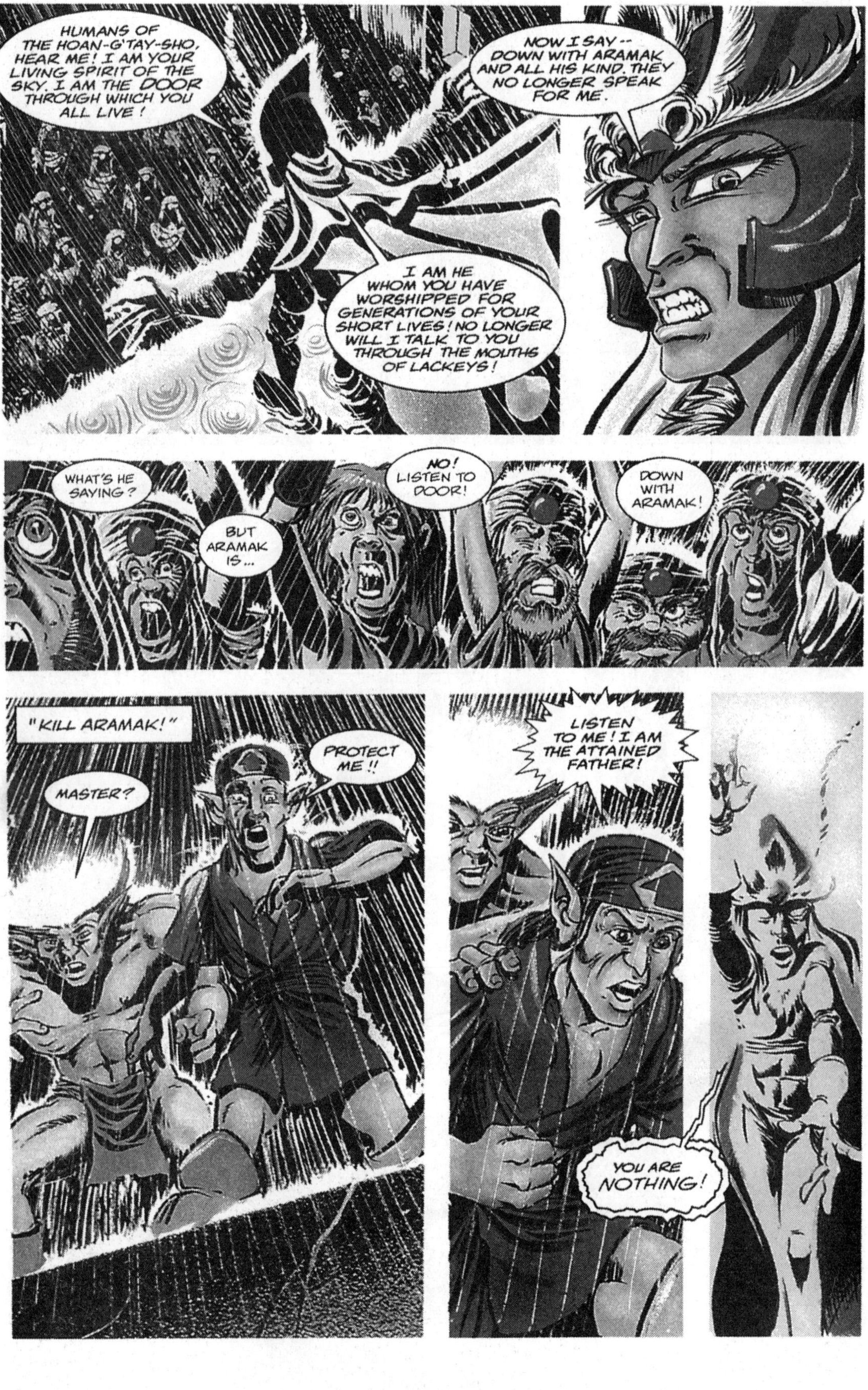
HUMANS OF THE HOAN-G'TAY-SHO, HEAR ME! I AM YOUR LIVING SPIRIT OF THE SKY. I AM THE DOOR THROUGH WHICH YOU ALL LIVE!
I AM HE WHOM YOU HAVE WORSHIPPED FOR GENERATIONS OF YOUR SHORT LIVES! NO LONGER WILL I TALK TO YOU THROUGH THE MOUTHS OF LACKEYS!
NOW I SAY -- DOWN WITH ARAMAK AND ALL HIS KIND. THEY NO LONGER SPEAK FOR ME.
WHAT'S HE SAYING?
BUT ARAMAK IS...
NO! LISTEN TO DOOR!
DOWN WITH ARAMAK!
"KILL ARAMAK!"
MASTER?
PROTECT ME!!
LISTEN TO ME! I AM THE ATTAINED FATHER!
YOU ARE NOTHING!

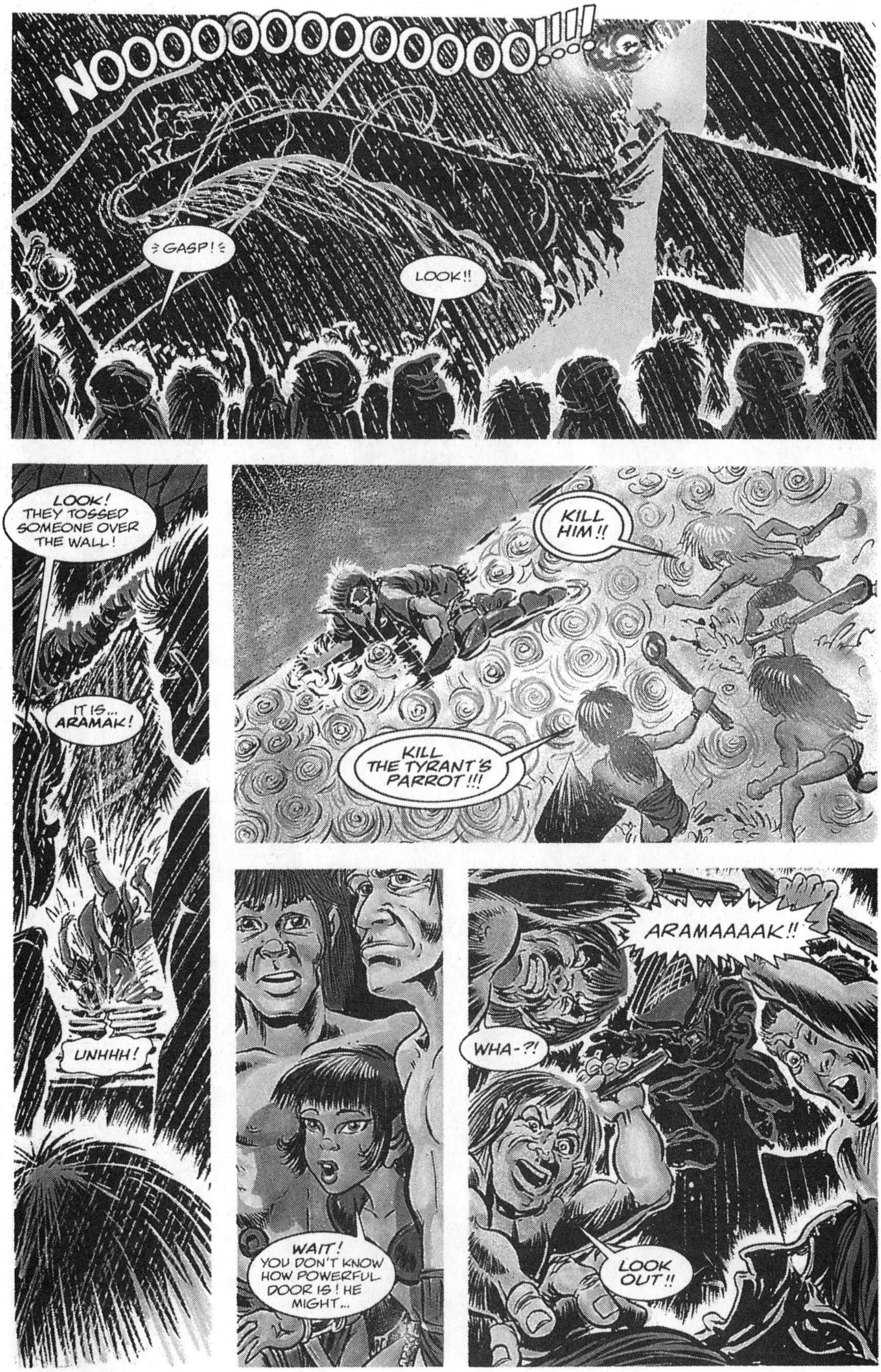
NOOOOOOOOOOOOOOO!!!!....
GASP!
LOOK!!
LOOK! THEY TOSSED SOMEONE OVER THE WALL!
IT IS... ARAMAK!
UNHHH!
KILL HIM!!
KILL THE TYRANT'S PARROT!!!
WAIT! YOU DON'T KNOW HOW POWERFUL DOOR IS! HE MIGHT...
ARAMAAAAK!!
WHA-?!
LOOK OUT!!

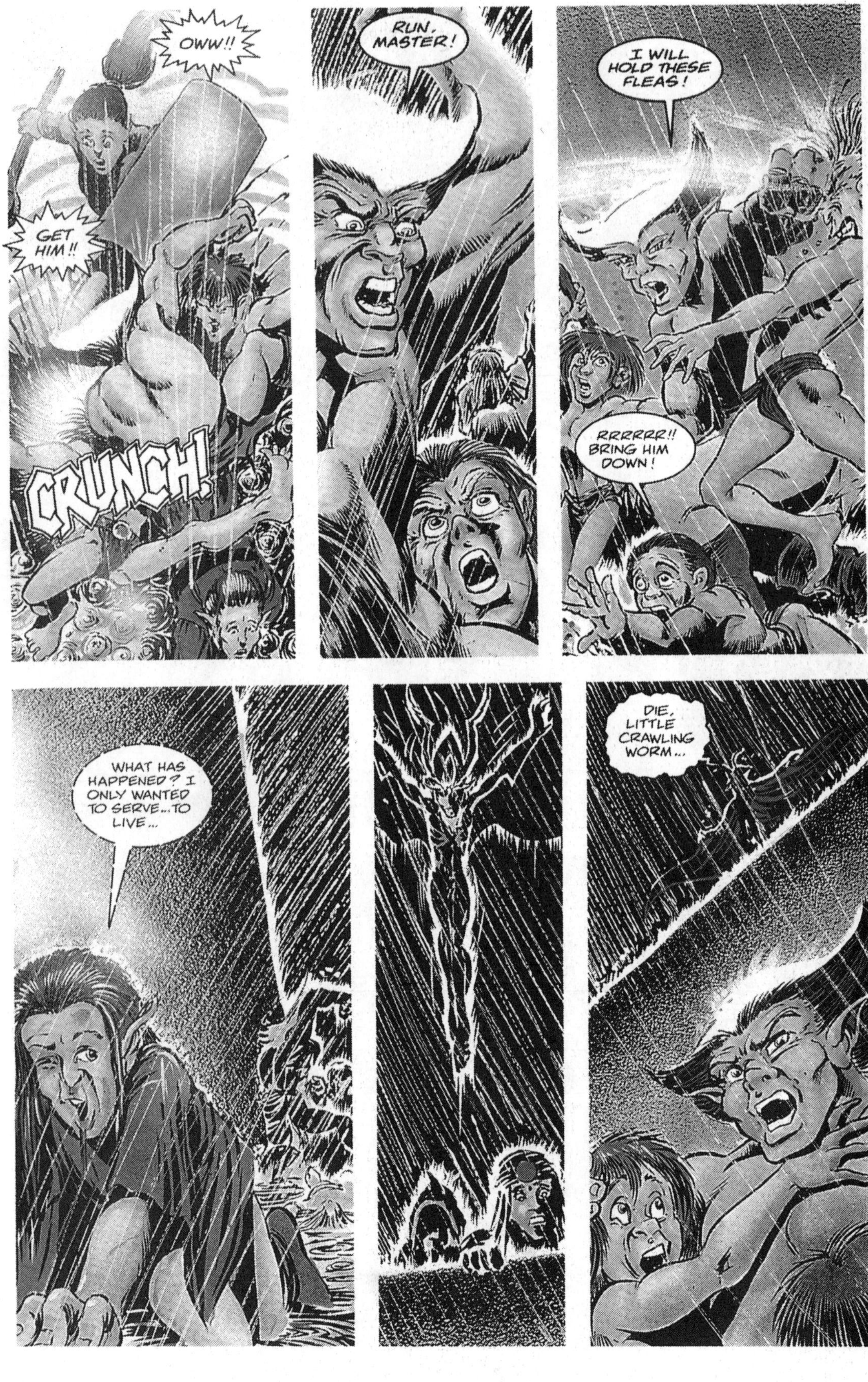
OWW!!
GET HIM!!
CRUNCH!
RUN, MASTER!
I WILL HOLD THESE FLEAS!
RRRRRR!! BRING HIM DOWN!
WHAT HAS HAPPENED? I ONLY WANTED TO SERVE...TO LIVE...
DIE, LITTLE CRAWLING WORM...

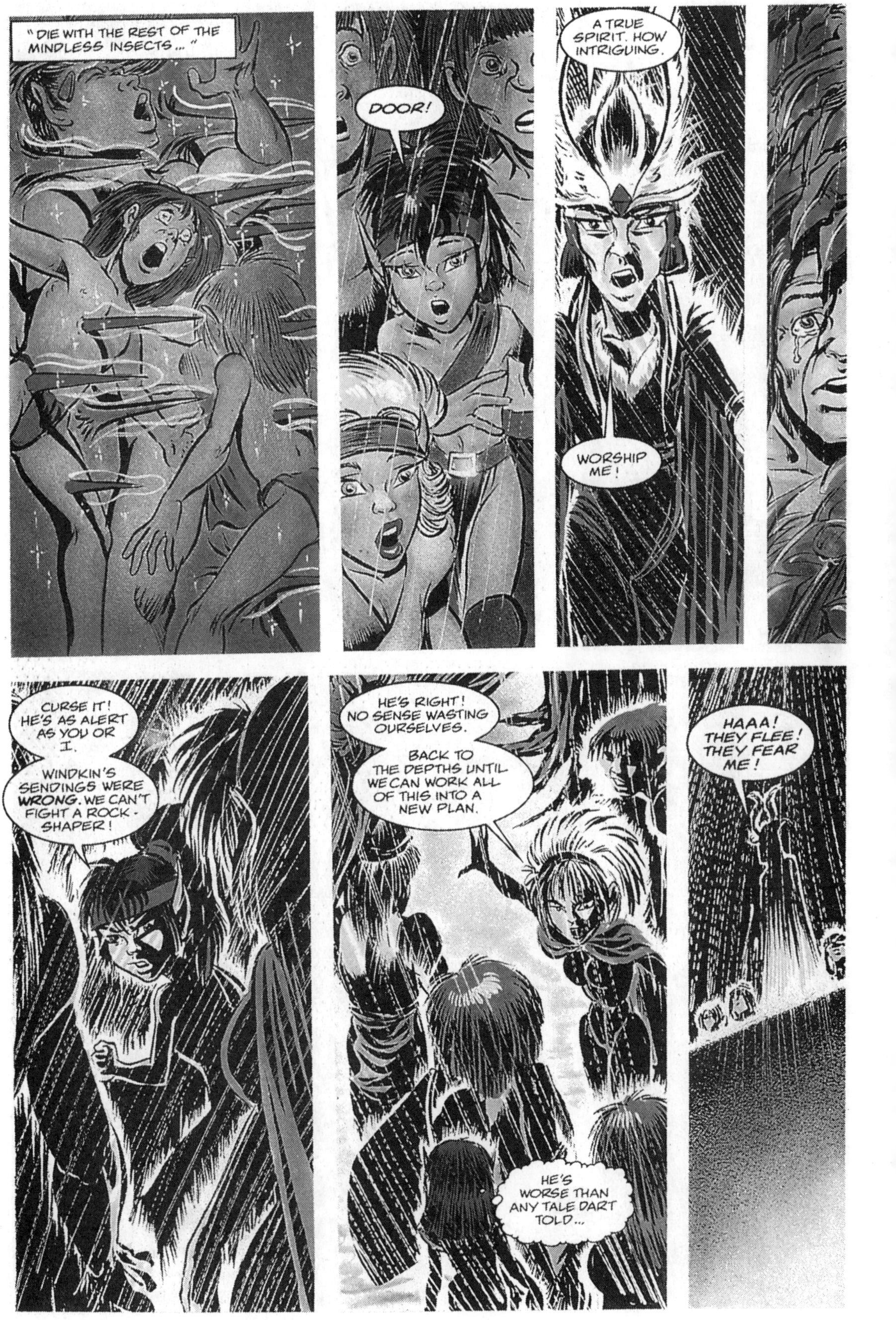
"DIE WITH THE REST OF THE MINDLESS INSECTS..."
DOOR!
A TRUE SPIRIT. HOW INTRIGUING.
WORSHIP ME!
CURSE IT! HE'S AS ALERT AS YOU OR I.
WINDKIN'S SENDINGS WERE **WRONG**. WE CAN'T FIGHT A ROCK-SHAPER!
HE'S RIGHT! NO SENSE WASTING OURSELVES.
BACK TO THE DEPTHS UNTIL WE CAN WORK ALL OF THIS INTO A NEW PLAN.
HE'S WORSE THAN ANY TALE DART TOLD...
HAAA! THEY FLEE! THEY FEAR ME!

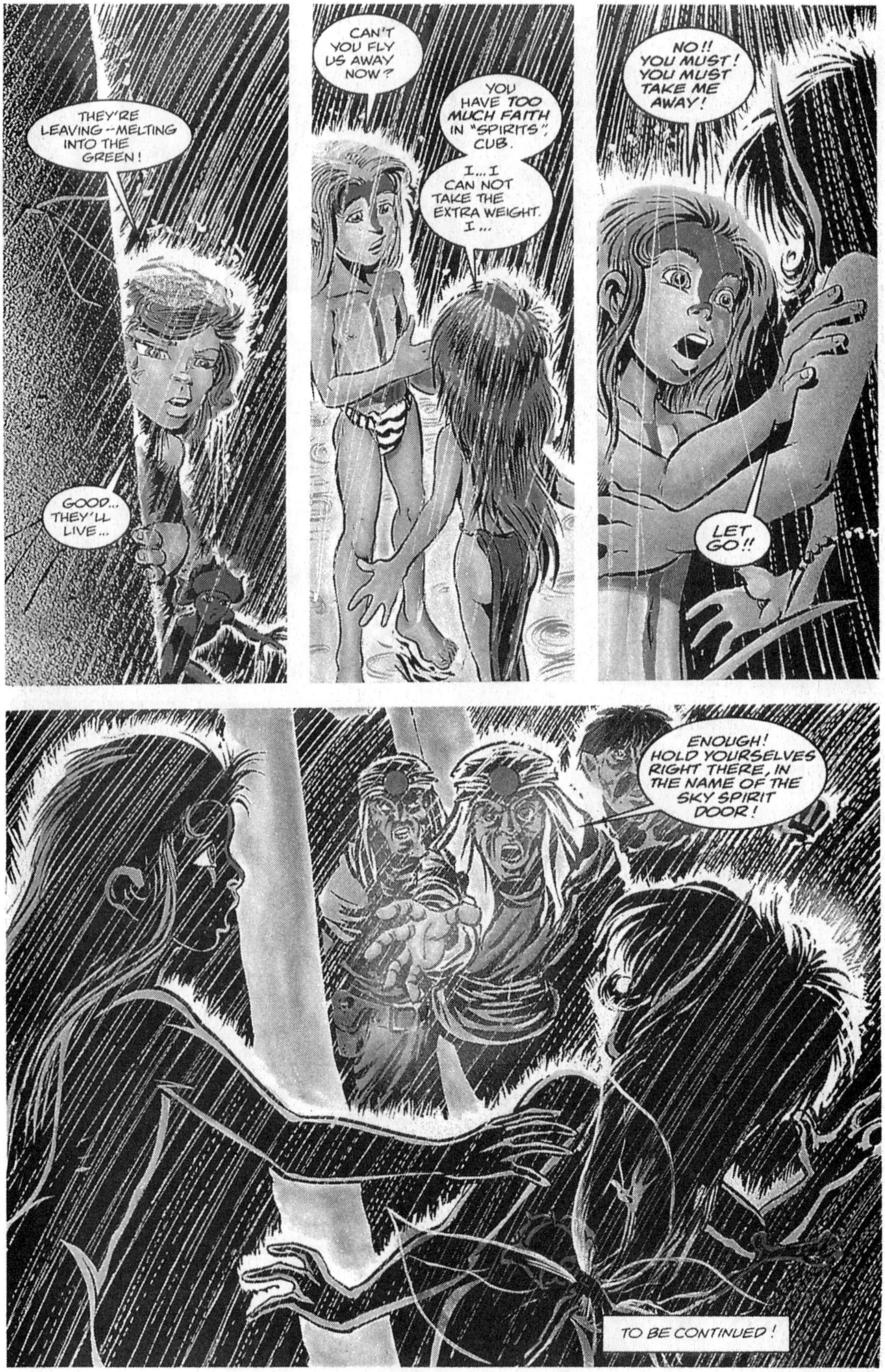
THEY'RE LEAVING--MELTING INTO THE GREEN!
GOOD... THEY'LL LIVE...
CAN'T YOU FLY US AWAY NOW?
YOU HAVE TOO MUCH FAITH IN "SPIRITS", CUB.
I... I CAN NOT TAKE THE EXTRA WEIGHT. I...
NO!! YOU MUST! YOU MUST TAKE ME AWAY!
LET GO!!
ENOUGH! HOLD YOURSELVES RIGHT THERE, IN THE NAME OF THE SKY SPIRIT DOOR!
TO BE CONTINUED!

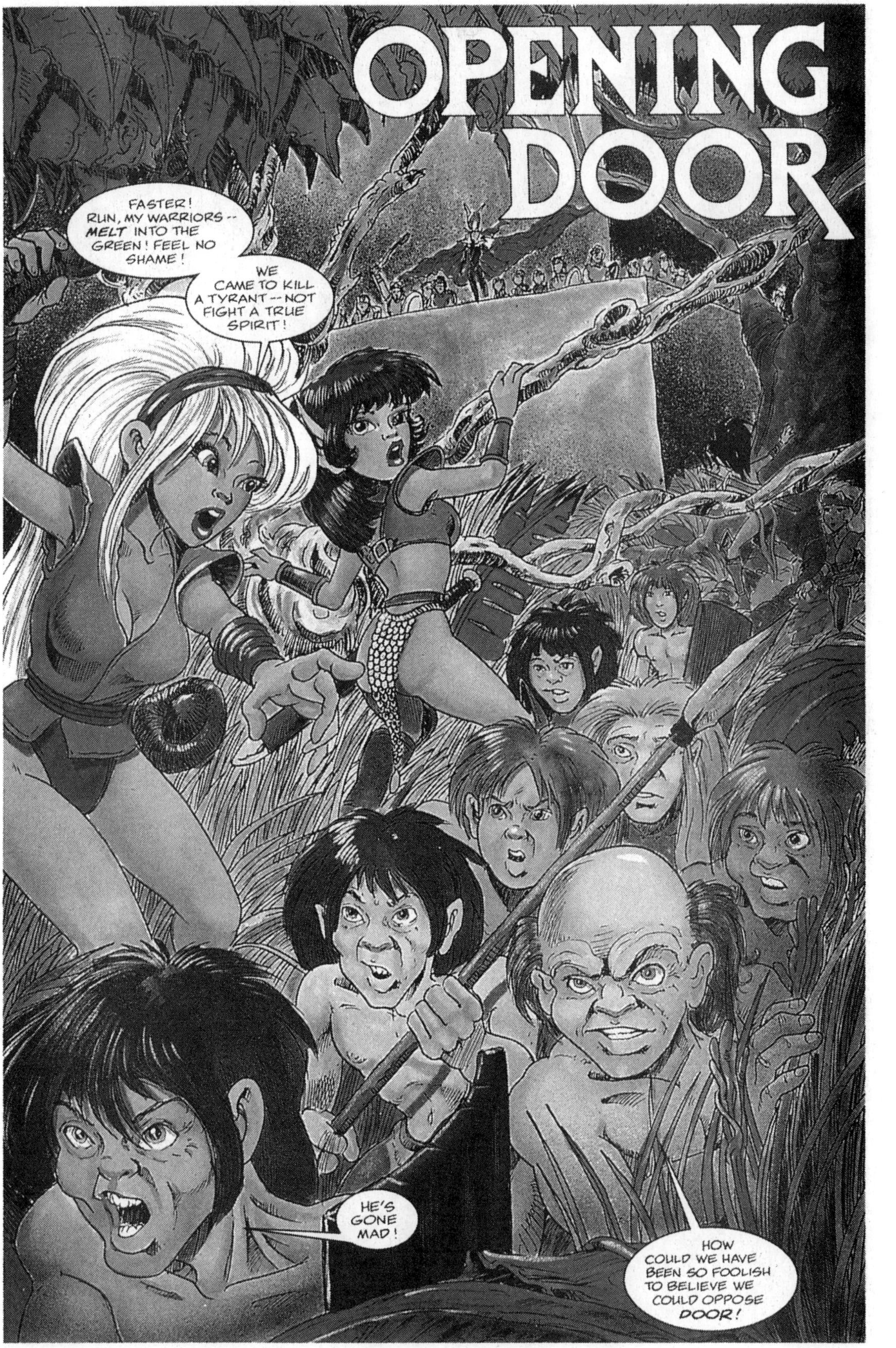
OPENING DOOR
FASTER! RUN, MY WARRIORS -- MELT INTO THE GREEN! FEEL NO SHAME!
WE CAME TO KILL A TYRANT -- NOT FIGHT A TRUE SPIRIT!
HE'S GONE MAD!
HOW COULD WE HAVE BEEN SO FOOLISH TO BELIEVE WE COULD OPPOSE DOOR!

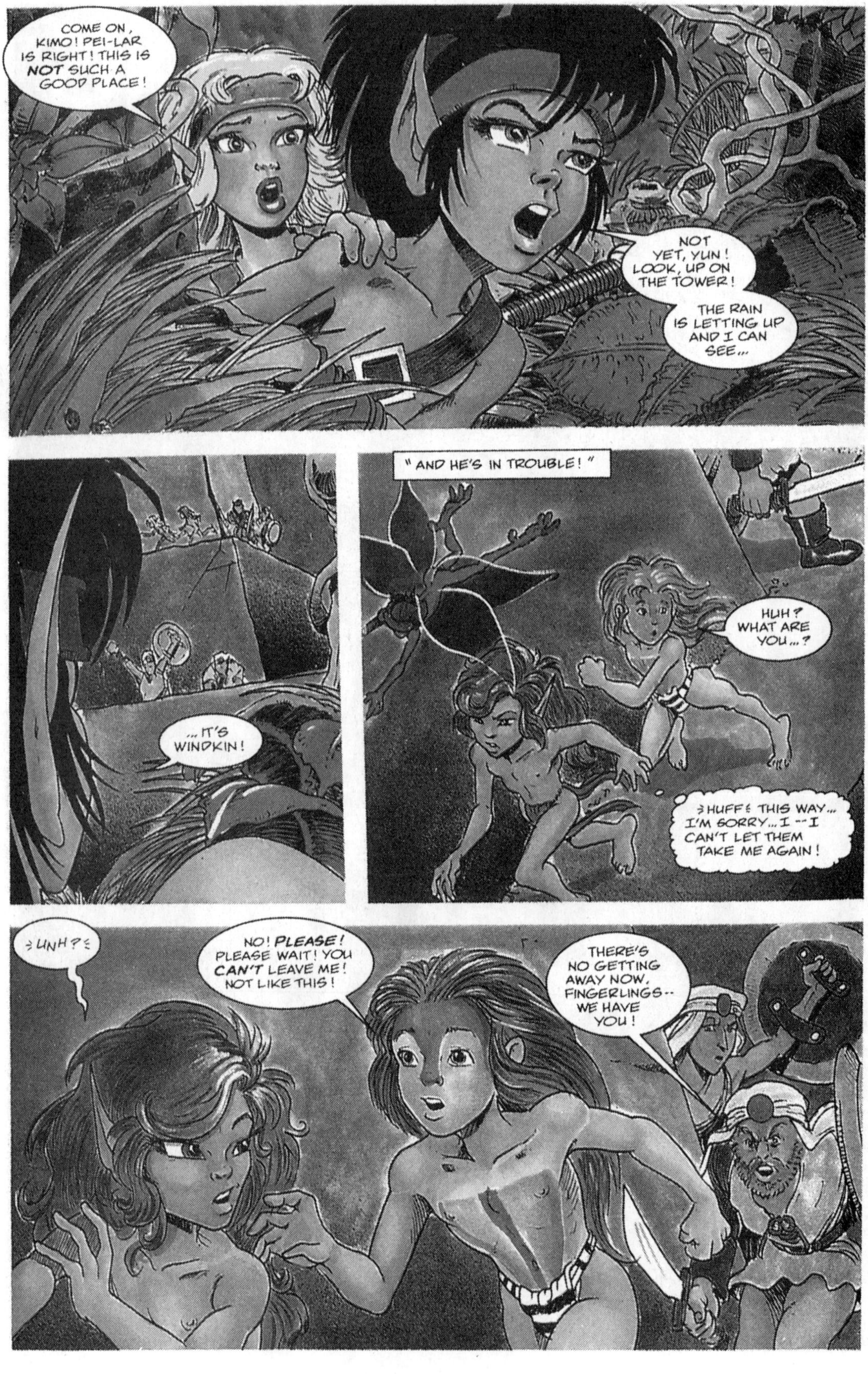
COME ON, KIMO! PEI-LAR IS RIGHT! THIS IS NOT SUCH A GOOD PLACE!
NOT YET, YUN! LOOK, UP ON THE TOWER!
THE RAIN IS LETTING UP AND I CAN SEE...
...IT'S WINDKIN!
"AND HE'S IN TROUBLE!"
HUH? WHAT ARE YOU...?
HUFF! THIS WAY... I'M SORRY... I --I CAN'T LET THEM TAKE ME AGAIN!
UNH?
NO! PLEASE! PLEASE WAIT! YOU CAN'T LEAVE ME! NOT LIKE THIS!
THERE'S NO GETTING AWAY NOW, FINGERLINGS-- WE HAVE YOU!

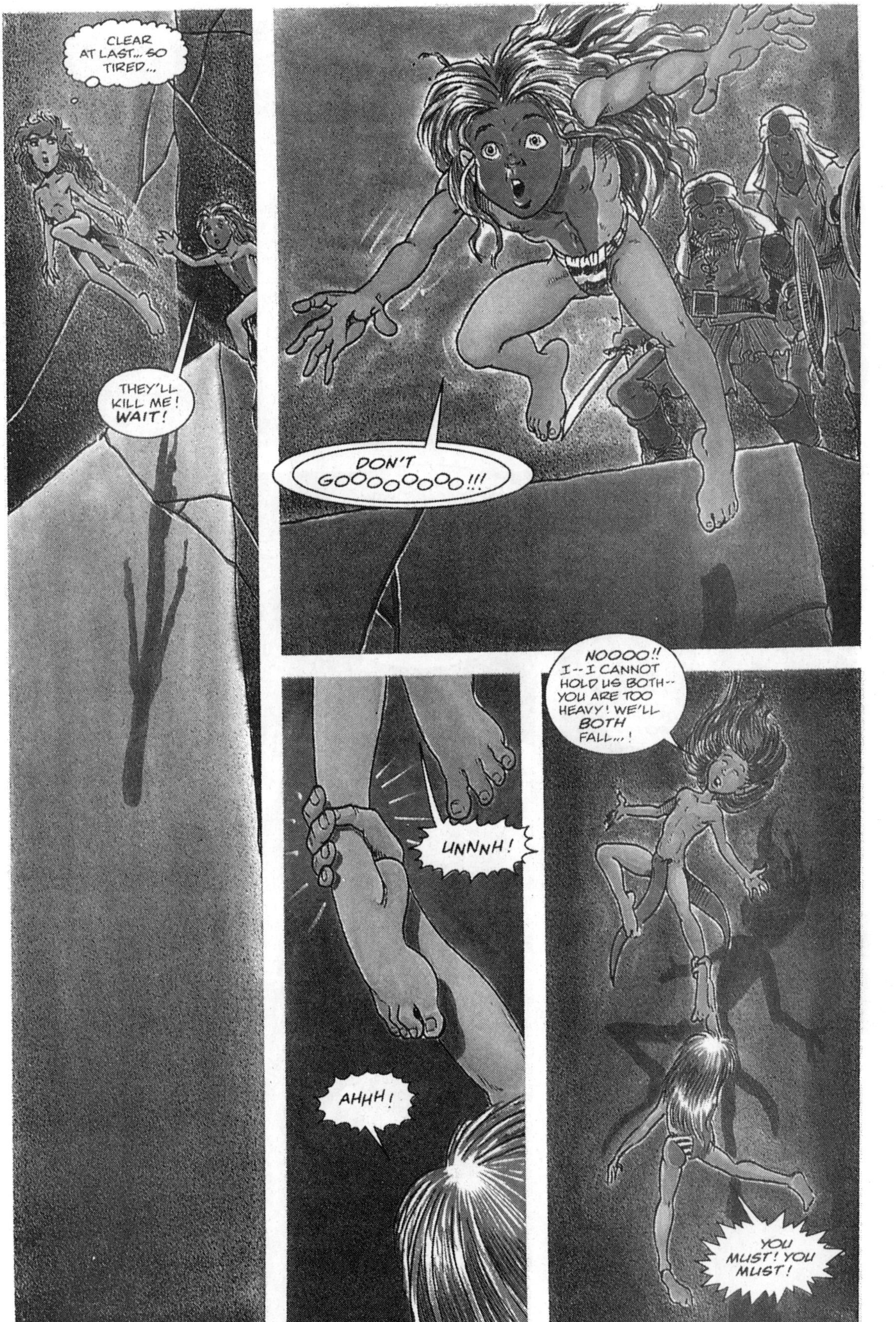
CLEAR AT LAST... SO TIRED...
THEY'LL KILL ME! WAIT!
DON'T GOOOOOOOO!!!
UNNNH!
AHHH!
NOOOO!! I-- I CANNOT HOLD US BOTH-- YOU ARE TOO HEAVY! WE'LL BOTH FALL...!
YOU MUST! YOU MUST!

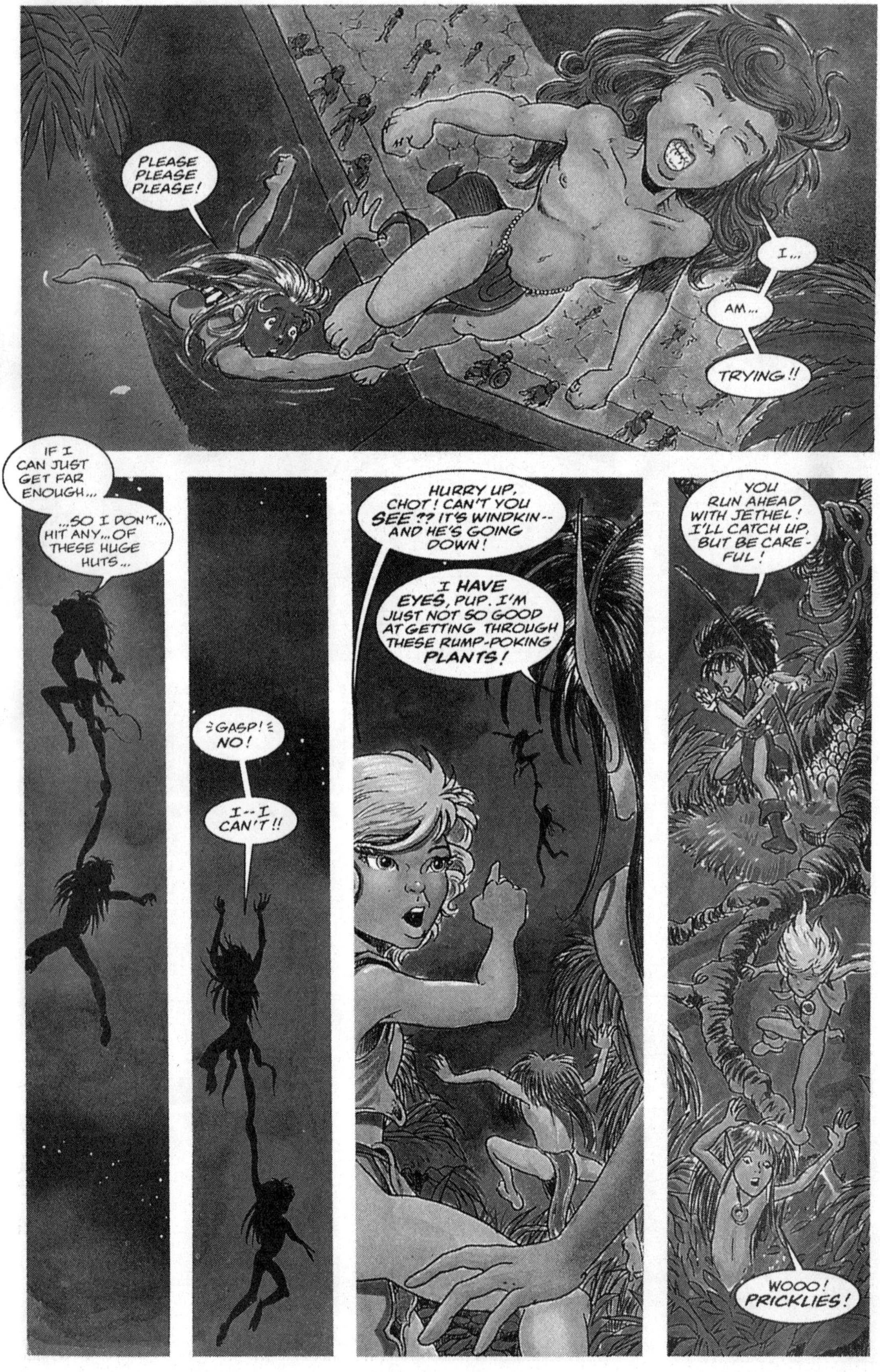
PLEASE PLEASE PLEASE!
I...
AM...
TRYING!!
IF I CAN JUST GET FAR ENOUGH...
...SO I DON'T... HIT ANY... OF THESE HUGE HUTS...
GASP! NO!
I-- I CAN'T!!
HURRY UP, CHOT! CAN'T YOU SEE?? IT'S WINDKIN-- AND HE'S GOING DOWN!
I HAVE EYES, PUP. I'M JUST NOT SO GOOD AT GETTING THROUGH THESE RUMP-POKING PLANTS!
YOU RUN AHEAD WITH JETHEL! I'LL CATCH UP, BUT BE CARE-FUL!
WOOO! PRICKLIES!

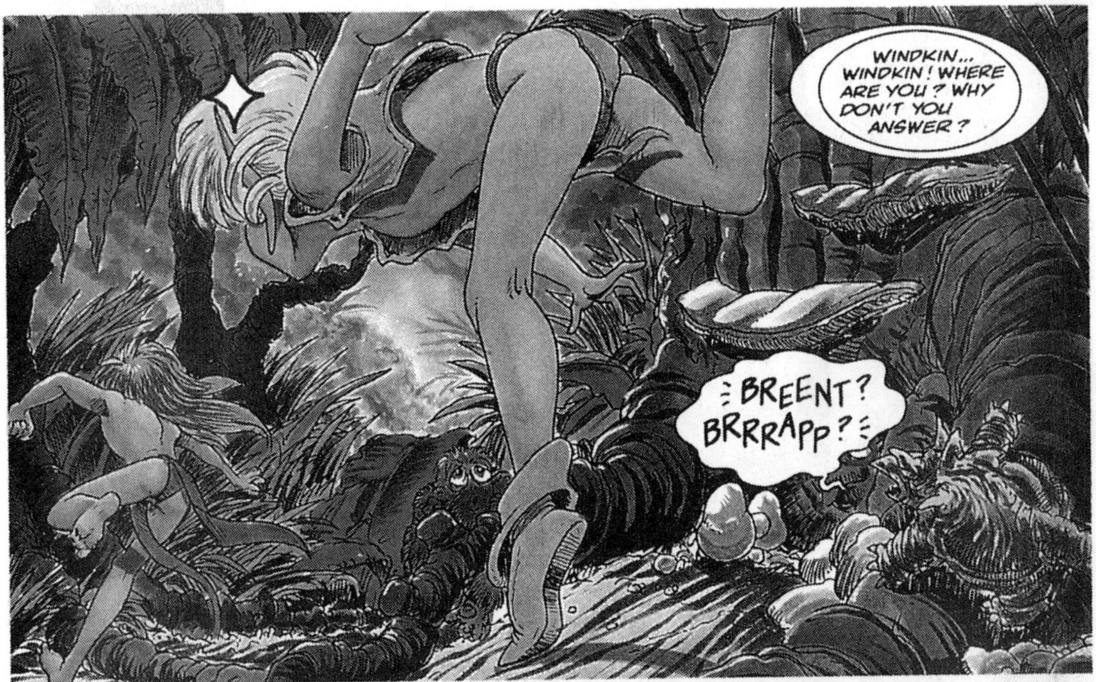
WINDKIN... WINDKIN! WHERE ARE YOU? WHY DON'T YOU ANSWER?
BREENT? BRRRAPP?

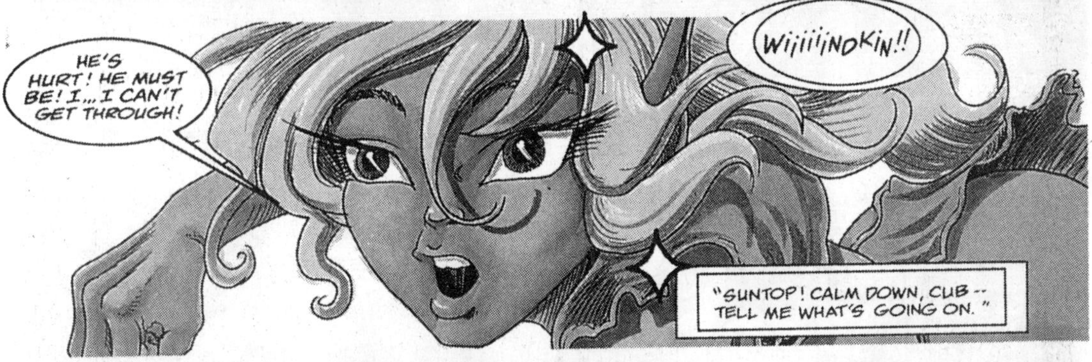
HE'S HURT! HE MUST BE! I... I CAN'T GET THROUGH!
WIIIIINDKIN!!
"SUNTOP! CALM DOWN, CUB -- TELL ME WHAT'S GOING ON."

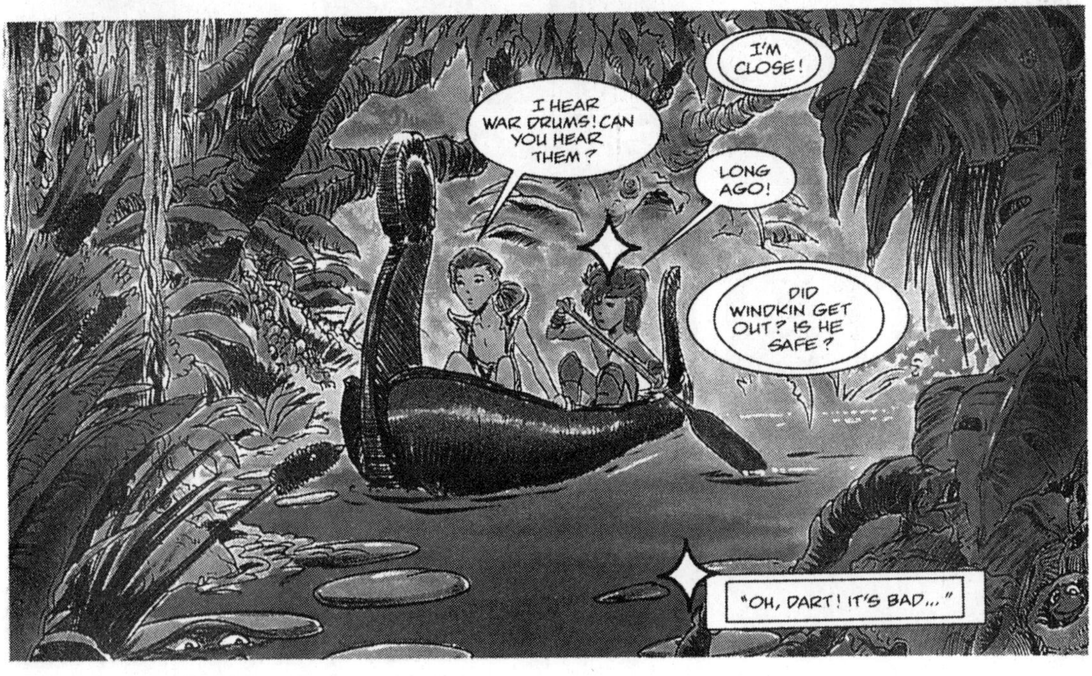
I HEAR WAR DRUMS! CAN YOU HEAR THEM?
I'M CLOSE!
LONG AGO!
DID WINDKIN GET OUT? IS HE SAFE?
"OH, DART! IT'S BAD..."

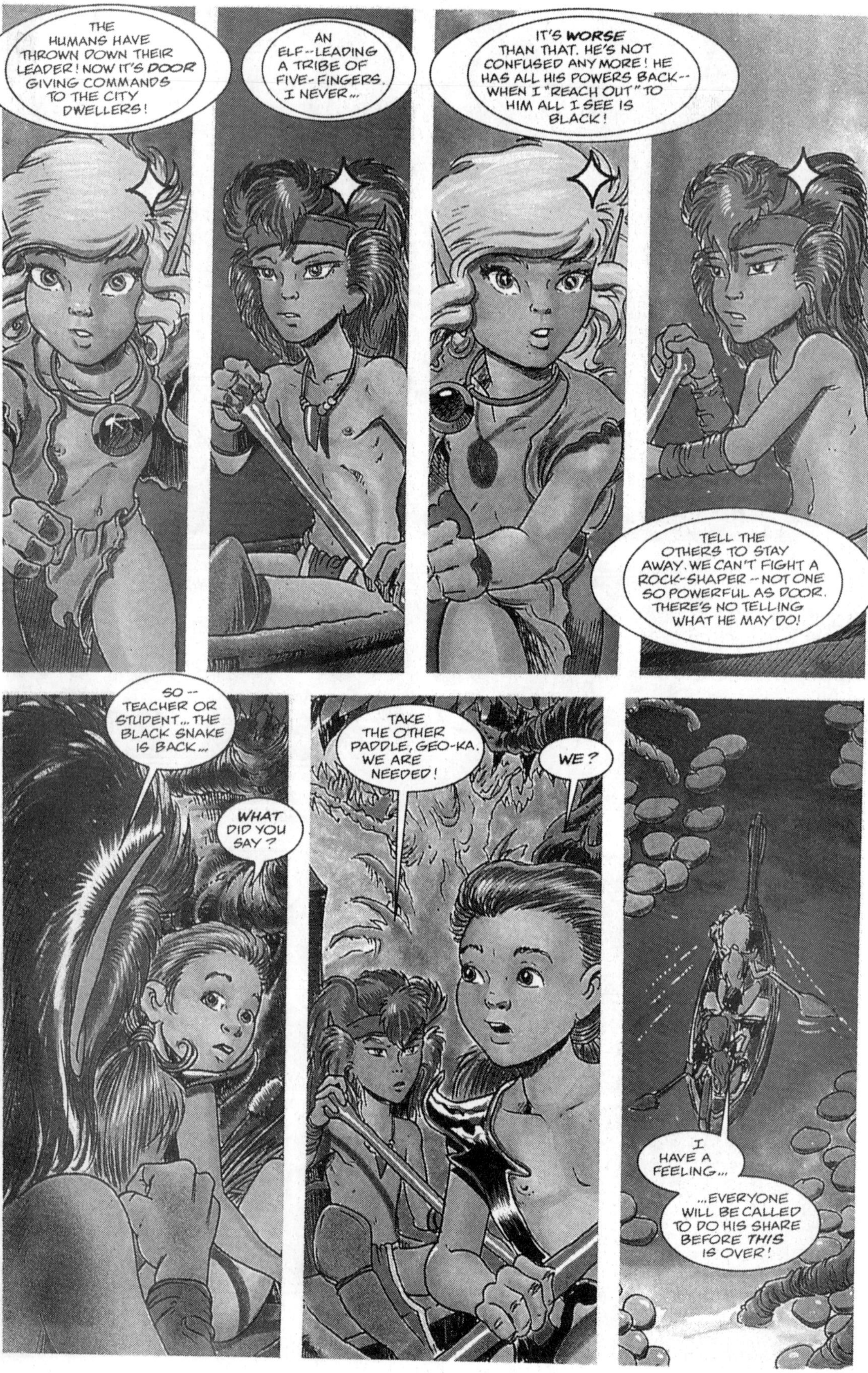
THE HUMANS HAVE THROWN DOWN THEIR LEADER! NOW IT'S DOOR GIVING COMMANDS TO THE CITY DWELLERS!
AN ELF--LEADING A TRIBE OF FIVE-FINGERS. I NEVER...
IT'S WORSE THAN THAT. HE'S NOT CONFUSED ANYMORE! HE HAS ALL HIS POWERS BACK--WHEN I "REACH OUT" TO HIM ALL I SEE IS BLACK!
TELL THE OTHERS TO STAY AWAY. WE CAN'T FIGHT A ROCK-SHAPER--NOT ONE SO POWERFUL AS DOOR. THERE'S NO TELLING WHAT HE MAY DO!
SO-- TEACHER OR STUDENT... THE BLACK SNAKE IS BACK...
WHAT DID YOU SAY?
TAKE THE OTHER PADDLE, GEO-KA. WE ARE NEEDED!
WE?
I HAVE A FEELING...
...EVERYONE WILL BE CALLED TO DO HIS SHARE BEFORE THIS IS OVER!

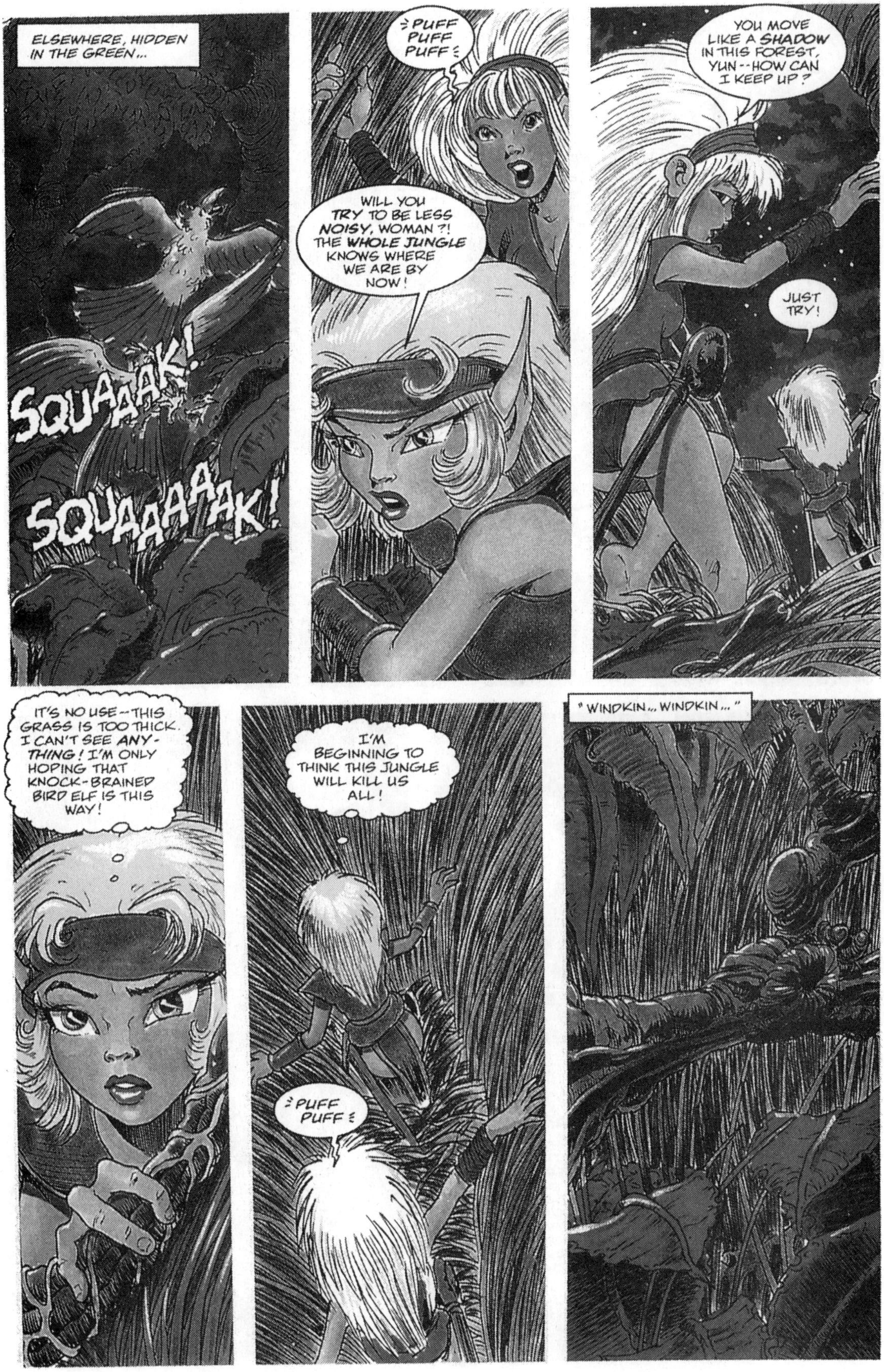
ELSEWHERE, HIDDEN IN THE GREEN...
SQUAAAK!
SQUAAAAAK!
PUFF PUFF PUFF
WILL YOU TRY TO BE LESS NOISY, WOMAN?! THE WHOLE JUNGLE KNOWS WHERE WE ARE BY NOW!
YOU MOVE LIKE A SHADOW IN THIS FOREST, YUN--HOW CAN I KEEP UP?
JUST TRY!
IT'S NO USE--THIS GRASS IS TOO THICK. I CAN'T SEE ANYTHING! I'M ONLY HOPING THAT KNOCK-BRAINED BIRD ELF IS THIS WAY!
I'M BEGINNING TO THINK THIS JUNGLE WILL KILL US ALL!
PUFF PUFF
"WINDKIN... WINDKIN..."

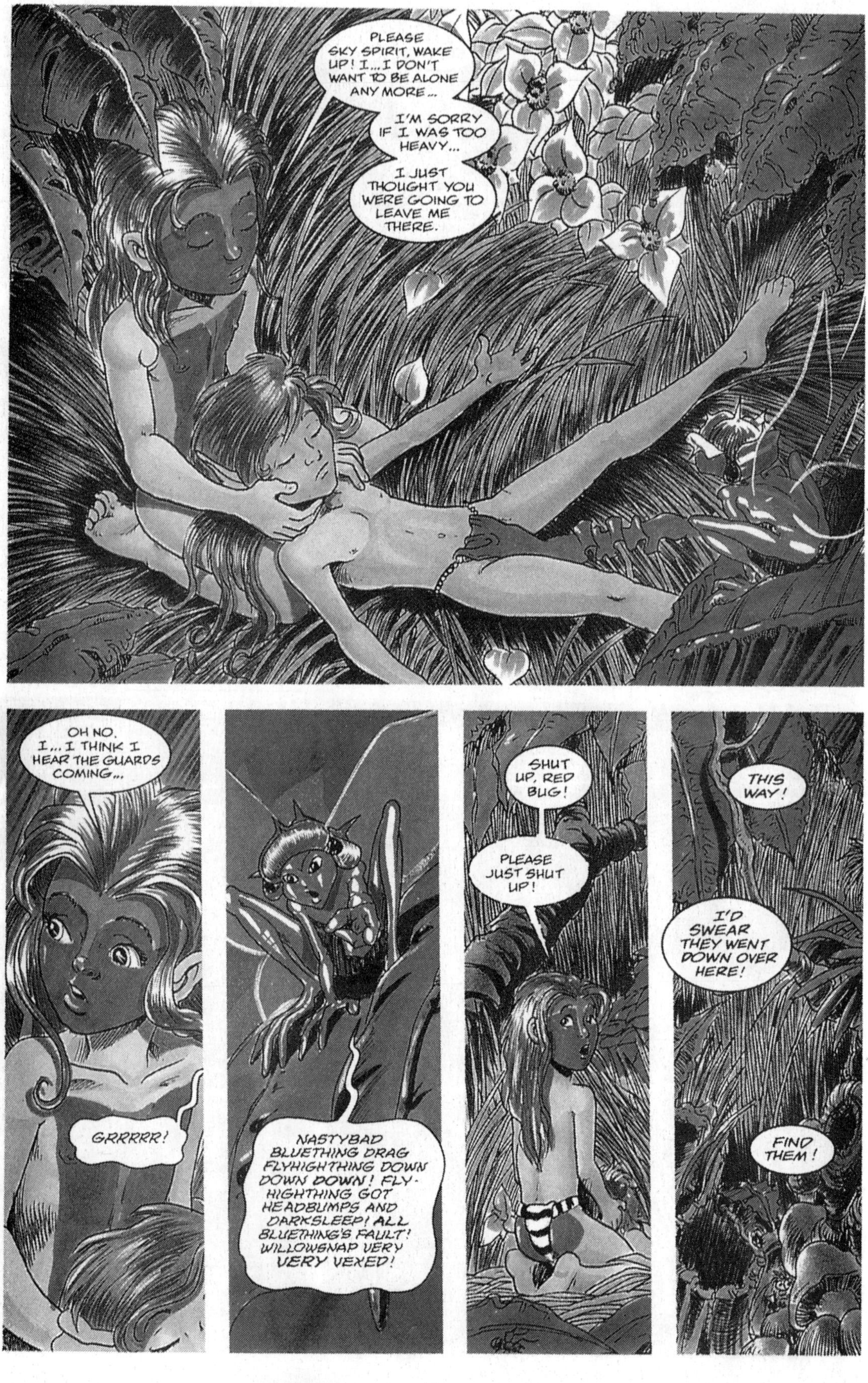
PLEASE SKY SPIRIT, WAKE UP! I... I DON'T WANT TO BE ALONE ANY MORE...
I'M SORRY IF I WAS TOO HEAVY...
I JUST THOUGHT YOU WERE GOING TO LEAVE ME THERE.
OH NO. I... I THINK I HEAR THE GUARDS COMING...
GRRRRR!
NASTYBAD BLUETHING DRAG FLYHIGHTHING DOWN DOWN DOWN! FLY-HIGHTHING GOT HEADBUMPS AND DARKSLEEP! ALL BLUETHING'S FAULT! WILLOWSNAP VERY VERY VEXED!
SHUT UP, RED BUG!
PLEASE JUST SHUT UP!
THIS WAY!
I'D SWEAR THEY WENT DOWN OVER HERE!
FIND THEM!

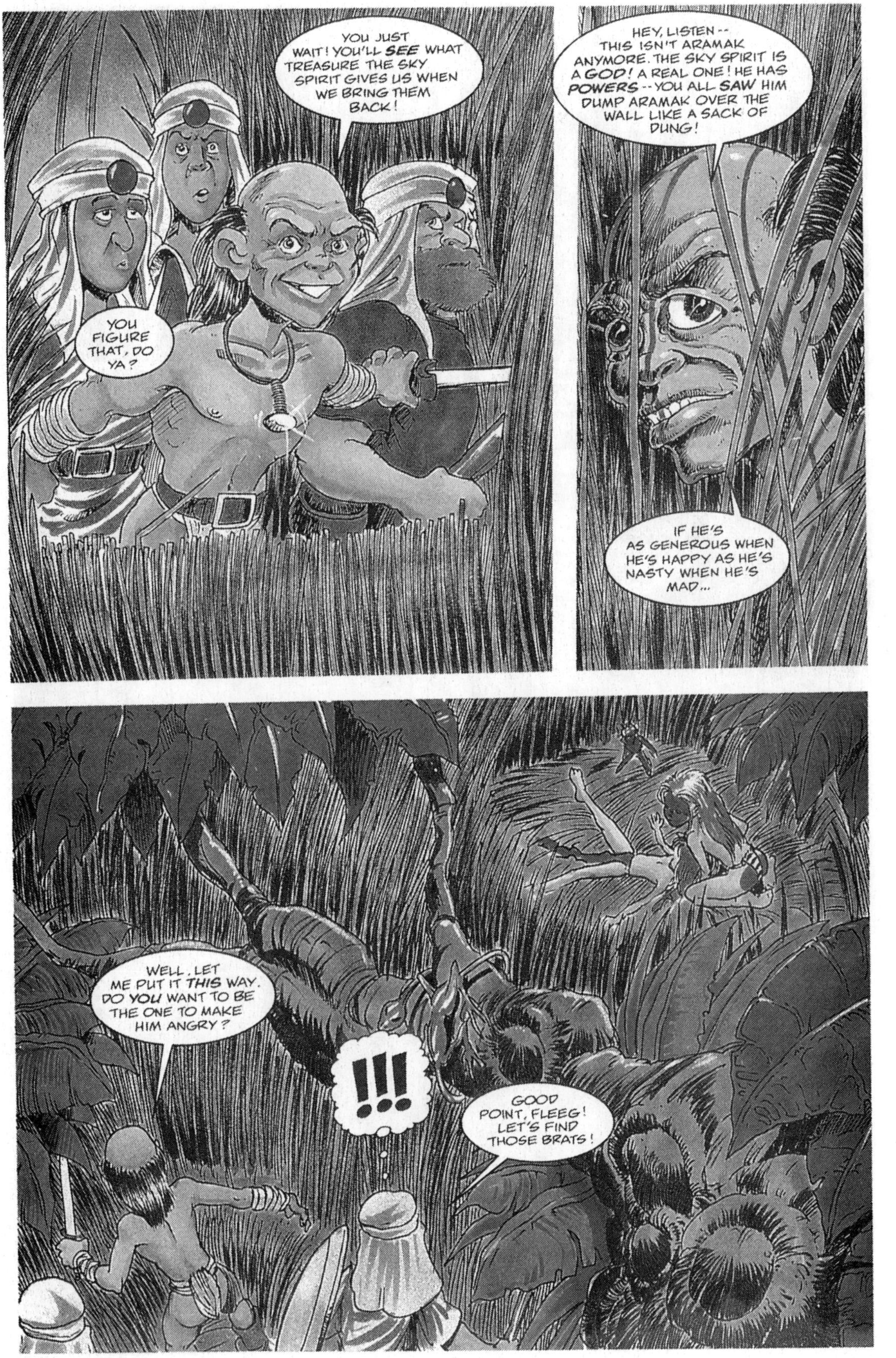
YOU JUST WAIT! YOU'LL SEE WHAT TREASURE THE SKY SPIRIT GIVES US WHEN WE BRING THEM BACK!
YOU FIGURE THAT, DO YA?
HEY, LISTEN -- THIS ISN'T ARAMAK ANYMORE. THE SKY SPIRIT IS A GOD! A REAL ONE! HE HAS POWERS -- YOU ALL SAW HIM DUMP ARAMAK OVER THE WALL LIKE A SACK OF DUNG!
IF HE'S AS GENEROUS WHEN HE'S HAPPY AS HE'S NASTY WHEN HE'S MAD...
WELL, LET ME PUT IT THIS WAY. DO YOU WANT TO BE THE ONE TO MAKE HIM ANGRY?
!!!
GOOD POINT, FLEEG! LET'S FIND THOSE BRATS!

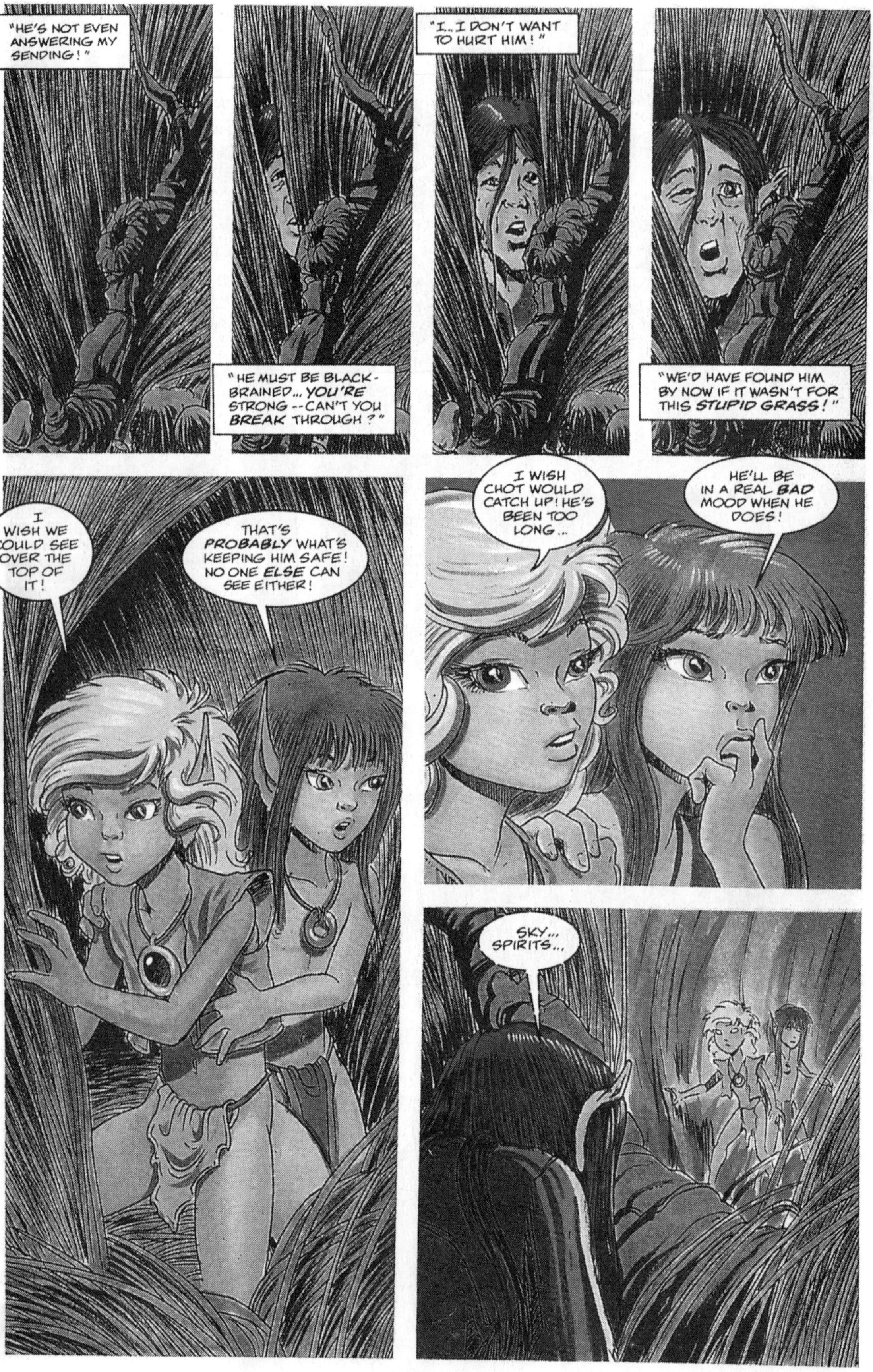
"HE'S NOT EVEN ANSWERING MY SENDING!"
"HE MUST BE BLACK-BRAINED... YOU'RE STRONG --CAN'T YOU BREAK THROUGH?"
"I... I DON'T WANT TO HURT HIM!"
"WE'D HAVE FOUND HIM BY NOW IF IT WASN'T FOR THIS STUPID GRASS!"
I WISH WE COULD SEE OVER THE TOP OF IT!
THAT'S PROBABLY WHAT'S KEEPING HIM SAFE! NO ONE ELSE CAN SEE EITHER!
I WISH CHOT WOULD CATCH UP! HE'S BEEN TOO LONG...
HE'LL BE IN A REAL BAD MOOD WHEN HE DOES!
SKY... SPIRITS...

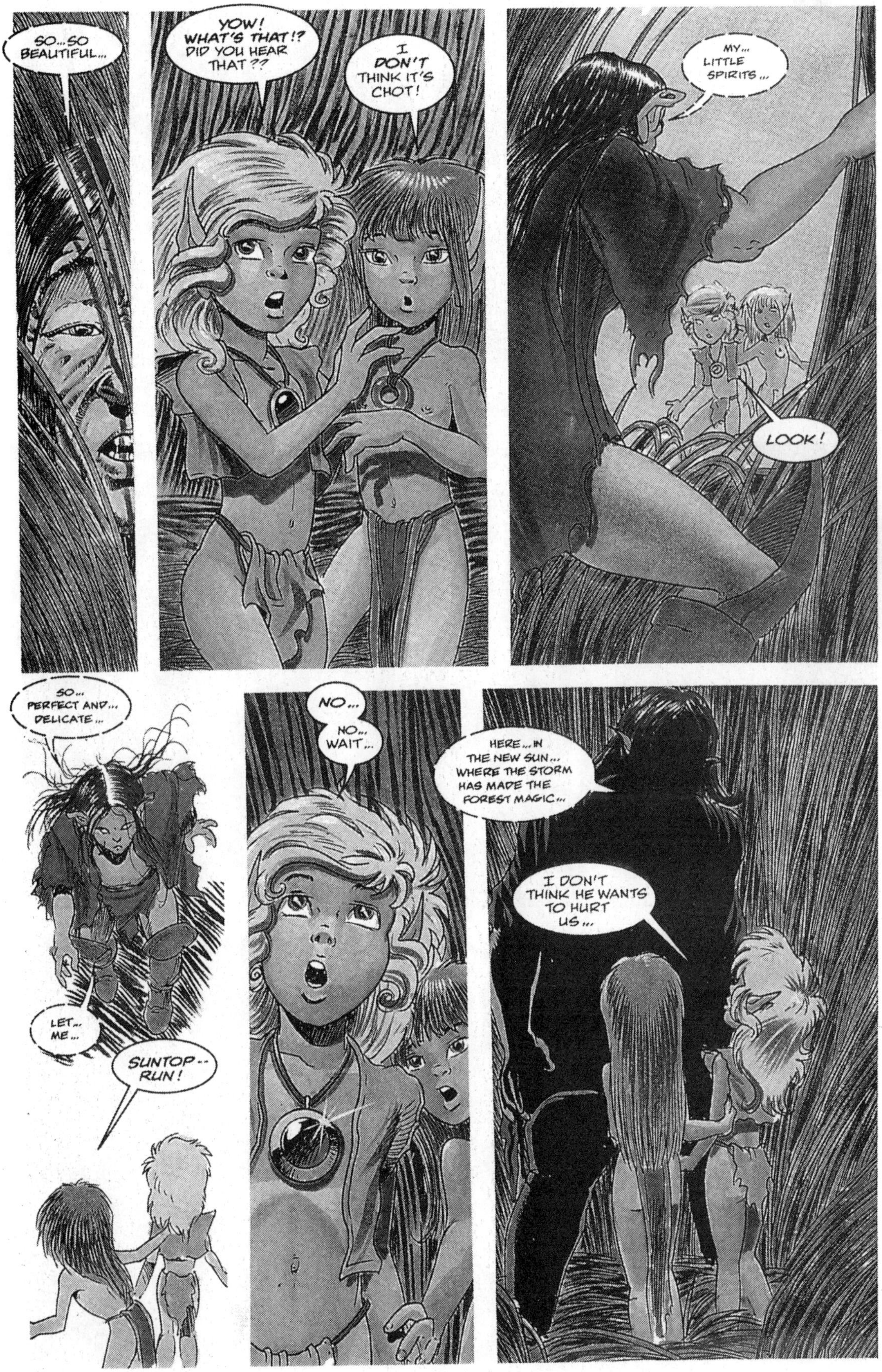
SO...SO BEAUTIFUL...
YOW! WHAT'S THAT!? DID YOU HEAR THAT??
I DON'T THINK IT'S CHOT!
MY... LITTLE SPIRITS...
LOOK!
SO... PERFECT AND... DELICATE...
LET... ME...
SUNTOP... RUN!
NO...
NO... WAIT...
HERE... IN THE NEW SUN... WHERE THE STORM HAS MADE THE FOREST MAGIC...
I DON'T THINK HE WANTS TO HURT US...

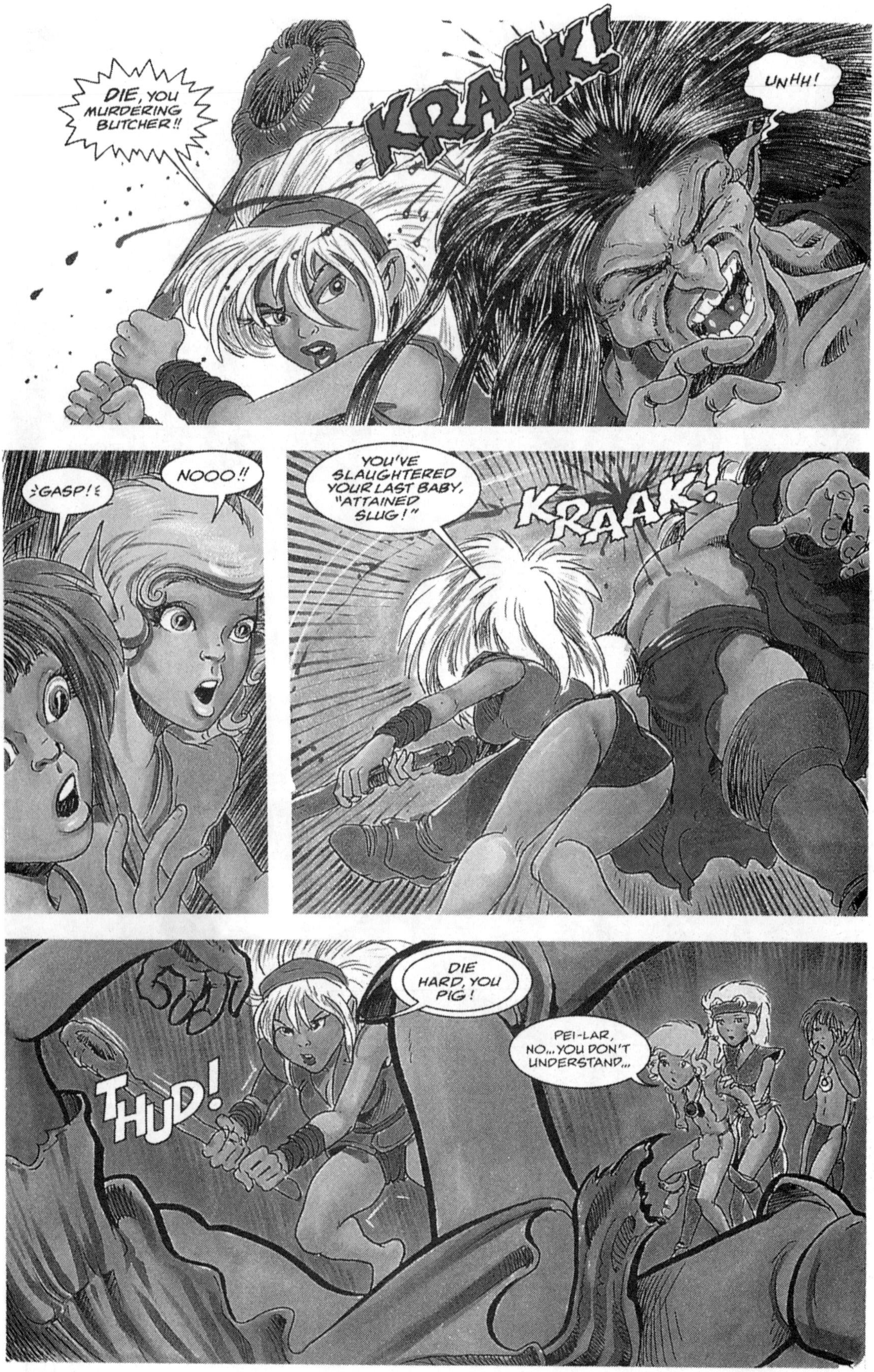

DIE, YOU MURDERING BUTCHER!!
KRAAK!
UNHH!
:GASP!:
NOOO!!
YOU'VE SLAUGHTERED YOUR LAST BABY, "ATTAINED SLUG!"
KRAAK!
DIE HARD, YOU PIG!
THUD!
PEI-LAR, NO...YOU DON'T UNDERSTAND...

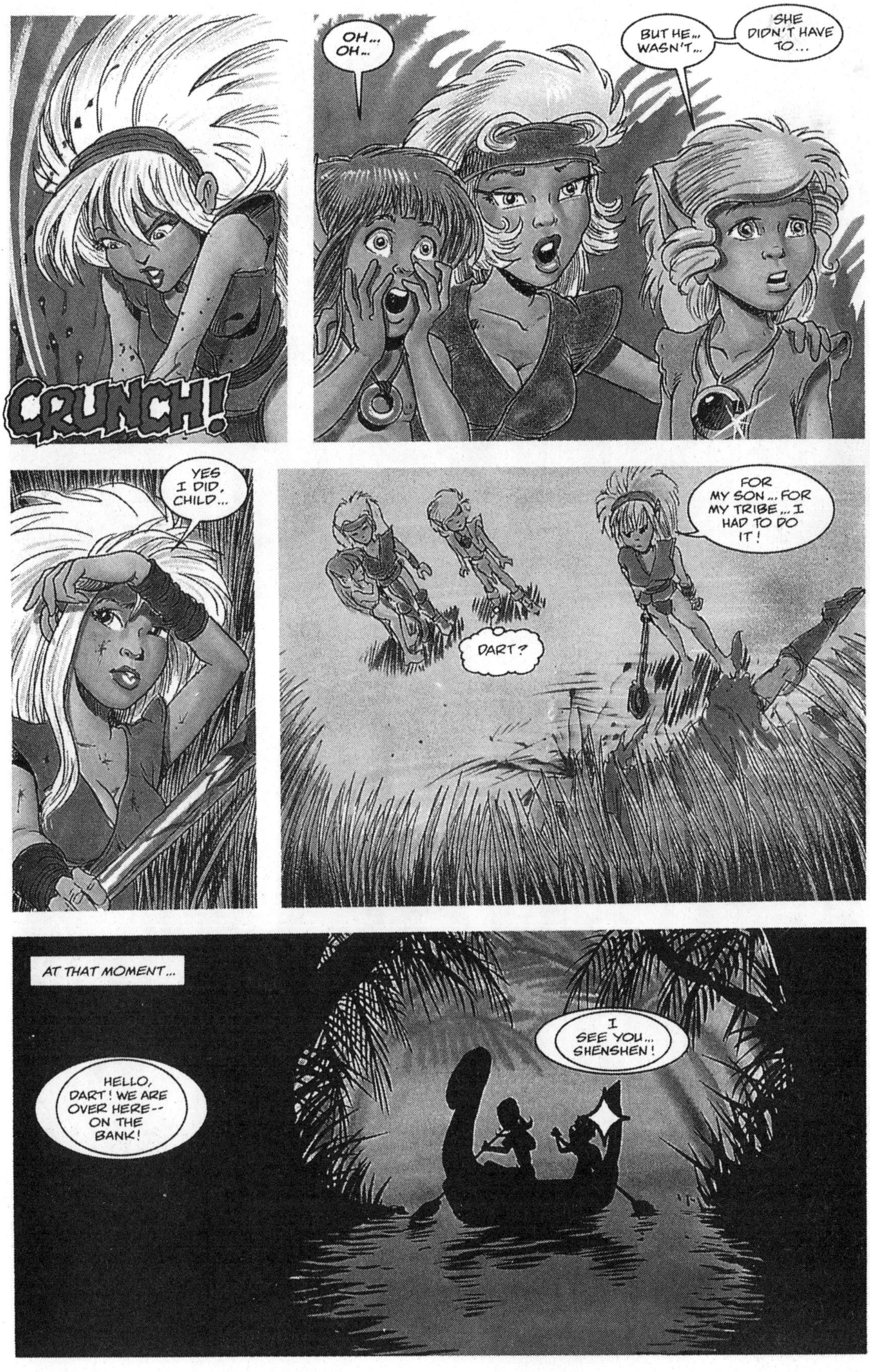
CRUNCH!
OH... OH...
BUT HE... WASN'T...
SHE DIDN'T HAVE TO...
YES I DID, CHILD...
FOR MY SON... FOR MY TRIBE... I HAD TO DO IT!
DART?
AT THAT MOMENT...
I SEE YOU... SHENSHEN!
HELLO, DART! WE ARE OVER HERE-- ON THE BANK!

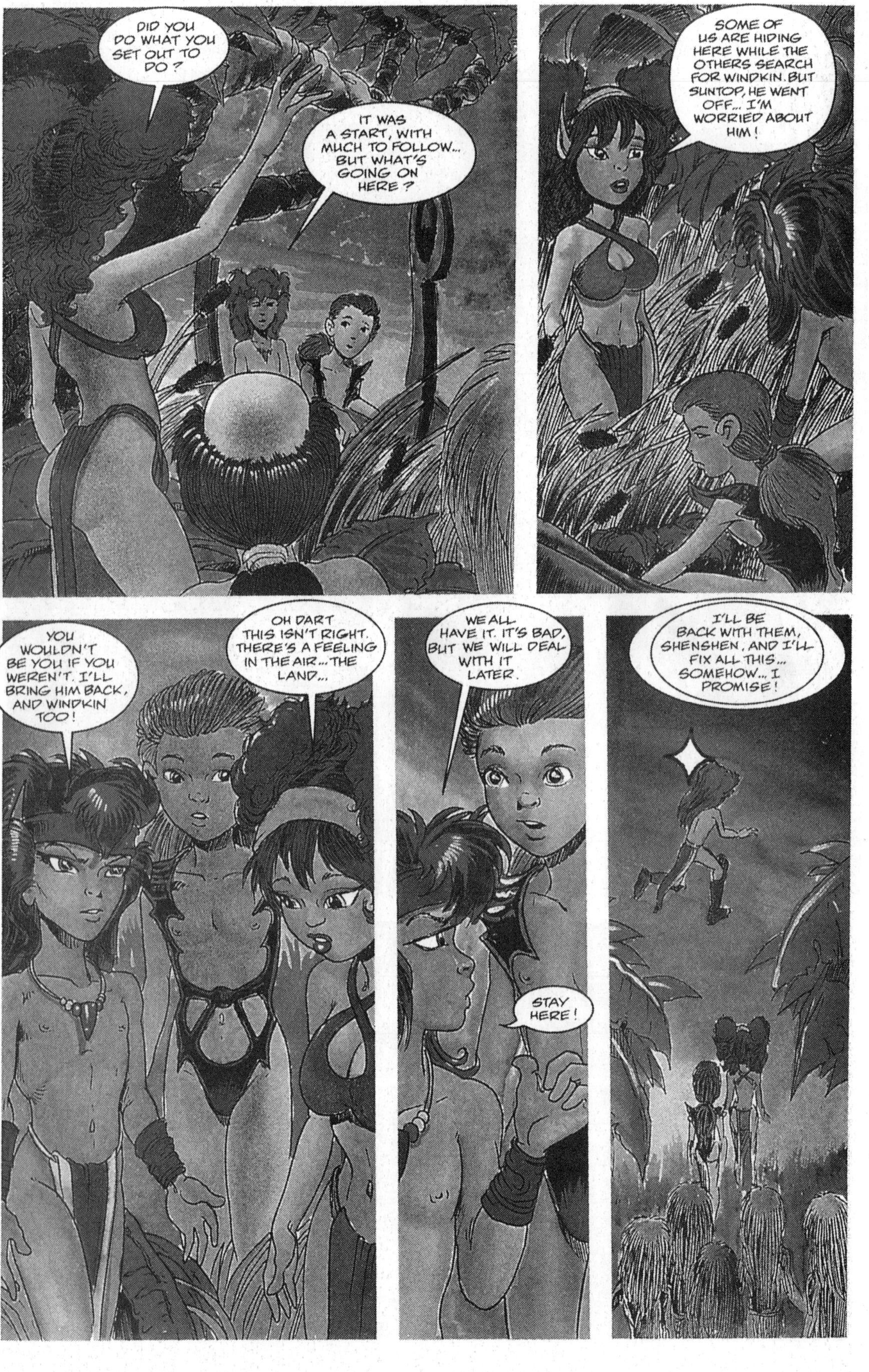
DID YOU DO WHAT YOU SET OUT TO DO ?
IT WAS A START, WITH MUCH TO FOLLOW... BUT WHAT'S GOING ON HERE ?
SOME OF US ARE HIDING HERE WHILE THE OTHERS SEARCH FOR WINDKIN. BUT SUNTOP, HE WENT OFF... I'M WORRIED ABOUT HIM !
YOU WOULDN'T BE YOU IF YOU WEREN'T. I'LL BRING HIM BACK, AND WINDKIN TOO !
OH DART THIS ISN'T RIGHT. THERE'S A FEELING IN THE AIR... THE LAND...
WE ALL HAVE IT. IT'S BAD, BUT WE WILL DEAL WITH IT LATER.
STAY HERE !
I'LL BE BACK WITH THEM, SHENSHEN, AND I'LL FIX ALL THIS... SOMEHOW... I PROMISE !

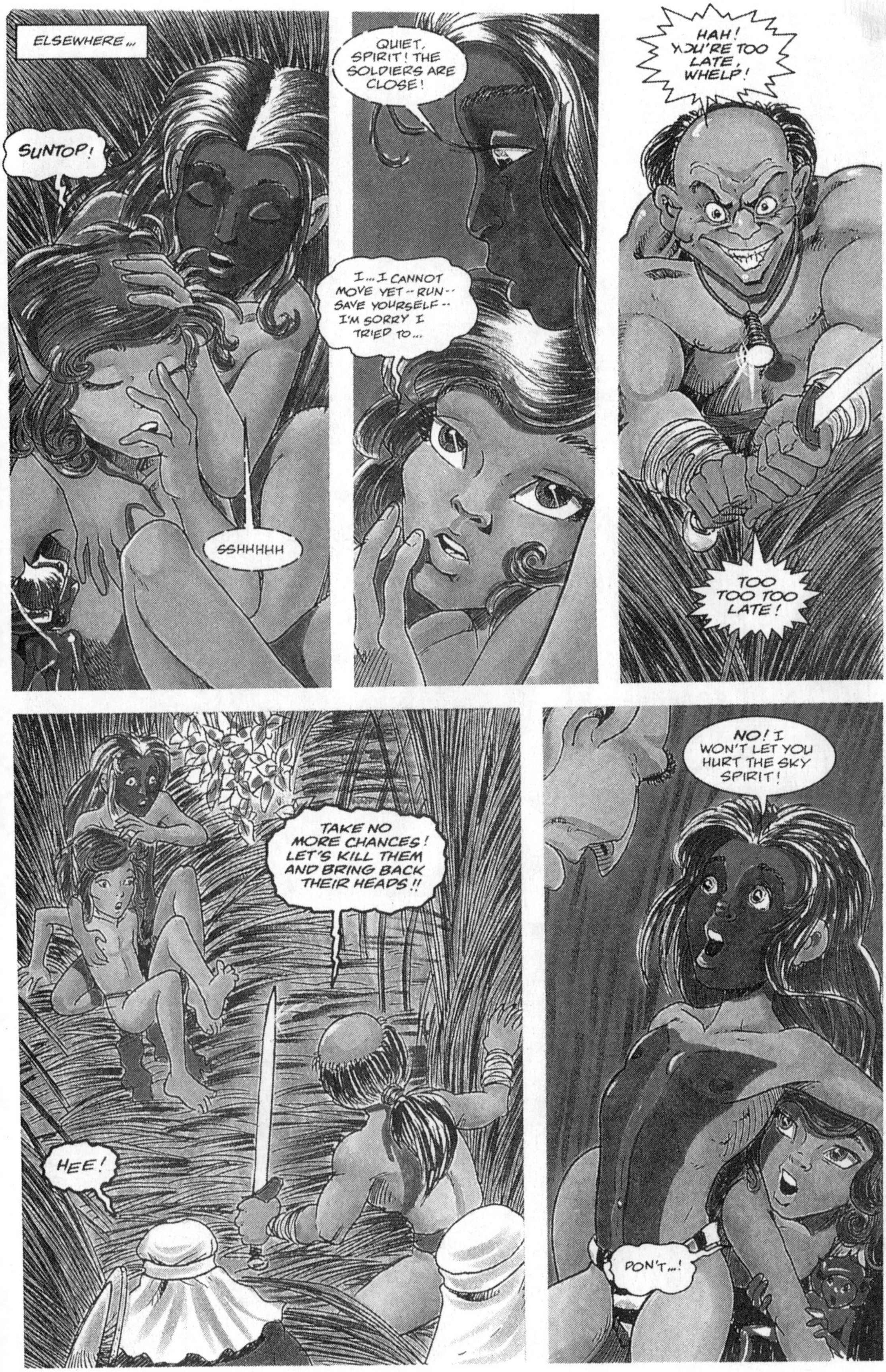
ELSEWHERE...
SUNTOP!
SSHHHHH
QUIET, SPIRIT! THE SOLDIERS ARE CLOSE!
I... I CANNOT MOVE YET -- RUN -- SAVE YOURSELF -- I'M SORRY I TRIED TO...
HAH! YOU'RE TOO LATE, WHELP!
TOO TOO TOO LATE!
TAKE NO MORE CHANCES! LET'S KILL THEM AND BRING BACK THEIR HEADS!!
HEE!
NO! I WON'T LET YOU HURT THE SKY SPIRIT!
DON'T...!

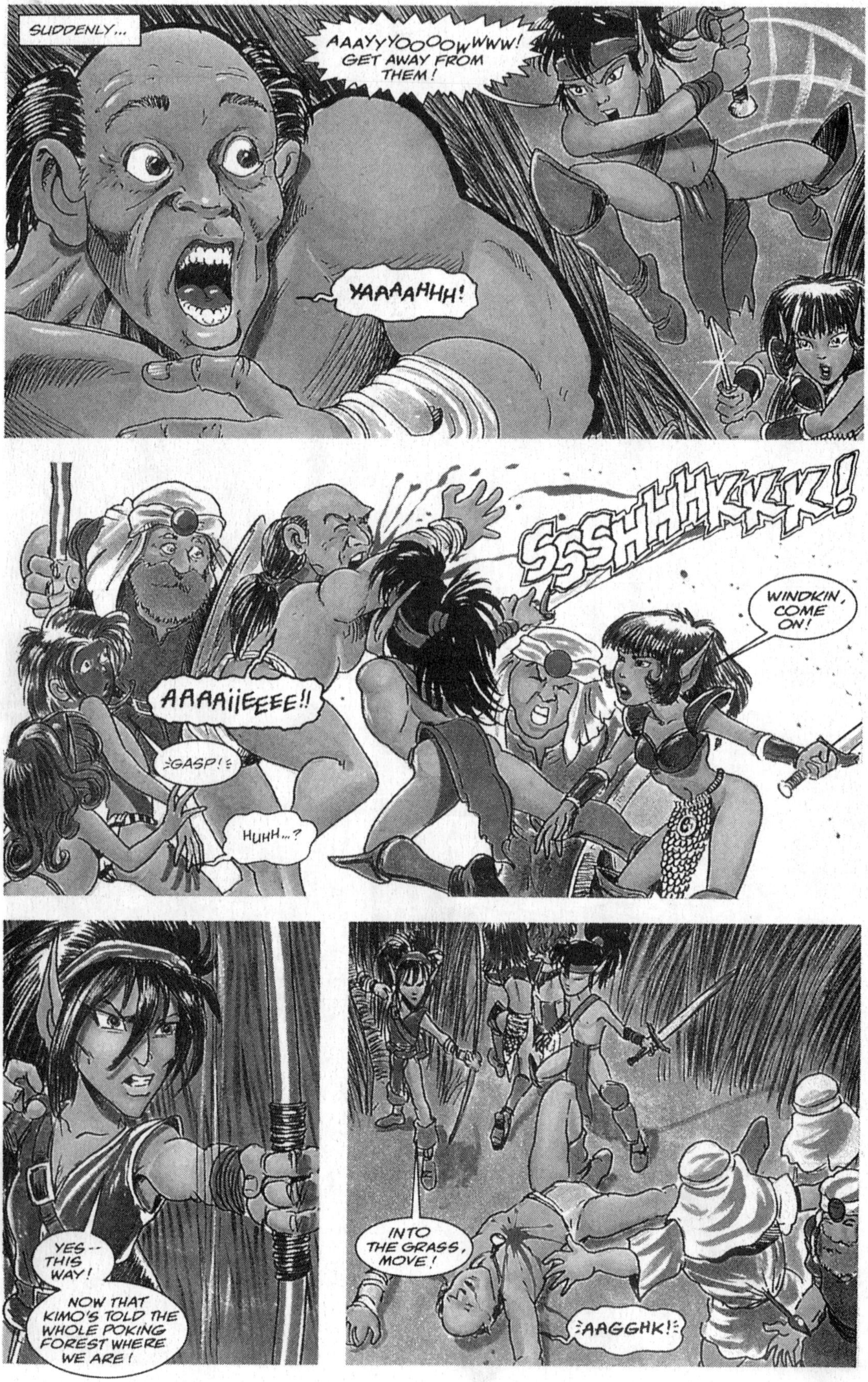
SUDDENLY...
AAAYYYOOOOWWWW! GET AWAY FROM THEM!
YAAAAHHH!
SSSHHHKKKK!
WINDKIN, COME ON!
AARAiiEEEE!!
GASP!
HUHH...?
YES -- THIS WAY!
NOW THAT KIMO'S TOLD THE WHOLE POKING FOREST WHERE WE ARE!
INTO THE GRASS, MOVE!
AAGGHK!

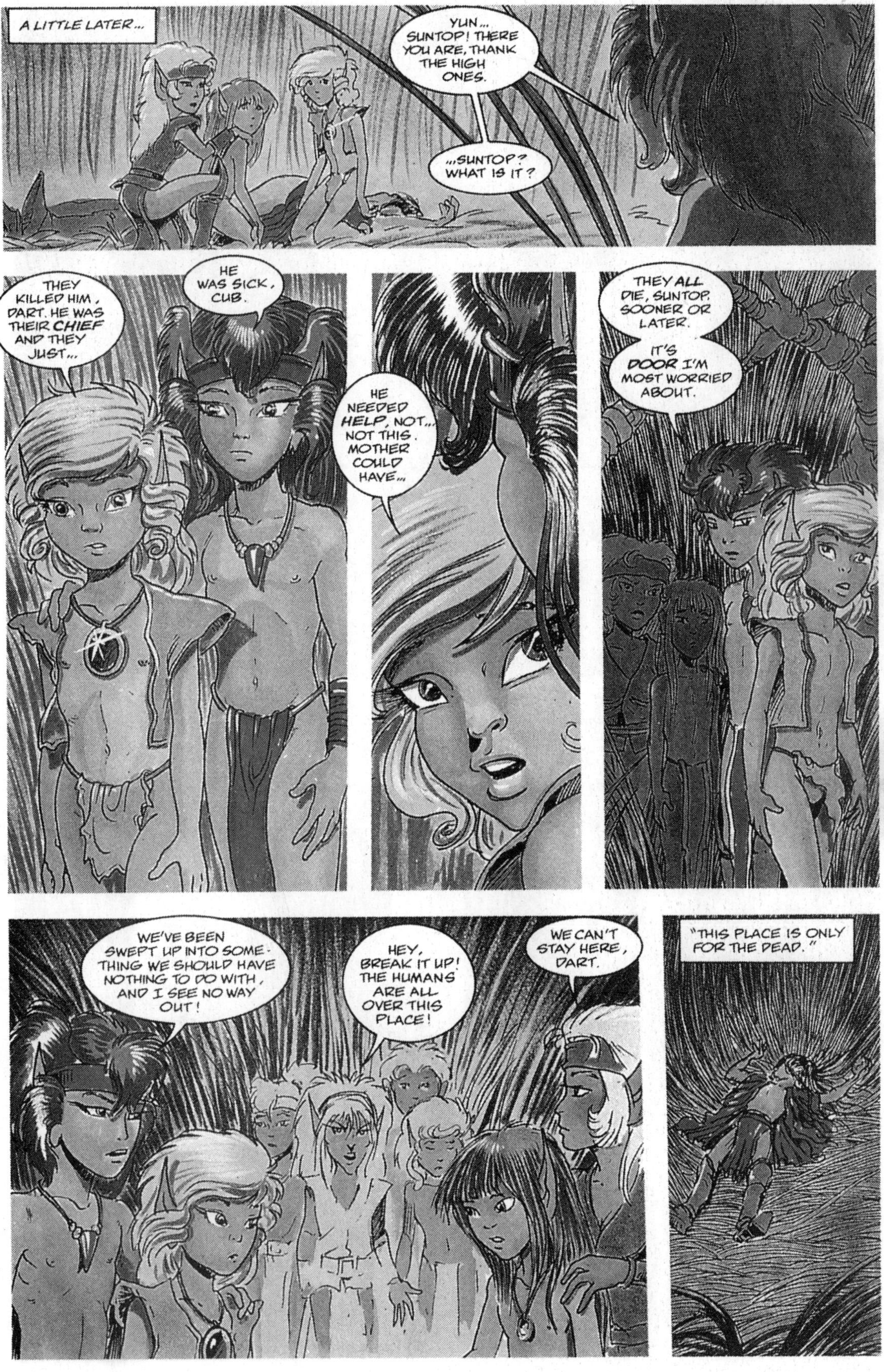
A LITTLE LATER...
YUN... SUNTOP! THERE YOU ARE, THANK THE HIGH ONES.
...SUNTOP? WHAT IS IT?
THEY KILLED HIM, DART. HE WAS THEIR CHIEF AND THEY JUST...
HE WAS SICK, CUB.
HE NEEDED HELP, NOT... NOT THIS. MOTHER COULD HAVE...
THEY ALL DIE, SUNTOP, SOONER OR LATER.
IT'S DOOR I'M MOST WORRIED ABOUT.
WE'VE BEEN SWEPT UP INTO SOME-THING WE SHOULD HAVE NOTHING TO DO WITH, AND I SEE NO WAY OUT!
HEY, BREAK IT UP! THE HUMANS ARE ALL OVER THIS PLACE!
WE CAN'T STAY HERE, DART.
"THIS PLACE IS ONLY FOR THE DEAD."

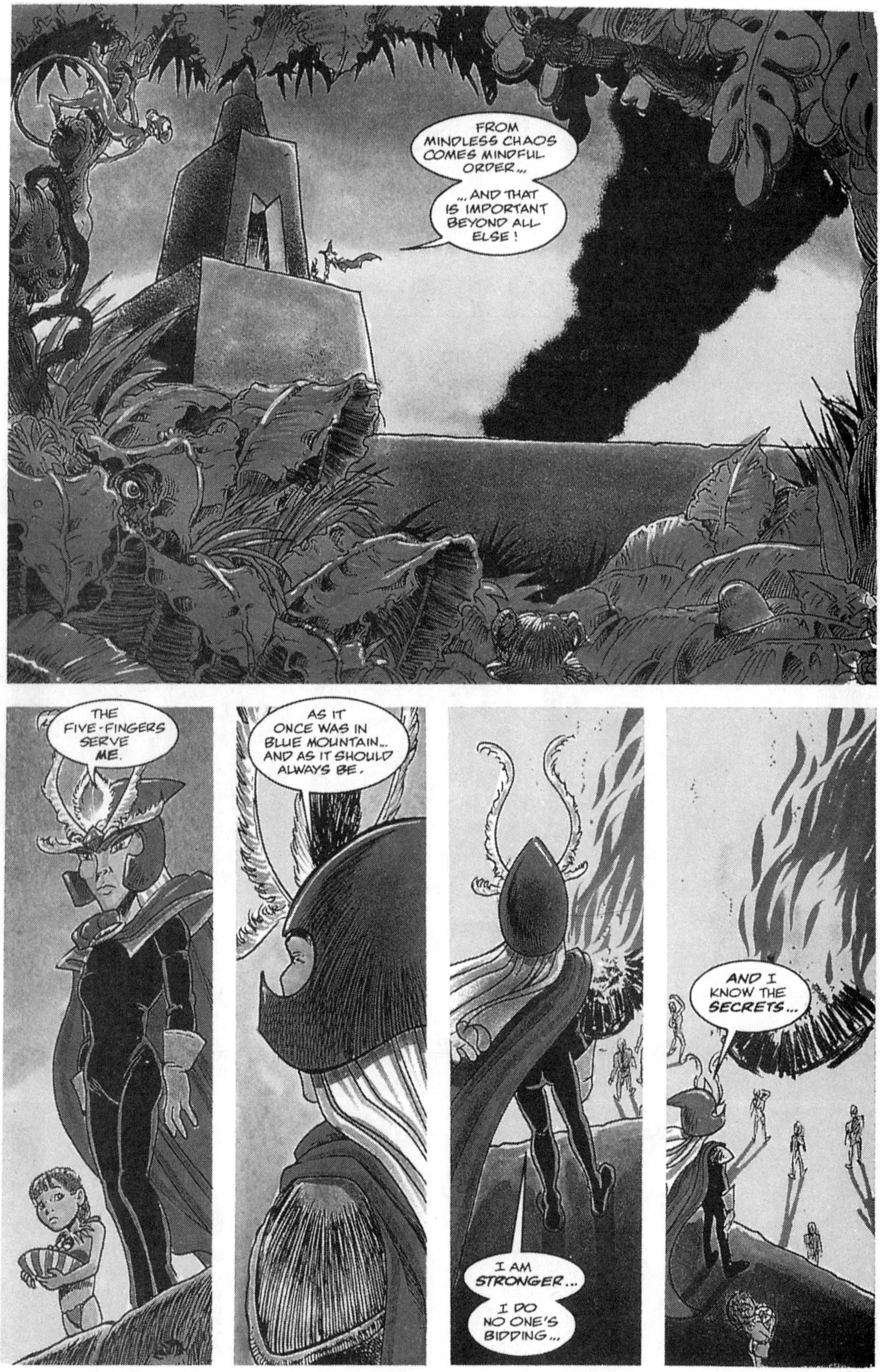
FROM MINDLESS CHAOS COMES MINDFUL ORDER...
...AND THAT IS IMPORTANT BEYOND ALL ELSE!
THE FIVE-FINGERS SERVE ME.
AS IT ONCE WAS IN BLUE MOUNTAIN... AND AS IT SHOULD ALWAYS BE.
I AM STRONGER...
I DO NO ONE'S BIDDING...
AND I KNOW THE SECRETS...

MASTER! WE FOUND ARAMAK'S BODY!

WHAT WILL YOU HAVE DONE WITH IT?

CAST IT INTO THE FIRE...

...WITH ALL THE OTHER USELESS RELICS!

LET HIM BURN WITH EVERYTHING ELSE THAT SPOKE OF THE FALSE WAYS!

CRACKLE!

I AM THE POWER!

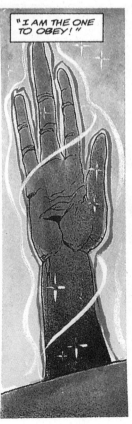

"I AM THE ONE TO OBEY!"

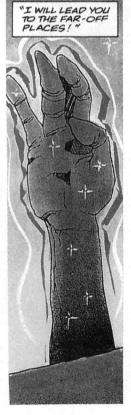

"I WILL LEAD YOU TO THE FAR-OFF PLACES!"

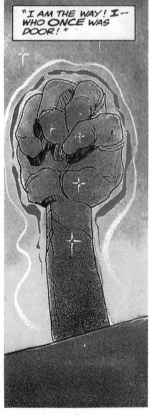

"I AM THE WAY! I-- WHO ONCE WAS DOOR!"

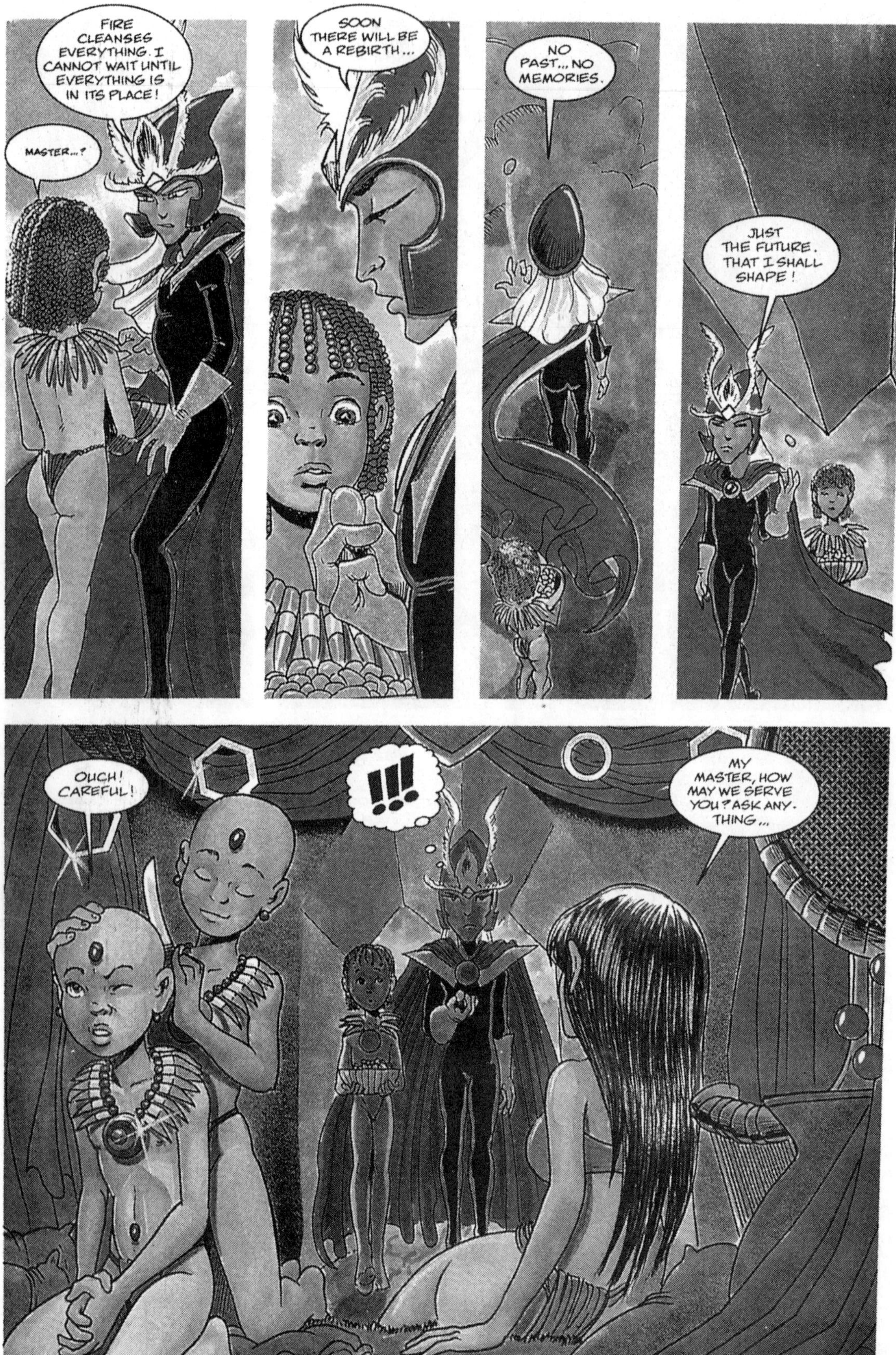
FIRE CLEANSES EVERYTHING. I CANNOT WAIT UNTIL EVERYTHING IS IN ITS PLACE!
MASTER...?
SOON THERE WILL BE A REBIRTH...
NO PAST... NO MEMORIES.
JUST THE FUTURE. THAT I SHALL SHAPE!
OUCH! CAREFUL!
!!!
MY MASTER, HOW MAY WE SERVE YOU? ASK ANY. THING...

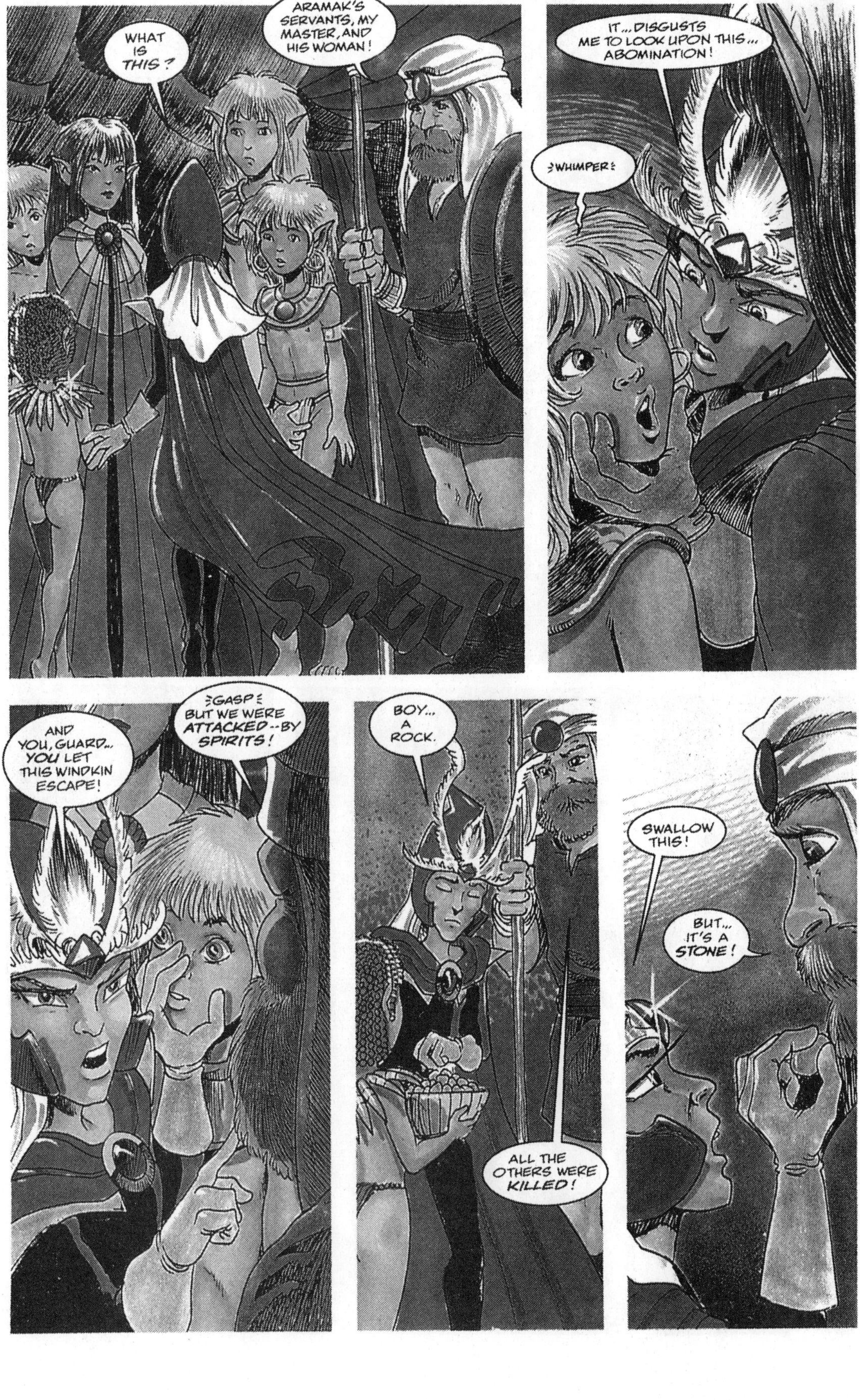
WHAT IS THIS?
ARAMAK'S SERVANTS, MY MASTER, AND HIS WOMAN!
IT... DISGUSTS ME TO LOOK UPON THIS... ABOMINATION!
WHIMPER
AND YOU, GUARD... YOU LET THIS WINDKIN ESCAPE!
GASP BUT WE WERE ATTACKED--BY SPIRITS!
BOY... A ROCK.
ALL THE OTHERS WERE KILLED!
SWALLOW THIS!
BUT... IT'S A STONE!

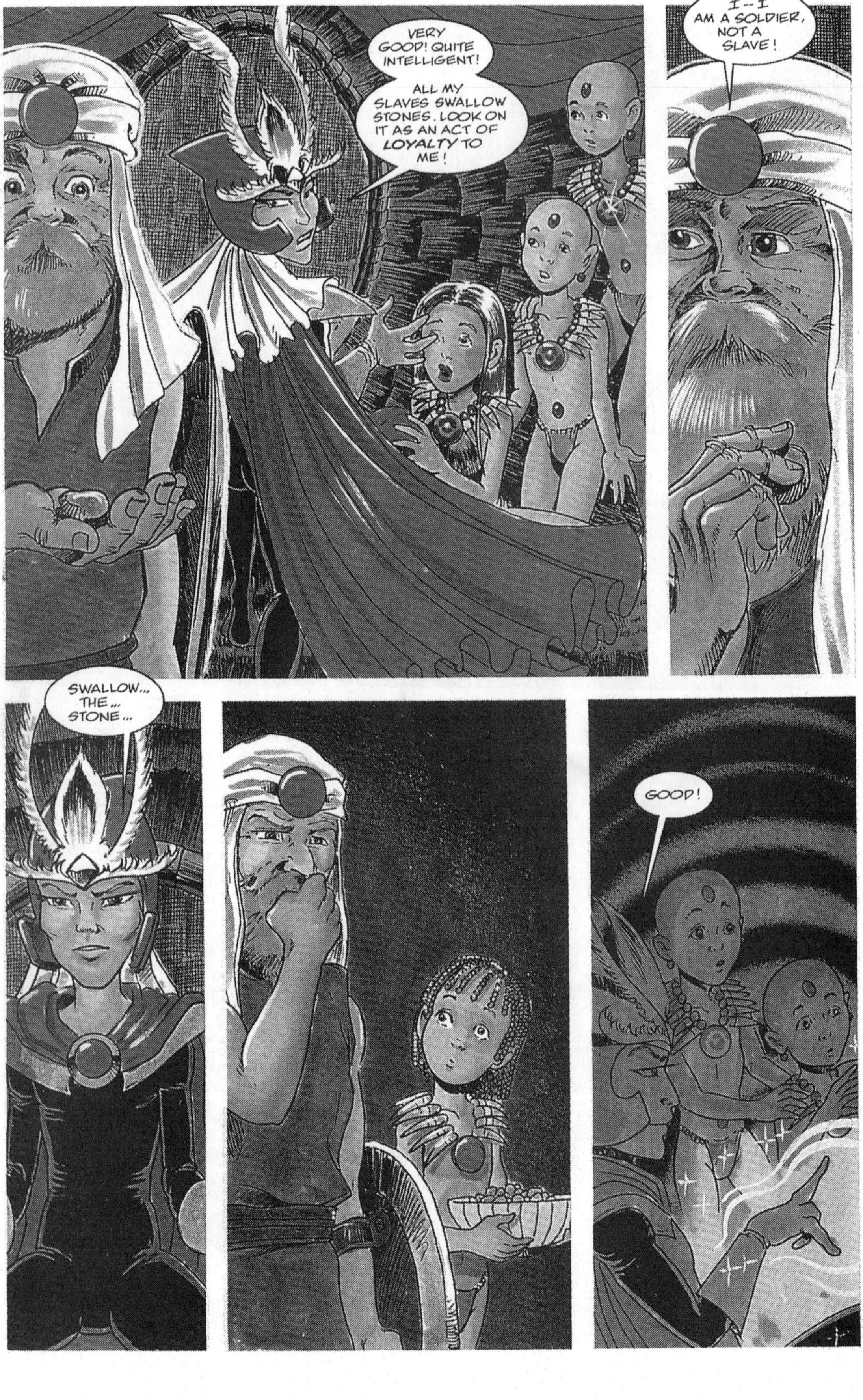
VERY GOOD! QUITE INTELLIGENT!
ALL MY SLAVES SWALLOW STONES. LOOK ON IT AS AN ACT OF LOYALTY TO ME!
I -- I AM A SOLDIER, NOT A SLAVE!
SWALLOW... THE... STONE...
GOOD!

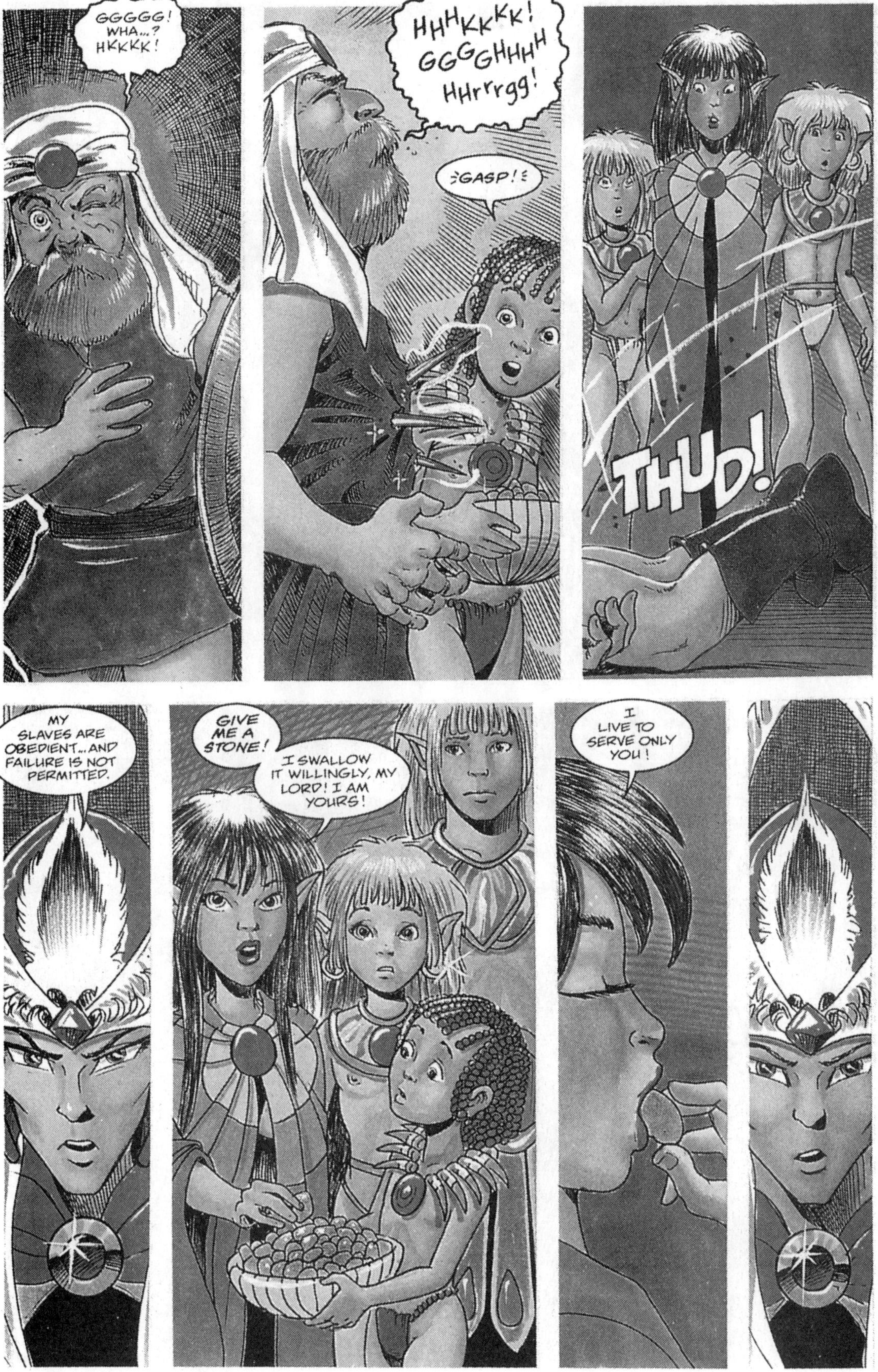
GGGGG! WHA...? HKKKK!
HHHKKKK! GGGGHHHH HHrrrgg!
GASP!
THUD!
MY SLAVES ARE OBEDIENT...AND FAILURE IS NOT PERMITTED.
GIVE ME A STONE!
I SWALLOW IT WILLINGLY, MY LORD! I AM YOURS!
I LIVE TO SERVE ONLY YOU!

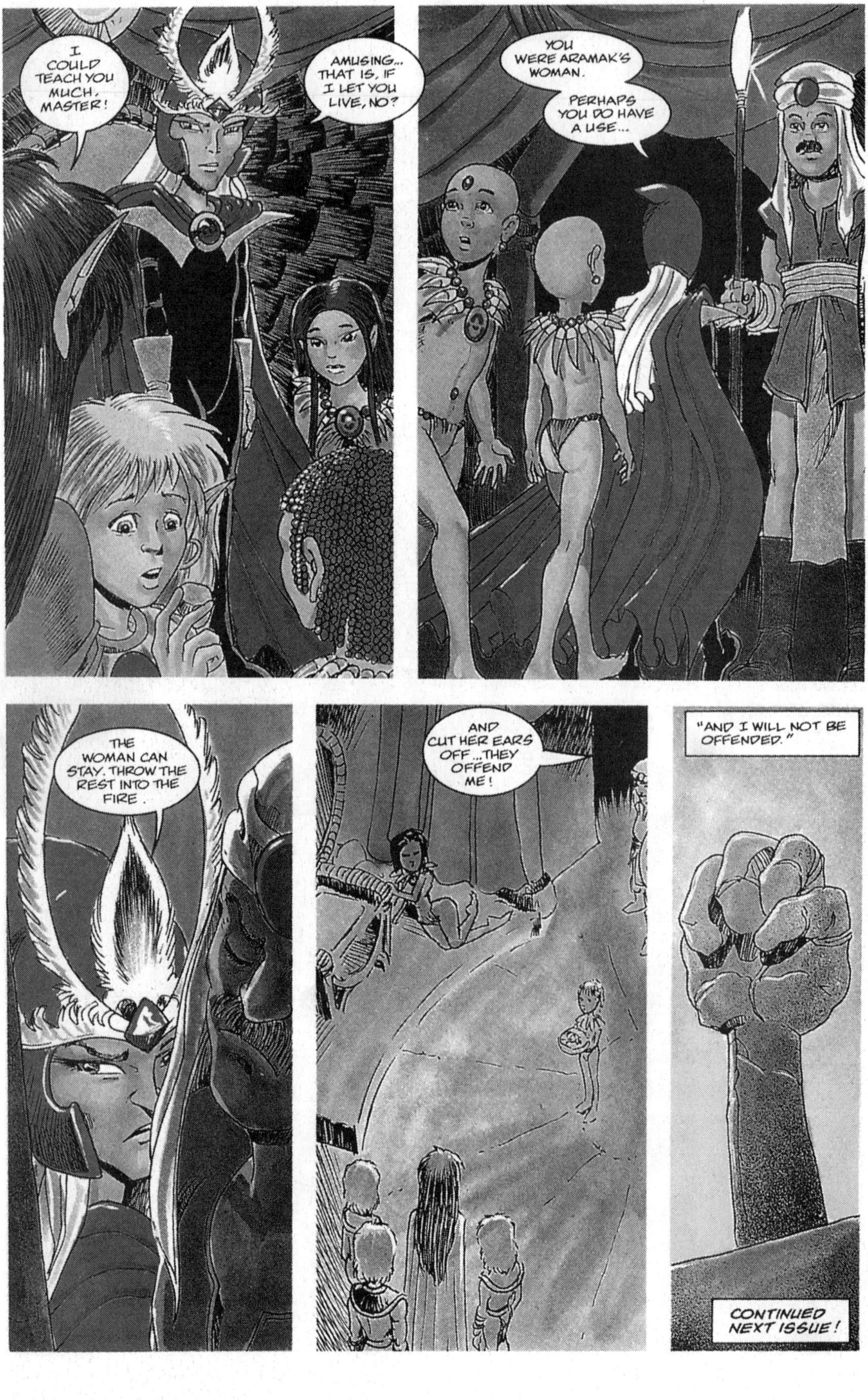
I COULD TEACH YOU MUCH, MASTER!
AMUSING... THAT IS, IF I LET YOU LIVE, NO?
YOU WERE ARAMAK'S WOMAN.
PERHAPS YOU DO HAVE A USE...
THE WOMAN CAN STAY. THROW THE REST INTO THE FIRE.
AND CUT HER EARS OFF... THEY OFFEND ME!
"AND I WILL NOT BE OFFENDED."
CONTINUED NEXT ISSUE!

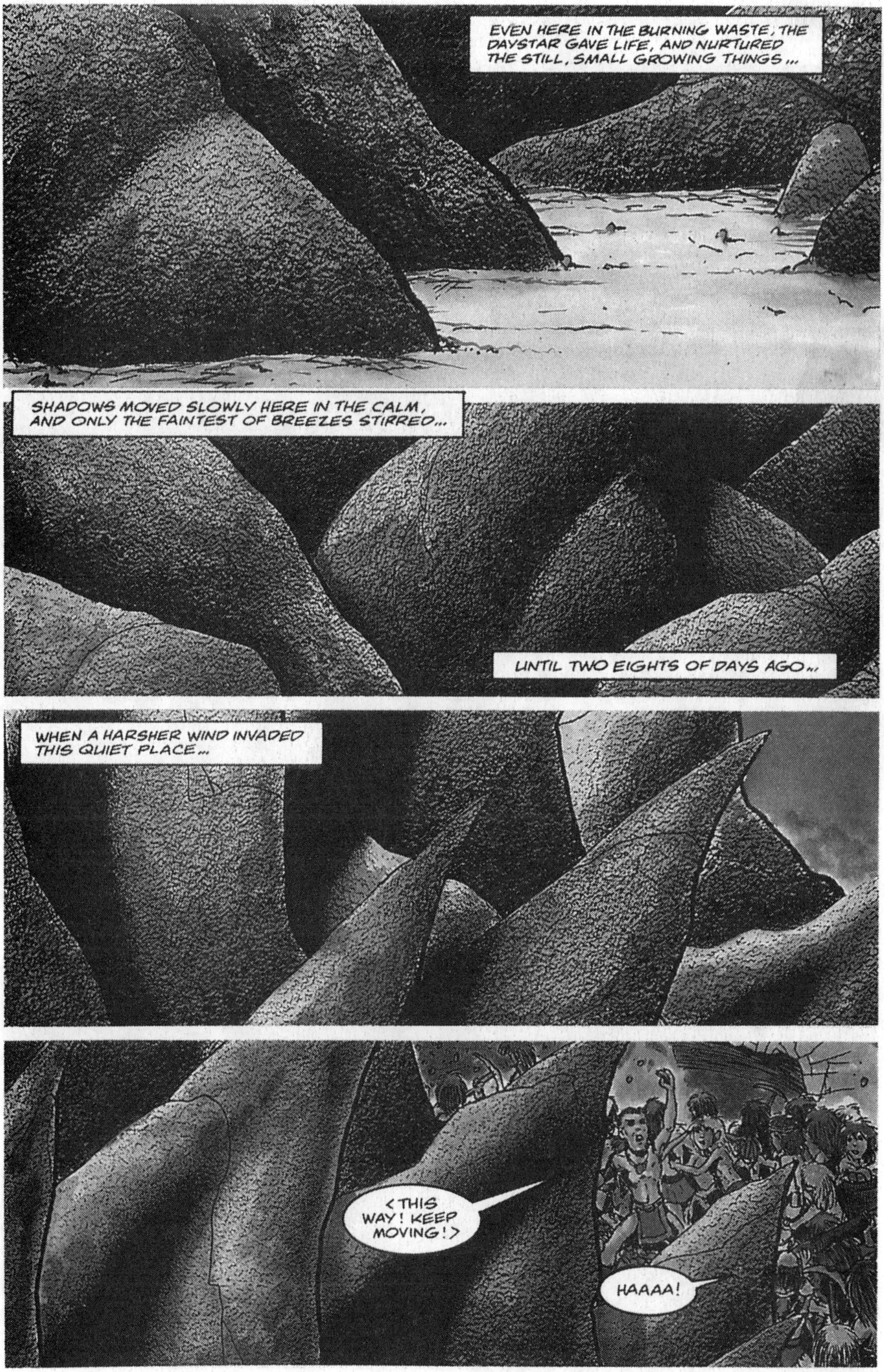
EVEN HERE IN THE BURNING WASTE, THE DAYSTAR GAVE LIFE, AND NURTURED THE STILL, SMALL GROWING THINGS...
SHADOWS MOVED SLOWLY HERE IN THE CALM, AND ONLY THE FAINTEST OF BREEZES STIRRED...
UNTIL TWO EIGHTS OF DAYS AGO...
WHEN A HARSHER WIND INVADED THIS QUIET PLACE...
<THIS WAY! KEEP MOVING!>
HAAAA!

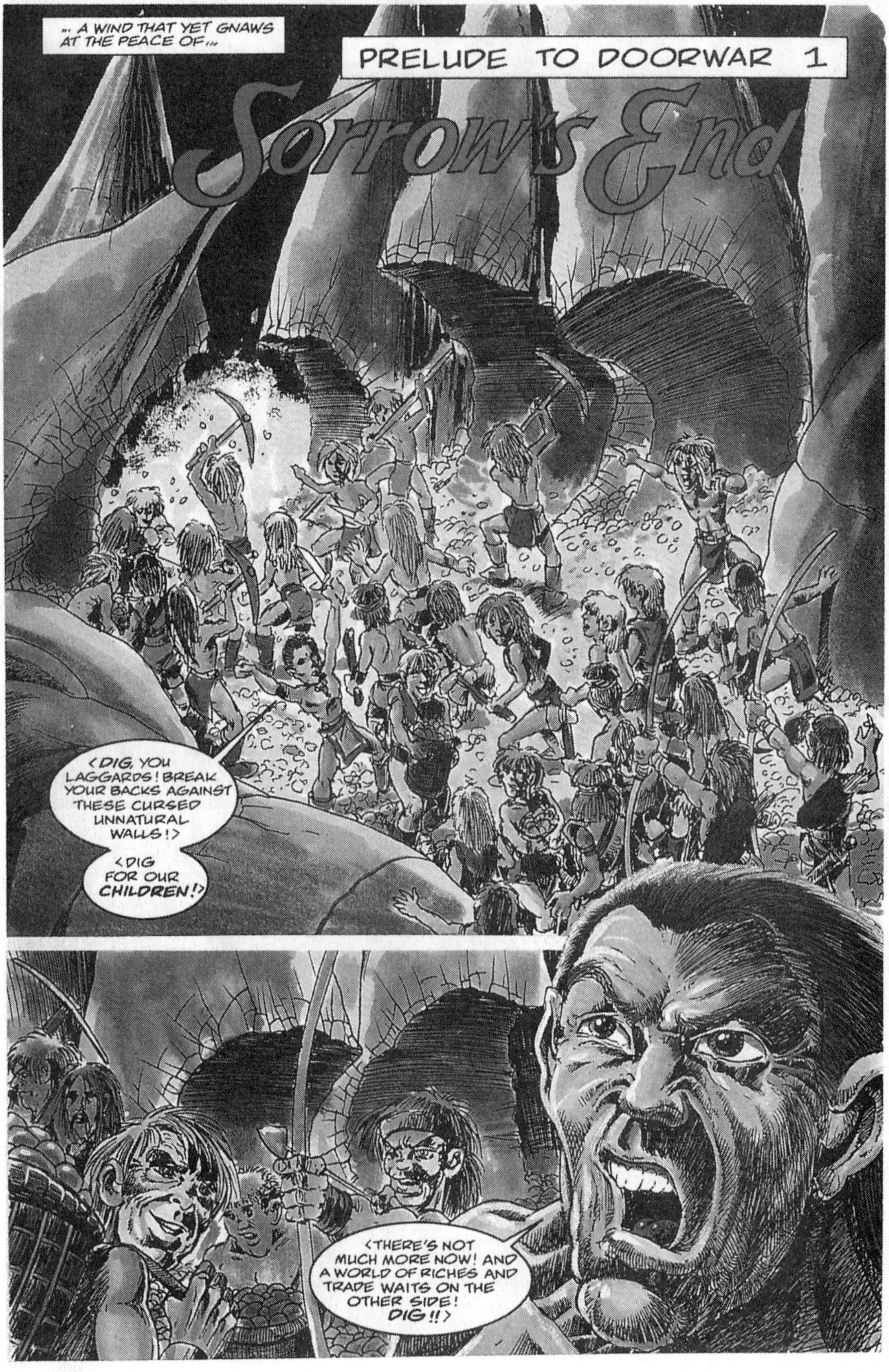

... A WIND THAT YET GNAWS AT THE PEACE OF...
PRELUDE TO DOORWAR 1
Sorrow's End
<DIG, YOU LAGGARDS! BREAK YOUR BACKS AGAINST THESE CURSED UNNATURAL WALLS!>
<DIG FOR OUR CHILDREN!>
<THERE'S NOT MUCH MORE NOW! AND A WORLD OF RICHES AND TRADE WAITS ON THE OTHER SIDE! DIG!!>

< THE GUARDS HAVE SPOTTED SPIRITS AGAIN, BAILON... IN THE ROCKS. WATCHING! >

< YES, THEY'RE QUICK, BUT NOT SO QUICK AS AN ARROW. AND THEY BLEED. >

< THEY KNOW THEY CANNOT STOP US THIS TIME. KEEP YOUR ARROW NOTCHED, BUT DON'T LET THEM DISTRACT YOU! >

< PUT YOUR SWEAT INTO IT! >

< WE'LL BE THROUGH THESE SPINES SOON! >

< I WANT TO LAY MY EYES ON THIS "SPIRIT" PLACE BY NIGHT-FALL! >

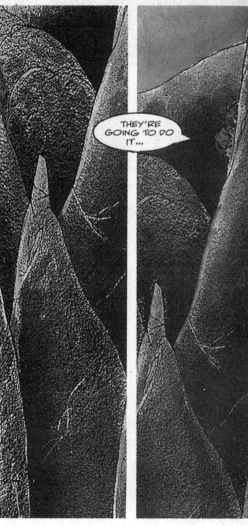
THEY'RE GOING TO DO IT...

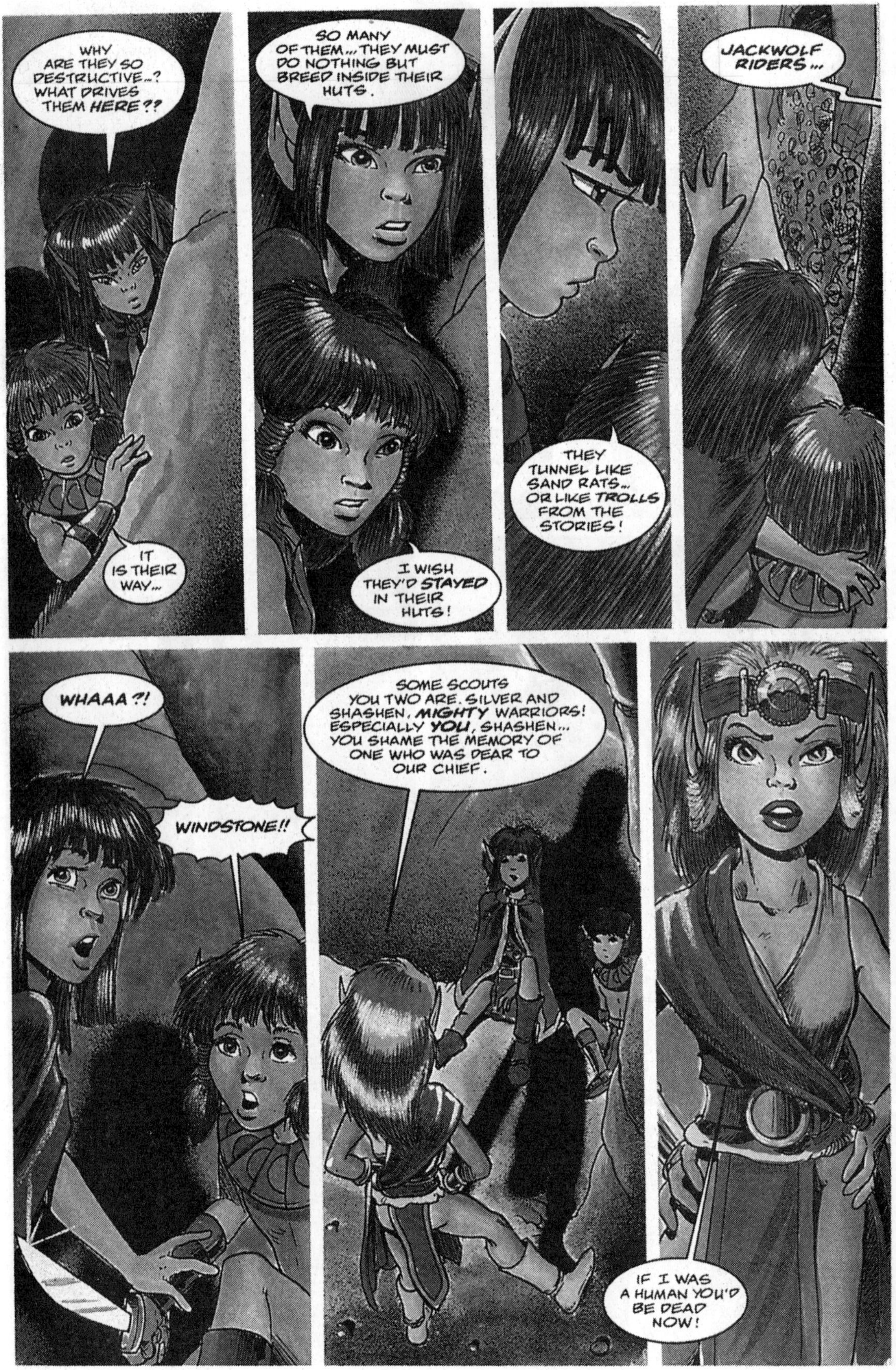
WHY ARE THEY SO DESTRUCTIVE...? WHAT DRIVES THEM HERE??
IT IS THEIR WAY...
SO MANY OF THEM... THEY MUST DO NOTHING BUT BREED INSIDE THEIR HUTS.
I WISH THEY'D STAYED IN THEIR HUTS!
THEY TUNNEL LIKE SAND RATS... OR LIKE TROLLS FROM THE STORIES!
JACKWOLF RIDERS...
WHAAA?!
WINDSTONE!!
SOME SCOUTS YOU TWO ARE. SILVER AND SHASHEN, MIGHTY WARRIORS! ESPECIALLY YOU, SHASHEN... YOU SHAME THE MEMORY OF ONE WHO WAS DEAR TO OUR CHIEF.
IF I WAS A HUMAN YOU'D BE DEAD NOW!

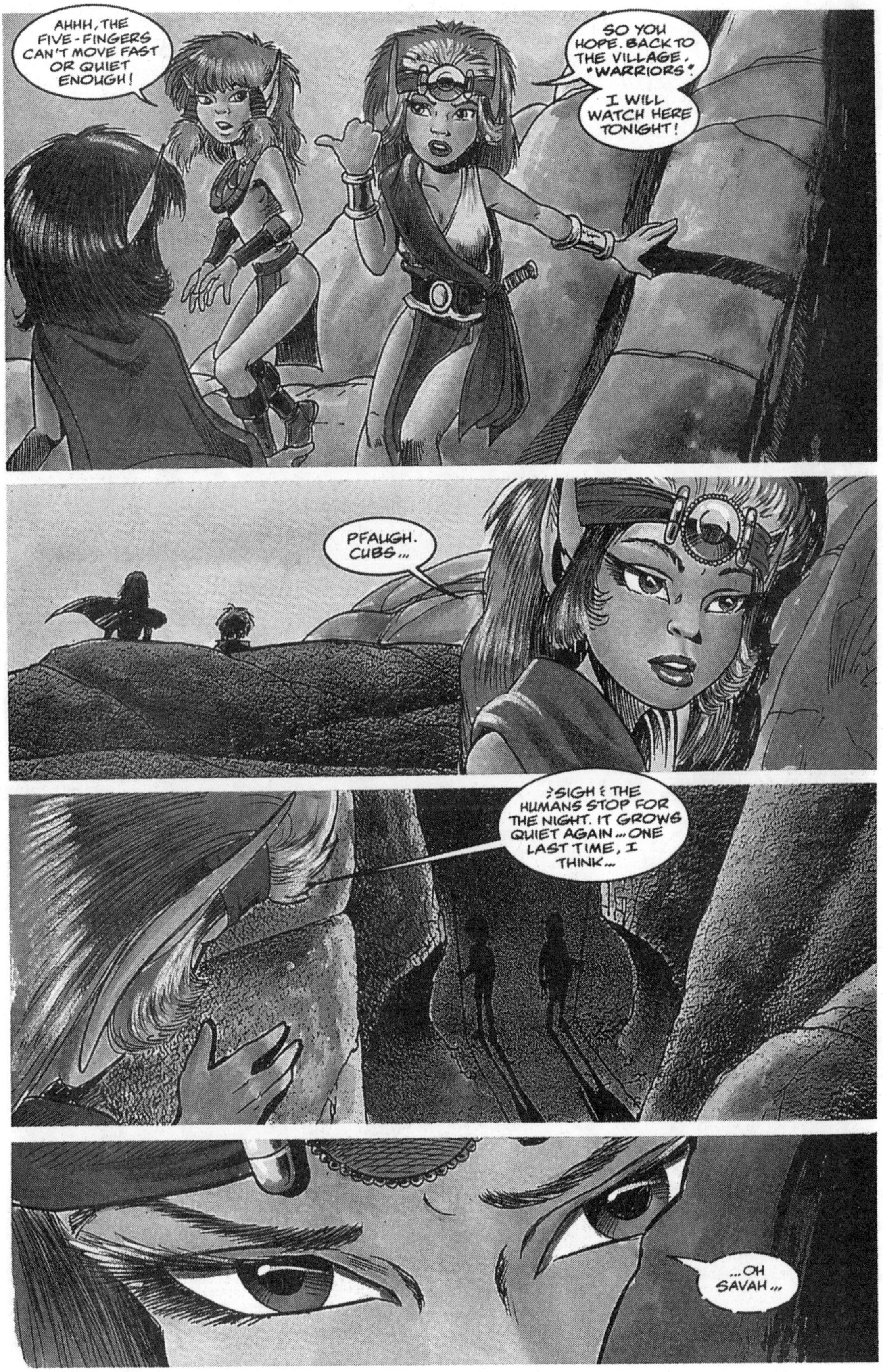
AHHH, THE FIVE-FINGERS CAN'T MOVE FAST OR QUIET ENOUGH!
SO YOU HOPE. BACK TO THE VILLAGE, "WARRIORS"
I WILL WATCH HERE TONIGHT!
PFAUGH. CUBS...
SIGH THE HUMANS STOP FOR THE NIGHT. IT GROWS QUIET AGAIN... ONE LAST TIME, I THINK...
...OH SAVAH...

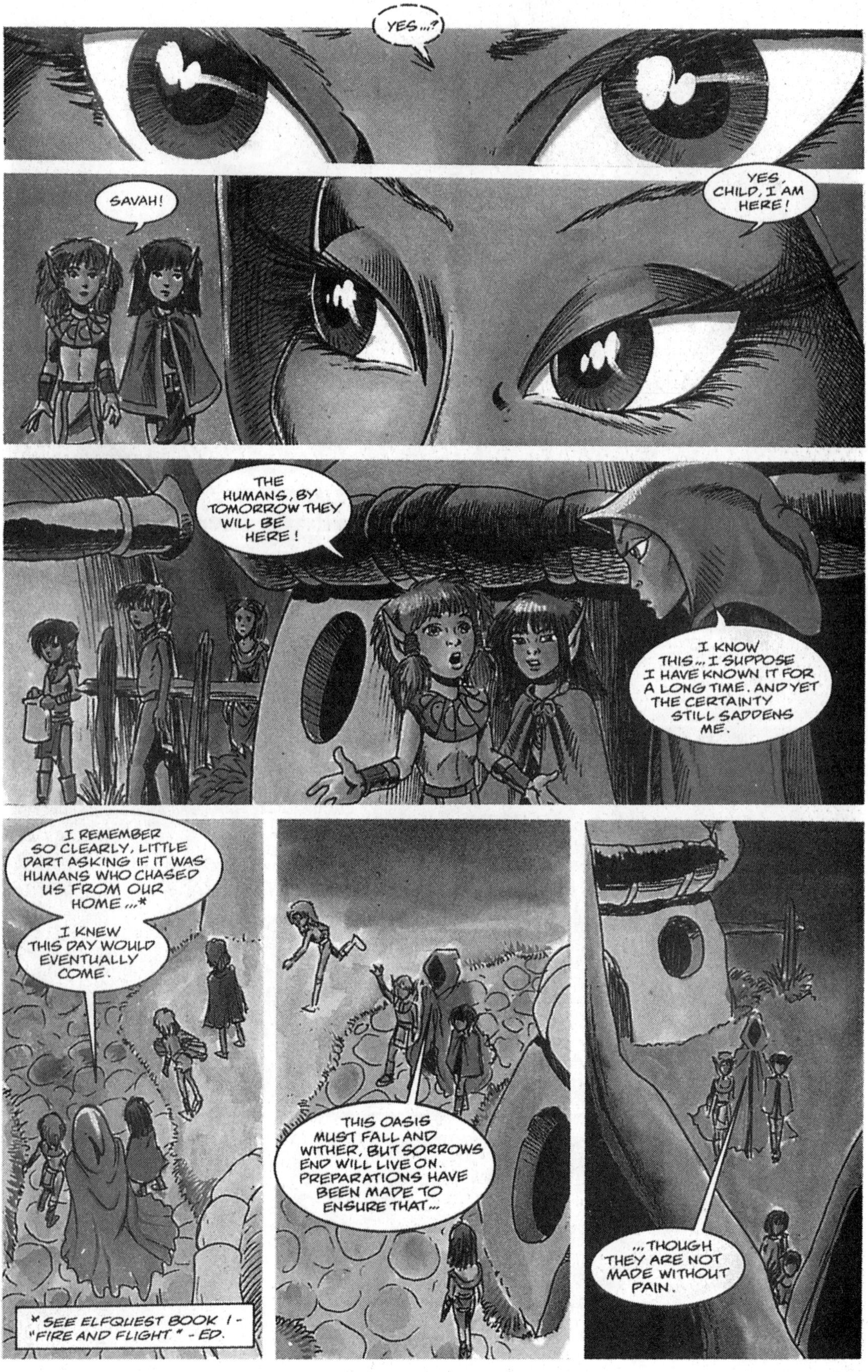
YES...?
SAVAH!
YES, CHILD, I AM HERE!
THE HUMANS, BY TOMORROW THEY WILL BE HERE!
I KNOW THIS... I SUPPOSE I HAVE KNOWN IT FOR A LONG TIME. AND YET THE CERTAINTY STILL SADDENS ME.
I REMEMBER SO CLEARLY, LITTLE DART ASKING IF IT WAS HUMANS WHO CHASED US FROM OUR HOME...*
I KNEW THIS DAY WOULD EVENTUALLY COME.
* SEE ELFQUEST BOOK 1 - "FIRE AND FLIGHT" - ED.
THIS OASIS MUST FALL AND WITHER, BUT SORROWS END WILL LIVE ON. PREPARATIONS HAVE BEEN MADE TO ENSURE THAT...
...THOUGH THEY ARE NOT MADE WITHOUT PAIN.

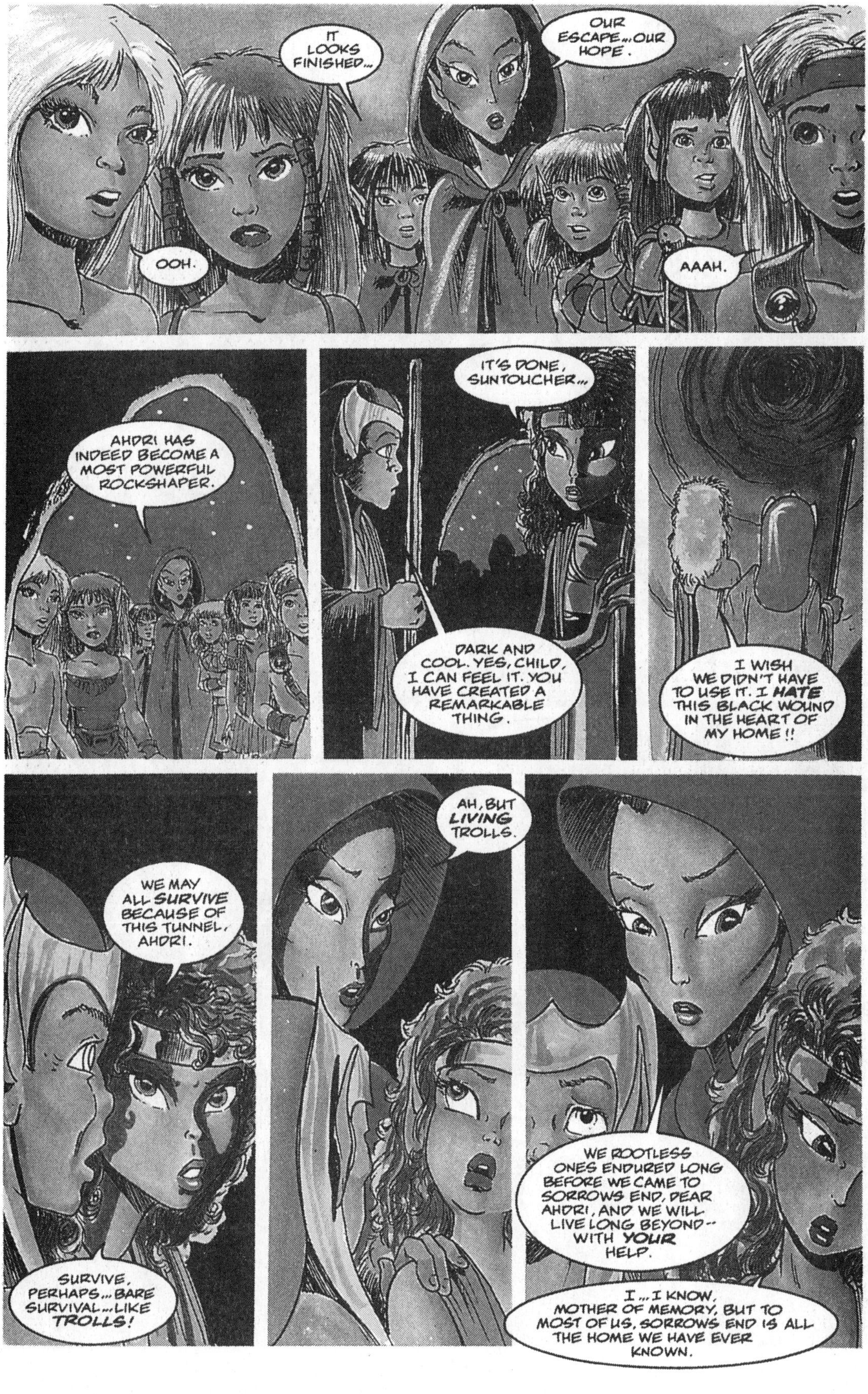
IT LOOKS FINISHED...
OUR ESCAPE...OUR HOPE.
OOH.
AAAH.
AHDRI HAS INDEED BECOME A MOST POWERFUL ROCKSHAPER.
IT'S DONE, SUNTOUCHER...
DARK AND COOL. YES, CHILD, I CAN FEEL IT. YOU HAVE CREATED A REMARKABLE THING.
I WISH WE DIDN'T HAVE TO USE IT. I HATE THIS BLACK WOUND IN THE HEART OF MY HOME!!
WE MAY ALL SURVIVE BECAUSE OF THIS TUNNEL, AHDRI.
SURVIVE, PERHAPS... BARE SURVIVAL... LIKE TROLLS!
AH, BUT LIVING TROLLS.
WE ROOTLESS ONES ENDURED LONG BEFORE WE CAME TO SORROWS END, DEAR AHDRI, AND WE WILL LIVE LONG BEYOND-- WITH YOUR HELP.
I... I KNOW, MOTHER OF MEMORY, BUT TO MOST OF US, SORROWS END IS ALL THE HOME WE HAVE EVER KNOWN.

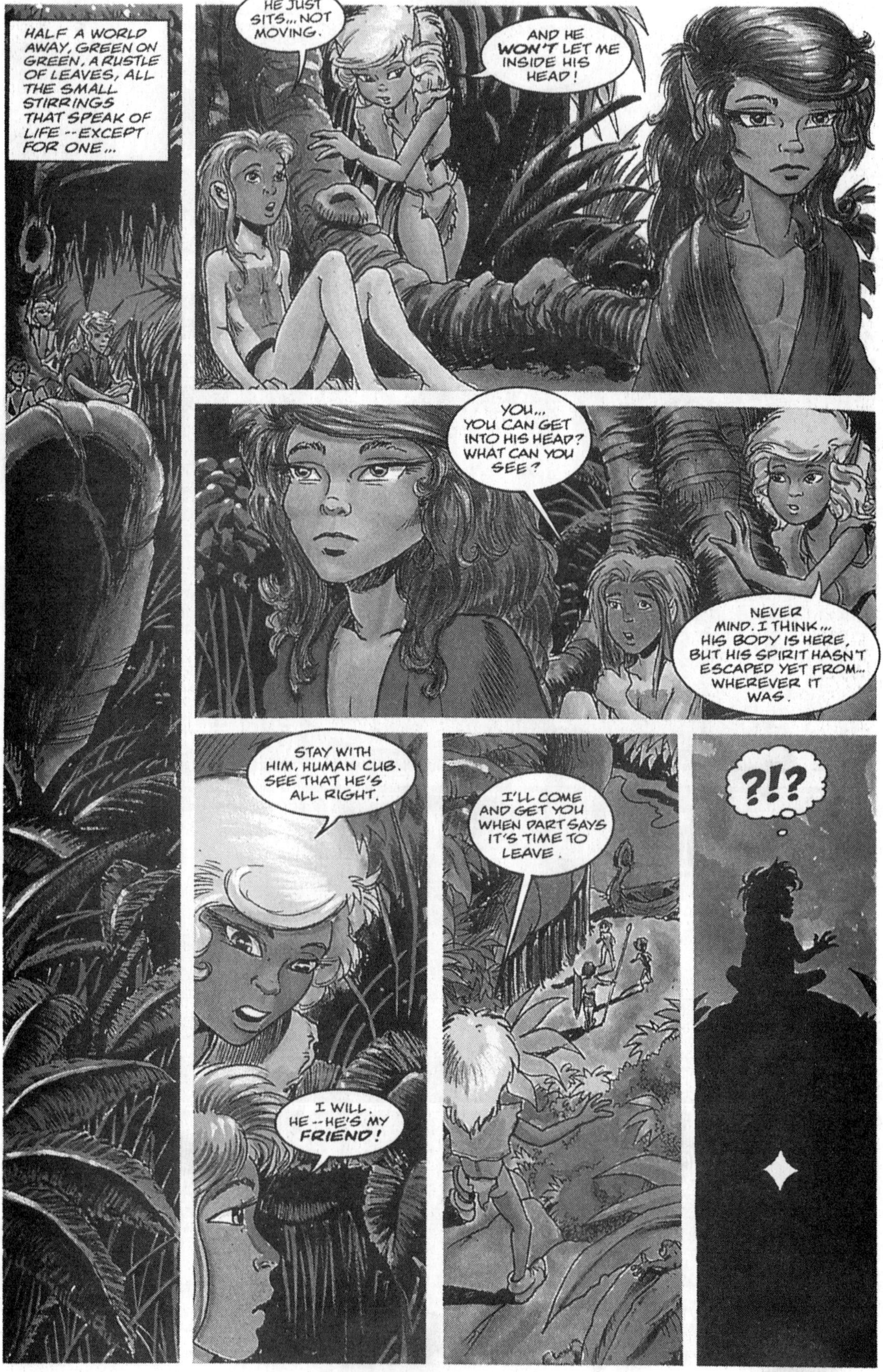
HALF A WORLD AWAY, GREEN ON GREEN, A RUSTLE OF LEAVES, ALL THE SMALL STIRRINGS THAT SPEAK OF LIFE --EXCEPT FOR ONE...
HE JUST SITS... NOT MOVING.
AND HE **WON'T** LET ME INSIDE HIS HEAD!
YOU... YOU CAN GET INTO HIS HEAD? WHAT CAN YOU SEE?
NEVER MIND. I THINK... HIS BODY IS HERE, BUT HIS SPIRIT HASN'T ESCAPED YET FROM... WHEREVER IT WAS.
STAY WITH HIM, HUMAN CUB. SEE THAT HE'S ALL RIGHT.
I WILL. HE--HE'S MY **FRIEND**!
I'LL COME AND GET YOU WHEN DART SAYS IT'S TIME TO LEAVE.
?!?

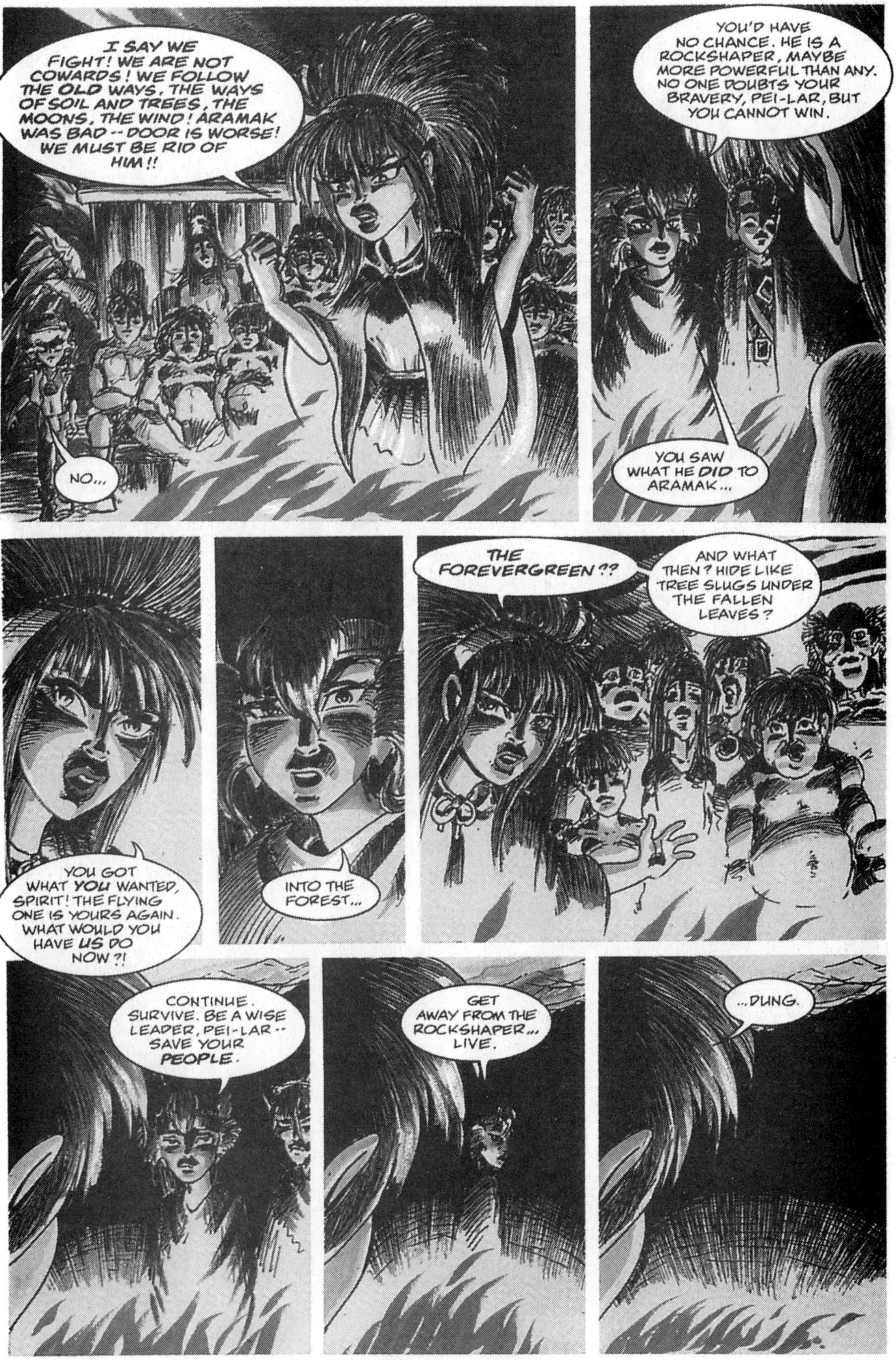
I SAY WE FIGHT! WE ARE NOT COWARDS! WE FOLLOW THE OLD WAYS, THE WAYS OF SOIL AND TREES, THE MOONS, THE WIND! ARAMAK WAS BAD -- DOOR IS WORSE! WE MUST BE RID OF HIM!!
NO...
YOU'D HAVE NO CHANCE. HE IS A ROCKSHAPER, MAYBE MORE POWERFUL THAN ANY. NO ONE DOUBTS YOUR BRAVERY, PEI-LAR, BUT YOU CANNOT WIN.
YOU SAW WHAT HE DID TO ARAMAK...
YOU GOT WHAT YOU WANTED, SPIRIT! THE FLYING ONE IS YOURS AGAIN. WHAT WOULD YOU HAVE US DO NOW?!
INTO THE FOREST...
THE FOREVERGREEN??
AND WHAT THEN? HIDE LIKE TREE SLUGS UNDER THE FALLEN LEAVES?
CONTINUE. SURVIVE. BE A WISE LEADER, PEI-LAR -- SAVE YOUR PEOPLE.
GET AWAY FROM THE ROCKSHAPER... LIVE.
...DUNG.

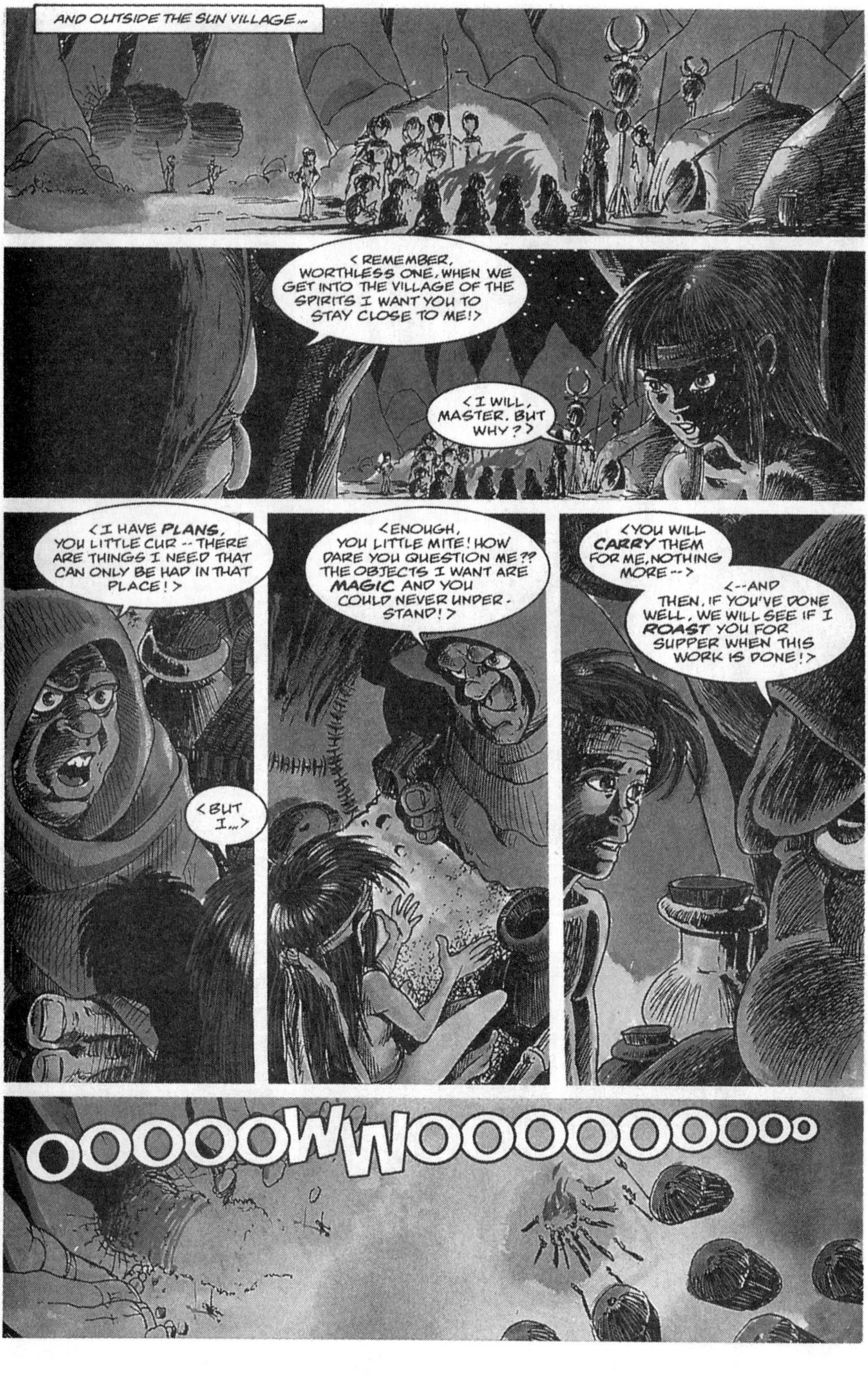
AND OUTSIDE THE SUN VILLAGE...
< REMEMBER, WORTHLESS ONE, WHEN WE GET INTO THE VILLAGE OF THE SPIRITS I WANT YOU TO STAY CLOSE TO ME! >
< I WILL, MASTER. BUT WHY? >
< I HAVE PLANS, YOU LITTLE CUR -- THERE ARE THINGS I NEED THAT CAN ONLY BE HAD IN THAT PLACE! >
< BUT I... >
< ENOUGH, YOU LITTLE MITE! HOW DARE YOU QUESTION ME?? THE OBJECTS I WANT ARE MAGIC AND YOU COULD NEVER UNDER-STAND! >
< YOU WILL CARRY THEM FOR ME, NOTHING MORE -- >
< --AND THEN, IF YOU'VE DONE WELL, WE WILL SEE IF I ROAST YOU FOR SUPPER WHEN THIS WORK IS DONE! >
OOOOOWWOOOOOOOOOo

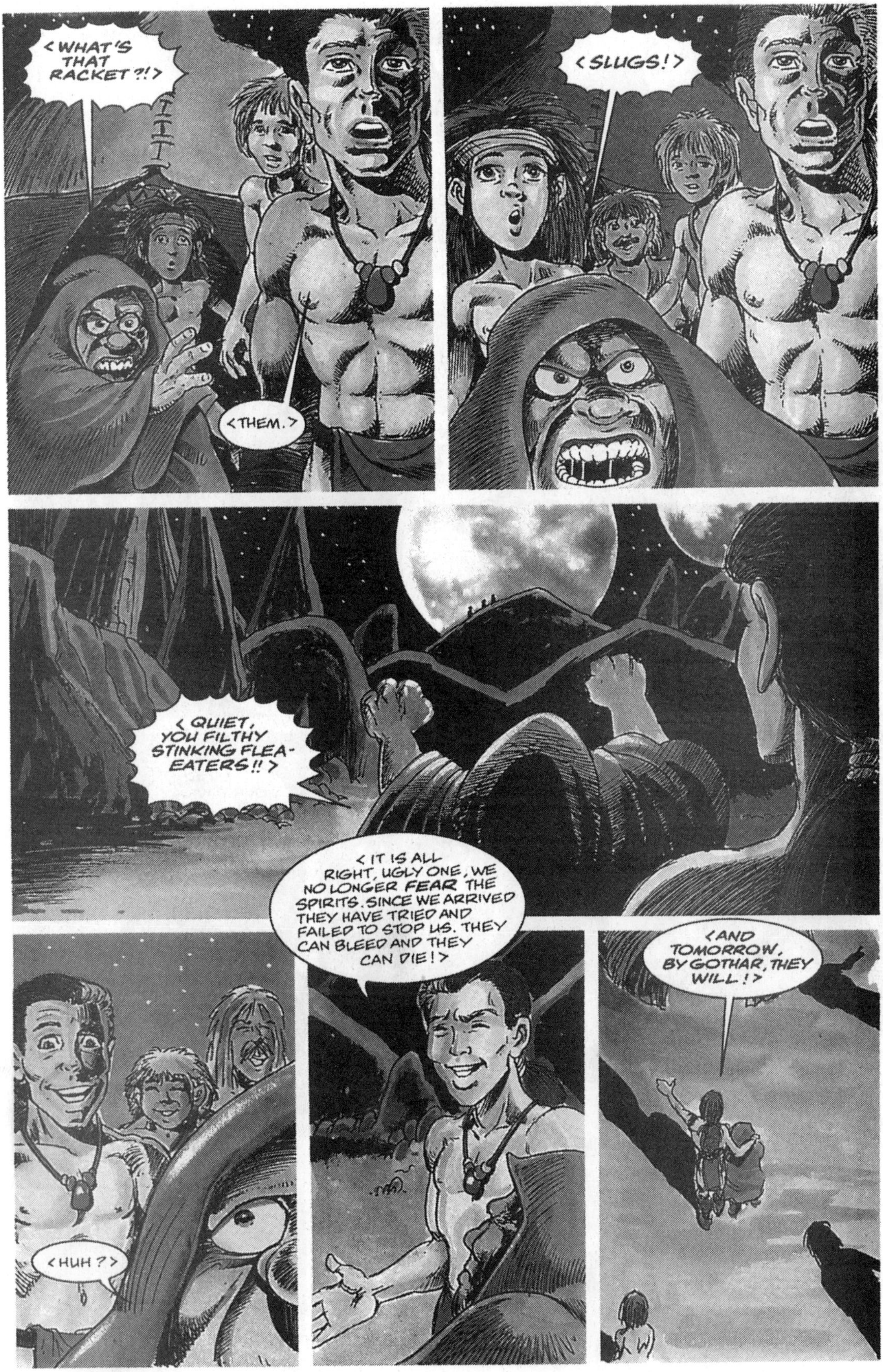
<WHAT'S THAT RACKET?!>
<THEM.>
<SLUGS!>
<QUIET, YOU FILTHY STINKING FLEA-EATERS!!>
<IT IS ALL RIGHT, UGLY ONE, WE NO LONGER FEAR THE SPIRITS. SINCE WE ARRIVED THEY HAVE TRIED AND FAILED TO STOP US. THEY CAN BLEED AND THEY CAN DIE!>
<HUH?>
<AND TOMORROW, BY GOTHAR, THEY WILL!>

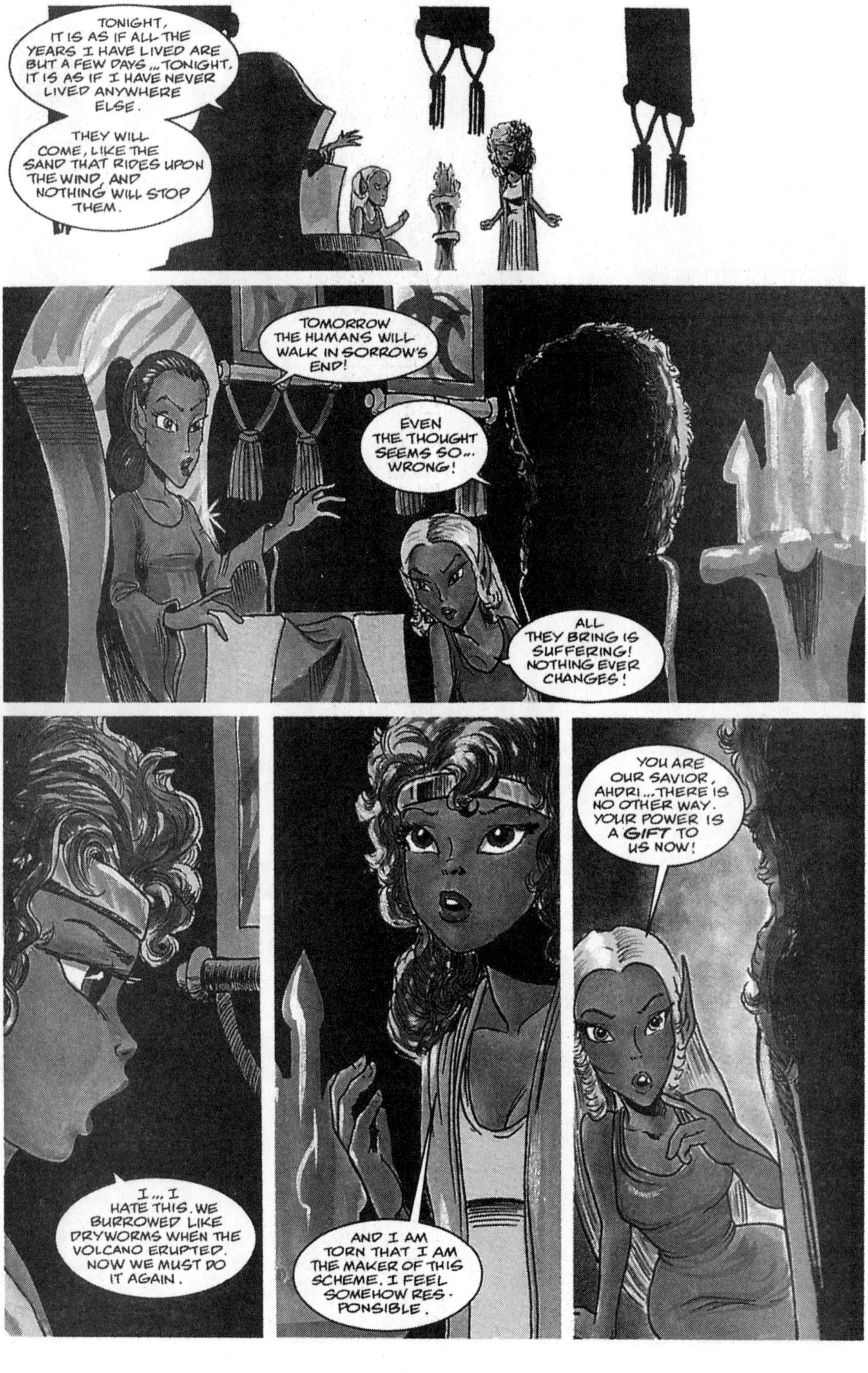
TONIGHT, IT IS AS IF ALL THE YEARS I HAVE LIVED ARE BUT A FEW DAYS... TONIGHT, IT IS AS IF I HAVE NEVER LIVED ANYWHERE ELSE.
THEY WILL COME, LIKE THE SAND THAT RIDES UPON THE WIND, AND NOTHING WILL STOP THEM.
TOMORROW THE HUMANS WILL WALK IN SORROW'S END!
EVEN THE THOUGHT SEEMS SO... WRONG!
ALL THEY BRING IS SUFFERING! NOTHING EVER CHANGES!
I... I HATE THIS. WE BURROWED LIKE DRYWORMS WHEN THE VOLCANO ERUPTED. NOW WE MUST DO IT AGAIN.
AND I AM TORN THAT I AM THE MAKER OF THIS SCHEME. I FEEL SOMEHOW RES-PONSIBLE.
YOU ARE OUR SAVIOR, AHDRI... THERE IS NO OTHER WAY. YOUR POWER IS A GIFT TO US NOW!

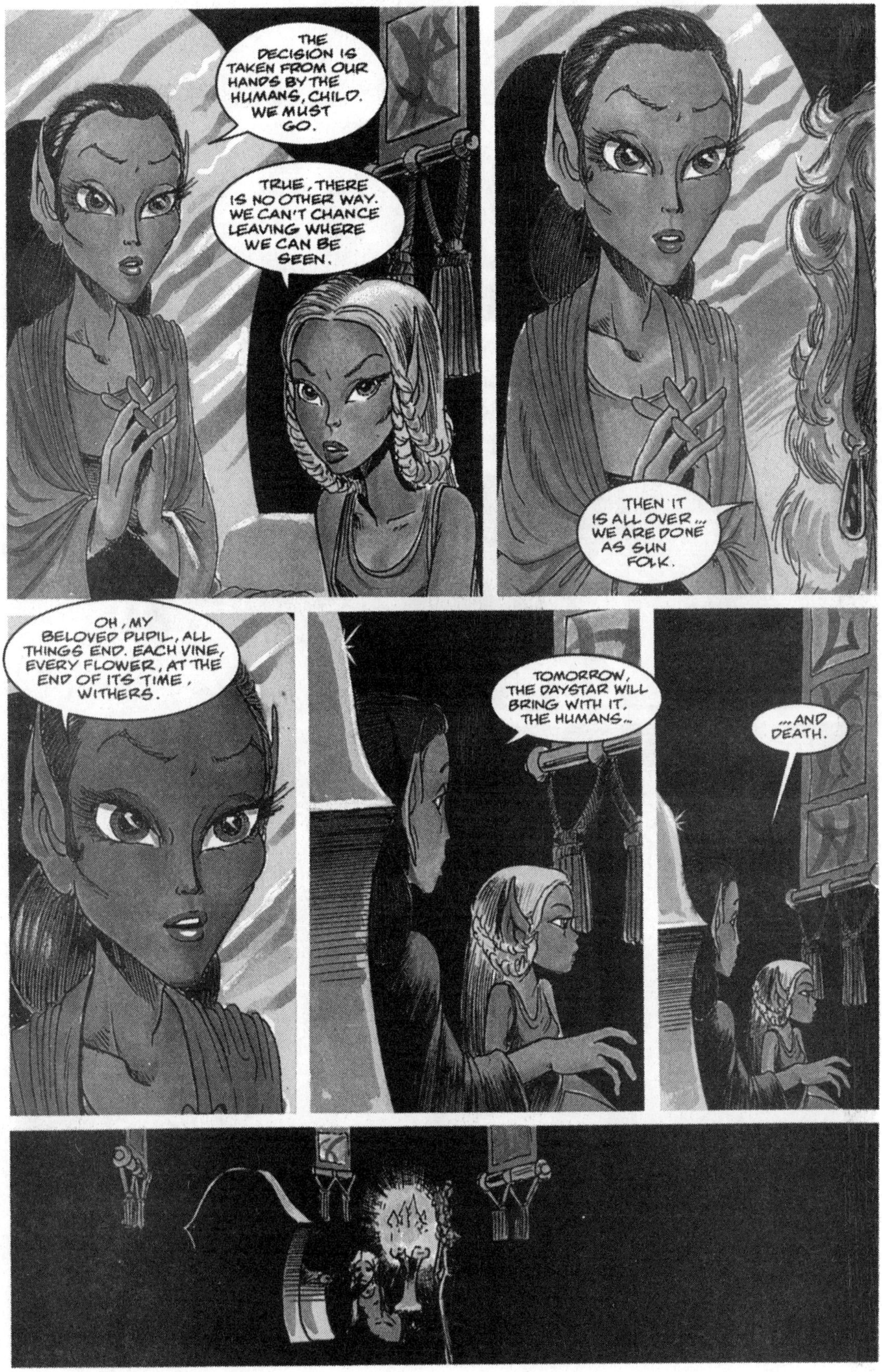
THE DECISION IS TAKEN FROM OUR HANDS BY THE HUMANS, CHILD. WE MUST GO.
TRUE, THERE IS NO OTHER WAY. WE CAN'T CHANCE LEAVING WHERE WE CAN BE SEEN.
THEN IT IS ALL OVER... WE ARE DONE AS SUN FOLK.
OH, MY BELOVED PUPIL, ALL THINGS END. EACH VINE, EVERY FLOWER, AT THE END OF ITS TIME, WITHERS.
TOMORROW, THE DAYSTAR WILL BRING WITH IT, THE HUMANS...
...AND DEATH.

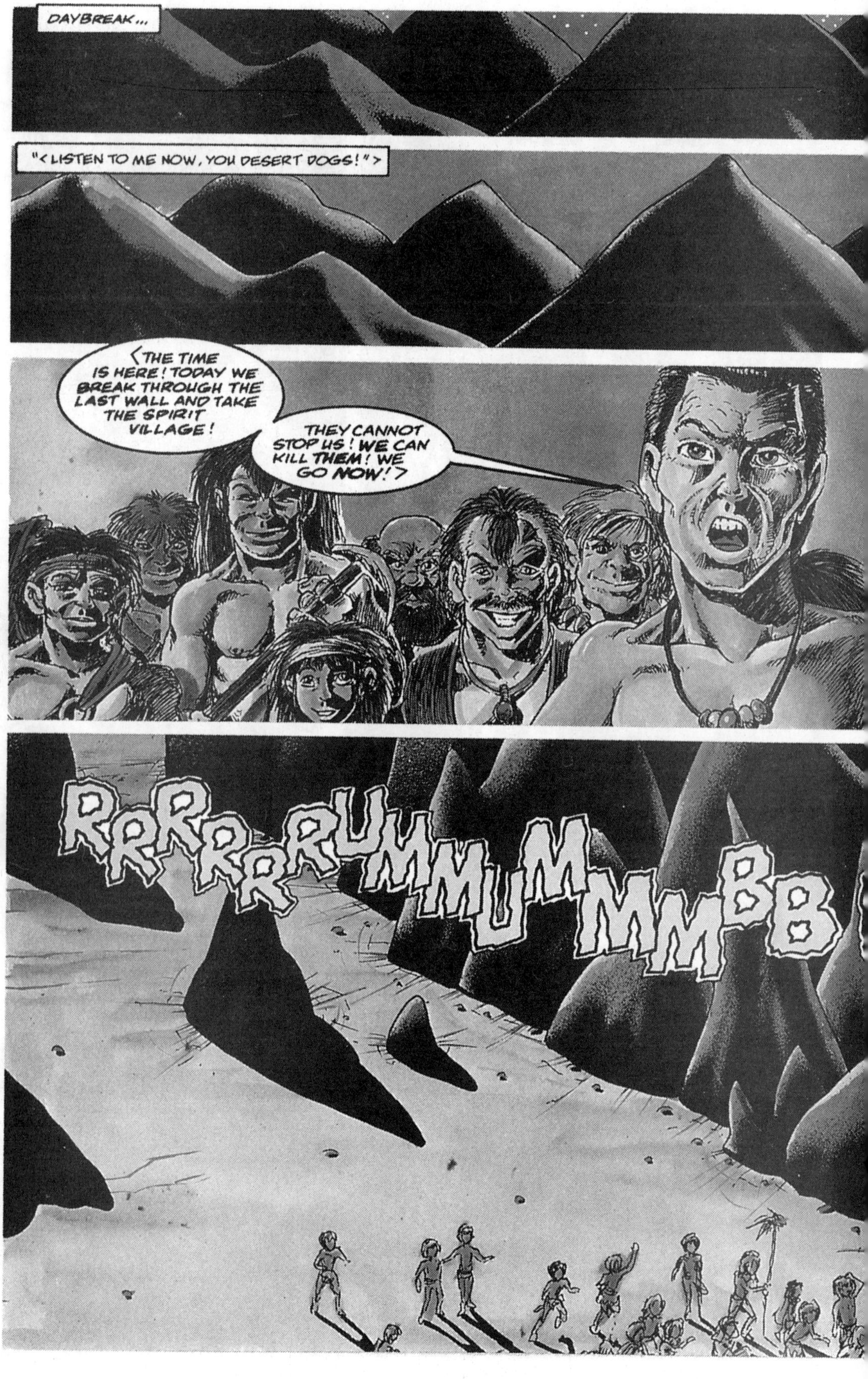
DAYBREAK...
"< LISTEN TO ME NOW, YOU DESERT DOGS!">
<THE TIME IS HERE! TODAY WE BREAK THROUGH THE LAST WALL AND TAKE THE SPIRIT VILLAGE!
THEY CANNOT STOP US! WE CAN KILL THEM! WE GO NOW!>
RRRRRRUMMMUMMMBB

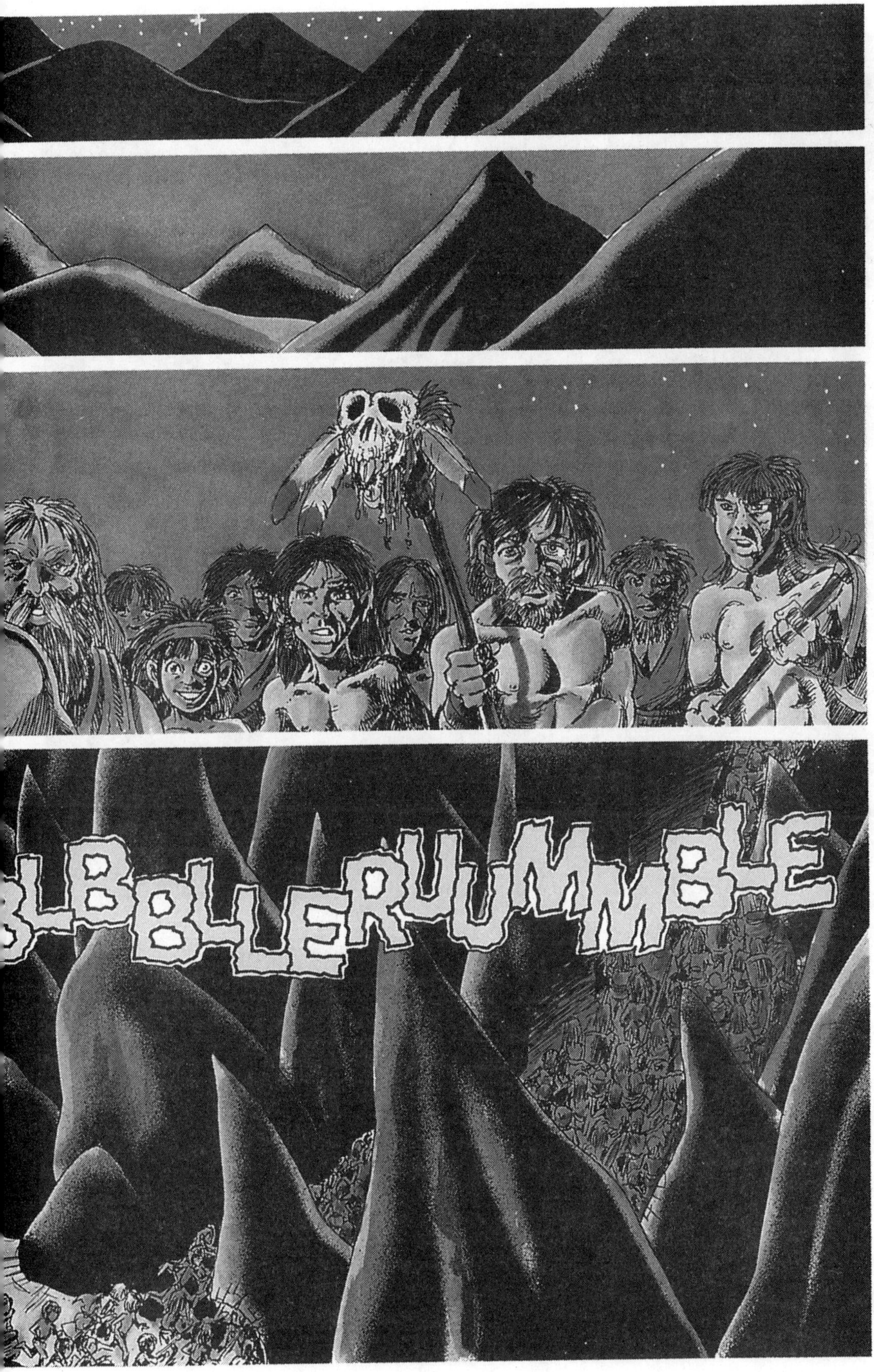
LBBLLERUUMMBLE

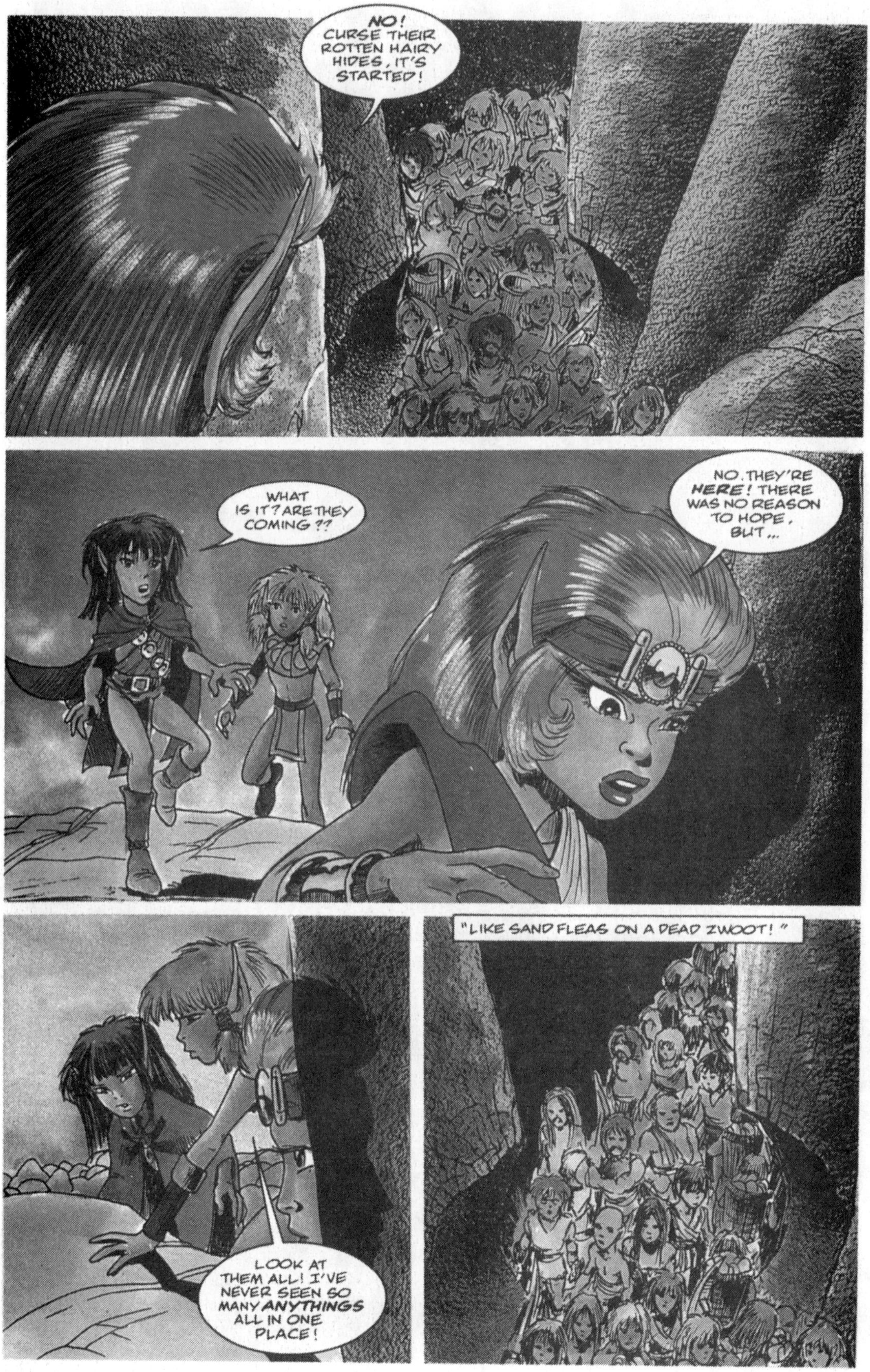
NO! CURSE THEIR ROTTEN HAIRY HIDES, IT'S STARTED!
WHAT IS IT? ARE THEY COMING??
NO. THEY'RE HERE! THERE WAS NO REASON TO HOPE, BUT...
LOOK AT THEM ALL! I'VE NEVER SEEN SO MANY ANYTHINGS ALL IN ONE PLACE!
"LIKE SAND FLEAS ON A DEAD ZWOOT!"

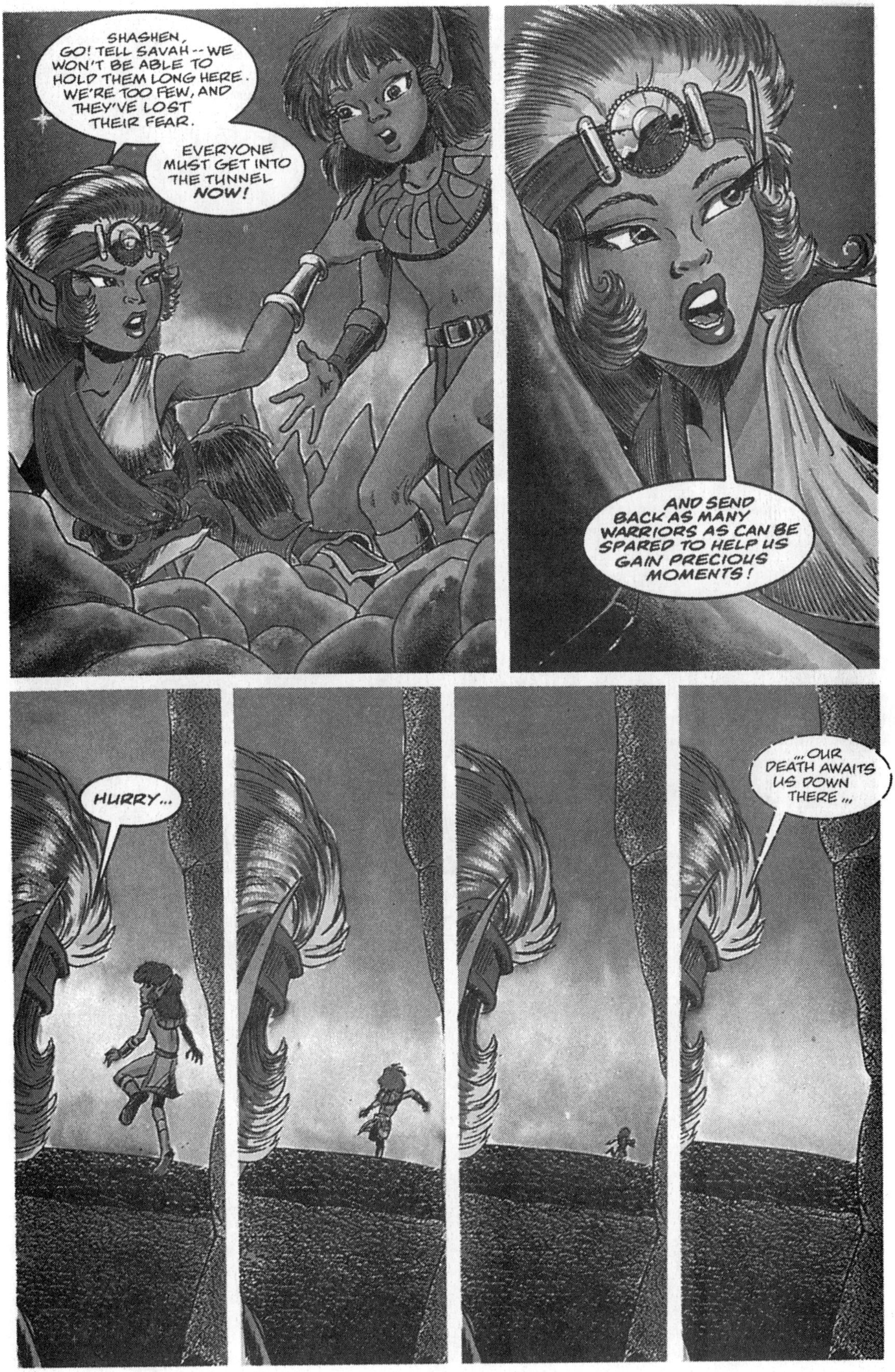
SHASHEN, GO! TELL SAVAH -- WE WON'T BE ABLE TO HOLD THEM LONG HERE. WE'RE TOO FEW, AND THEY'VE LOST THEIR FEAR.
EVERYONE MUST GET INTO THE TUNNEL NOW!
AND SEND BACK AS MANY WARRIORS AS CAN BE SPARED TO HELP US GAIN PRECIOUS MOMENTS!
HURRY...
...OUR DEATH AWAITS US DOWN THERE...

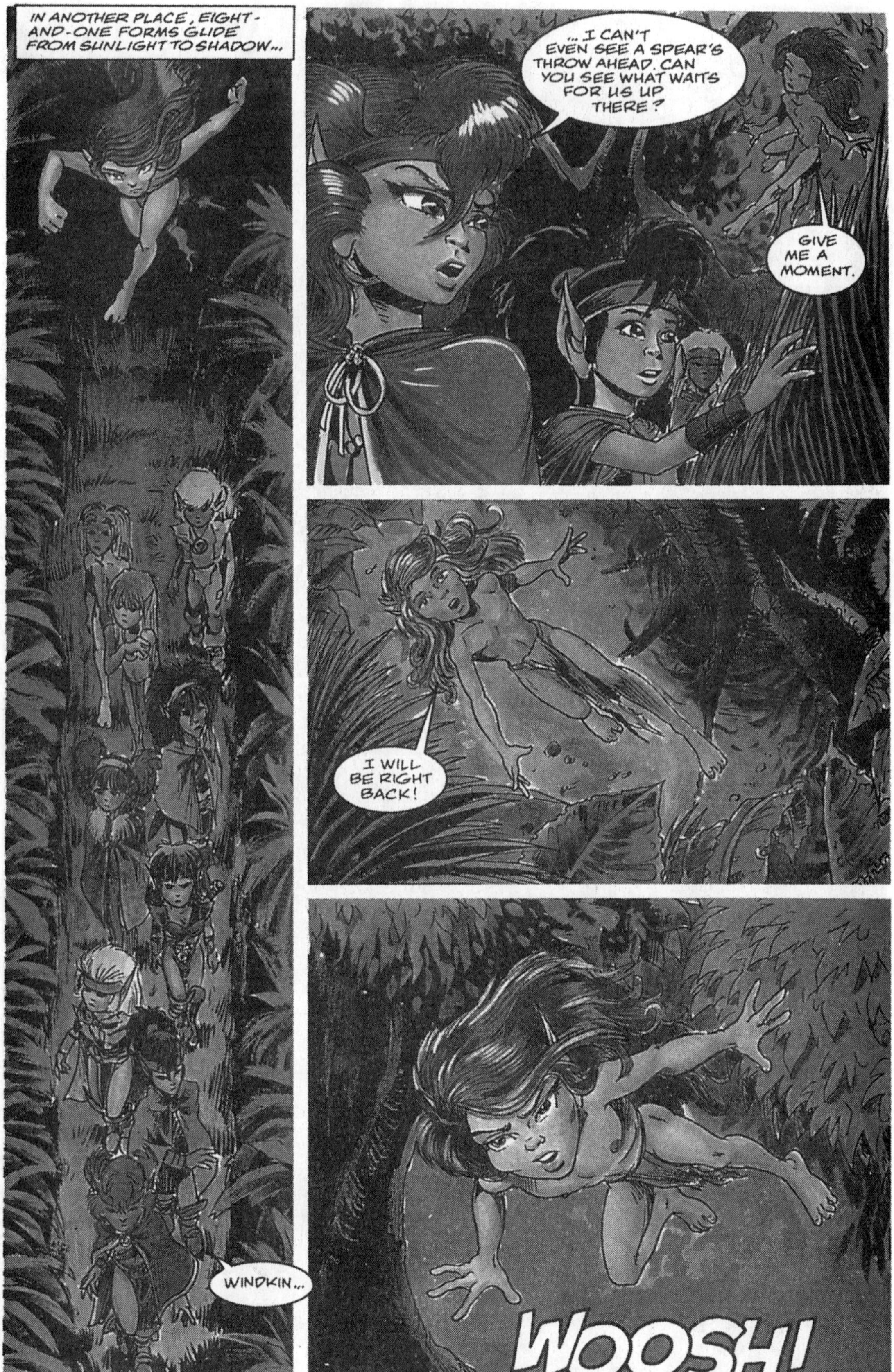
IN ANOTHER PLACE, EIGHT-AND-ONE FORMS GLIDE FROM SUNLIGHT TO SHADOW...
WINDKIN...
...I CAN'T EVEN SEE A SPEAR'S THROW AHEAD. CAN YOU SEE WHAT WAITS FOR US UP THERE?
GIVE ME A MOMENT.
I WILL BE RIGHT BACK!
WOOSH!

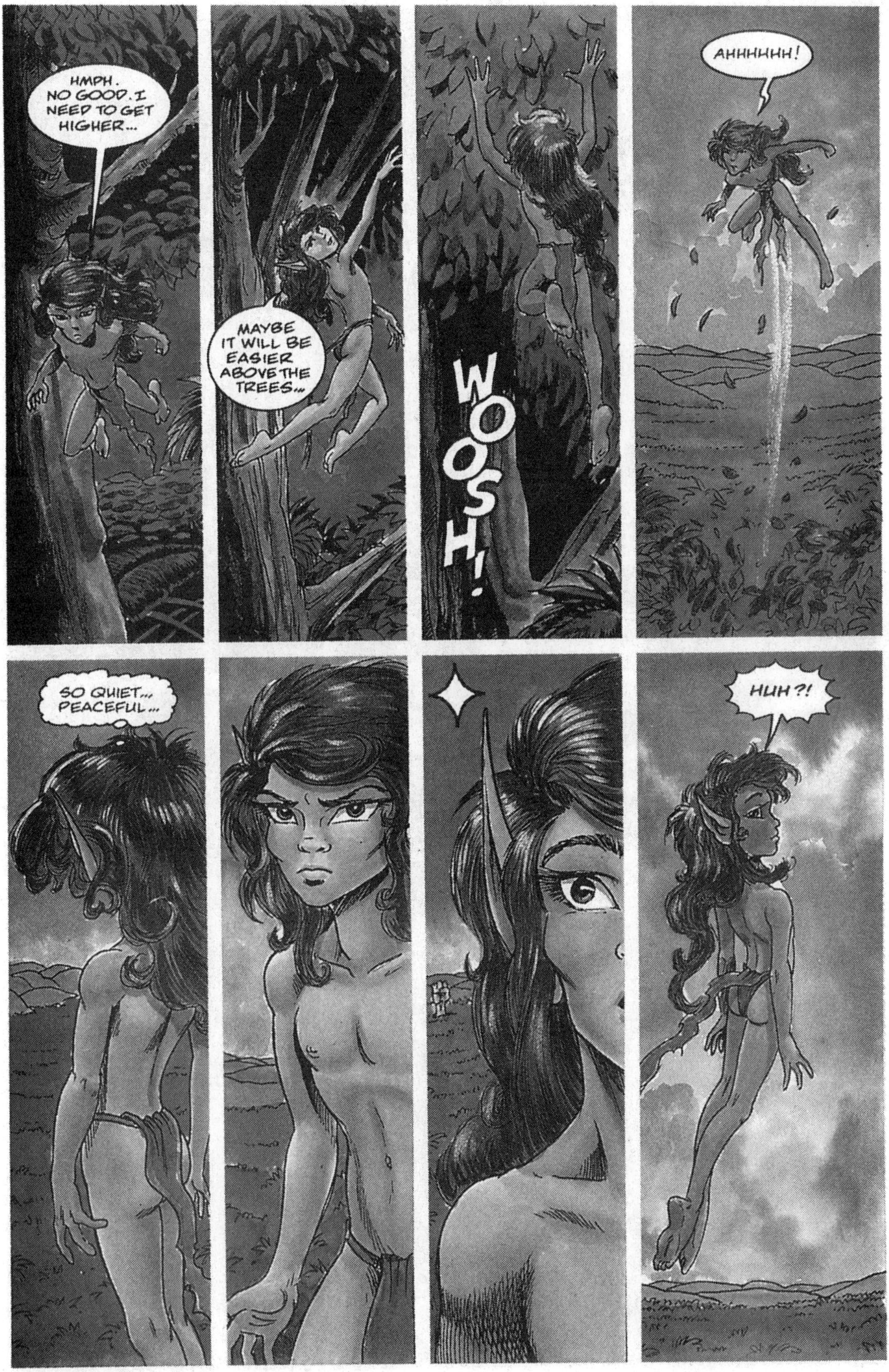
HMPH. NO GOOD. I NEED TO GET HIGHER...
MAYBE IT WILL BE EASIER ABOVE THE TREES...
WOOSH!
AHHHHHH!
SO QUIET... PEACEFUL...
HUH?!

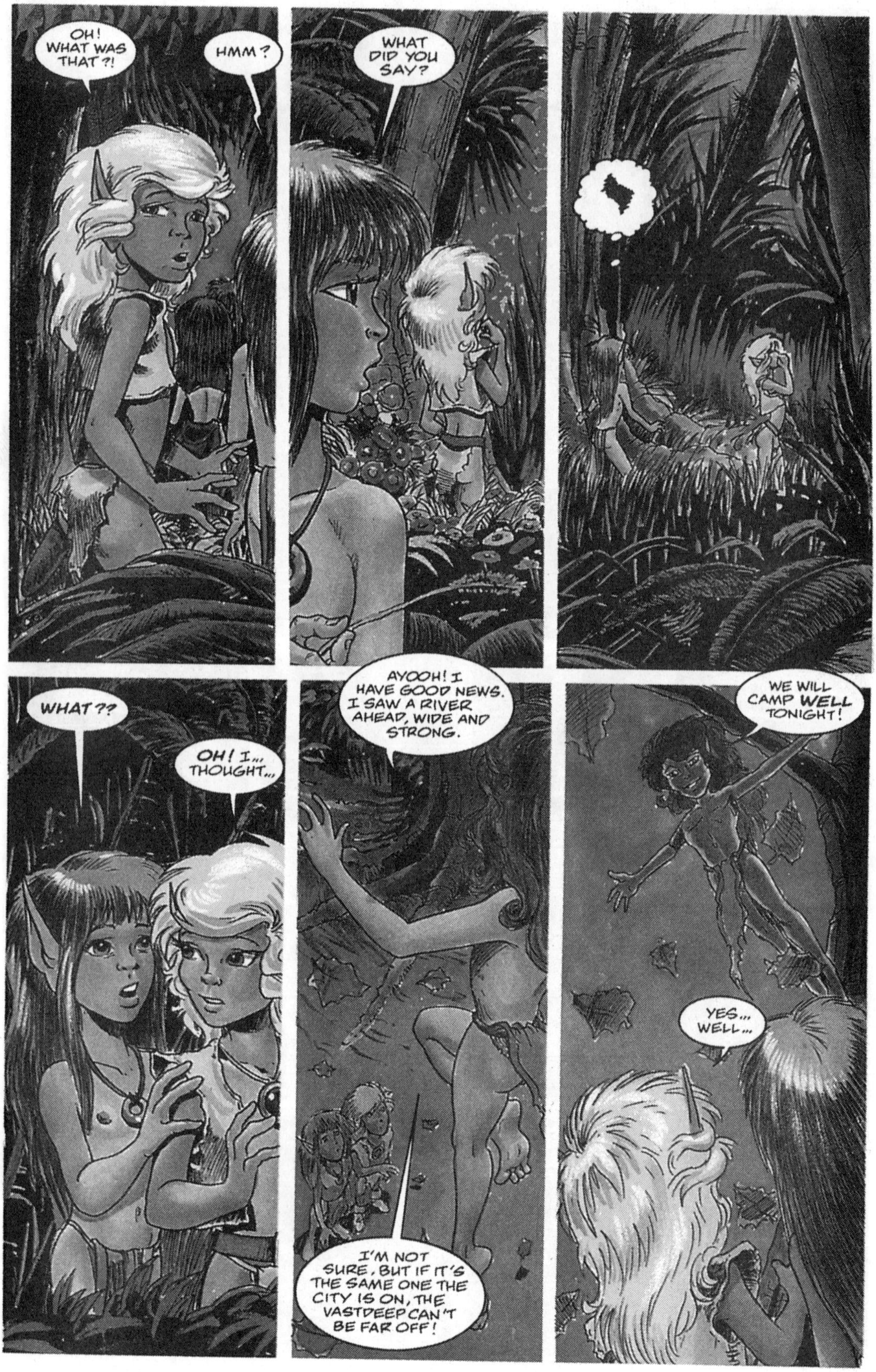
OH! WHAT WAS THAT?!
HMM?
WHAT DID YOU SAY?
WHAT??
OH! I... THOUGHT...
AYOOH! I HAVE GOOD NEWS. I SAW A RIVER AHEAD, WIDE AND STRONG.
I'M NOT SURE, BUT IF IT'S THE SAME ONE THE CITY IS ON, THE VASTDEEP CAN'T BE FAR OFF!
WE WILL CAMP **WELL** TONIGHT!
YES... WELL...

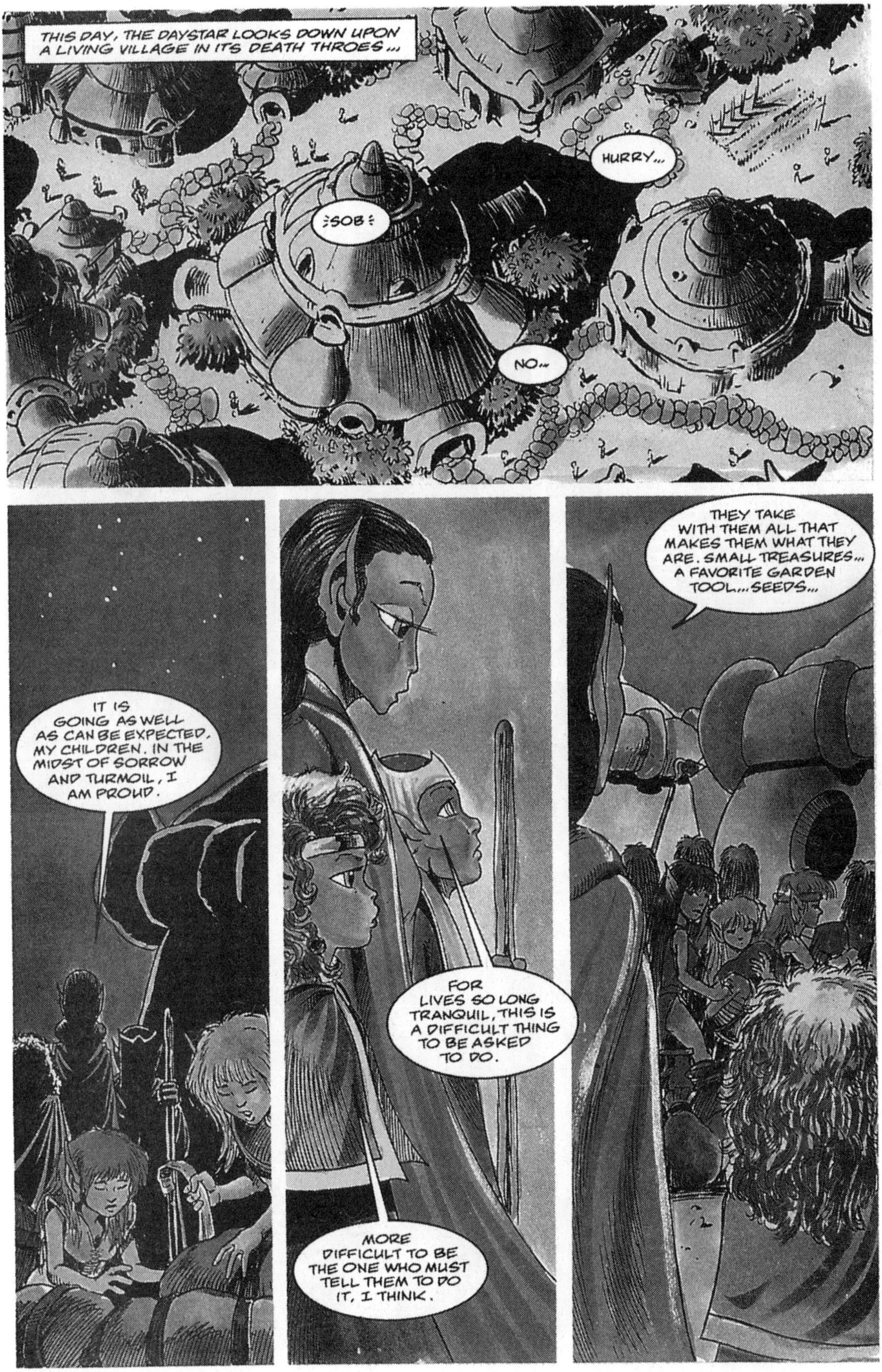
THIS DAY, THE DAYSTAR LOOKS DOWN UPON A LIVING VILLAGE IN ITS DEATH THROES...
HURRY...
SOB
NO...
IT IS GOING AS WELL AS CAN BE EXPECTED, MY CHILDREN. IN THE MIDST OF SORROW AND TURMOIL, I AM PROUD.
FOR LIVES SO LONG TRANQUIL, THIS IS A DIFFICULT THING TO BE ASKED TO DO.
MORE DIFFICULT TO BE THE ONE WHO MUST TELL THEM TO DO IT, I THINK.
THEY TAKE WITH THEM ALL THAT MAKES THEM WHAT THEY ARE. SMALL TREASURES... A FAVORITE GARDEN TOOL... SEEDS...

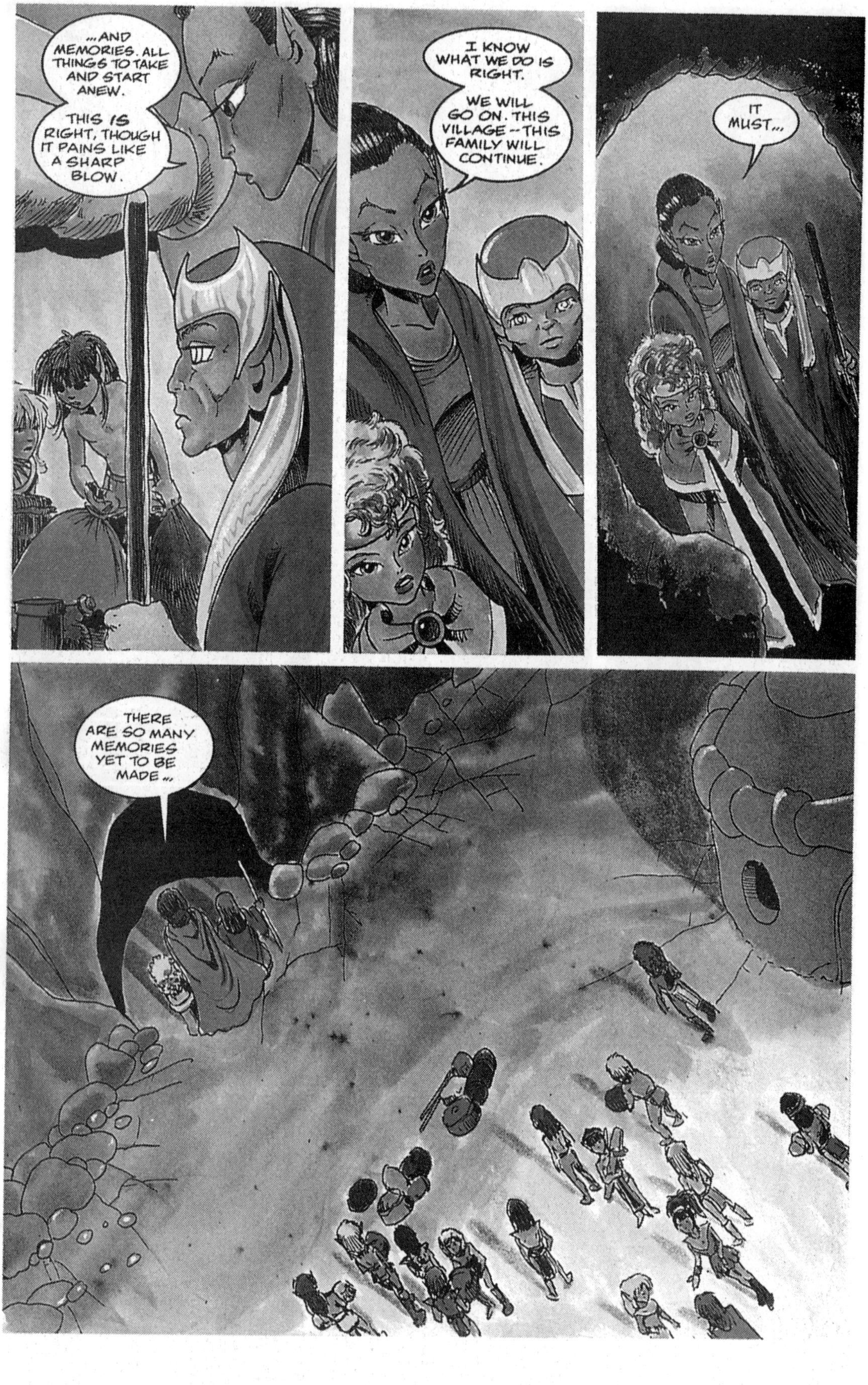
...AND MEMORIES. ALL THINGS TO TAKE AND START ANEW.
THIS IS RIGHT, THOUGH IT PAINS LIKE A SHARP BLOW.
I KNOW WHAT WE DO IS RIGHT.
WE WILL GO ON. THIS VILLAGE -- THIS FAMILY WILL CONTINUE.
IT MUST...
THERE ARE SO MANY MEMORIES YET TO BE MADE...

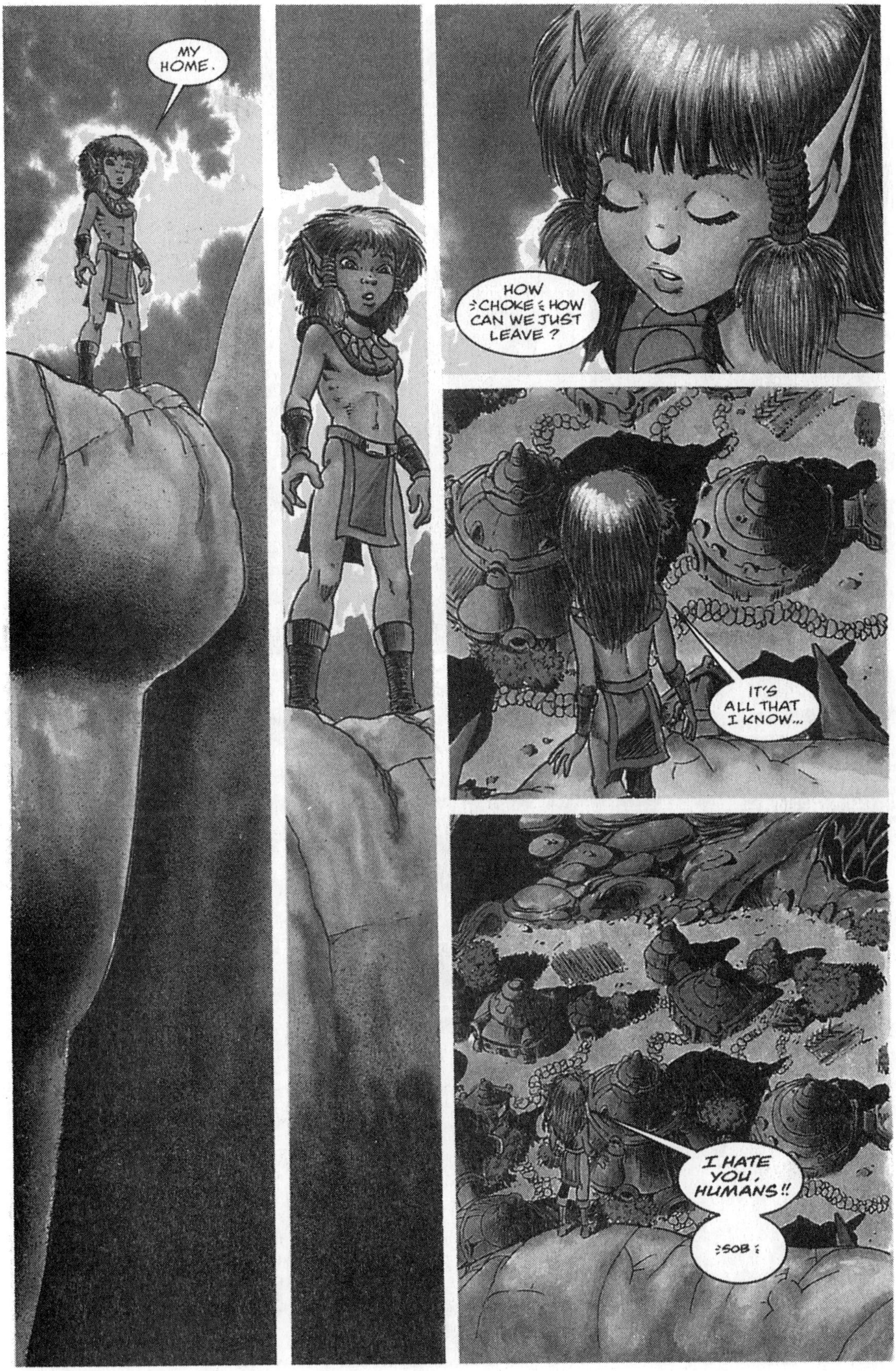
MY HOME.
HOW *CHOKE* HOW CAN WE JUST LEAVE?
IT'S ALL THAT I KNOW...
I HATE YOU, HUMANS!!
SOB

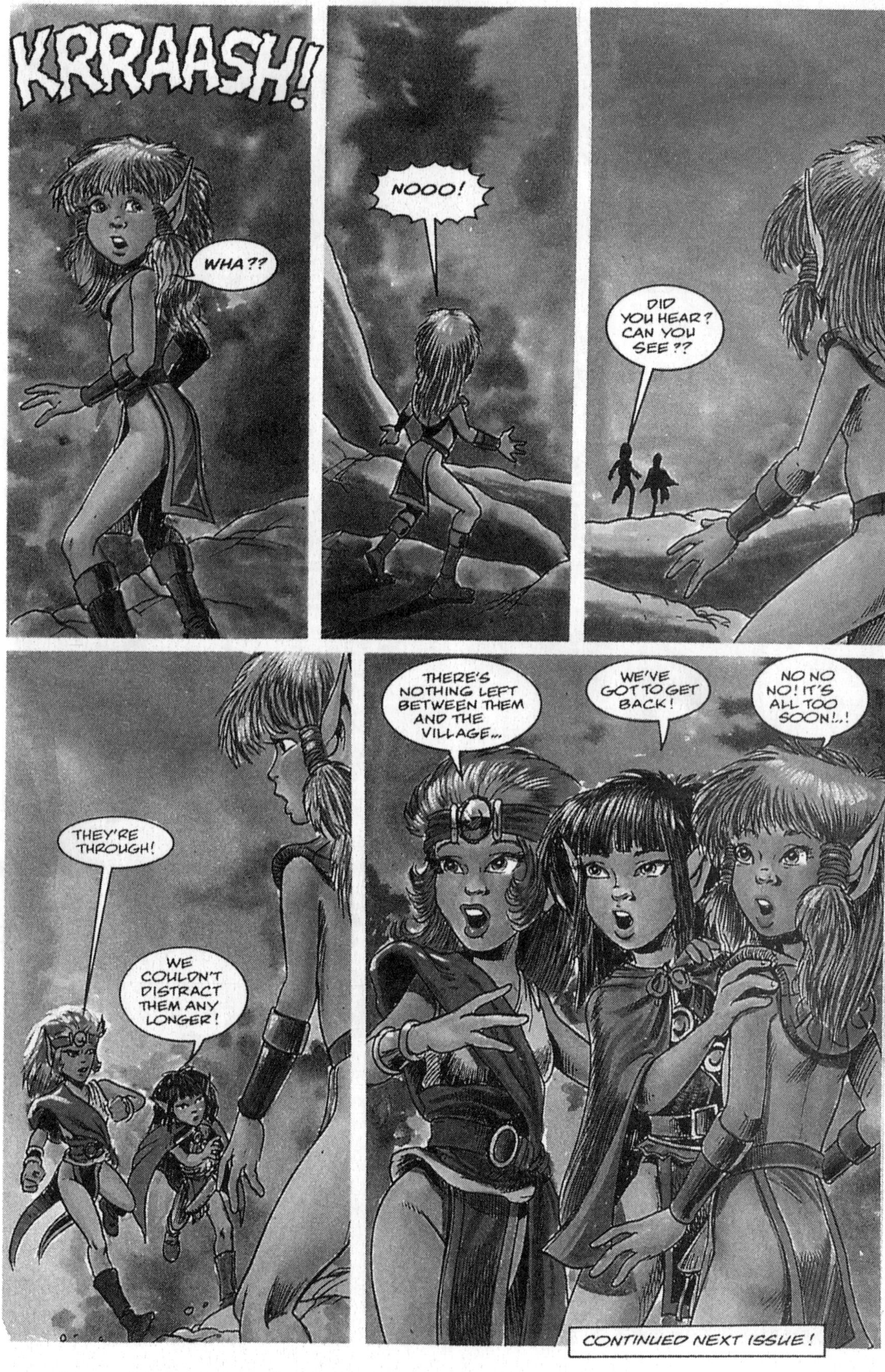
KRRAASH!
WHA??
NOOO!
DID YOU HEAR? CAN YOU SEE??
THEY'RE THROUGH!
WE COULDN'T DISTRACT THEM ANY LONGER!
THERE'S NOTHING LEFT BETWEEN THEM AND THE VILLAGE...
WE'VE GOT TO GET BACK!
NO NO NO! IT'S ALL TOO SOON!.!
CONTINUED NEXT ISSUE!

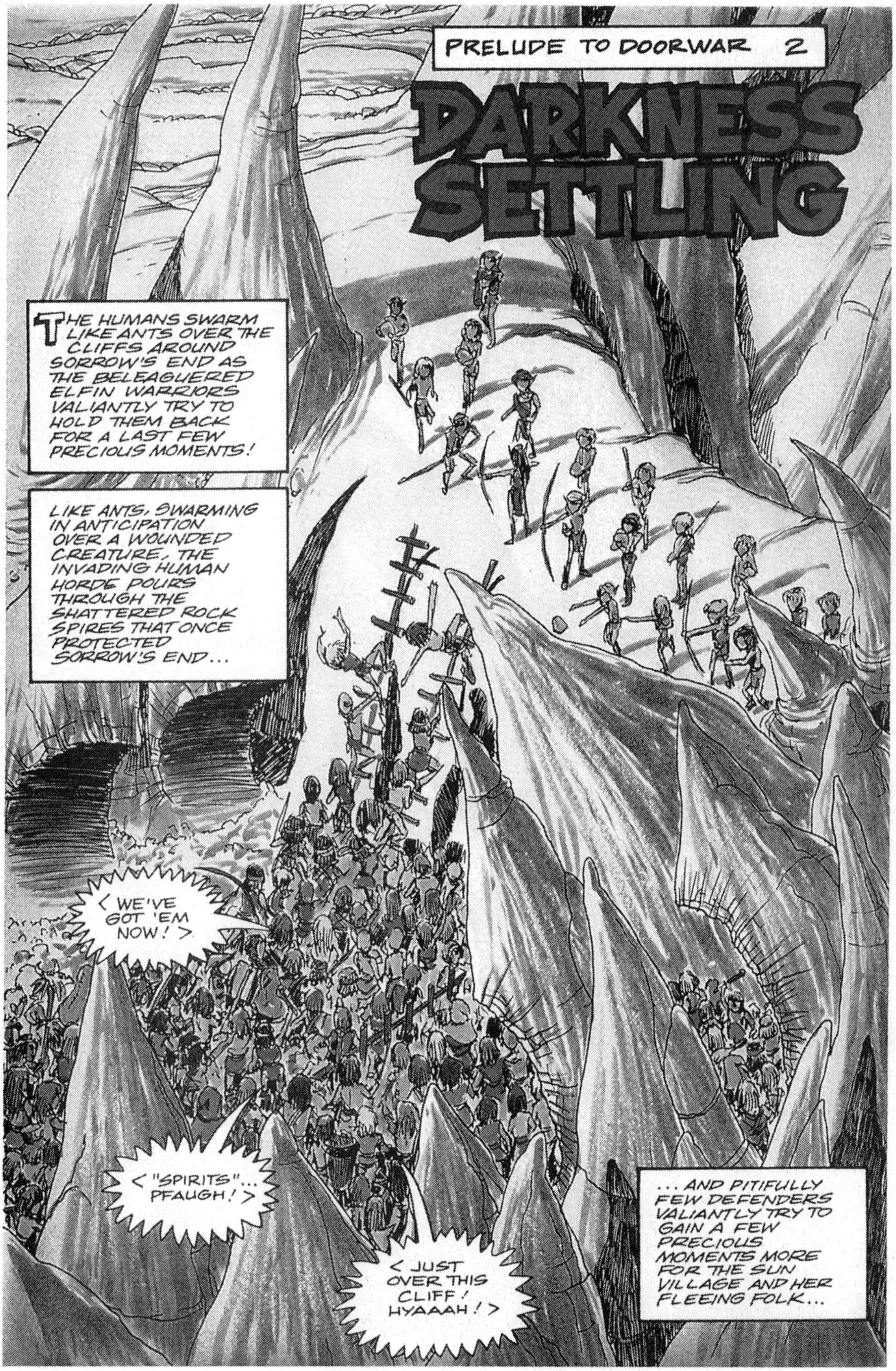
PRELUDE TO DOORWAR 2
DARKNESS SETTLING
THE HUMANS SWARM LIKE ANTS OVER THE CLIFFS AROUND SORROW'S END AS THE BELEAGUERED ELFIN WARRIORS VALIANTLY TRY TO HOLD THEM BACK FOR A LAST FEW PRECIOUS MOMENTS!
LIKE ANTS, SWARMING IN ANTICIPATION OVER A WOUNDED CREATURE, THE INVADING HUMAN HORDE POURS THROUGH THE SHATTERED ROCK SPIRES THAT ONCE PROTECTED SORROW'S END...
< WE'VE GOT 'EM NOW! >
< "SPIRITS"... PFAUGH! >
< JUST OVER THIS CLIFF! HYAAAH! >
... AND PITIFULLY FEW DEFENDERS VALIANTLY TRY TO GAIN A FEW PRECIOUS MOMENTS MORE FOR THE SUN VILLAGE AND HER FLEEING FOLK...

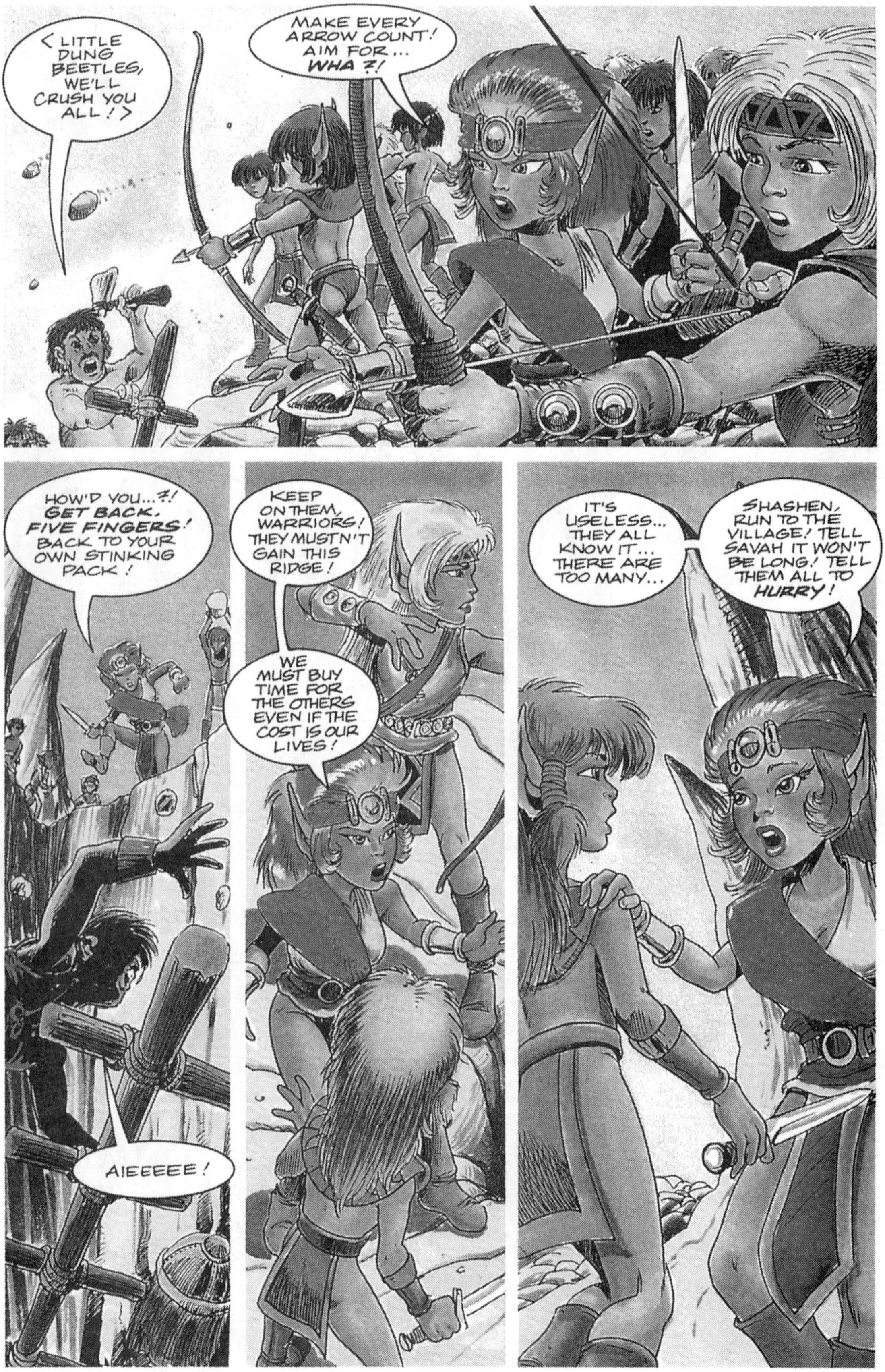

< LITTLE DUNG BEETLES, WE'LL CRUSH YOU ALL ! >
MAKE EVERY ARROW COUNT! AIM FOR... WHA ?!
HOW'D YOU...?! GET BACK, FIVE FINGERS! BACK TO YOUR OWN STINKING PACK!
AIEEEEE!
KEEP ON THEM, WARRIORS! THEY MUSTN'T GAIN THIS RIDGE!
WE MUST BUY TIME FOR THE OTHERS EVEN IF THE COST IS OUR LIVES!
IT'S USELESS... THEY ALL KNOW IT... THERE ARE TOO MANY...
SHASHEN, RUN TO THE VILLAGE! TELL SAVAH IT WON'T BE LONG! TELL THEM ALL TO HURRY!

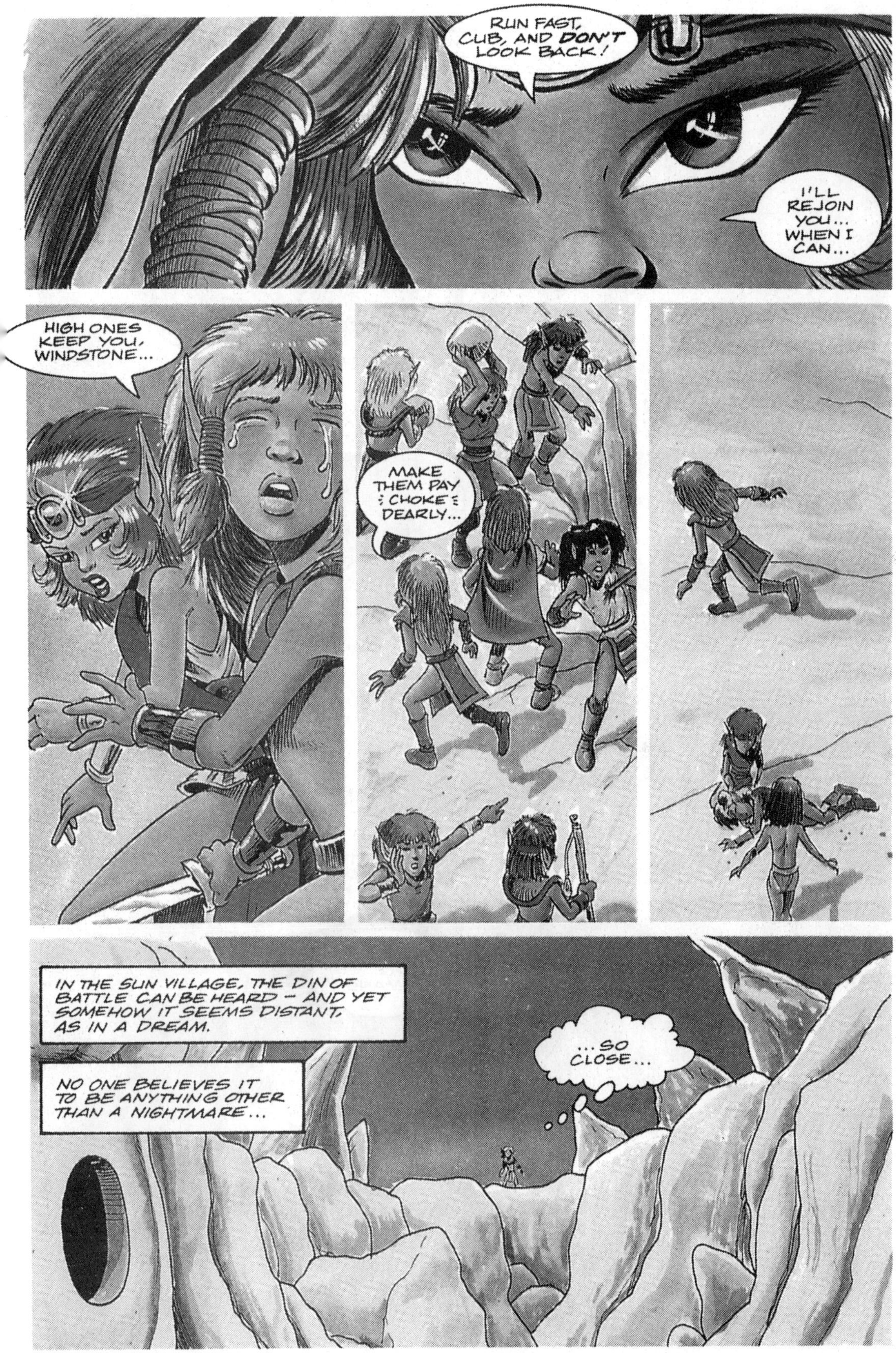
RUN FAST, CUB, AND DON'T LOOK BACK!
I'LL REJOIN YOU... WHEN I CAN...
HIGH ONES KEEP YOU, WINDSTONE...
MAKE THEM PAY DEARLY...
CHOKE
IN THE SUN VILLAGE, THE DIN OF BATTLE CAN BE HEARD — AND YET SOMEHOW IT SEEMS DISTANT, AS IN A DREAM.
NO ONE BELIEVES IT TO BE ANYTHING OTHER THAN A NIGHTMARE...
...SO CLOSE...

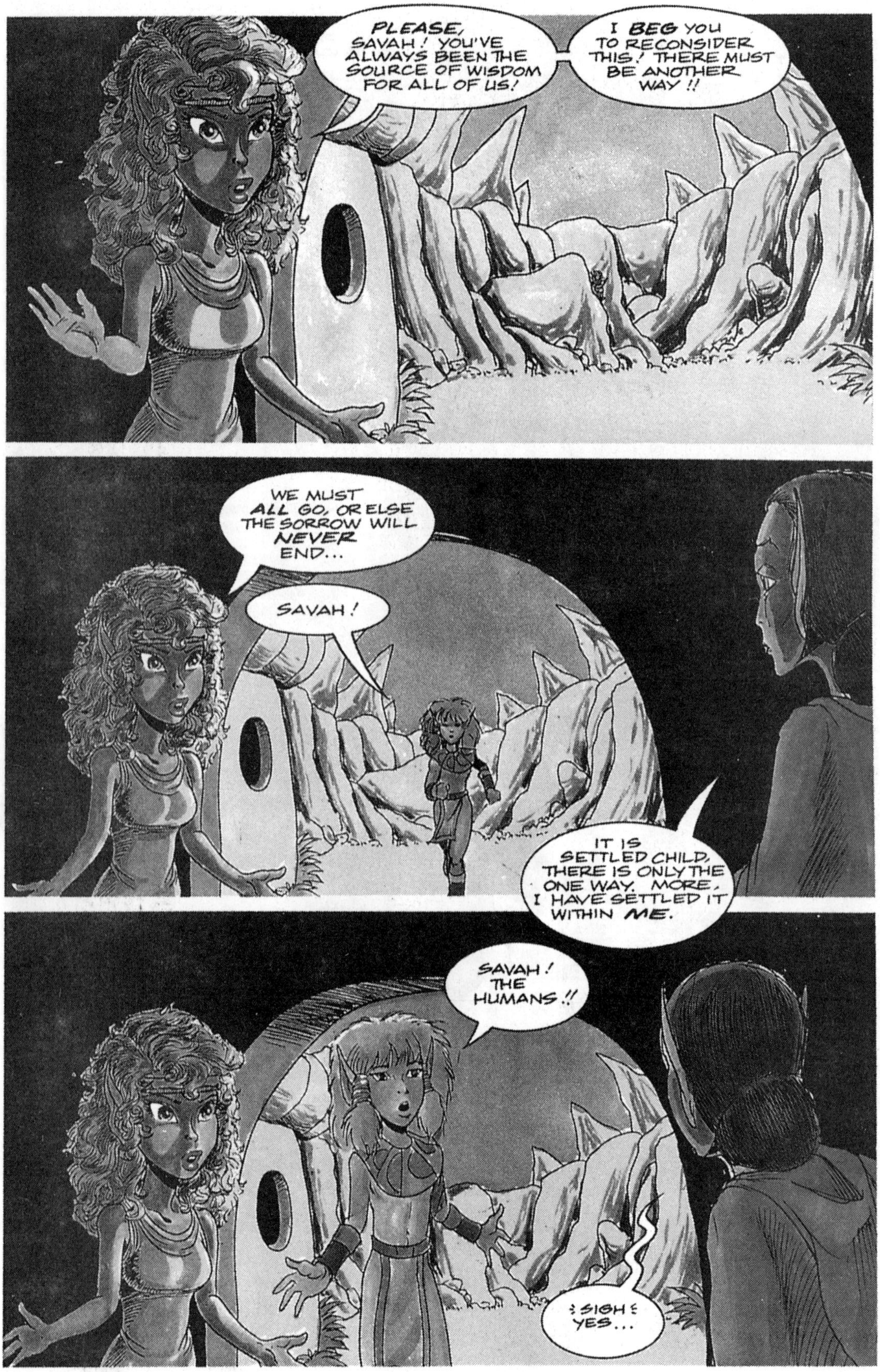
PLEASE, SAVAH! YOU'VE ALWAYS BEEN THE SOURCE OF WISDOM FOR ALL OF US!
I BEG YOU TO RECONSIDER THIS! THERE MUST BE ANOTHER WAY!!
WE MUST ALL GO, OR ELSE THE SORROW WILL NEVER END...
SAVAH!
IT IS SETTLED CHILD, THERE IS ONLY THE ONE WAY. MORE, I HAVE SETTLED IT WITHIN ME.
SAVAH! THE HUMANS!!
SIGH YES...

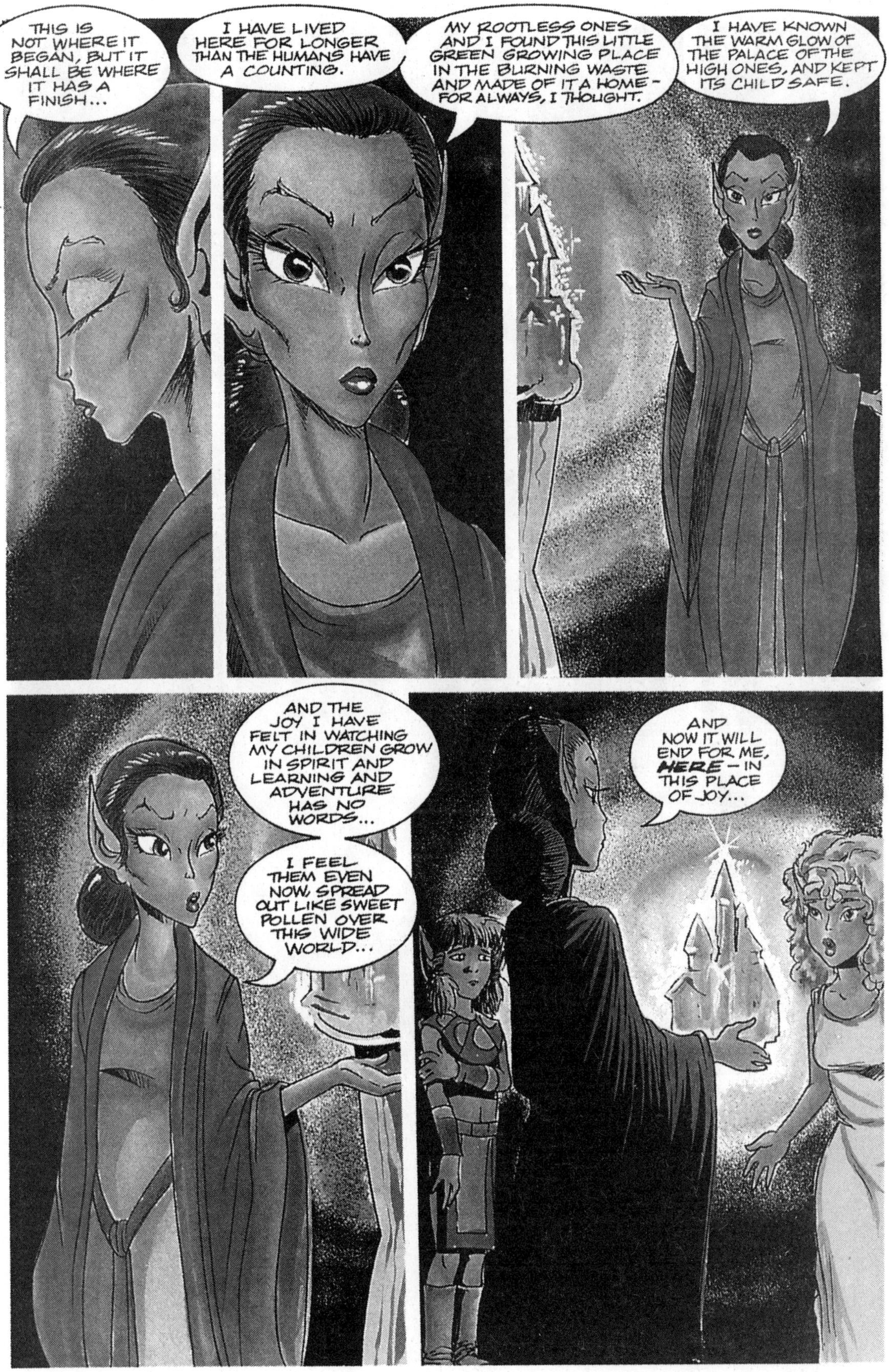
THIS IS NOT WHERE IT BEGAN, BUT IT SHALL BE WHERE IT HAS A FINISH...
I HAVE LIVED HERE FOR LONGER THAN THE HUMANS HAVE A COUNTING.
MY ROOTLESS ONES AND I FOUND THIS LITTLE GREEN GROWING PLACE IN THE BURNING WASTE AND MADE OF IT A HOME — FOR ALWAYS, I THOUGHT.
I HAVE KNOWN THE WARM GLOW OF THE PALACE OF THE HIGH ONES, AND KEPT ITS CHILD SAFE.
AND THE JOY I HAVE FELT IN WATCHING MY CHILDREN GROW IN SPIRIT AND LEARNING AND ADVENTURE HAS NO WORDS...
I FEEL THEM EVEN NOW, SPREAD OUT LIKE SWEET POLLEN OVER THIS WIDE WORLD...
AND NOW IT WILL END FOR ME, HERE — IN THIS PLACE OF JOY...

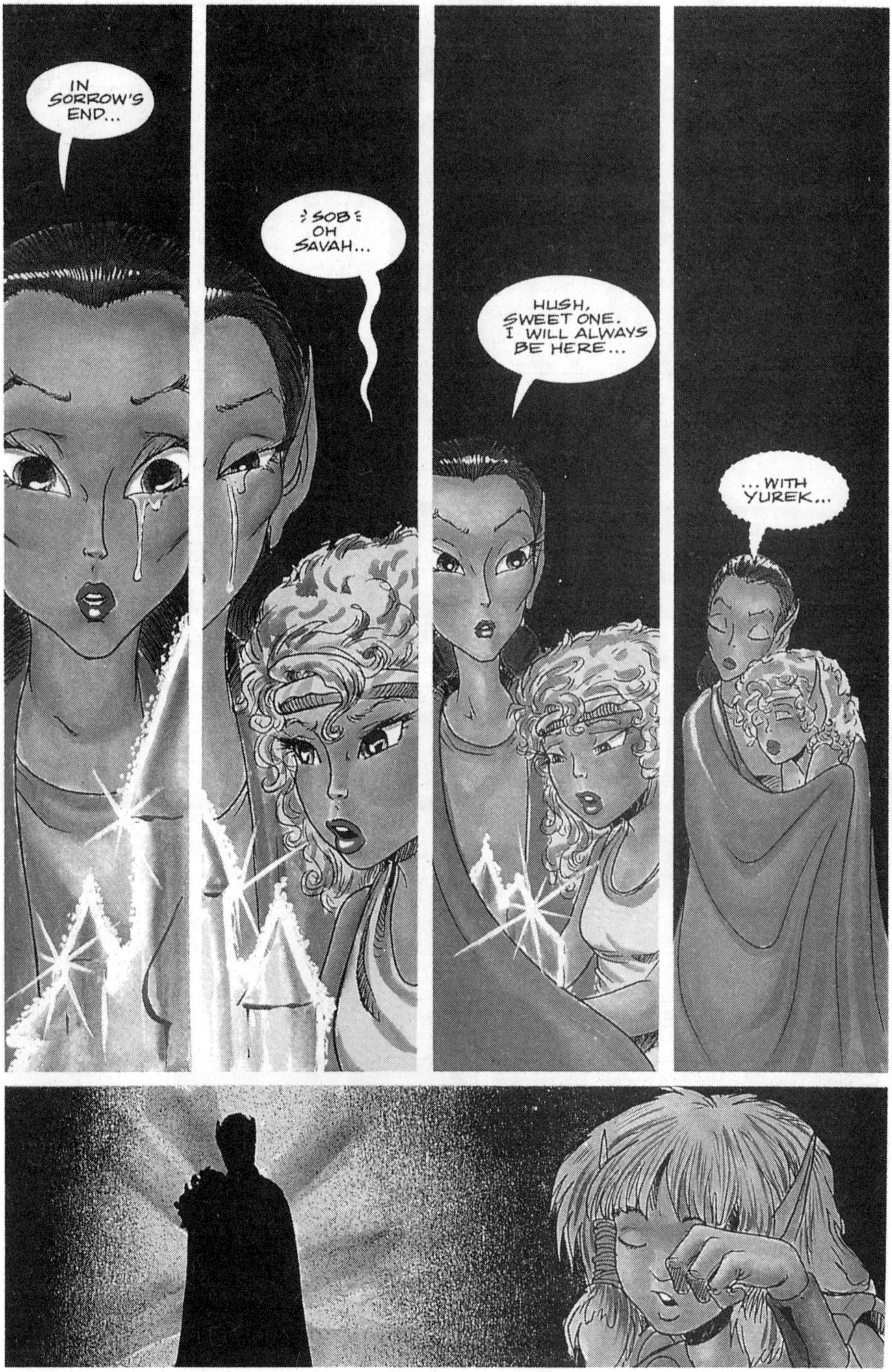
IN SORROW'S END...
SOB OH SAVAH...
HUSH, SWEET ONE. I WILL ALWAYS BE HERE...
...WITH YUREK...

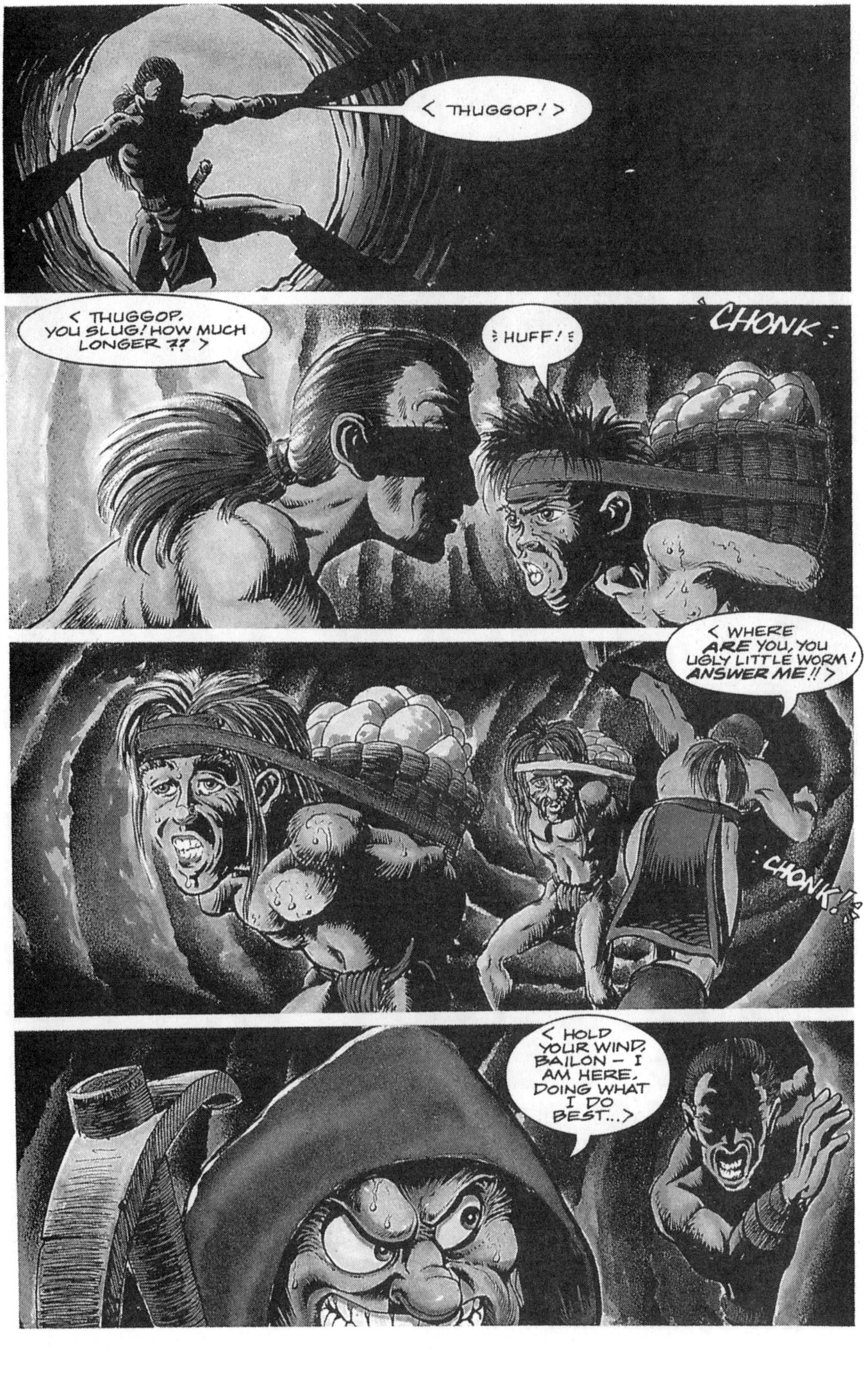
< THUGGOP! >
< THUGGOP, YOU SLUG! HOW MUCH LONGER ?? >
HUFF!
CHONK
< WHERE ARE YOU, YOU UGLY LITTLE WORM! ANSWER ME!! >
CHONK!
< HOLD YOUR WIND, BAILON - I AM HERE, DOING WHAT I DO BEST... >

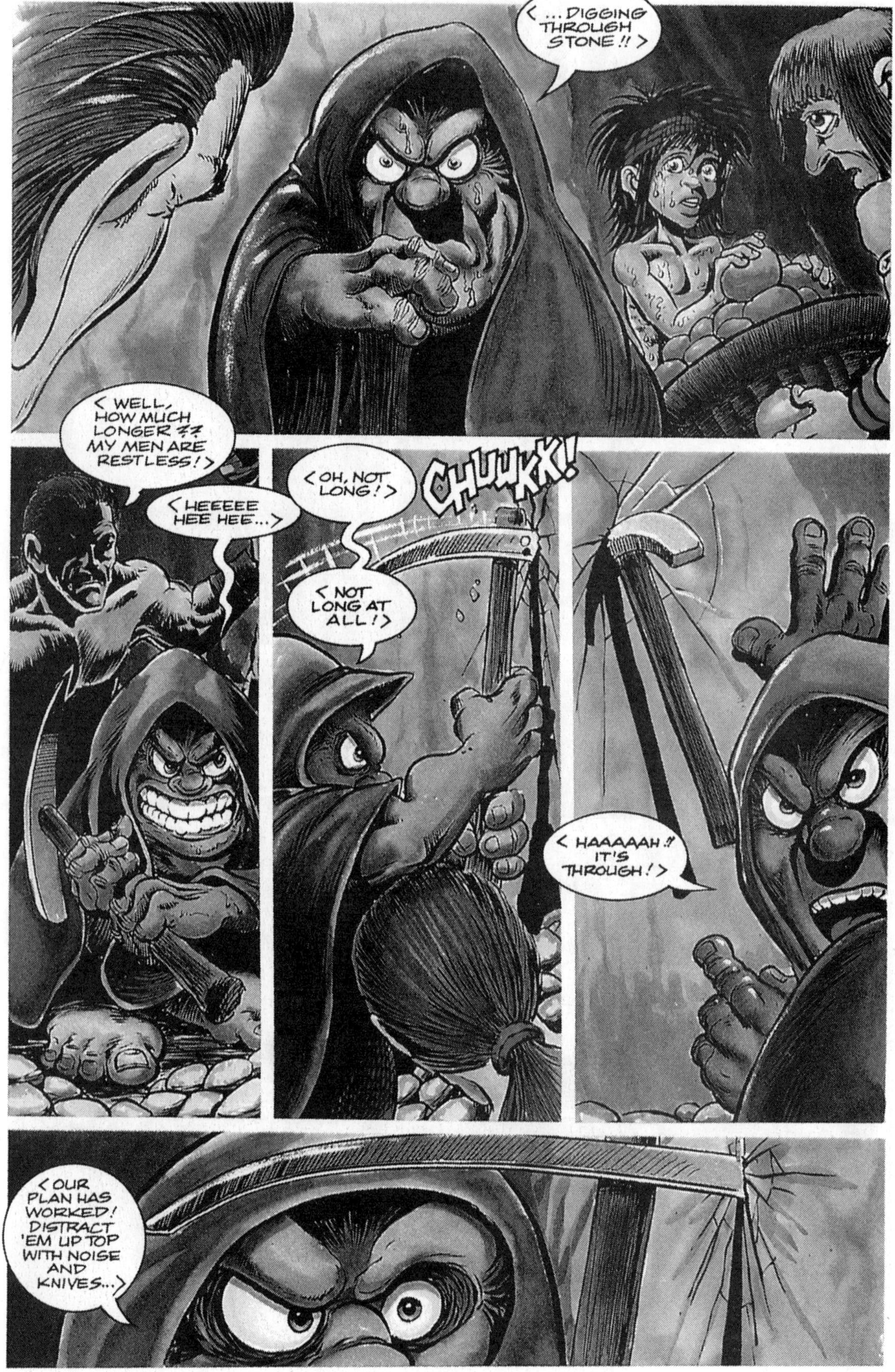
< ...DIGGING THROUGH STONE!! >
< WELL, HOW MUCH LONGER ?? MY MEN ARE RESTLESS! >
< HEEEEE HEE HEE... >
< OH, NOT LONG! >
< NOT LONG AT ALL! >
CHUUKK!
< HAAAAAH!! IT'S THROUGH! >
< OUR PLAN HAS WORKED! DISTRACT 'EM UP TOP WITH NOISE AND KNIVES... >

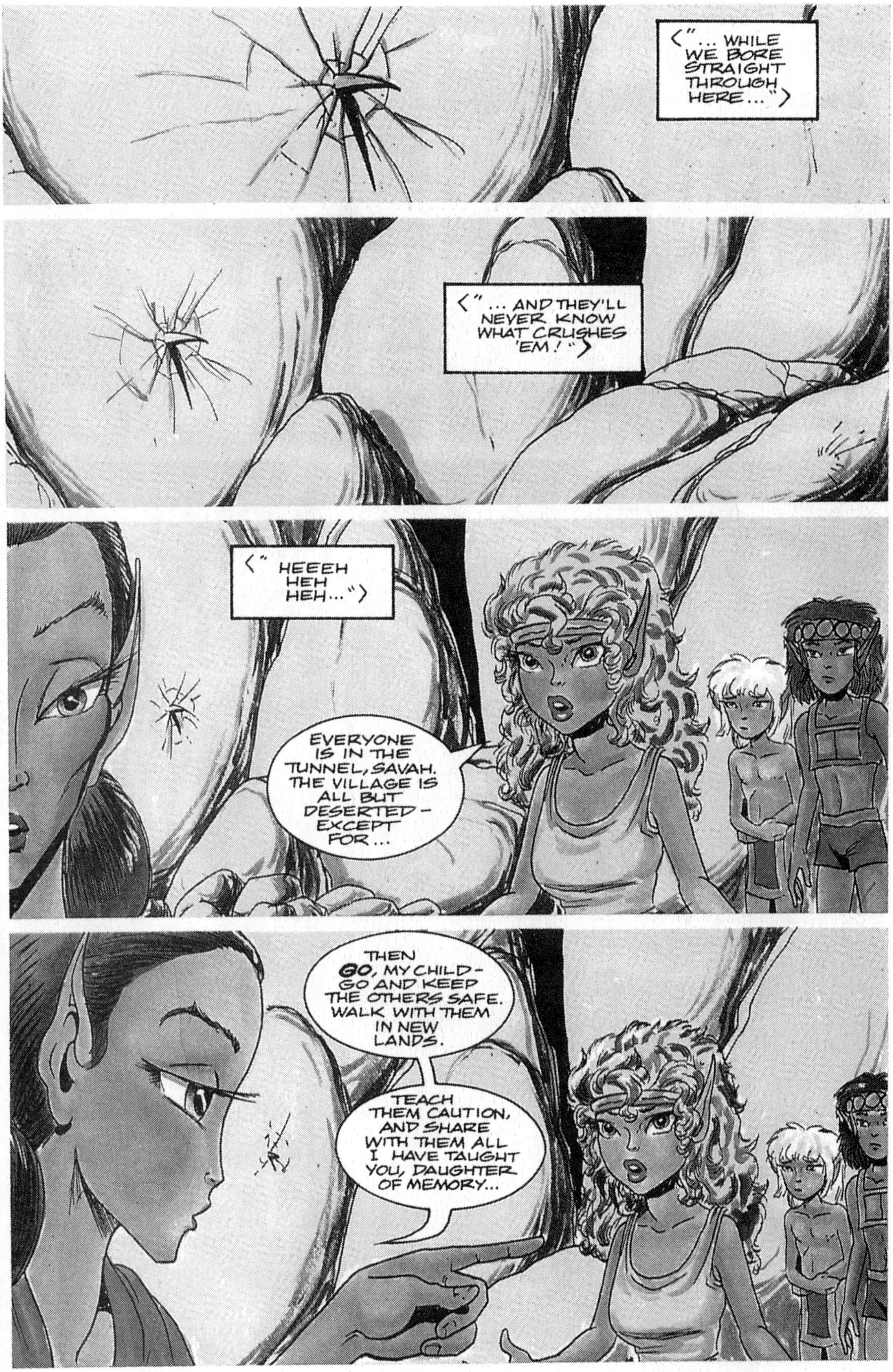
<"... WHILE WE BORE STRAIGHT THROUGH HERE...">
<"... AND THEY'LL NEVER KNOW WHAT CRUSHES 'EM!">
<" HEEEH HEH HEH...">
EVERYONE IS IN THE TUNNEL, SAVAH. THE VILLAGE IS ALL BUT DESERTED - EXCEPT FOR...
THEN GO, MY CHILD - GO AND KEEP THE OTHERS SAFE. WALK WITH THEM IN NEW LANDS.
TEACH THEM CAUTION, AND SHARE WITH THEM ALL I HAVE TAUGHT YOU, DAUGHTER OF MEMORY...

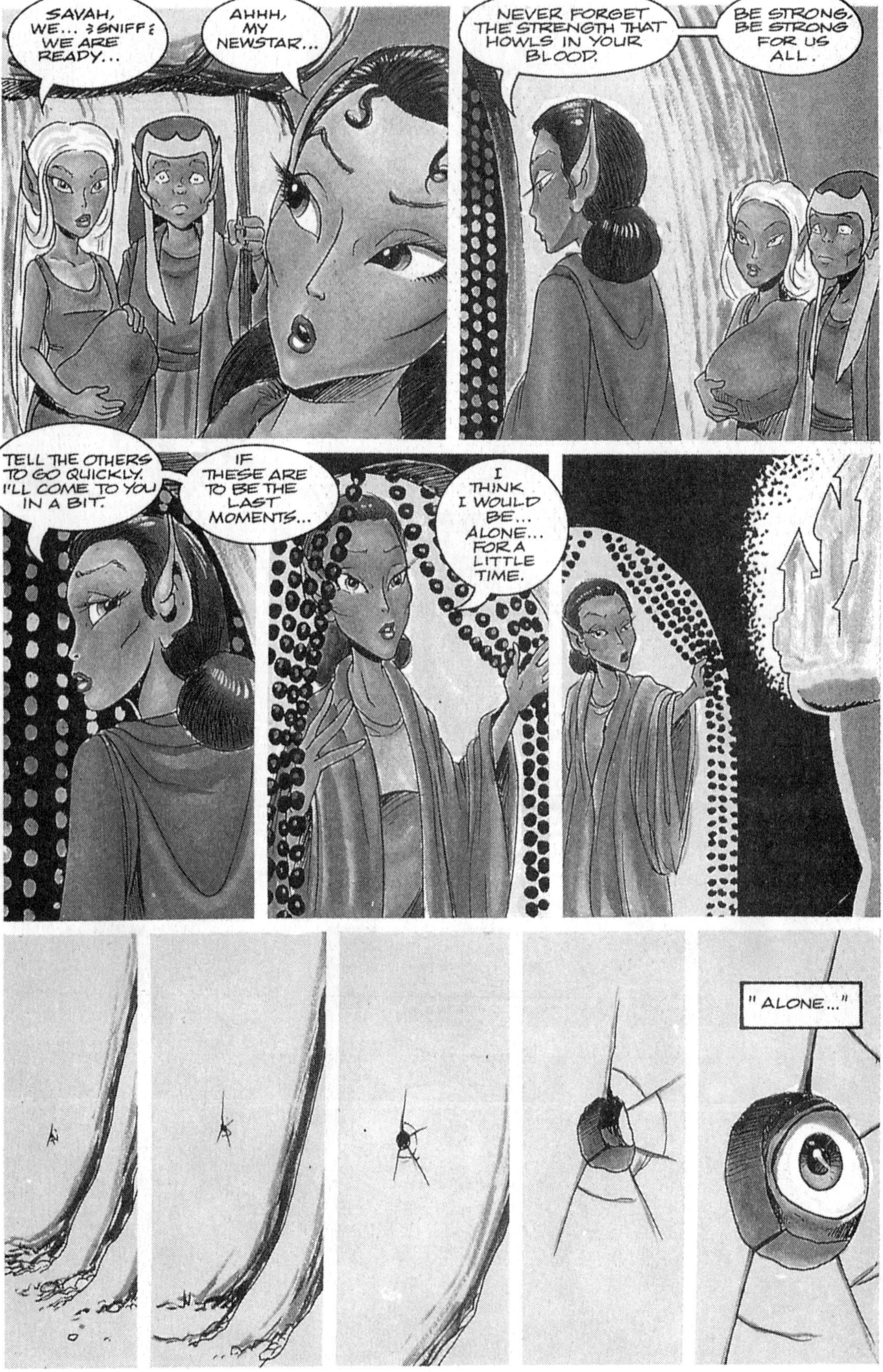
SAVAH, WE... ;SNIFF; WE ARE READY...
AHHH, MY NEWSTAR...
NEVER FORGET THE STRENGTH THAT HOWLS IN YOUR BLOOD.
BE STRONG, BE STRONG FOR US ALL.
TELL THE OTHERS TO GO QUICKLY. I'LL COME TO YOU IN A BIT.
IF THESE ARE TO BE THE LAST MOMENTS...
I THINK I WOULD BE... ALONE... FOR A LITTLE TIME.
"ALONE..."

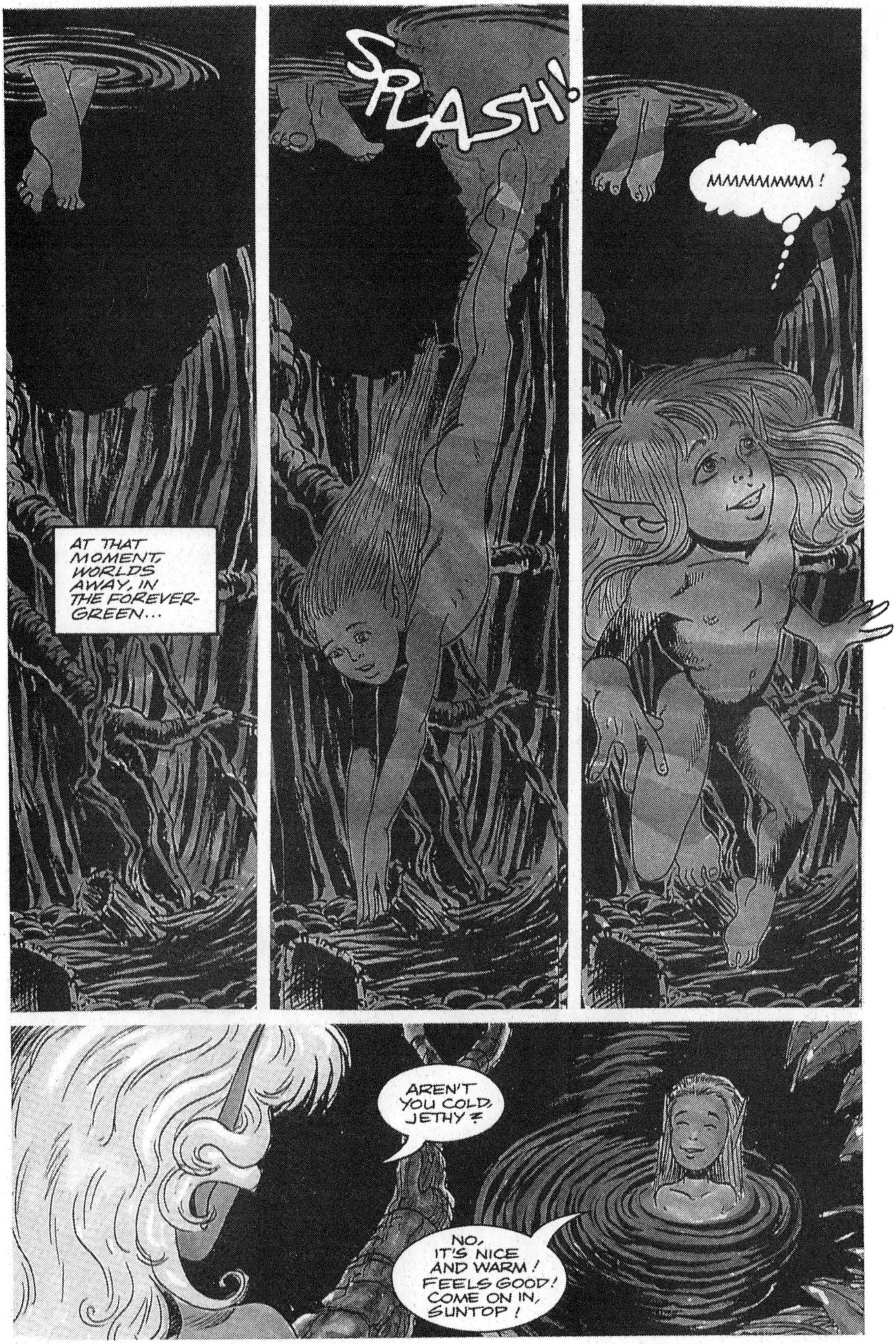
AT THAT MOMENT, WORLDS AWAY, IN THE FOREVER-GREEN...
SPLASH!
MMMMMMMM!
AREN'T YOU COLD, JETHY?
NO, IT'S NICE AND WARM! FEELS GOOD! COME ON IN, SUNTOP!

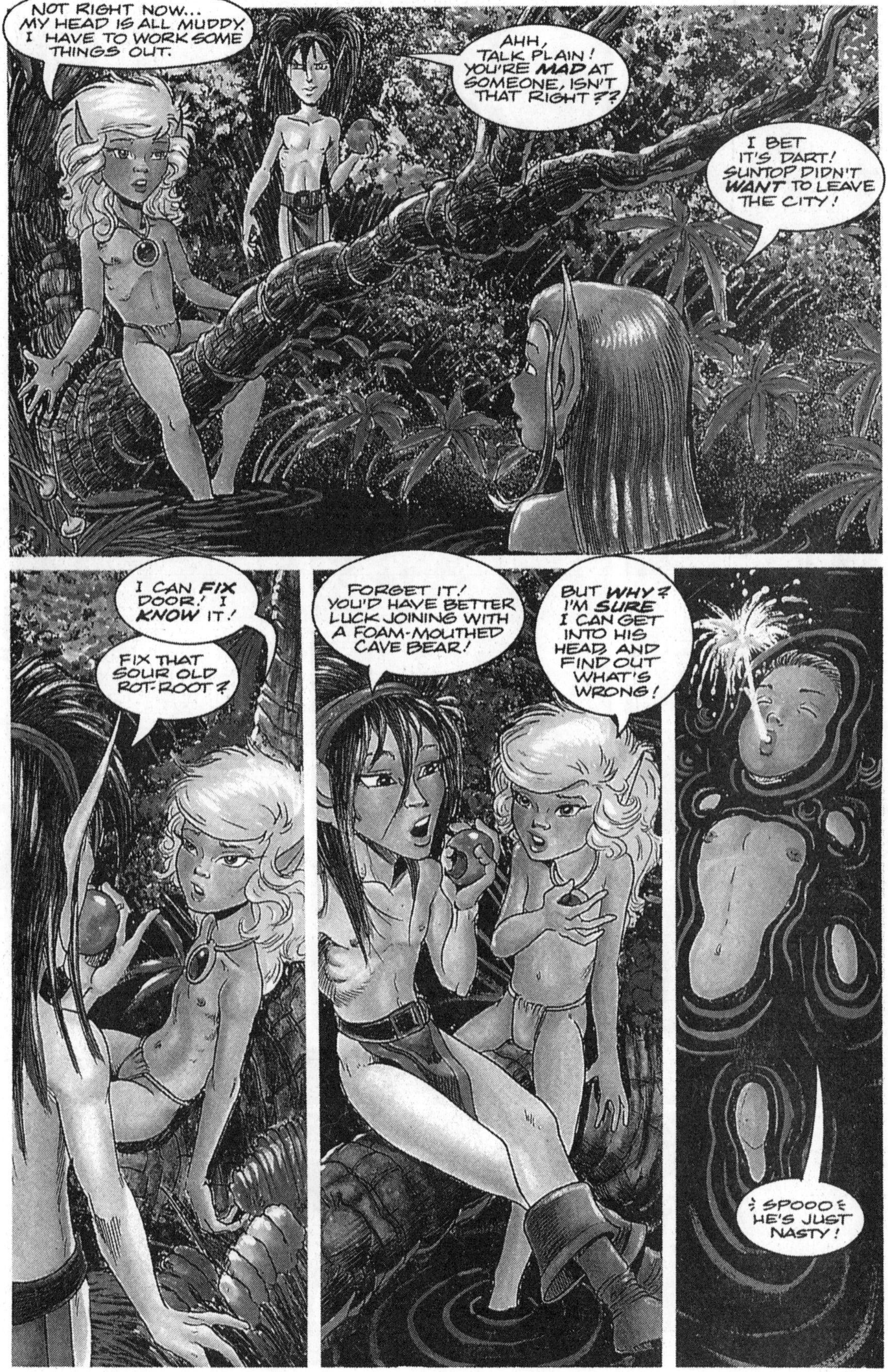
NOT RIGHT NOW... MY HEAD IS ALL MUDDY. I HAVE TO WORK SOME THINGS OUT.
AHH, TALK PLAIN! YOU'RE **MAD** AT SOMEONE, ISN'T THAT RIGHT??
I BET IT'S DART! SUNTOP DIDN'T **WANT** TO LEAVE THE CITY!
I CAN **FIX** DOOR! I **KNOW** IT!
FIX THAT SOUR OLD ROT-ROOT?
FORGET IT! YOU'D HAVE BETTER LUCK JOINING WITH A FOAM-MOUTHED CAVE BEAR!
BUT **WHY**? I'M **SURE** I CAN GET INTO HIS HEAD AND FIND OUT WHAT'S WRONG!
SPOOO HE'S JUST NASTY!

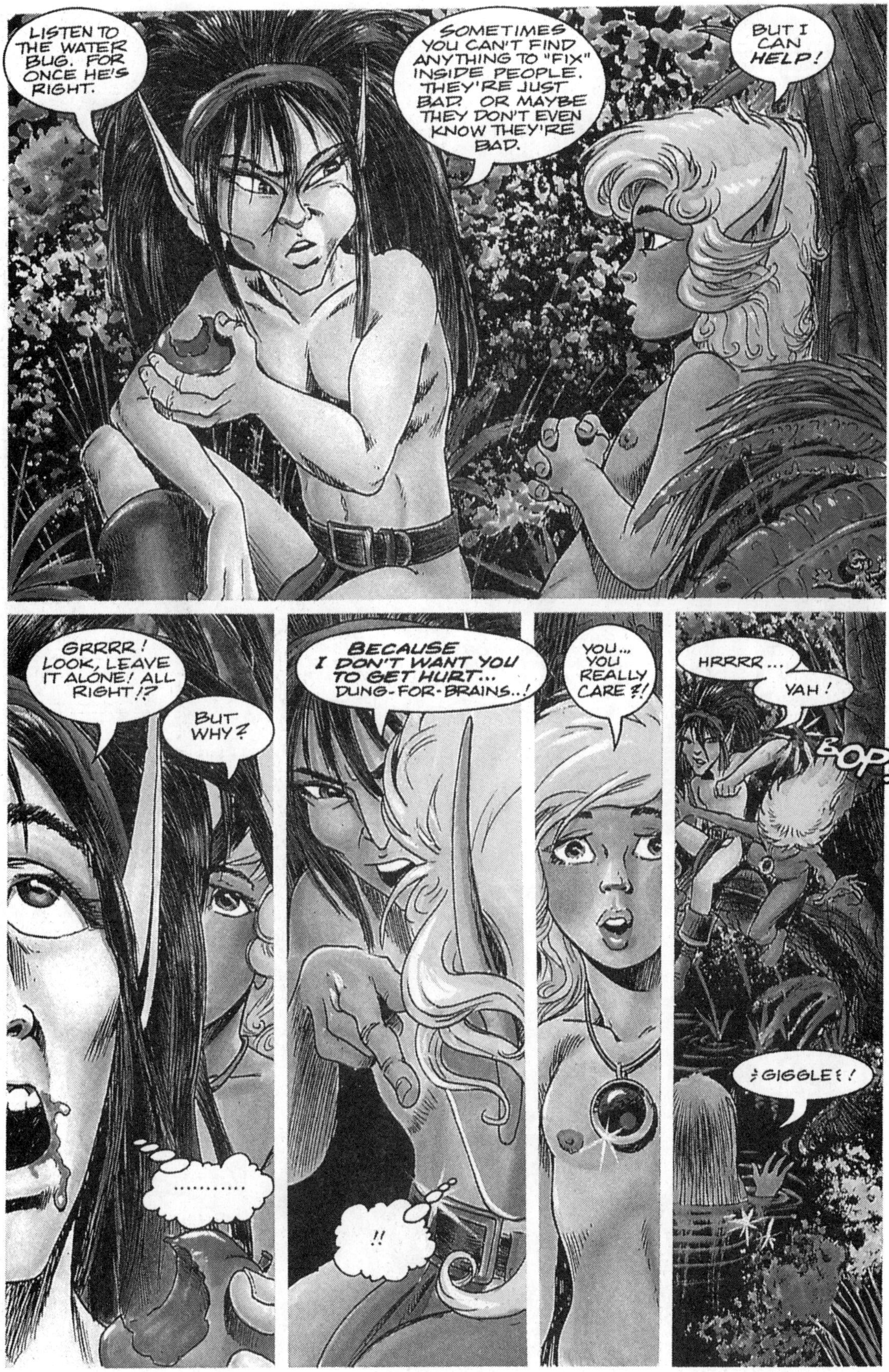
LISTEN TO THE WATER BUG. FOR ONCE HE'S RIGHT.
SOMETIMES YOU CAN'T FIND ANYTHING TO "FIX" INSIDE PEOPLE. THEY'RE JUST BAD. OR MAYBE THEY DON'T EVEN KNOW THEY'RE BAD.
BUT I CAN HELP!
GRRRR! LOOK, LEAVE IT ALONE! ALL RIGHT!?
BUT WHY?
....
BECAUSE I DON'T WANT YOU TO GET HURT... DUNG-FOR-BRAINS..!
!!
YOU... YOU REALLY CARE?!
HRRRR...
YAH!
BOP!
{GIGGLE}!

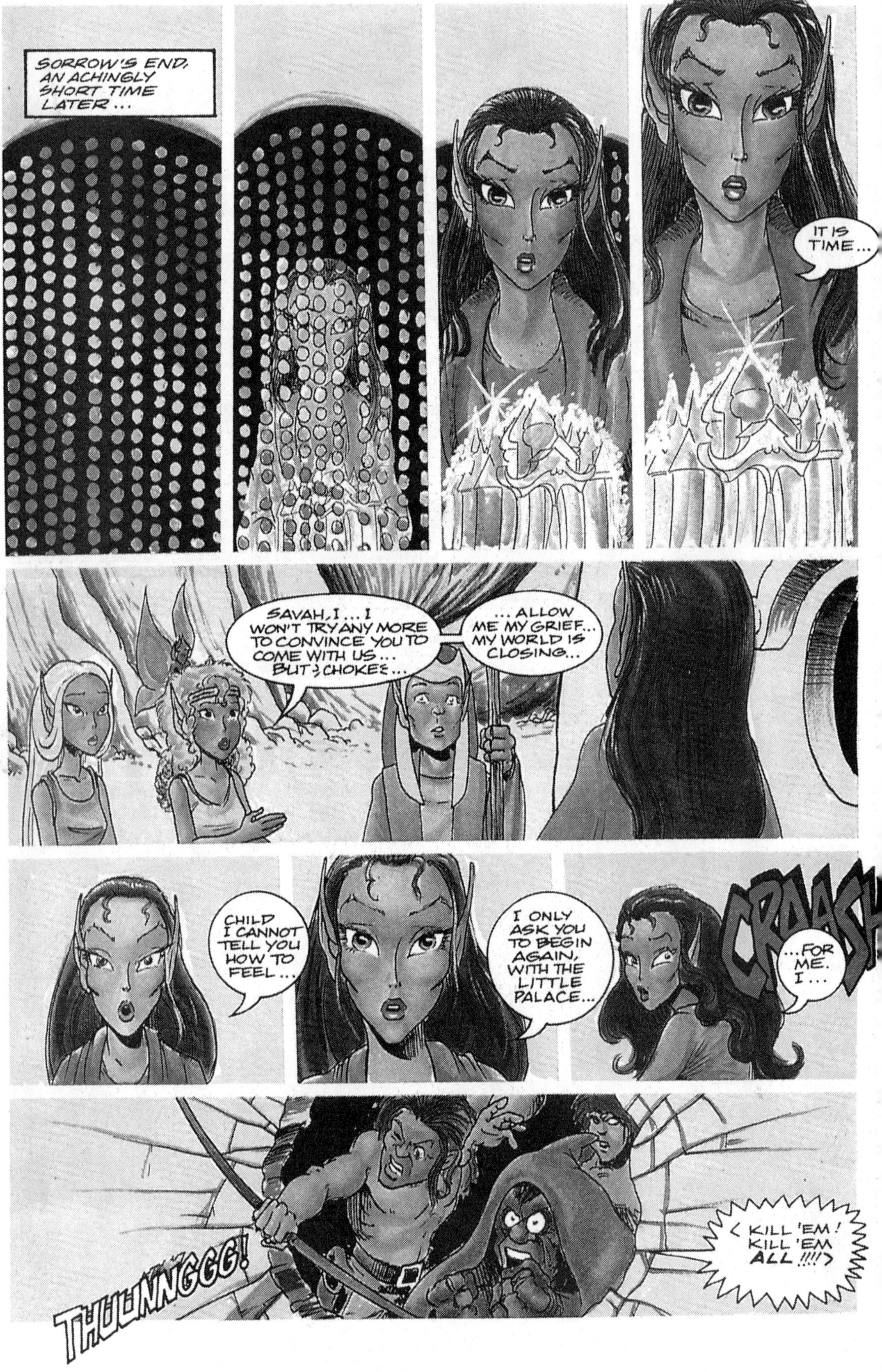

SORROW'S END, AN ACHINGLY SHORT TIME LATER...
IT IS TIME...
SAVAH, I... I WON'T TRY ANY MORE TO CONVINCE YOU TO COME WITH US... BUT ¿CHOKE¿...
...ALLOW ME MY GRIEF... MY WORLD IS CLOSING...
CHILD I CANNOT TELL YOU HOW TO FEEL...
I ONLY ASK YOU TO BEGIN AGAIN, WITH THE LITTLE PALACE...
...FOR ME. I...
CRASH
THUUNNGGG!
< KILL 'EM! KILL 'EM ALL!!!! >

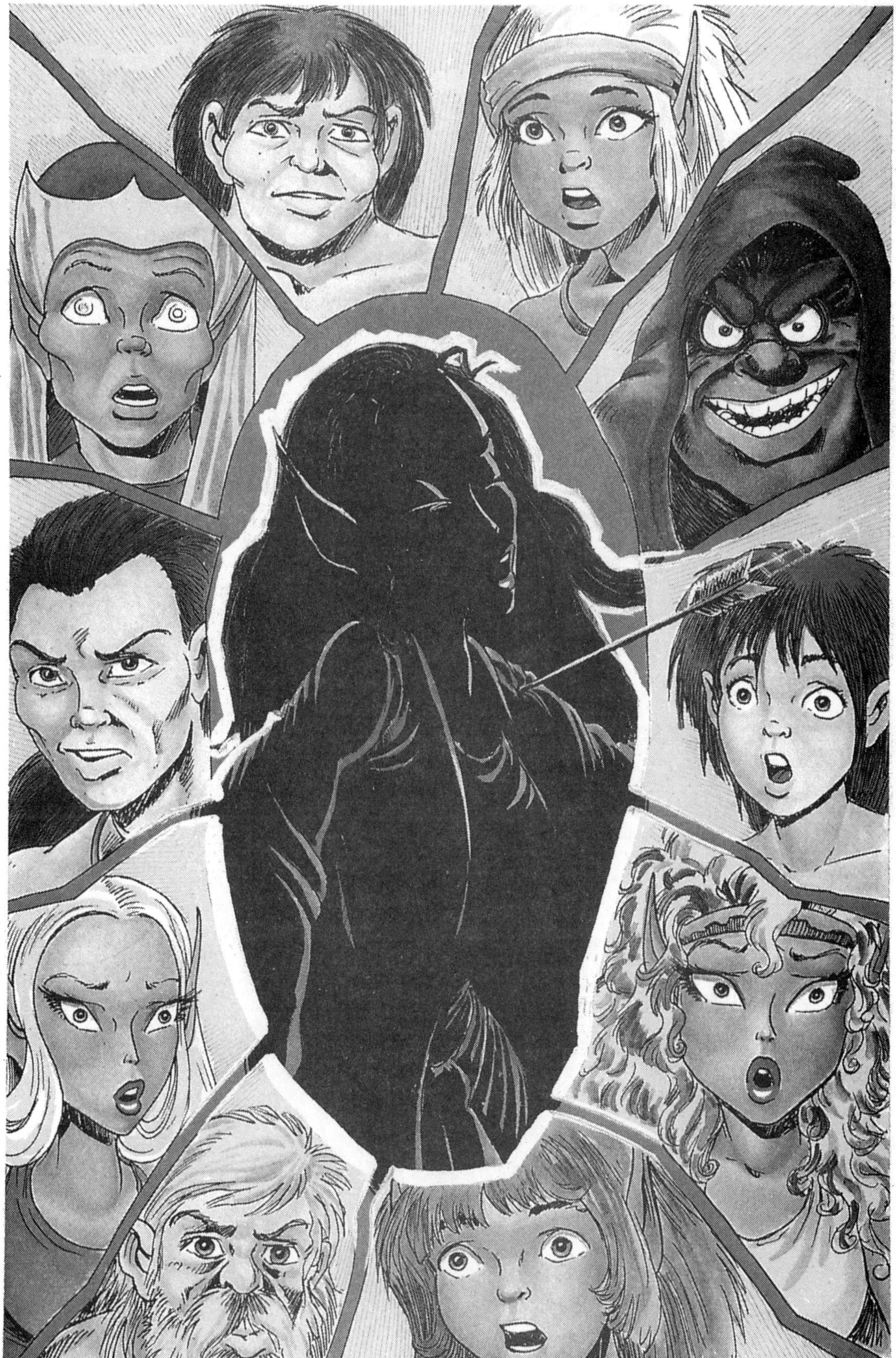

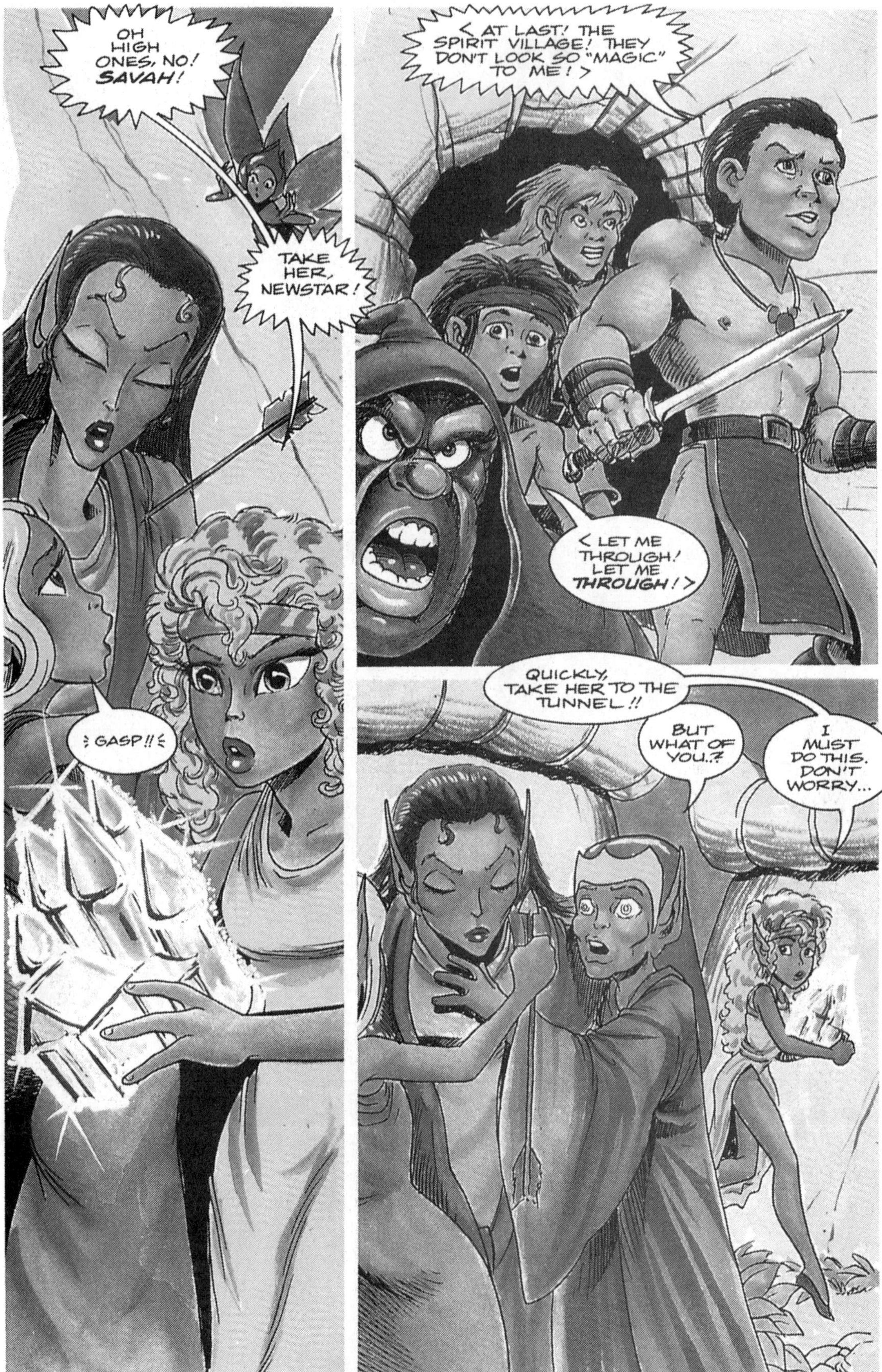

OH HIGH ONES, NO! SAVAH!
TAKE HER, NEWSTAR!
GASP!!
< AT LAST! THE SPIRIT VILLAGE! THEY DON'T LOOK SO "MAGIC" TO ME! >
< LET ME THROUGH! LET ME THROUGH! >
QUICKLY, TAKE HER TO THE TUNNEL!!
BUT WHAT OF YOU..?
I MUST DO THIS. DON'T WORRY...

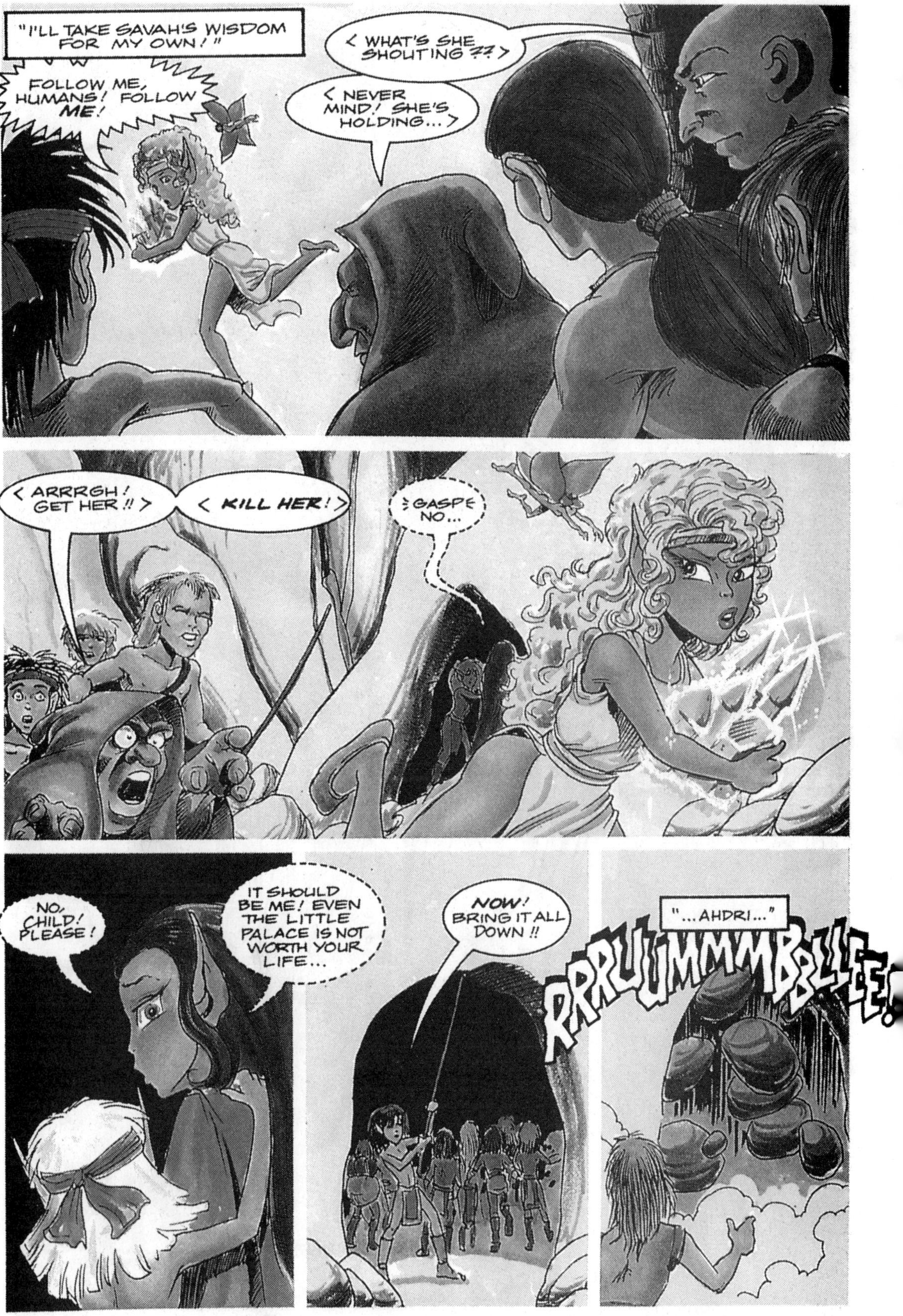
"I'LL TAKE SAVAH'S WISDOM FOR MY OWN!"
FOLLOW ME, HUMANS! FOLLOW ME!
< WHAT'S SHE SHOUTING ?? >
< NEVER MIND! SHE'S HOLDING... >
< ARRRGH! GET HER!! >
< KILL HER! >
GASP NO...
NO, CHILD! PLEASE!
IT SHOULD BE ME! EVEN THE LITTLE PALACE IS NOT WORTH YOUR LIFE...
NOW! BRING IT ALL DOWN!!
"...AHDRI..."
RRRUUMMMBBLLEE!

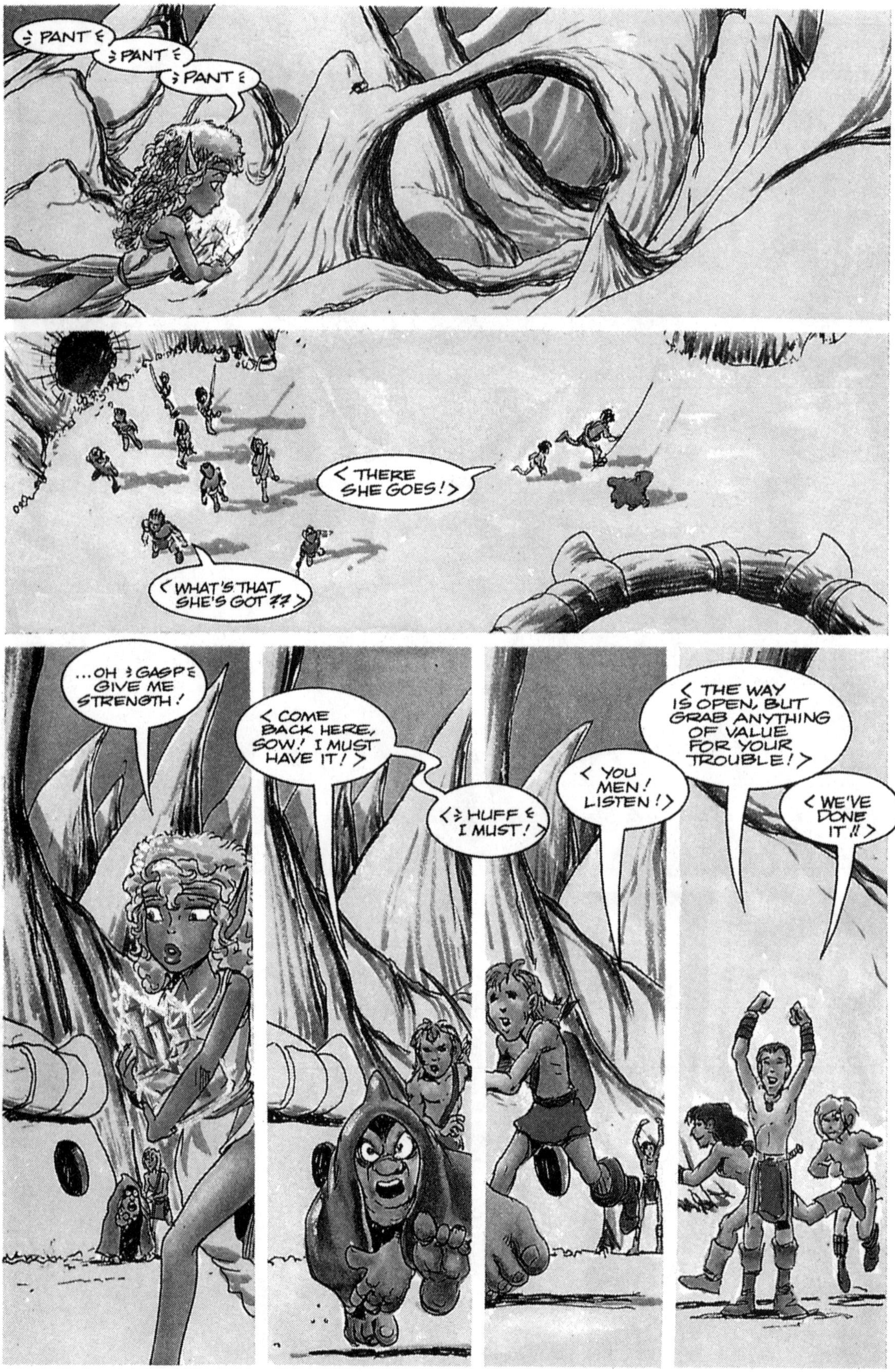

⋛ PANT ⋚
⋛ PANT ⋚
⋛ PANT ⋚
< THERE SHE GOES! >
< WHAT'S THAT SHE'S GOT ?? >
...OH ⋛ GASP ⋚ GIVE ME STRENGTH!
< COME BACK HERE, SOW! I MUST HAVE IT! >
< ⋛ HUFF ⋚ I MUST! >
< YOU MEN! LISTEN! >
< THE WAY IS OPEN, BUT GRAB ANYTHING OF VALUE FOR YOUR TROUBLE! >
< WE'VE DONE IT!! >

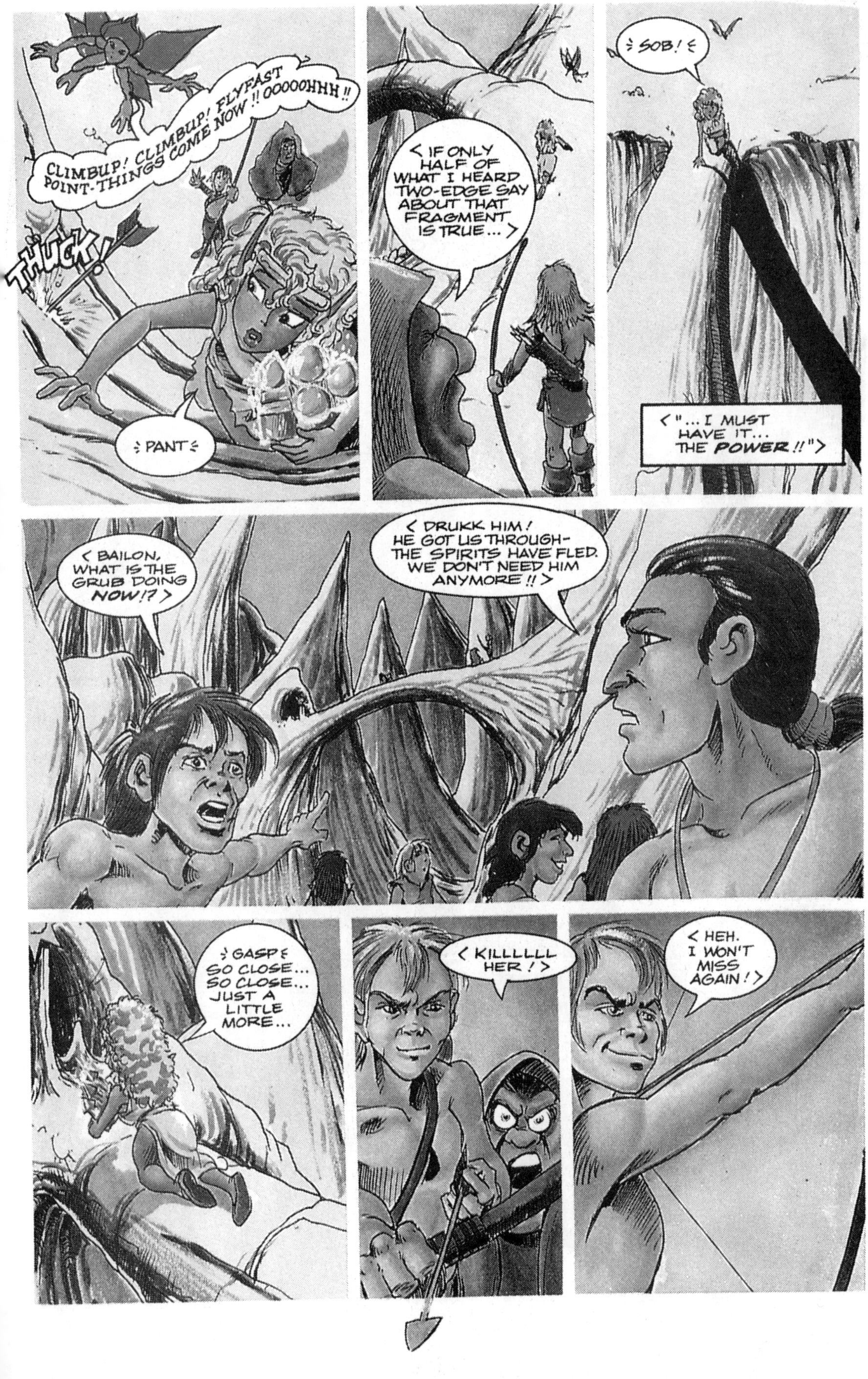
CLIMBUP! CLIMBUP! FLYFAST POINT-THINGS COME NOW!! OOOOOHHH!!
THUCK!
PANT
< IF ONLY HALF OF WHAT I HEARD TWO-EDGE SAY ABOUT THAT FRAGMENT IS TRUE... >
SOB!
< "...I MUST HAVE IT... THE POWER!!" >
< BAILON, WHAT IS THE GRUB DOING NOW!? >
< DRUKK HIM! HE GOT US THROUGH- THE SPIRITS HAVE FLED. WE DON'T NEED HIM ANYMORE!! >
GASP SO CLOSE... SO CLOSE... JUST A LITTLE MORE...
< KILLLLLL HER! >
< HEH. I WON'T MISS AGAIN! >

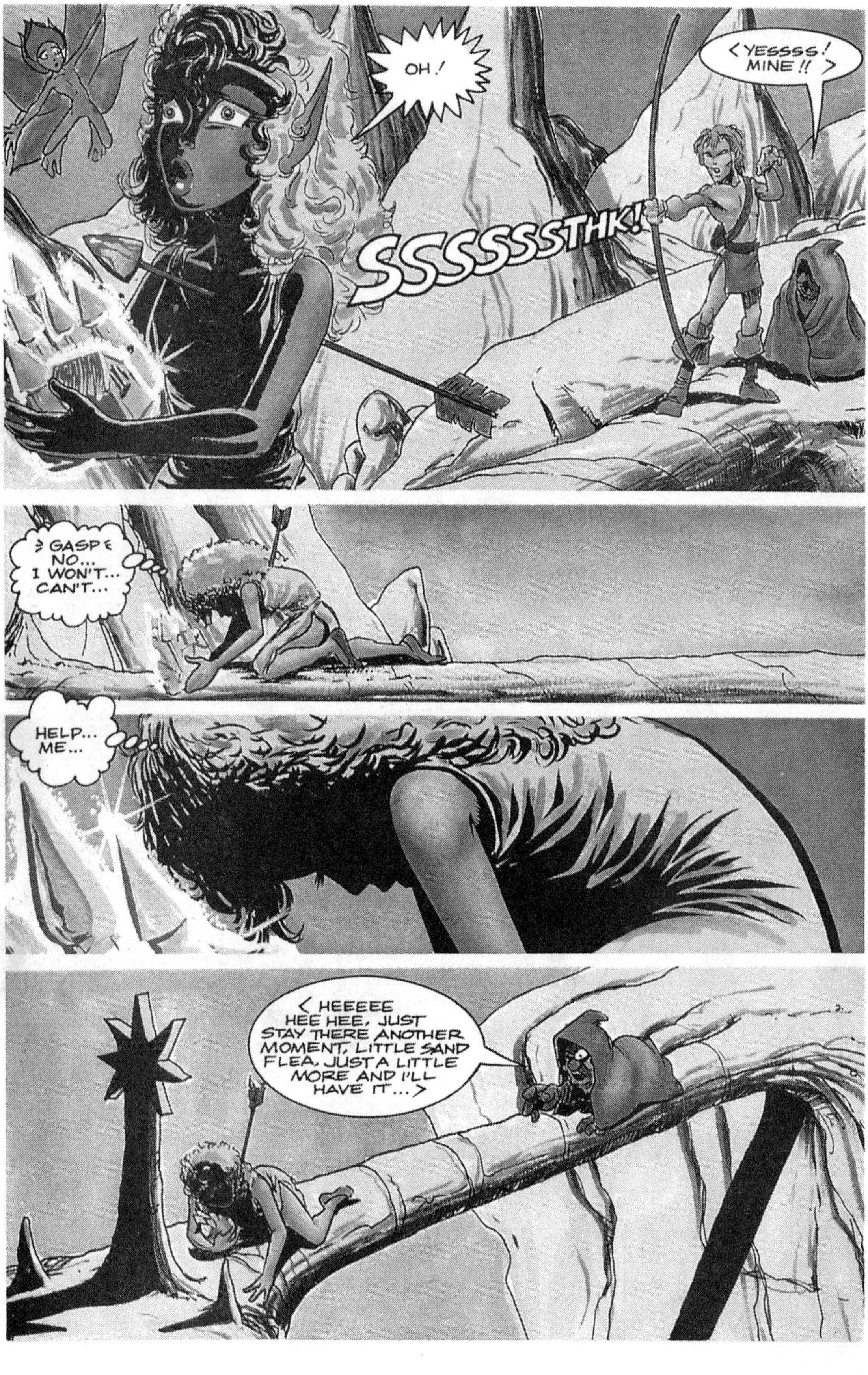
OH!
<YESSSS! MINE!!>
SSSSSSSTHK!
≥GASP≤ NO... I WON'T... CAN'T...
HELP... ME...
<HEEEEE HEE HEE, JUST STAY THERE ANOTHER MOMENT, LITTLE SAND FLEA. JUST A LITTLE MORE AND I'LL HAVE IT...>

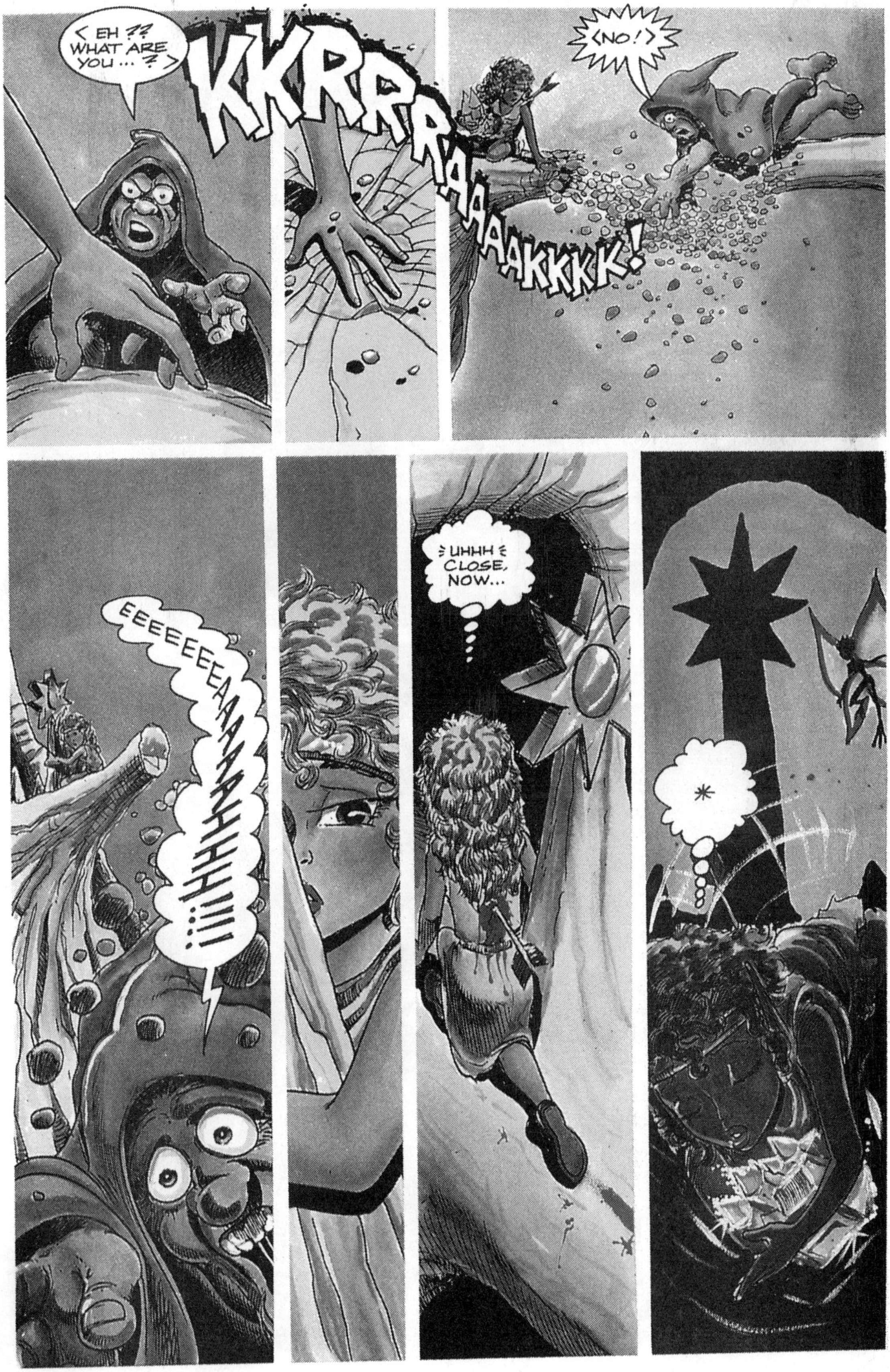
< EH ?? WHAT ARE YOU ... ? >
KKRRRAAAAAKKKK!
<NO!>
EEEEEEEAAAAAAHHHH!!!!!
UHHH CLOSE, NOW...
*

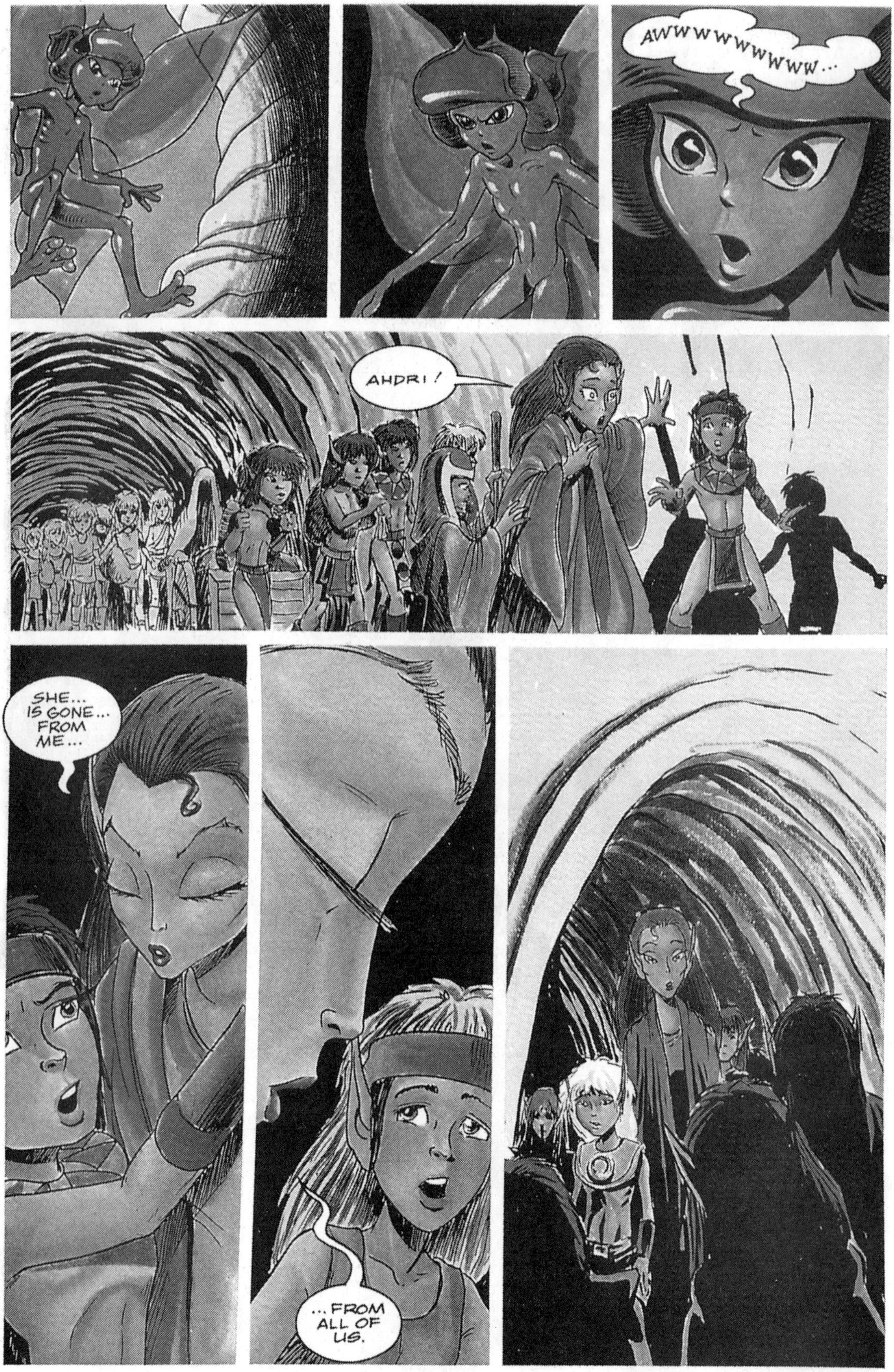
AWWWWWWWWW...
AHDRI!
SHE... IS GONE... FROM ME...
...FROM ALL OF US.

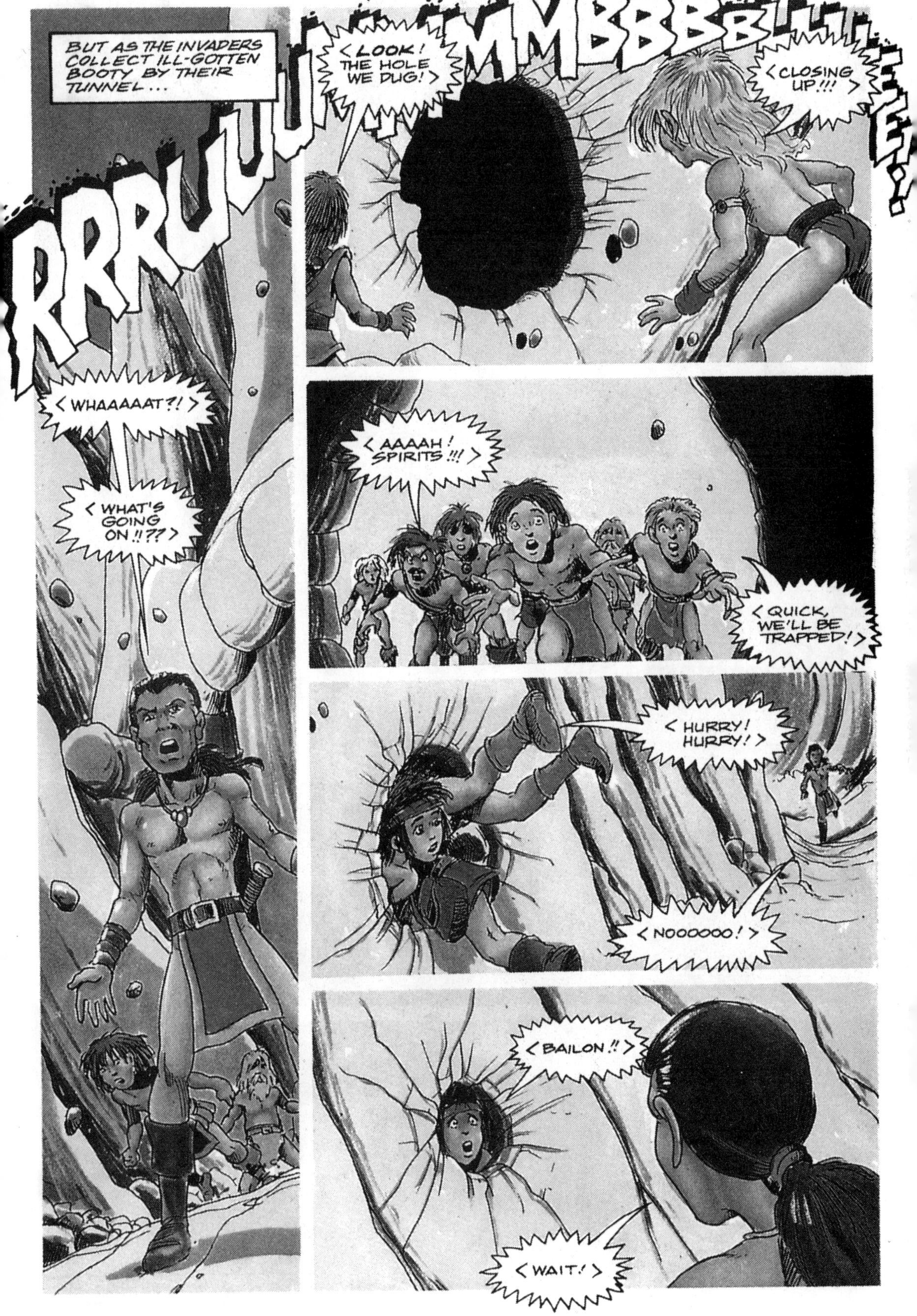
BUT AS THE INVADERS COLLECT ILL-GOTTEN BOOTY BY THEIR TUNNEL...
RRRUUUU...MMBBBBLLLEE!!
< LOOK! THE HOLE WE DUG! >
< CLOSING UP!!! >
< WHAAAAAT?! >
< WHAT'S GOING ON!!??? >
< AAAAH! SPIRITS!!! >
< QUICK, WE'LL BE TRAPPED! >
< HURRY! HURRY! >
< NOOOOOO! >
< BAILON!! >
< WAIT! >

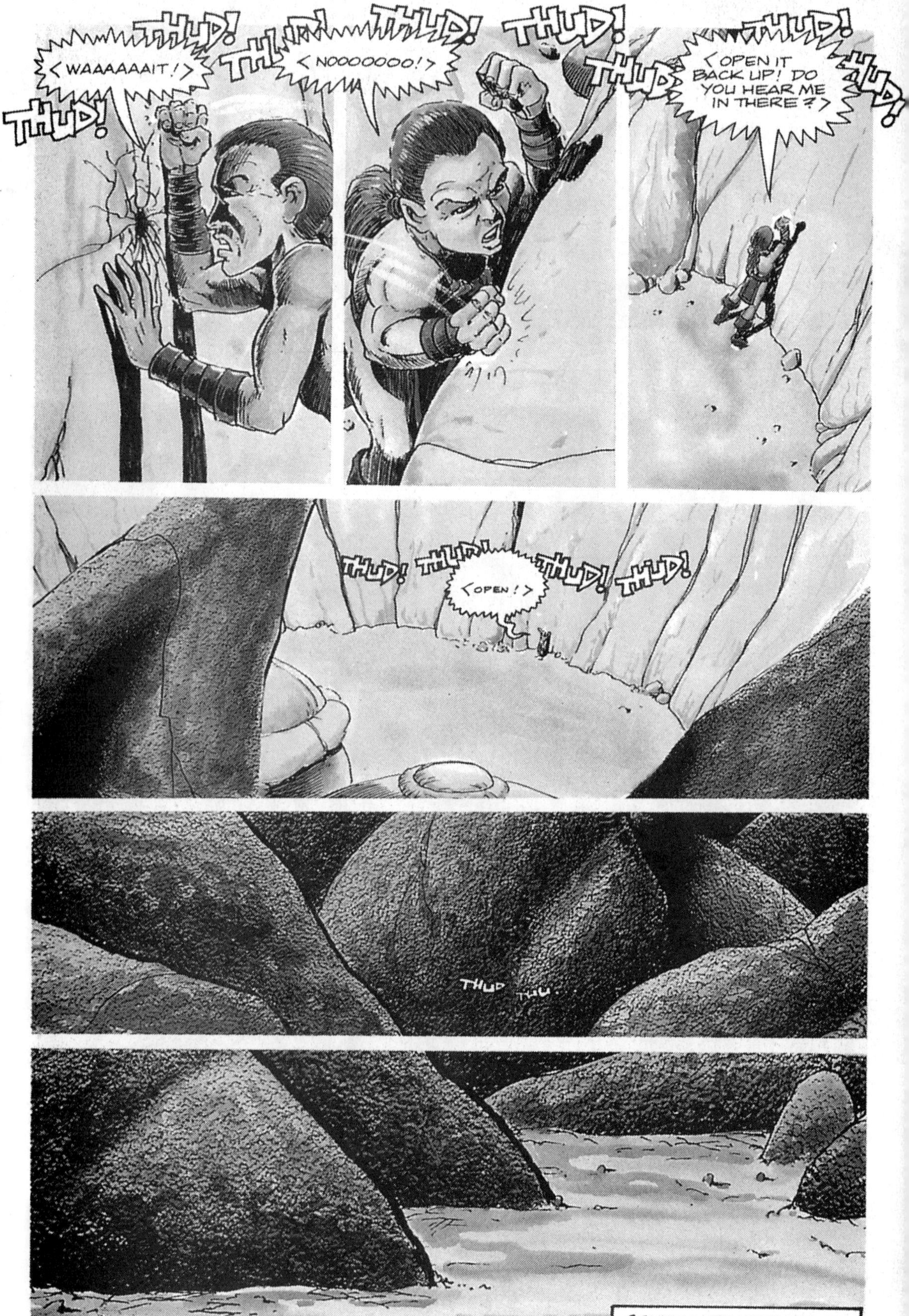
THUD!
<WAAAAAAIT!>
THUD!
THUD!
<NOOOOOOO!>
THUD!
THUD!
THUD!
THUD!
<OPEN IT BACK UP! DO YOU HEAR ME IN THERE?>
THUD!
THUD!
THUD!
<OPEN!>
THUD!
THUD!
THUD THU
CONTINUED NEXT ISSUE...

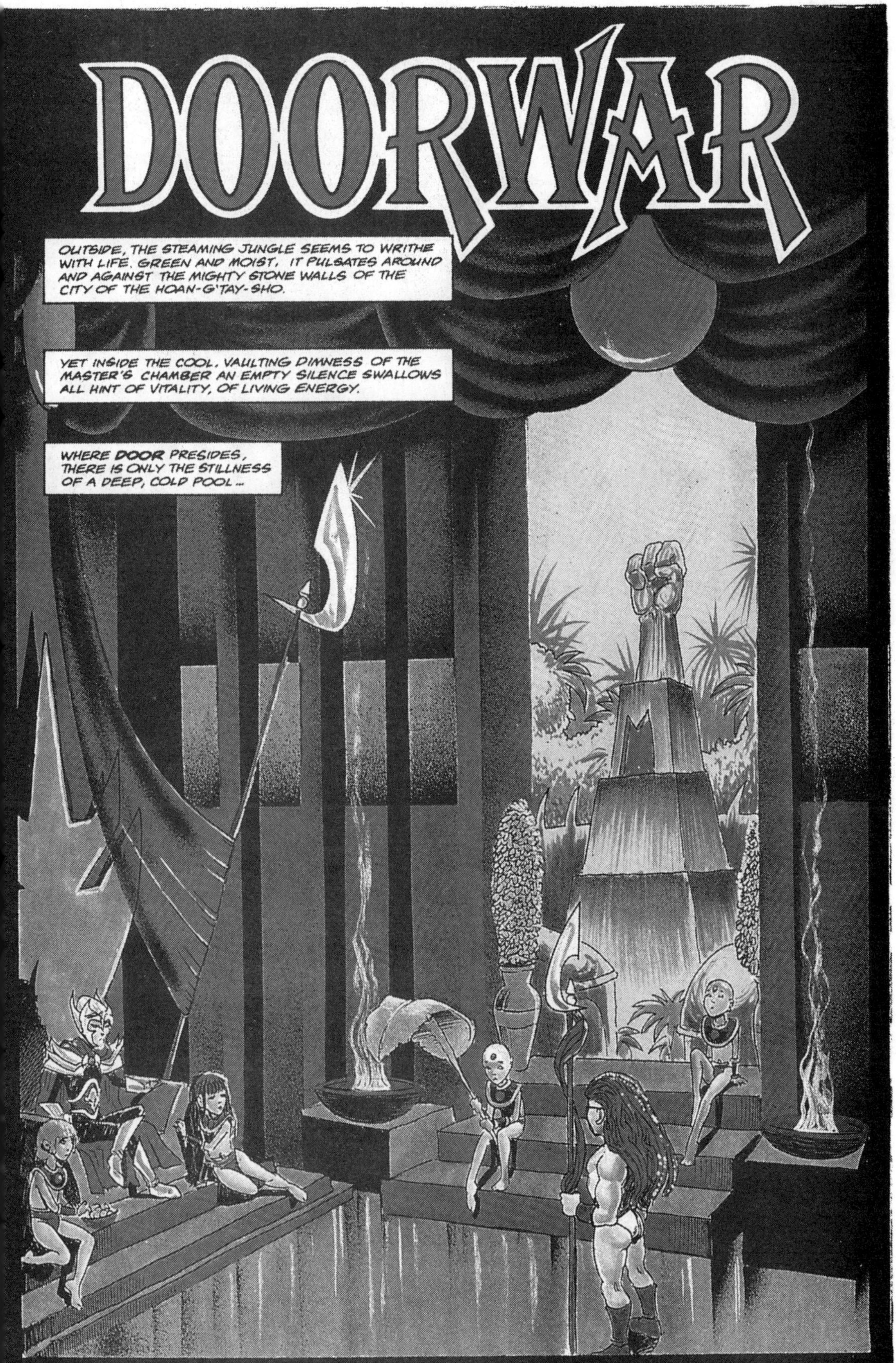
DOORWAR
OUTSIDE, THE STEAMING JUNGLE SEEMS TO WRITHE WITH LIFE. GREEN AND MOIST, IT PULSATES AROUND AND AGAINST THE MIGHTY STONE WALLS OF THE CITY OF THE HOAN-G'TAY-SHO.
YET INSIDE THE COOL, VAULTING DIMNESS OF THE MASTER'S CHAMBER AN EMPTY SILENCE SWALLOWS ALL HINT OF VITALITY, OF LIVING ENERGY.
WHERE DOOR PRESIDES, THERE IS ONLY THE STILLNESS OF A DEEP, COLD POOL...

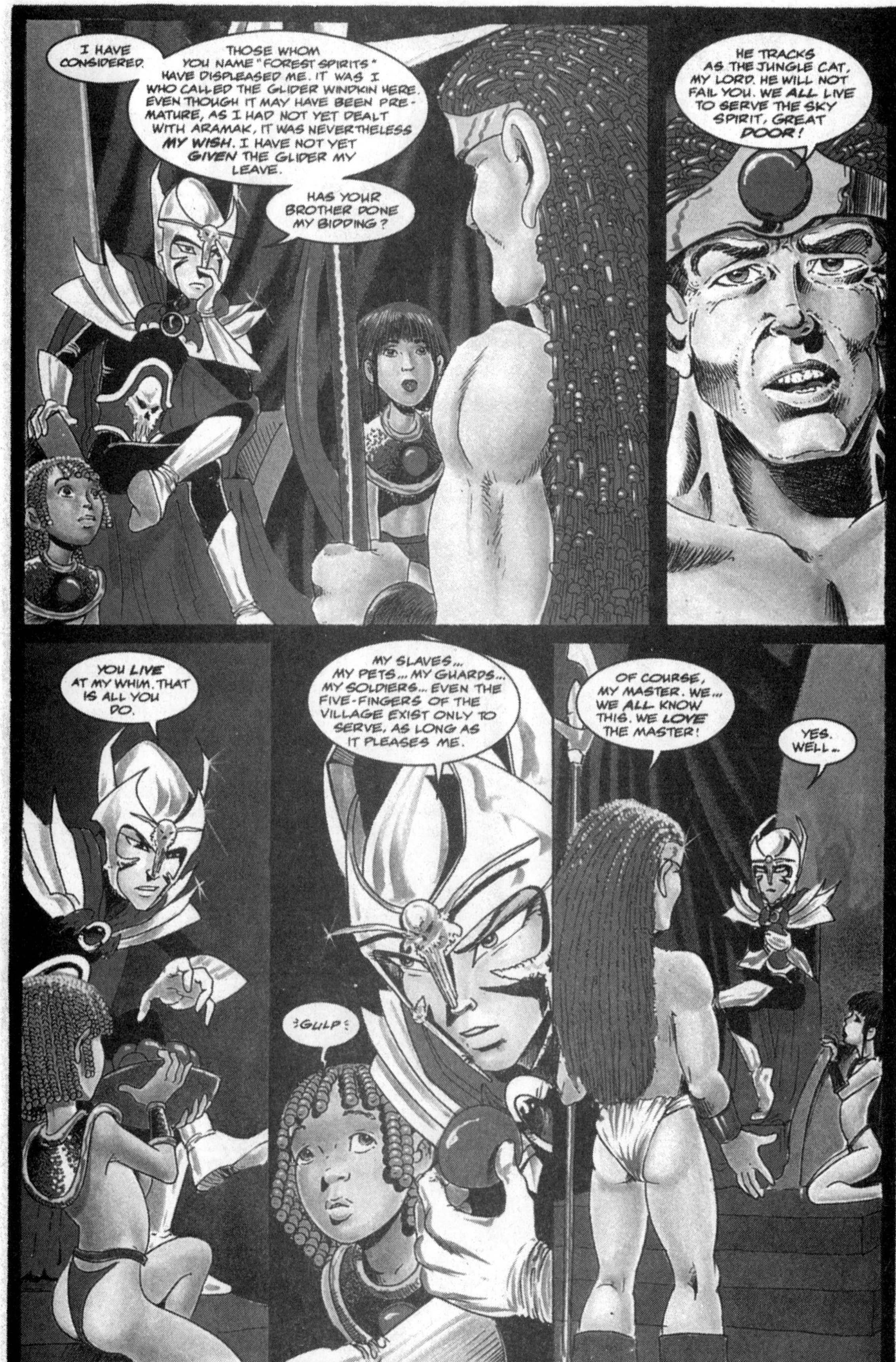
I HAVE CONSIDERED.
THOSE WHOM YOU NAME "FOREST SPIRITS" HAVE DISPLEASED ME. IT WAS I WHO CALLED THE GLIDER WINDKIN HERE. EVEN THOUGH IT MAY HAVE BEEN PRE-MATURE, AS I HAD NOT YET DEALT WITH ARAMAK, IT WAS NEVERTHELESS MY WISH. I HAVE NOT YET GIVEN THE GLIDER MY LEAVE.
HAS YOUR BROTHER DONE MY BIDDING?
HE TRACKS AS THE JUNGLE CAT, MY LORD. HE WILL NOT FAIL YOU. WE ALL LIVE TO SERVE THE SKY SPIRIT, GREAT DOOR!
YOU LIVE AT MY WHIM. THAT IS ALL YOU DO.
MY SLAVES... MY PETS... MY GUARDS... MY SOLDIERS... EVEN THE FIVE-FINGERS OF THE VILLAGE EXIST ONLY TO SERVE, AS LONG AS IT PLEASES ME.
:GULP:
OF COURSE, MY MASTER. WE... WE ALL KNOW THIS. WE LOVE THE MASTER!
YES. WELL...

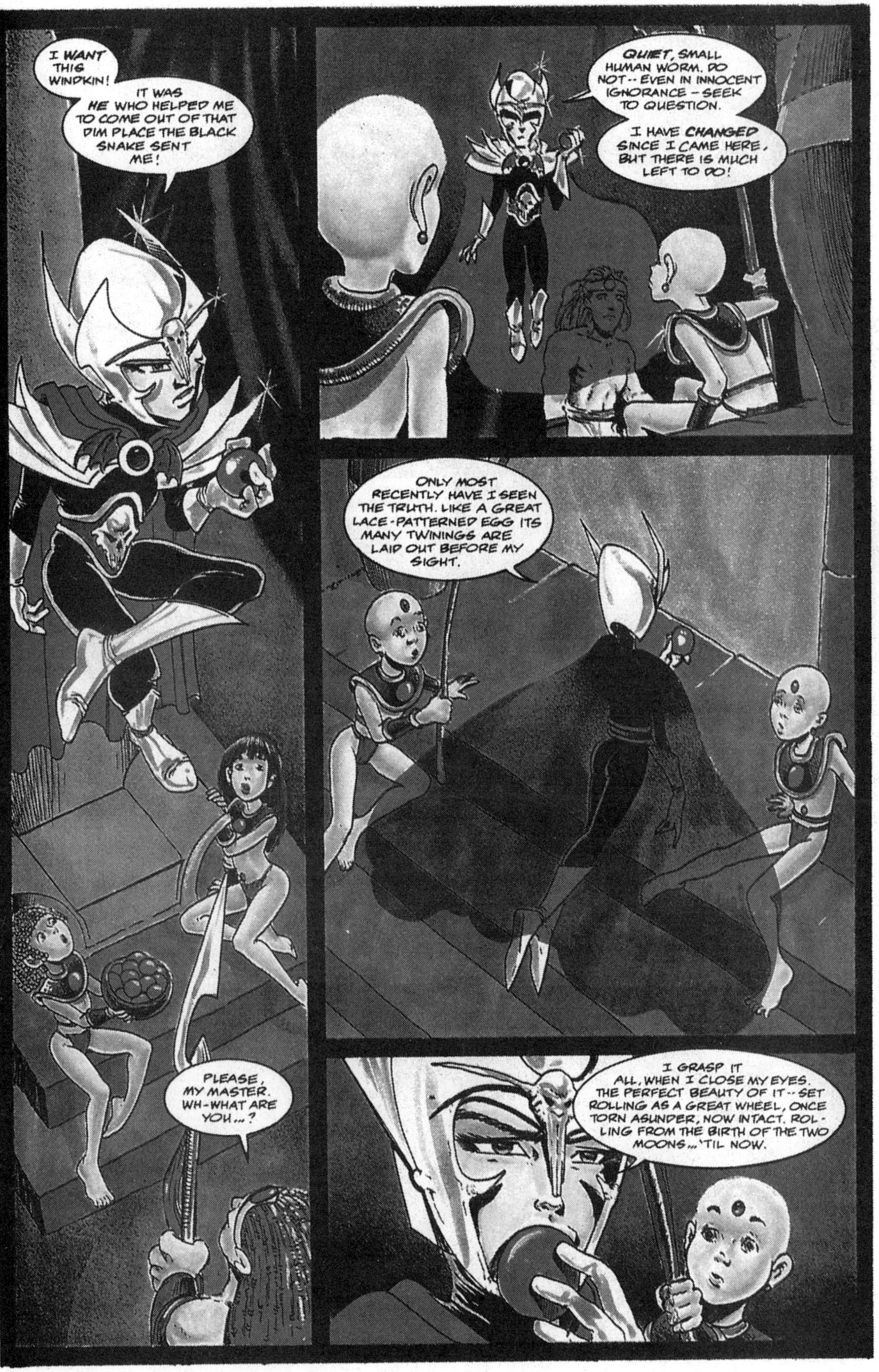

I WANT THIS WINDKIN!
IT WAS HE WHO HELPED ME TO COME OUT OF THAT DIM PLACE THE BLACK SNAKE SENT ME!
PLEASE, MY MASTER. WH-WHAT ARE YOU...?
QUIET, SMALL HUMAN WORM. DO NOT-- EVEN IN INNOCENT IGNORANCE - SEEK TO QUESTION.
I HAVE CHANGED SINCE I CAME HERE, BUT THERE IS MUCH LEFT TO DO!
ONLY MOST RECENTLY HAVE I SEEN THE TRUTH. LIKE A GREAT LACE-PATTERNED EGG ITS MANY TWININGS ARE LAID OUT BEFORE MY SIGHT.
I GRASP IT ALL, WHEN I CLOSE MY EYES. THE PERFECT BEAUTY OF IT-- SET ROLLING AS A GREAT WHEEL, ONCE TORN ASUNDER, NOW INTACT. ROL-LING FROM THE BIRTH OF THE TWO MOONS...'TIL NOW.

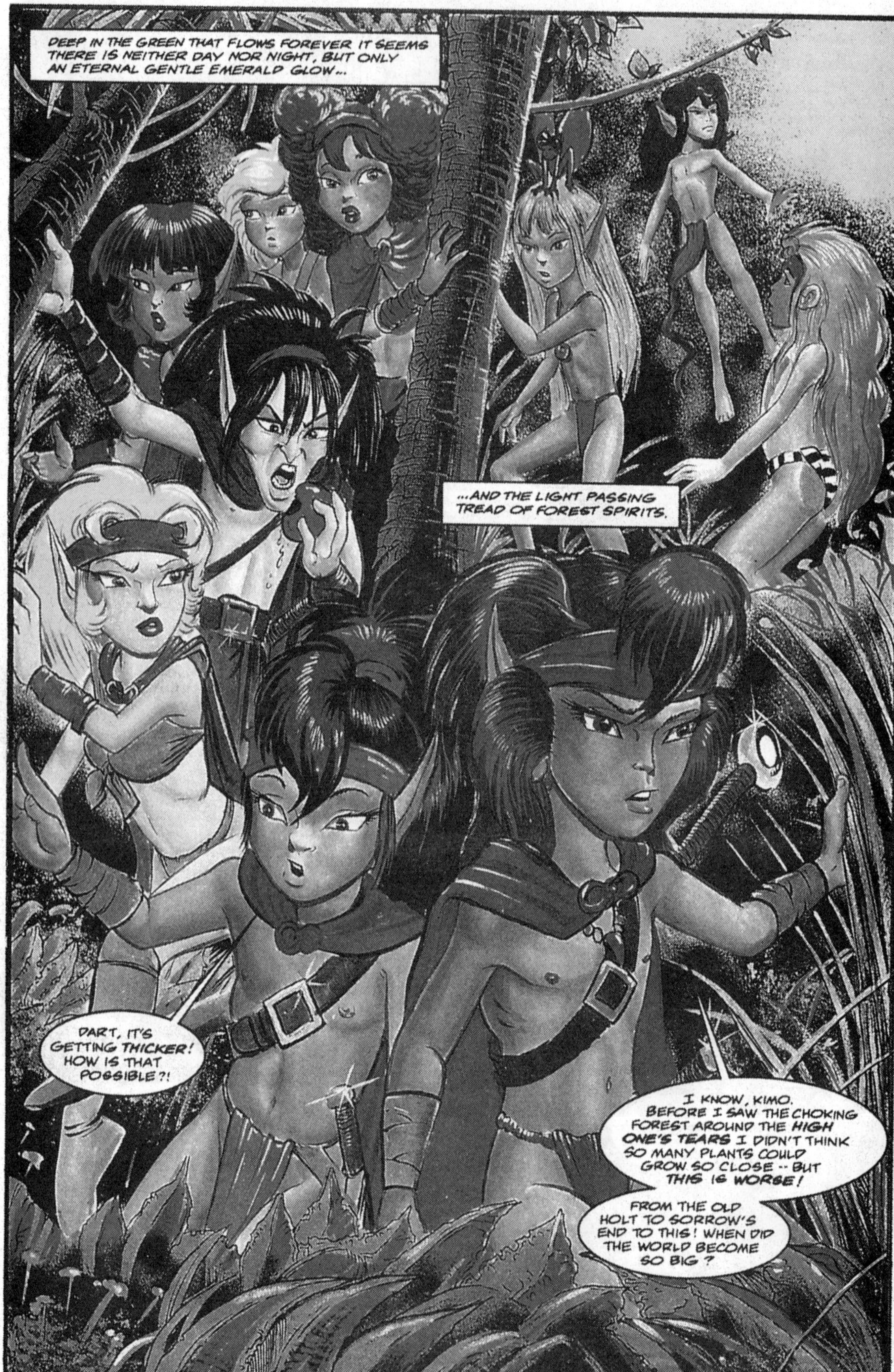
DEEP IN THE GREEN THAT FLOWS FOREVER IT SEEMS THERE IS NEITHER DAY NOR NIGHT, BUT ONLY AN ETERNAL GENTLE EMERALD GLOW...
...AND THE LIGHT PASSING TREAD OF FOREST SPIRITS.
DART, IT'S GETTING THICKER! HOW IS THAT POSSIBLE?!
I KNOW, KIMO. BEFORE I SAW THE CHOKING FOREST AROUND THE HIGH ONE'S TEARS I DIDN'T THINK SO MANY PLANTS COULD GROW SO CLOSE -- BUT THIS IS WORSE!
FROM THE OLD HOLT TO SORROW'S END TO THIS! WHEN DID THE WORLD BECOME SO BIG?

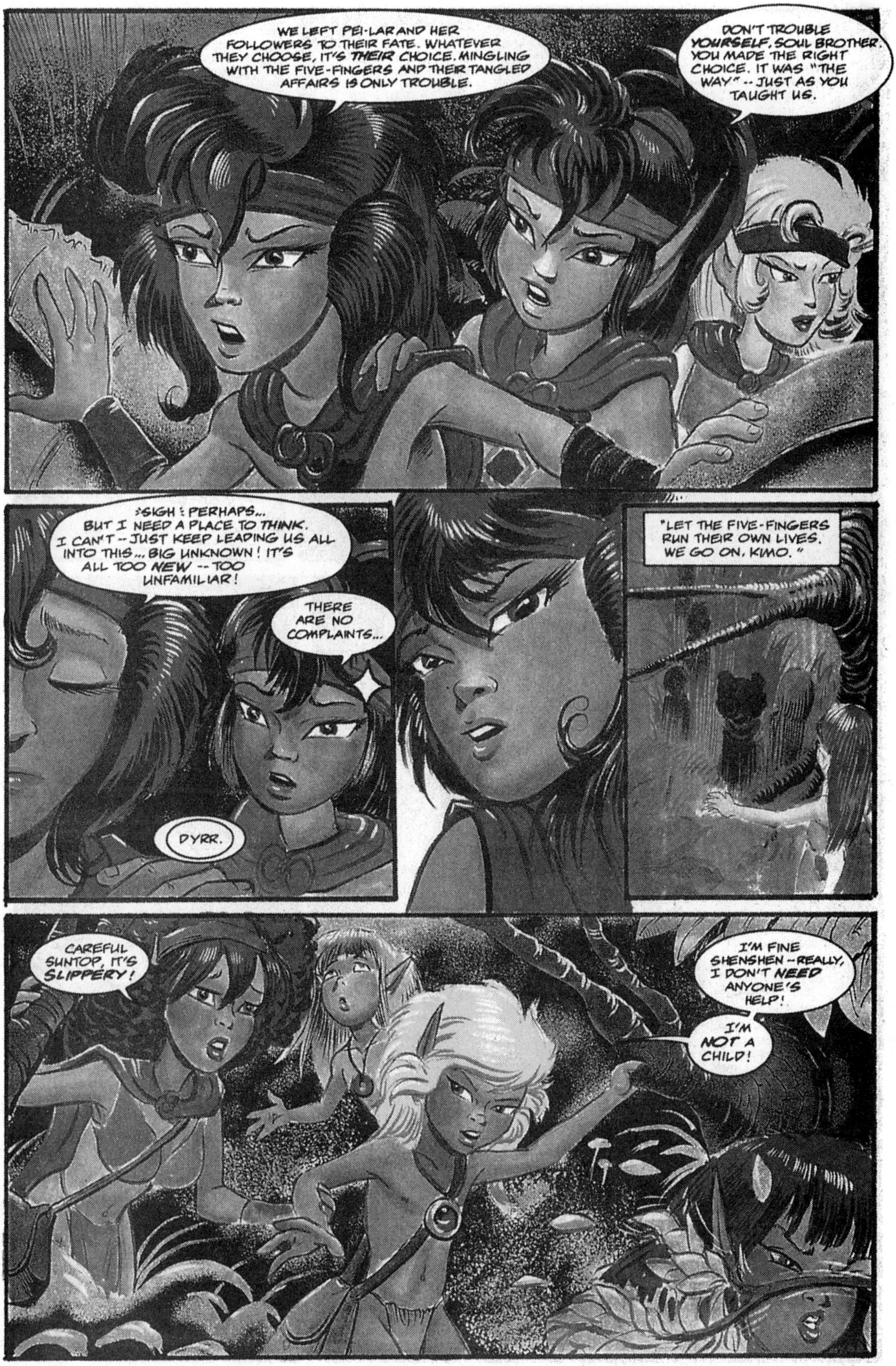

WE LEFT PEI-LAR AND HER FOLLOWERS TO THEIR FATE. WHATEVER THEY CHOOSE, IT'S *THEIR* CHOICE. MINGLING WITH THE FIVE-FINGERS AND THEIR TANGLED AFFAIRS IS ONLY TROUBLE.
DON'T TROUBLE *YOURSELF*, SOUL BROTHER. YOU MADE THE RIGHT CHOICE. IT WAS "THE WAY" -- JUST AS YOU TAUGHT US.
>SIGH< PERHAPS... BUT I NEED A PLACE TO *THINK*. I CAN'T -- JUST KEEP LEADING US ALL INTO THIS... BIG UNKNOWN! IT'S ALL TOO *NEW* -- TOO UNFAMILIAR!
THERE ARE NO COMPLAINTS...
DYRR.
"LET THE FIVE-FINGERS RUN THEIR OWN LIVES. WE GO ON, KIMO."
CAREFUL SUNTOP, IT'S *SLIPPERY*!
I'M FINE SHENSHEN -- REALLY, I DON'T *NEED* ANYONE'S HELP!
I'M *NOT* A CHILD!

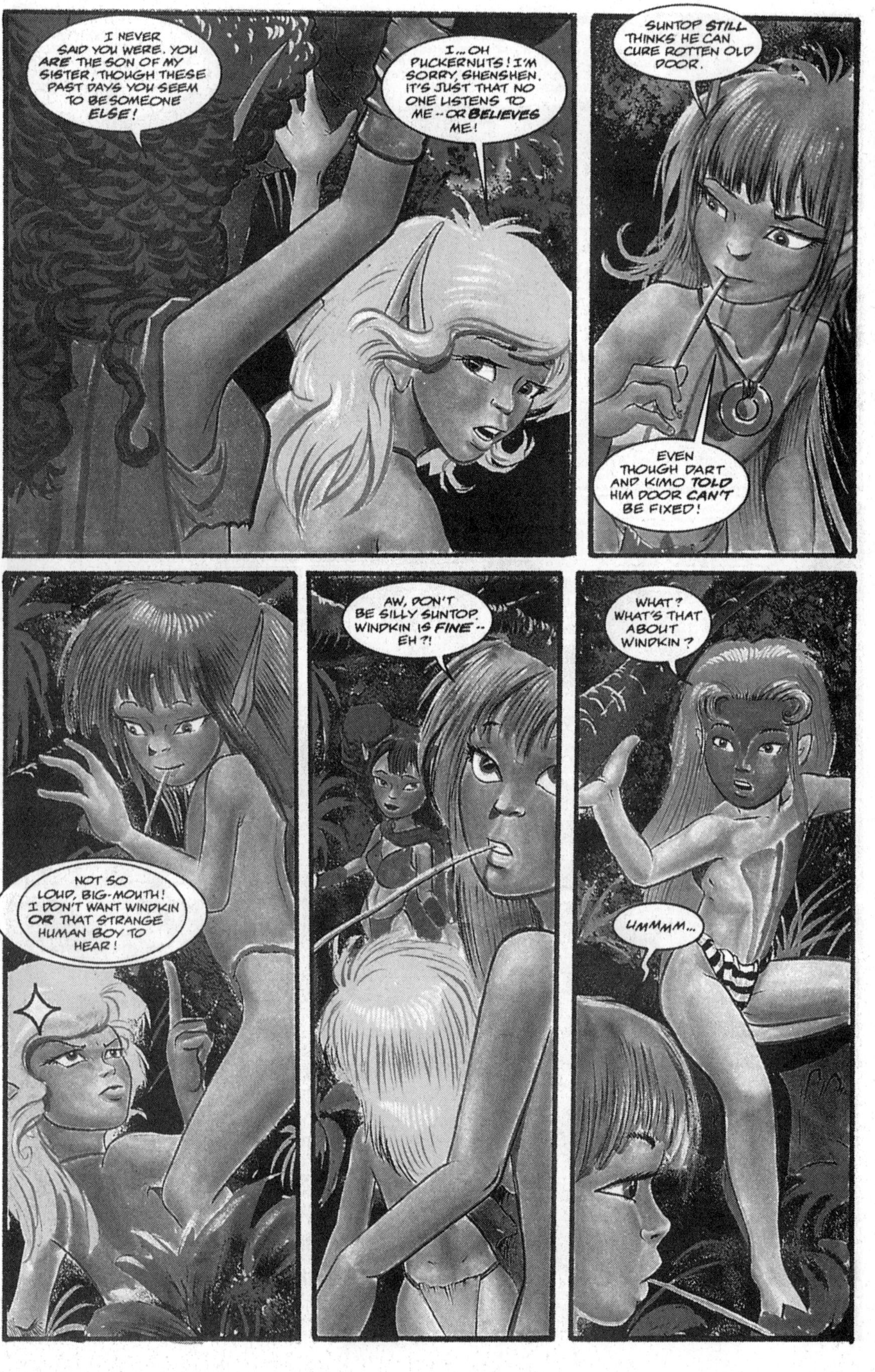
I NEVER SAID YOU WERE. YOU ARE THE SON OF MY SISTER, THOUGH THESE PAST DAYS YOU SEEM TO BE SOMEONE ELSE!
I... OH PUCKERNUTS! I'M SORRY, SHENSHEN. IT'S JUST THAT NO ONE LISTENS TO ME -- OR BELIEVES ME!
SUNTOP STILL THINKS HE CAN CURE ROTTEN OLD DOOR.
EVEN THOUGH DART AND KIMO TOLD HIM DOOR CAN'T BE FIXED!
NOT SO LOUD, BIG-MOUTH! I DON'T WANT WINDKIN OR THAT STRANGE HUMAN BOY TO HEAR!
AW, DON'T BE SILLY SUNTOP. WINDKIN IS FINE -- EH ?!
WHAT? WHAT'S THAT ABOUT WINDKIN?
UMMMM...

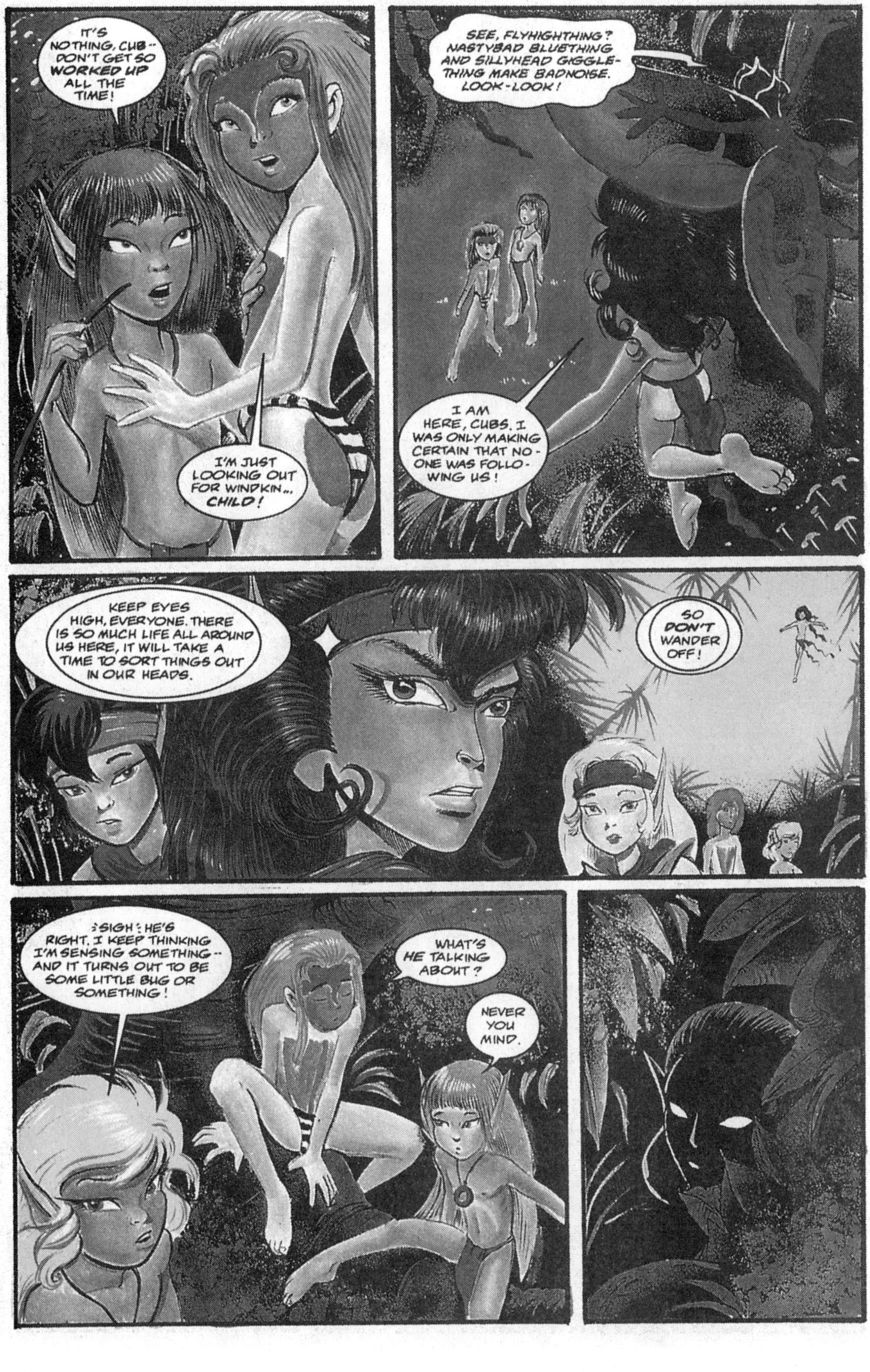

IT'S NOTHING, CUB -- DON'T GET SO WORKED UP ALL THE TIME!
I'M JUST LOOKING OUT FOR WINDKIN... CHILD!
SEE, FLYHIGHTHING? NASTYBAD BLUETHING AND SILLYHEAD GIGGLE-THING MAKE BADNOISE. LOOK-LOOK!
I AM HERE, CUBS. I WAS ONLY MAKING CERTAIN THAT NO-ONE WAS FOLLO-WING US!
KEEP EYES HIGH, EVERYONE. THERE IS SO MUCH LIFE ALL AROUND US HERE, IT WILL TAKE A TIME TO SORT THINGS OUT IN OUR HEADS.
SO DON'T WANDER OFF!
:SIGH: HE'S RIGHT. I KEEP THINKING I'M SENSING SOMETHING -- AND IT TURNS OUT TO BE SOME LITTLE BUG OR SOMETHING!
WHAT'S HE TALKING ABOUT?
NEVER YOU MIND.

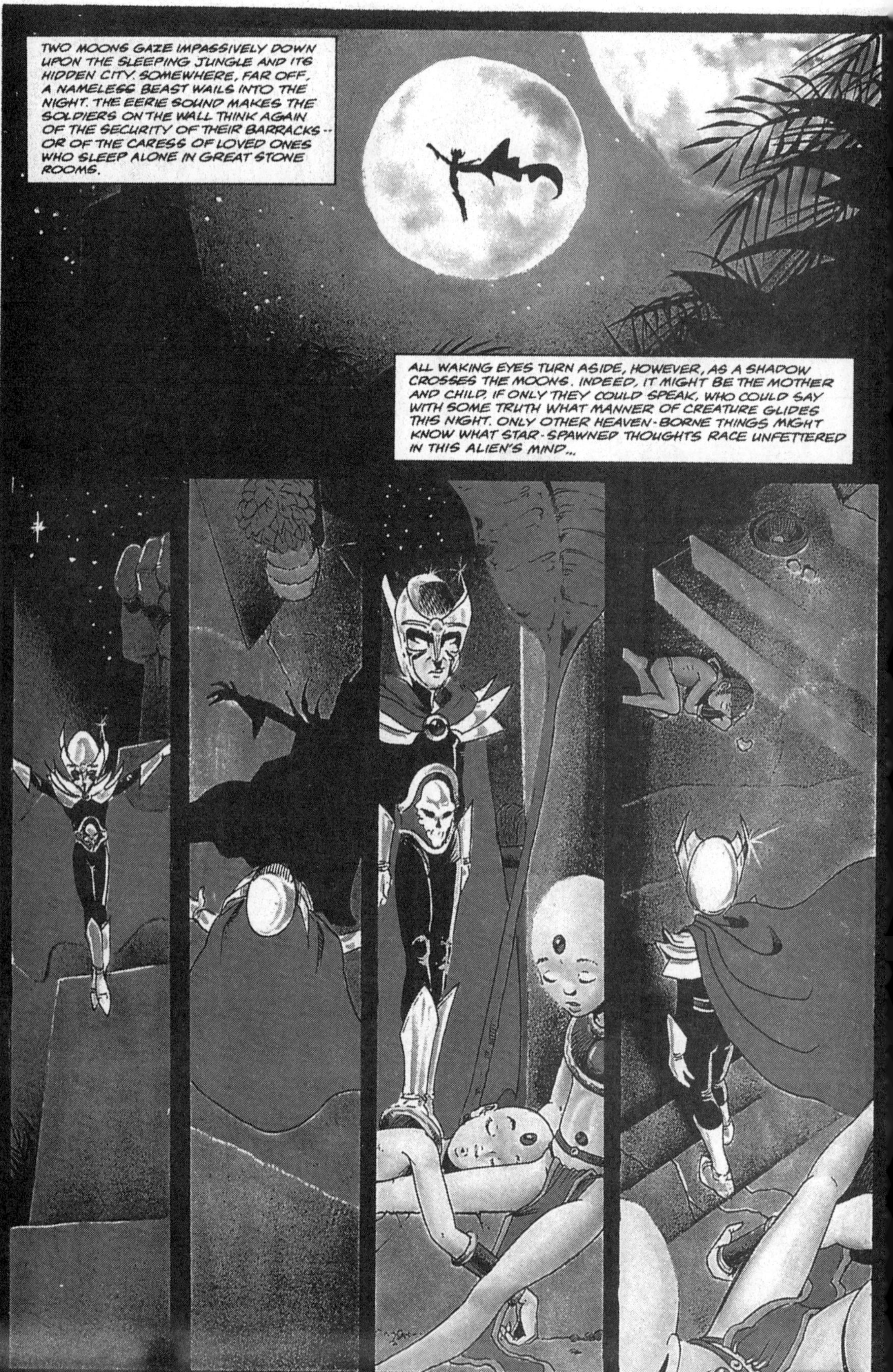
TWO MOONS GAZE IMPASSIVELY DOWN UPON THE SLEEPING JUNGLE AND ITS HIDDEN CITY. SOMEWHERE, FAR OFF, A NAMELESS BEAST WAILS INTO THE NIGHT. THE EERIE SOUND MAKES THE SOLDIERS ON THE WALL THINK AGAIN OF THE SECURITY OF THEIR BARRACKS -- OR OF THE CARESS OF LOVED ONES WHO SLEEP ALONE IN GREAT STONE ROOMS.
ALL WAKING EYES TURN ASIDE, HOWEVER, AS A SHADOW CROSSES THE MOONS. INDEED, IT MIGHT BE THE MOTHER AND CHILD, IF ONLY THEY COULD SPEAK, WHO COULD SAY WITH SOME TRUTH WHAT MANNER OF CREATURE GLIDES THIS NIGHT. ONLY OTHER HEAVEN-BORNE THINGS MIGHT KNOW WHAT STAR-SPAWNED THOUGHTS RACE UNFETTERED IN THIS ALIEN'S MIND...

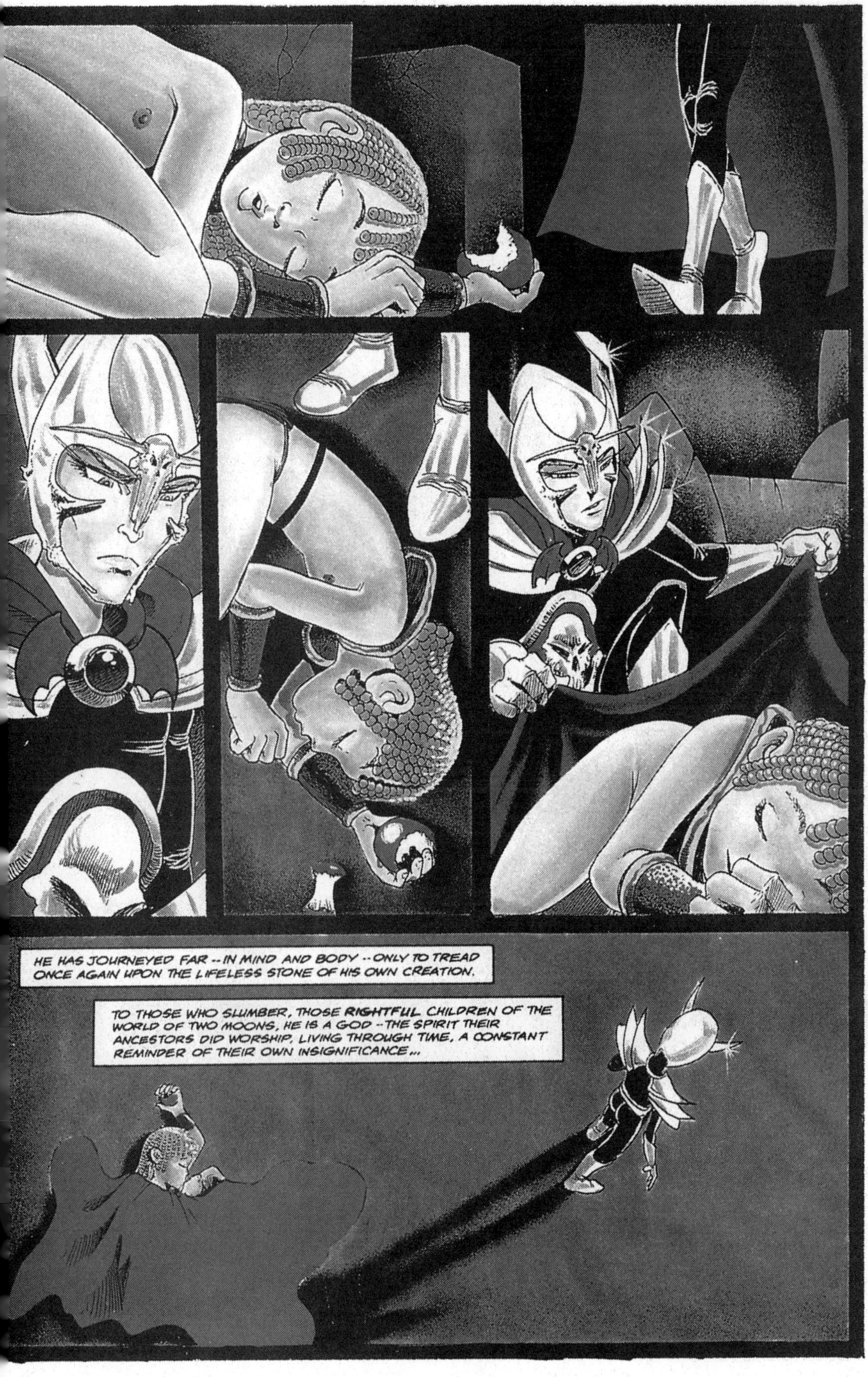
HE HAS JOURNEYED FAR -- IN MIND AND BODY -- ONLY TO TREAD ONCE AGAIN UPON THE LIFELESS STONE OF HIS OWN CREATION.
TO THOSE WHO SLUMBER, THOSE RIGHTFUL CHILDREN OF THE WORLD OF TWO MOONS, HE IS A GOD -- THE SPIRIT THEIR ANCESTORS DID WORSHIP, LIVING THROUGH TIME, A CONSTANT REMINDER OF THEIR OWN INSIGNIFICANCE...

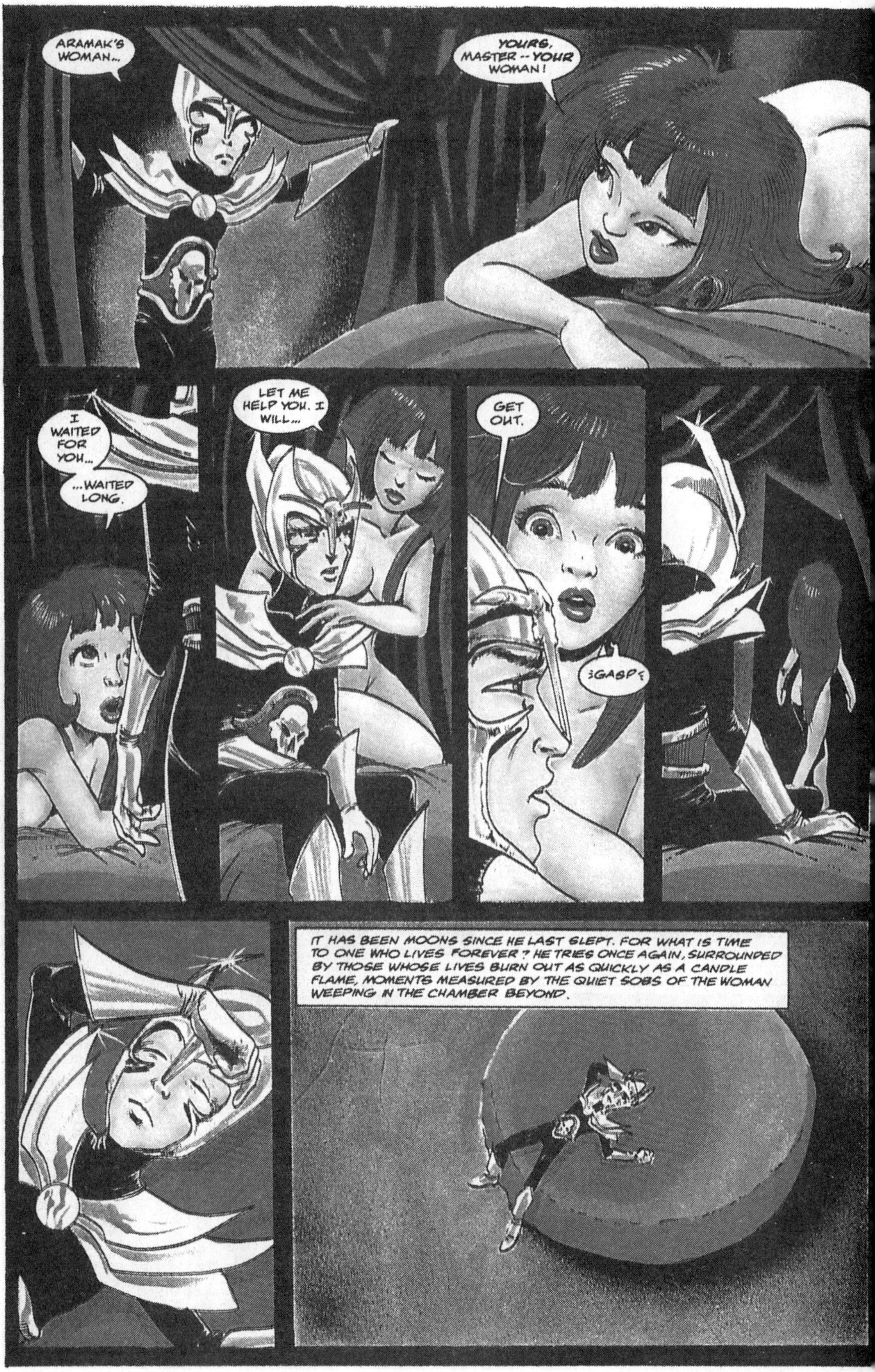
ARAMAK'S WOMAN...
YOURS, MASTER -- YOUR WOMAN!
I WAITED FOR YOU...
...WAITED LONG.
LET ME HELP YOU. I WILL...
GET OUT.
¡GASP!
IT HAS BEEN MOONS SINCE HE LAST SLEPT. FOR WHAT IS TIME TO ONE WHO LIVES FOREVER ? HE TRIES ONCE AGAIN, SURROUNDED BY THOSE WHOSE LIVES BURN OUT AS QUICKLY AS A CANDLE FLAME, MOMENTS MEASURED BY THE QUIET SOBS OF THE WOMAN WEEPING IN THE CHAMBER BEYOND.

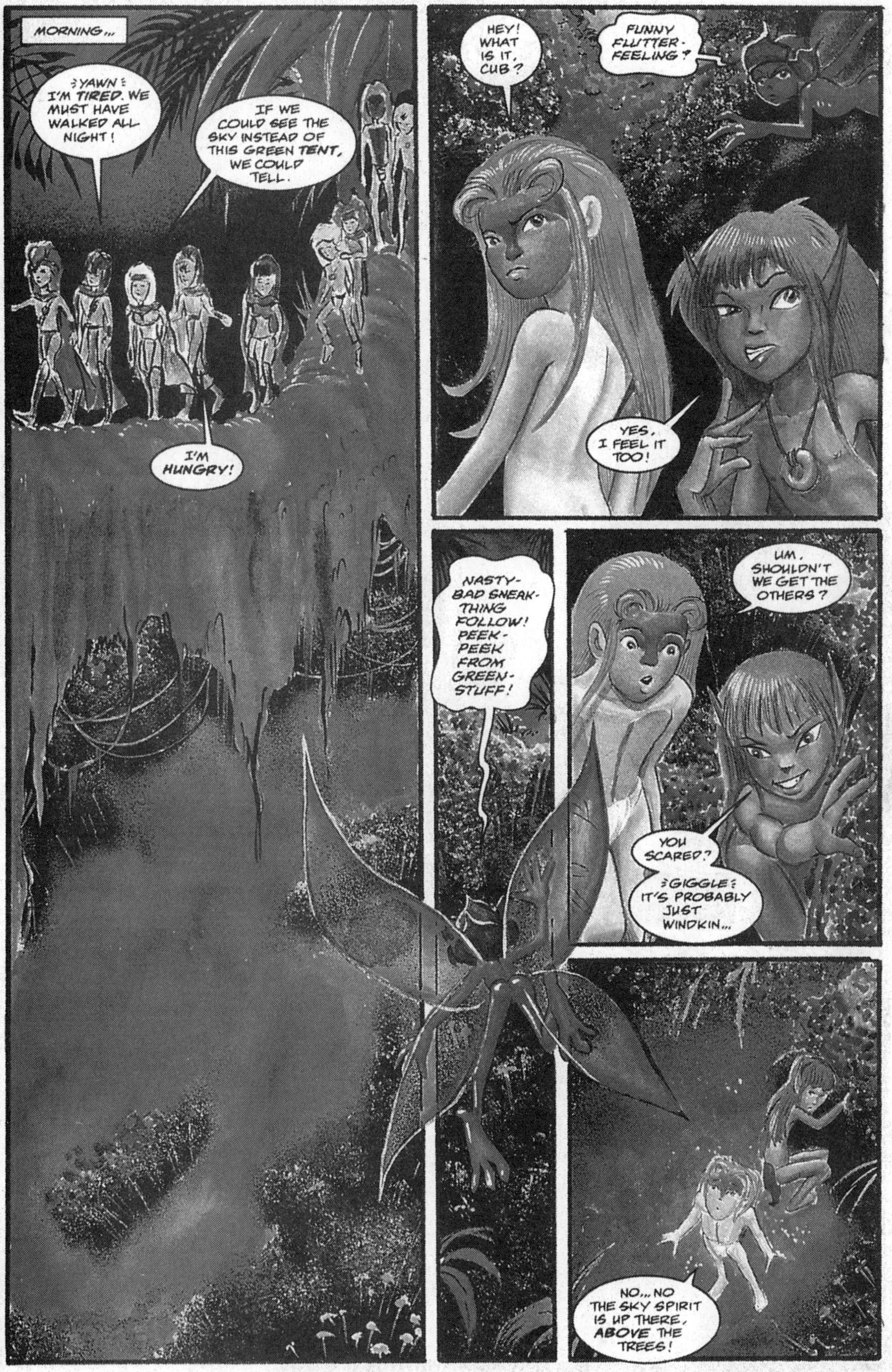
MORNING...
:YAWN: I'M TIRED. WE MUST HAVE WALKED ALL NIGHT!
IF WE COULD SEE THE SKY INSTEAD OF THIS GREEN TENT, WE COULD TELL.
I'M HUNGRY!
HEY! WHAT IS IT, CUB?
FUNNY FLUTTER-FEELING?
YES, I FEEL IT TOO!
NASTY-BAD SNEAK-THING FOLLOW! PEEK-PEEK FROM GREEN-STUFF!
UM, SHOULDN'T WE GET THE OTHERS?
YOU SCARED?
:GIGGLE: IT'S PROBABLY JUST WINDKIN...
NO... NO THE SKY SPIRIT IS UP THERE, ABOVE THE TREES!

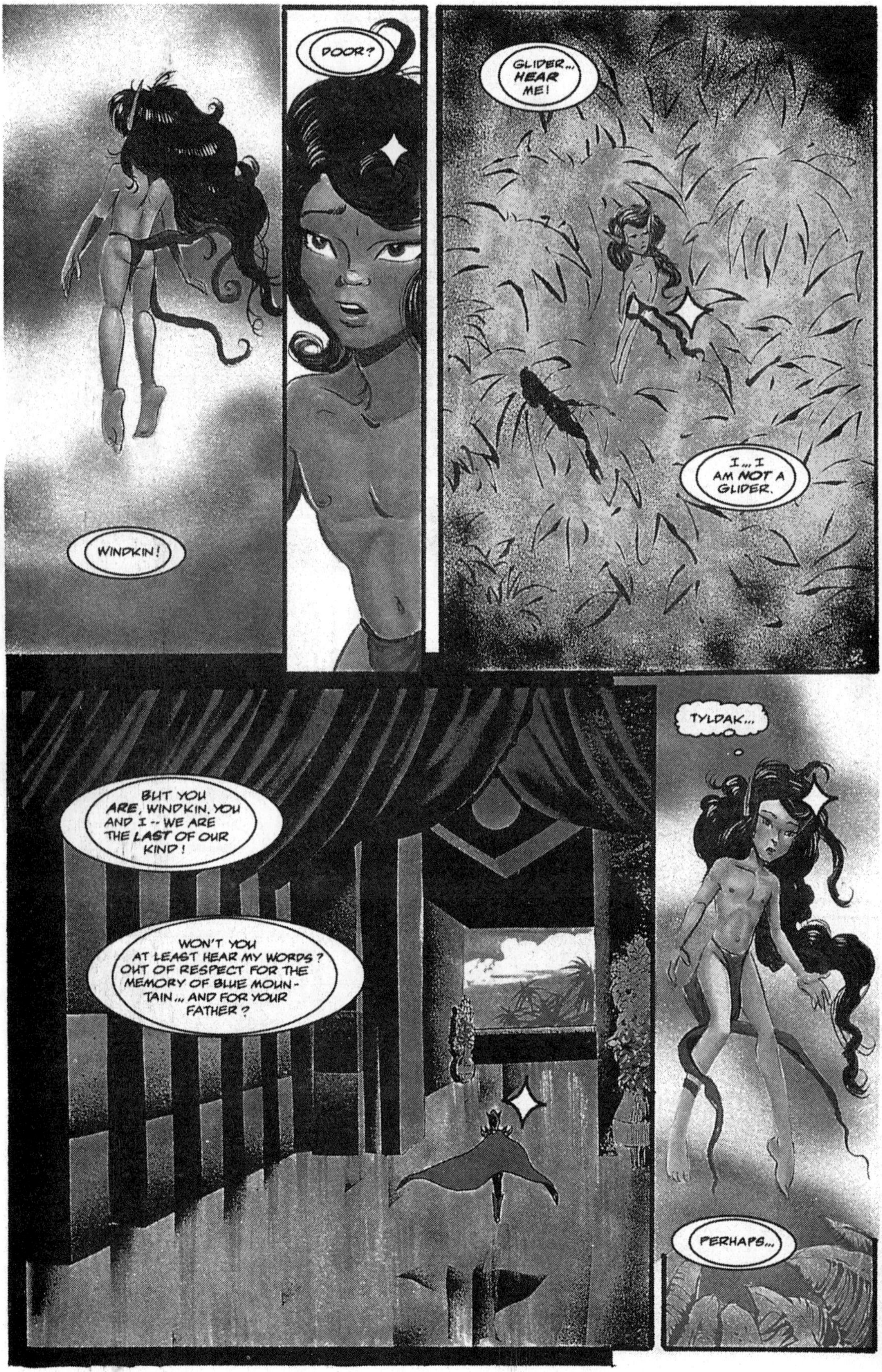
WINDKIN!
DOOR?
GLIDER... HEAR ME!
I... I AM NOT A GLIDER.
BUT YOU ARE, WINDKIN. YOU AND I -- WE ARE THE LAST OF OUR KIND!
WON'T YOU AT LEAST HEAR MY WORDS? OUT OF RESPECT FOR THE MEMORY OF BLUE MOUNTAIN... AND FOR YOUR FATHER?
TYLDAK...
PERHAPS...

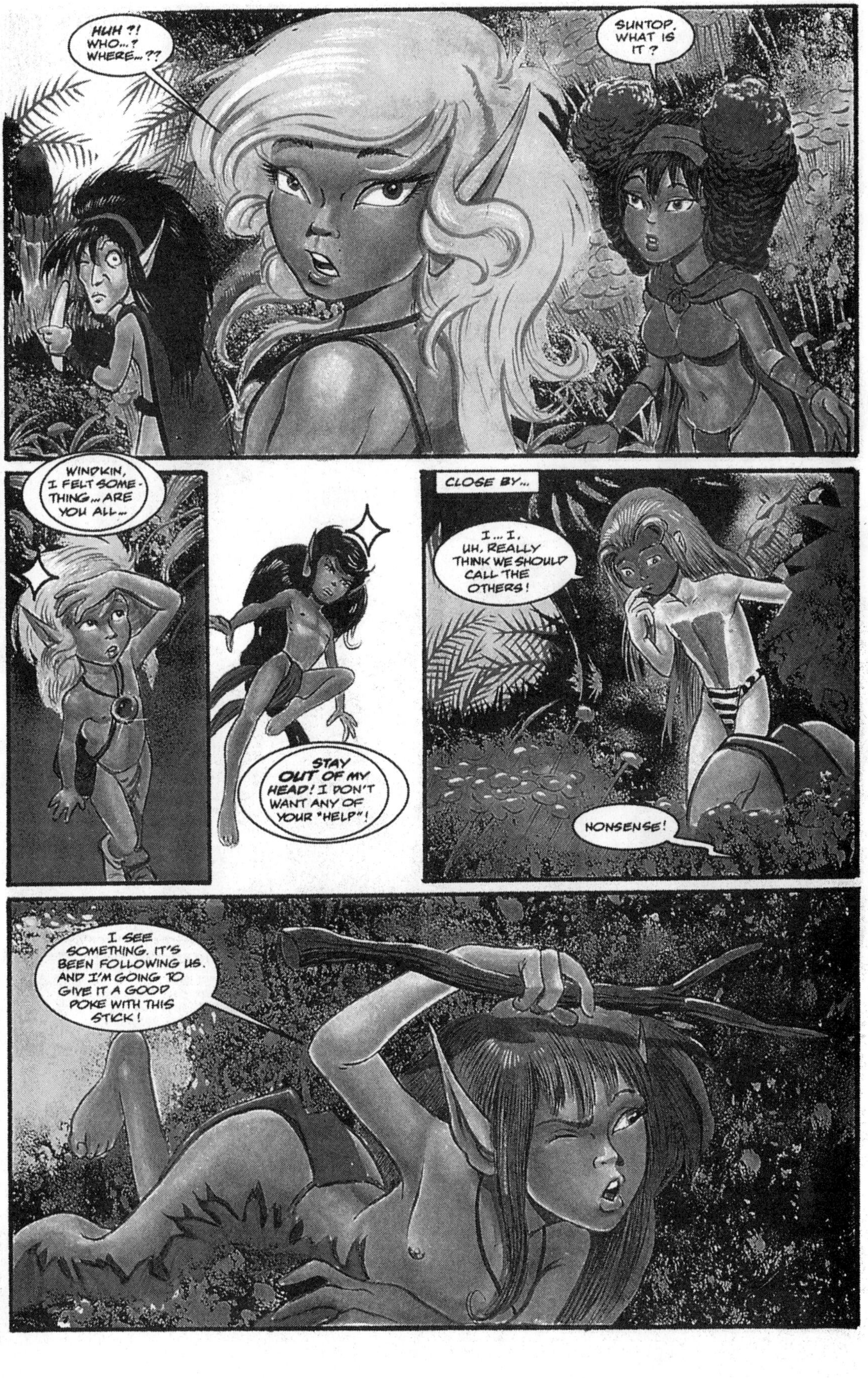
HUH ?! WHO...? WHERE...??
SUNTOP. WHAT IS IT ?
WINDKIN, I FELT SOME-THING... ARE YOU ALL...
STAY OUT OF MY HEAD! I DON'T WANT ANY OF YOUR "HELP"!
CLOSE BY...
I... I, UH, REALLY THINK WE SHOULD CALL THE OTHERS!
NONSENSE!
I SEE SOMETHING. IT'S BEEN FOLLOWING US. AND I'M GOING TO GIVE IT A GOOD POKE WITH THIS STICK!

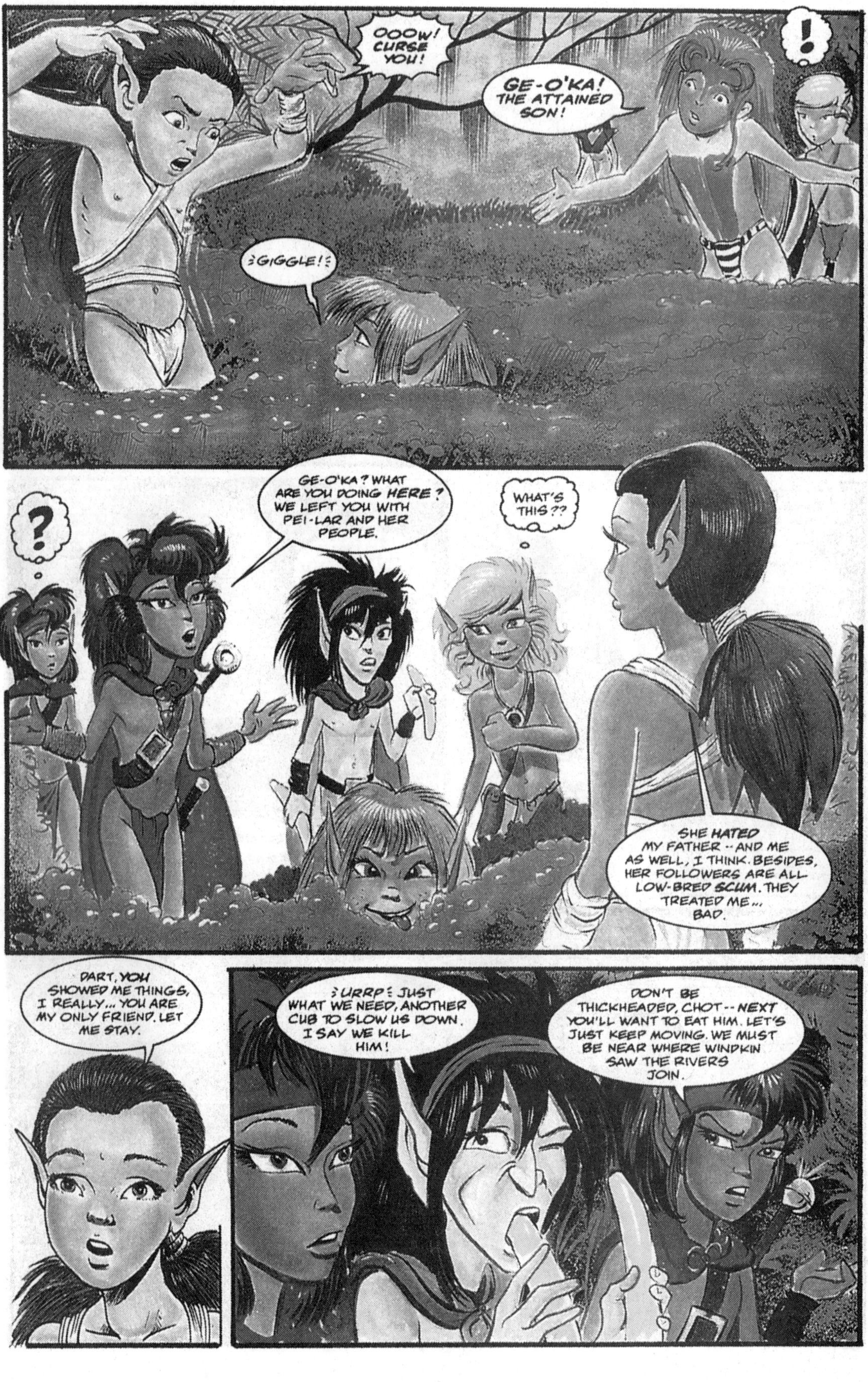
OOOW! CURSE YOU!
!
GE-O'KA! THE ATTAINED SON!
GIGGLE!
?
GE-O'KA? WHAT ARE YOU DOING HERE? WE LEFT YOU WITH PEI-LAR AND HER PEOPLE.
WHAT'S THIS??
SHE HATED MY FATHER -- AND ME AS WELL, I THINK. BESIDES, HER FOLLOWERS ARE ALL LOW-BRED SCUM. THEY TREATED ME... BAD.
DART, YOU SHOWED ME THINGS, I REALLY... YOU ARE MY ONLY FRIEND. LET ME STAY.
URRP JUST WHAT WE NEED, ANOTHER CUB TO SLOW US DOWN. I SAY WE KILL HIM!
DON'T BE THICKHEADED, CHOT -- NEXT YOU'LL WANT TO EAT HIM. LET'S JUST KEEP MOVING. WE MUST BE NEAR WHERE WINDKIN SAW THE RIVERS JOIN.

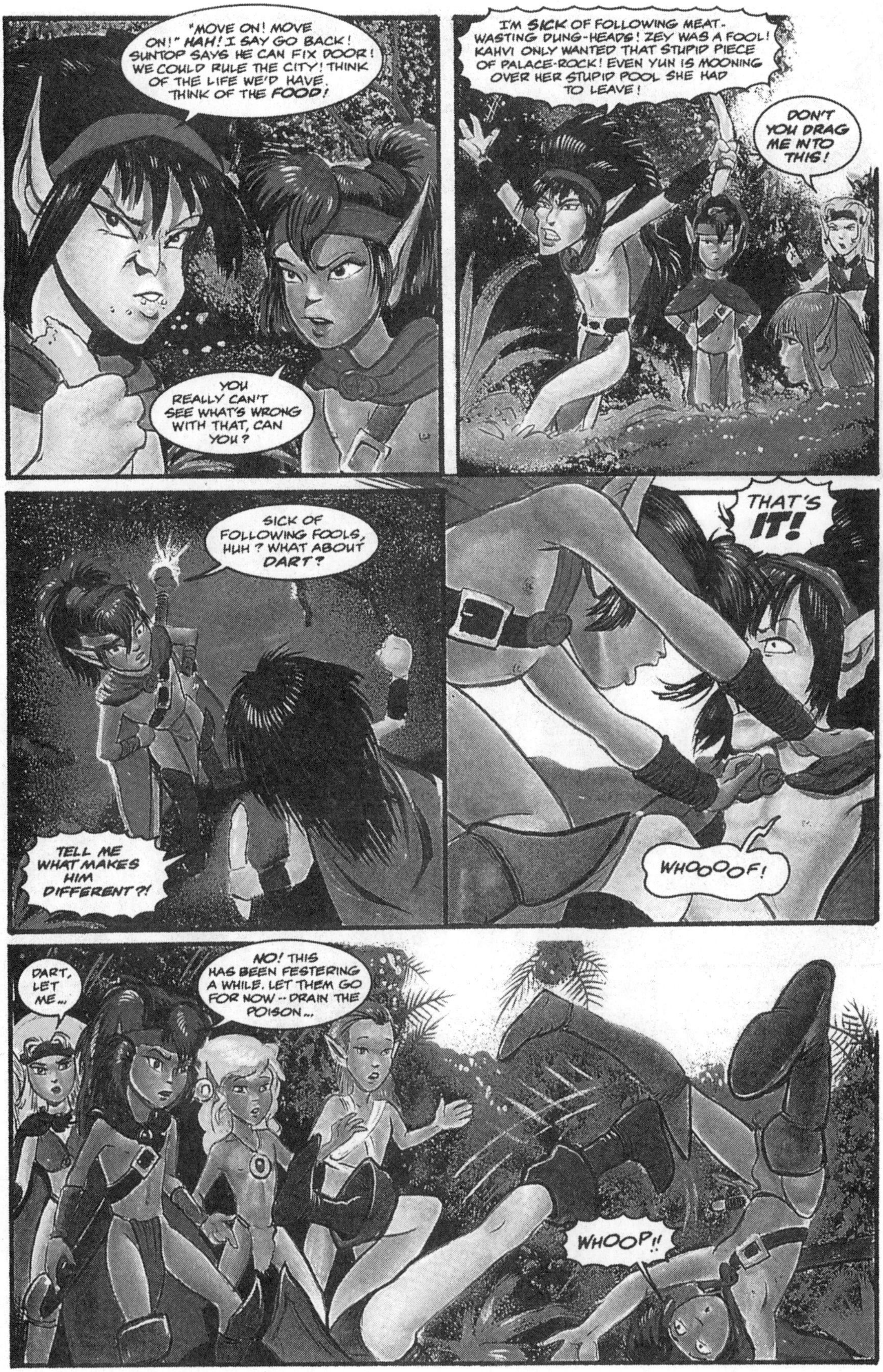
"MOVE ON! MOVE ON!" HAH! I SAY GO BACK! SUNTOP SAYS HE CAN FIX DOOR! WE COULD RULE THE CITY! THINK OF THE LIFE WE'D HAVE. THINK OF THE FOOD!
YOU REALLY CAN'T SEE WHAT'S WRONG WITH THAT, CAN YOU?
I'M SICK OF FOLLOWING MEAT-WASTING DUNG-HEADS! ZEY WAS A FOOL! KAHVI ONLY WANTED THAT STUPID PIECE OF PALACE-ROCK! EVEN YUN IS MOONING OVER HER STUPID POOL SHE HAD TO LEAVE!
DON'T YOU DRAG ME INTO THIS!
SICK OF FOLLOWING FOOLS, HUH? WHAT ABOUT DART?
TELL ME WHAT MAKES HIM DIFFERENT?!
THAT'S IT!
WHOOOOF!
DART, LET ME...
NO! THIS HAS BEEN FESTERING A WHILE. LET THEM GO FOR NOW -- DRAIN THE POISON...
WHOOP!!

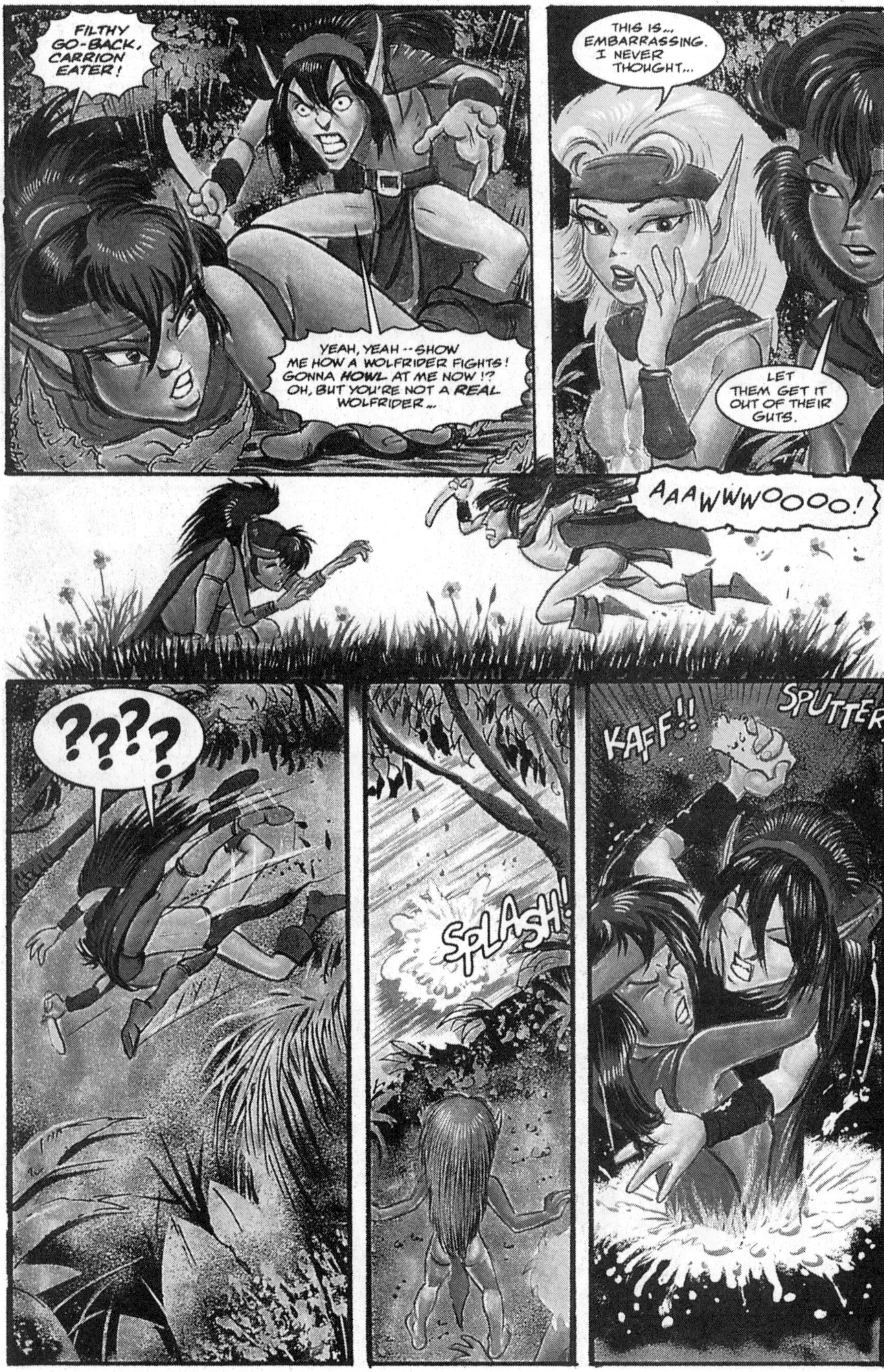
FILTHY GO-BACK, CARRION EATER!
YEAH, YEAH -- SHOW ME HOW A WOLFRIDER FIGHTS! GONNA HOWL AT ME NOW!? OH, BUT YOU'RE NOT A REAL WOLFRIDER...
THIS IS... EMBARRASSING. I NEVER THOUGHT...
LET THEM GET IT OUT OF THEIR GUTS.
AAAWWWOOOOO!
????
SPLASH!
KAFF!!
SPUTTER!

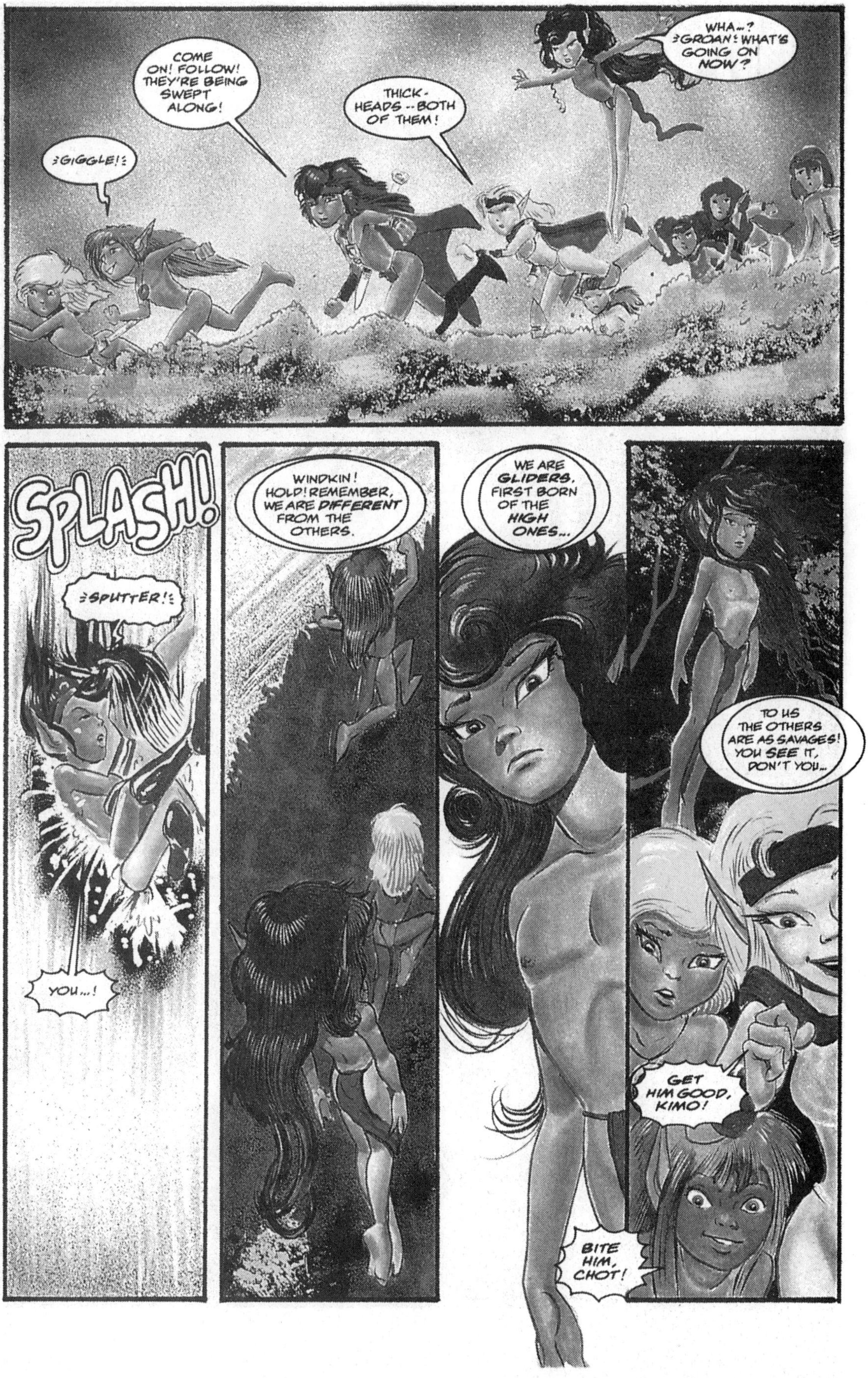

:GIGGLE!:
COME ON! FOLLOW! THEY'RE BEING SWEPT ALONG!
THICK-HEADS -- BOTH OF THEM!
WHA...? :GROAN!: WHAT'S GOING ON NOW?
SPLASH!
:SPUTTER!:
YOU...!
WINDKIN! HOLD! REMEMBER, WE ARE DIFFERENT FROM THE OTHERS.
WE ARE GLIDERS, FIRST BORN OF THE HIGH ONES...
TO US THE OTHERS ARE AS SAVAGES! YOU SEE IT, DON'T YOU...
GET HIM GOOD, KIMO!
BITE HIM, CHOT!

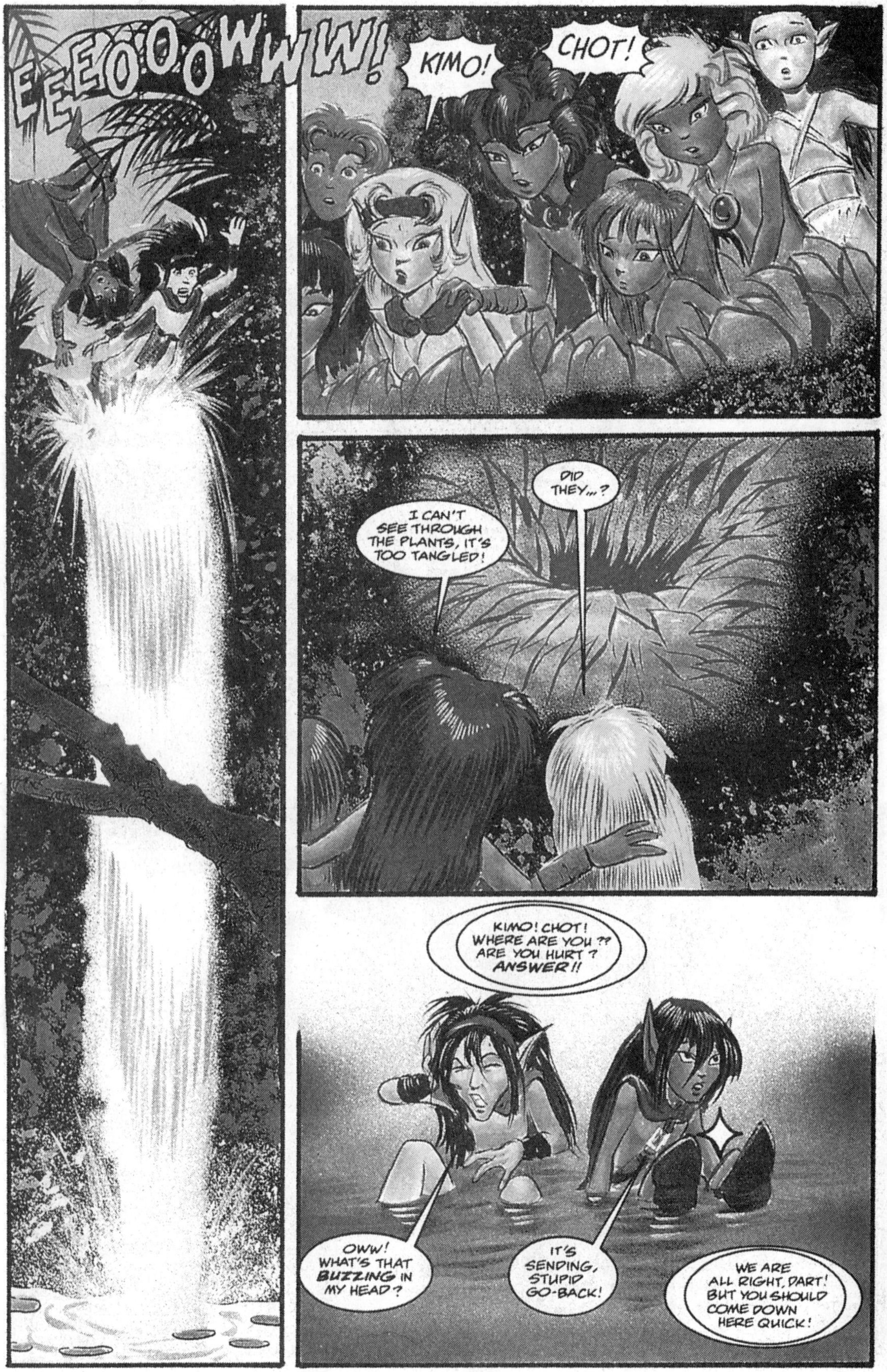
EEEOOOWWW!
KIMO!
CHOT!
I CAN'T SEE THROUGH THE PLANTS, IT'S TOO TANGLED!
DID THEY...?
KIMO! CHOT! WHERE ARE YOU?? ARE YOU HURT? ANSWER!!
OWW! WHAT'S THAT BUZZING IN MY HEAD?
IT'S SENDING, STUPID GO-BACK!
WE ARE ALL RIGHT, DART! BUT YOU SHOULD COME DOWN HERE QUICK!

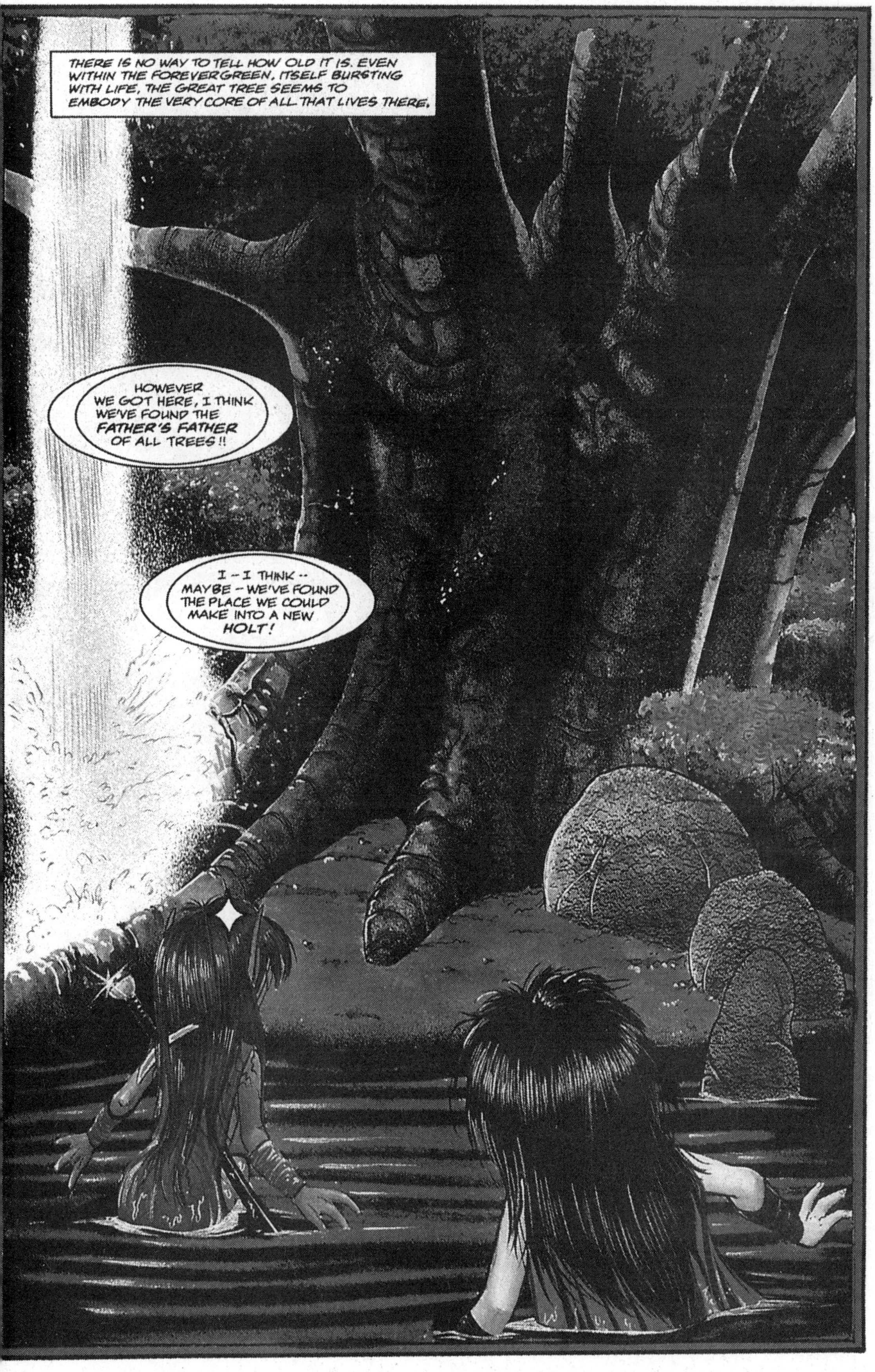
THERE IS NO WAY TO TELL HOW OLD IT IS. EVEN WITHIN THE FOREVERGREEN, ITSELF BURSTING WITH LIFE, THE GREAT TREE SEEMS TO EMBODY THE VERY CORE OF ALL THAT LIVES THERE.
HOWEVER WE GOT HERE, I THINK WE'VE FOUND THE FATHER'S FATHER OF ALL TREES!!
I -- I THINK -- MAYBE -- WE'VE FOUND THE PLACE WE COULD MAKE INTO A NEW HOLT!

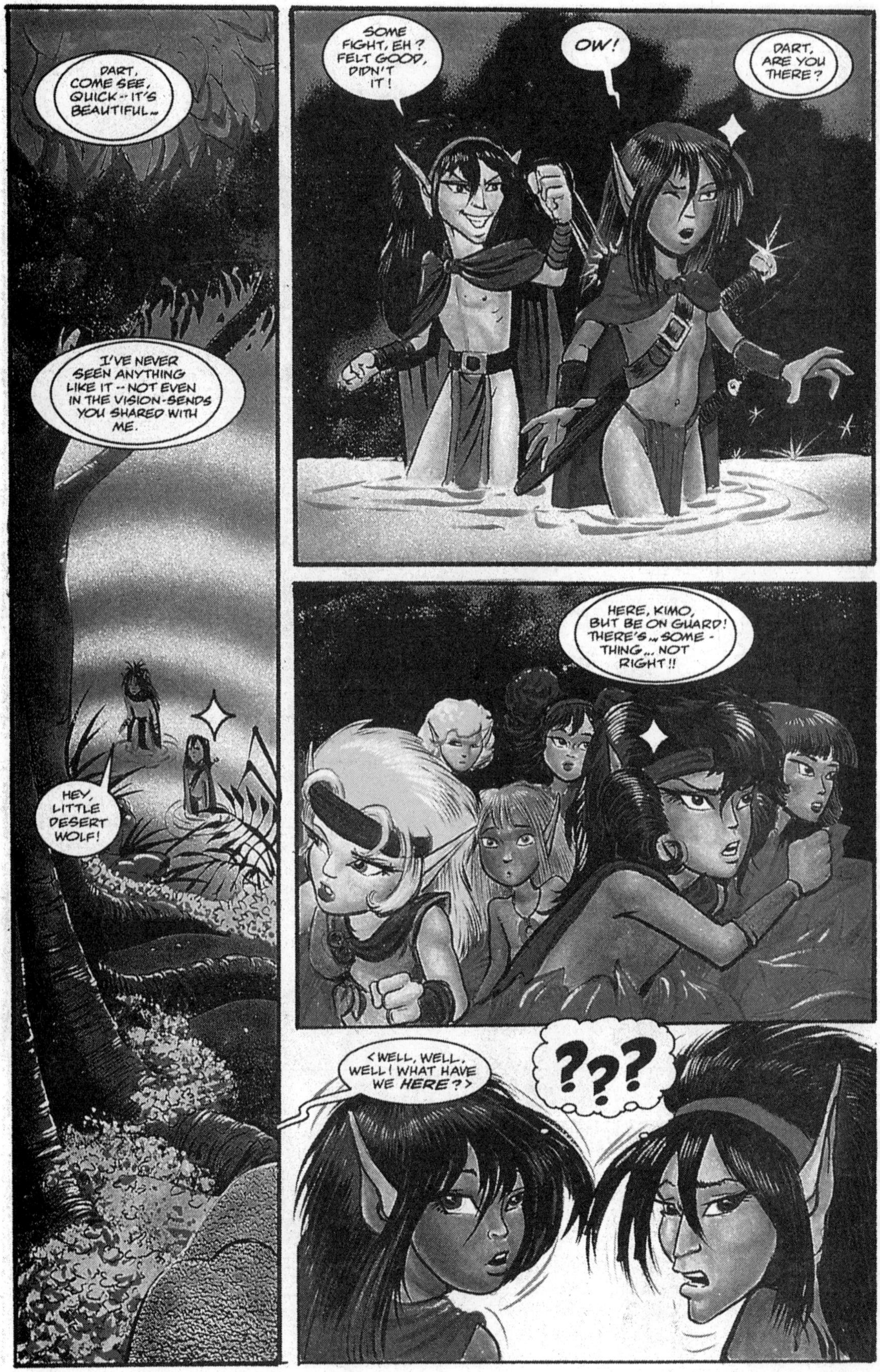
DART, COME SEE, QUICK -- IT'S BEAUTIFUL...
I'VE NEVER SEEN ANYTHING LIKE IT -- NOT EVEN IN THE VISION-SENDS YOU SHARED WITH ME.
HEY, LITTLE DESERT WOLF!
SOME FIGHT, EH? FELT GOOD, DIDN'T IT!
OW!
DART, ARE YOU THERE?
HERE, KIMO, BUT BE ON GUARD! THERE'S... SOME-THING... NOT RIGHT!!
<WELL, WELL, WELL! WHAT HAVE WE HERE?>
???

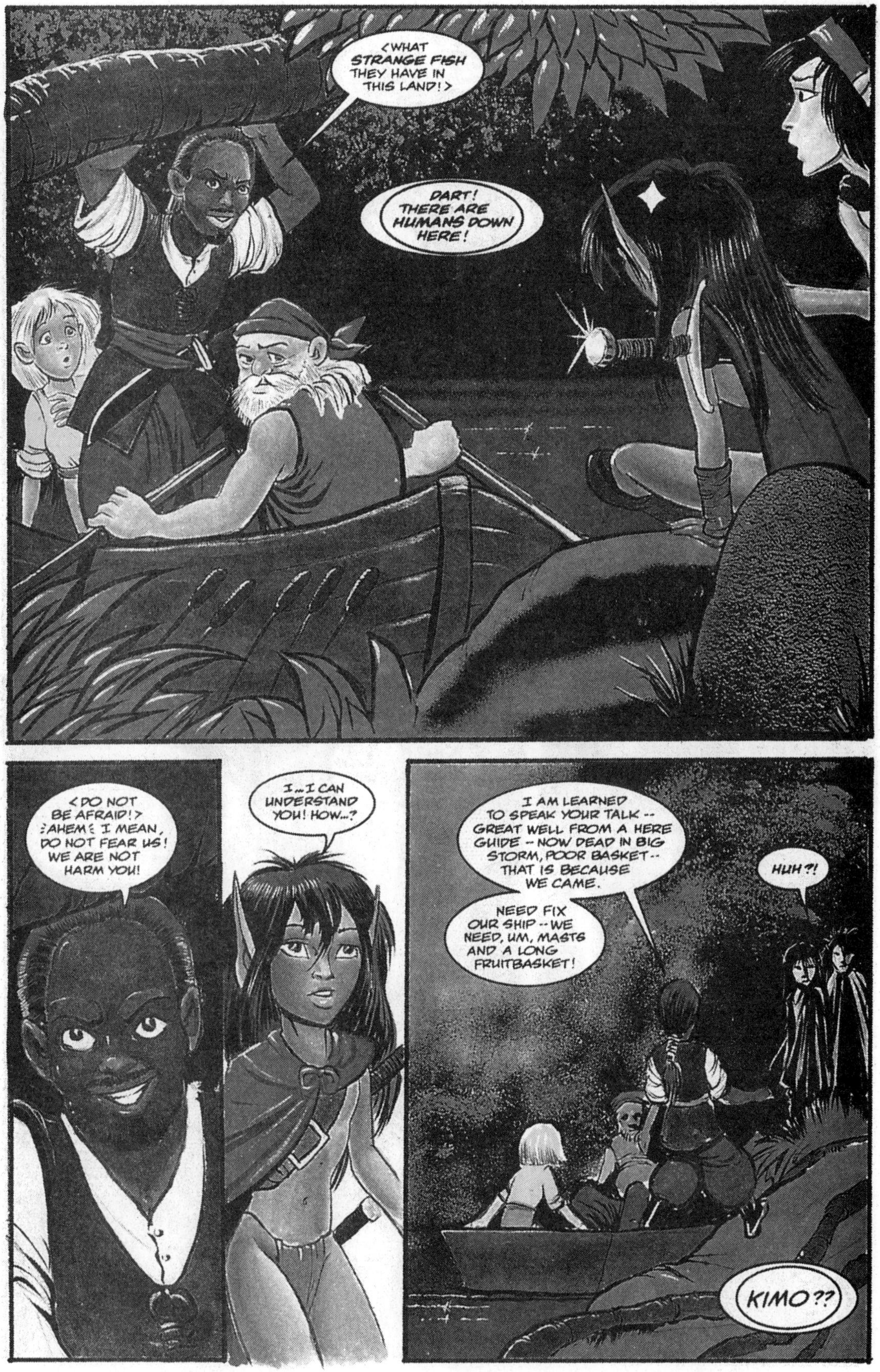
<WHAT STRANGE FISH THEY HAVE IN THIS LAND!>
DART! THERE ARE HUMANS DOWN HERE!
<DO NOT BE AFRAID!> AHEM I MEAN, DO NOT FEAR US! WE ARE NOT HARM YOU!
I...I CAN UNDERSTAND YOU! HOW...?
I AM LEARNED TO SPEAK YOUR TALK -- GREAT WELL FROM A HERE GUIDE -- NOW DEAD IN BIG STORM, POOR BASKET -- THAT IS BECAUSE WE CAME.
NEED FIX OUR SHIP -- WE NEED, UM, MASTS AND A LONG FRUITBASKET!
HUH?!
KIMO??

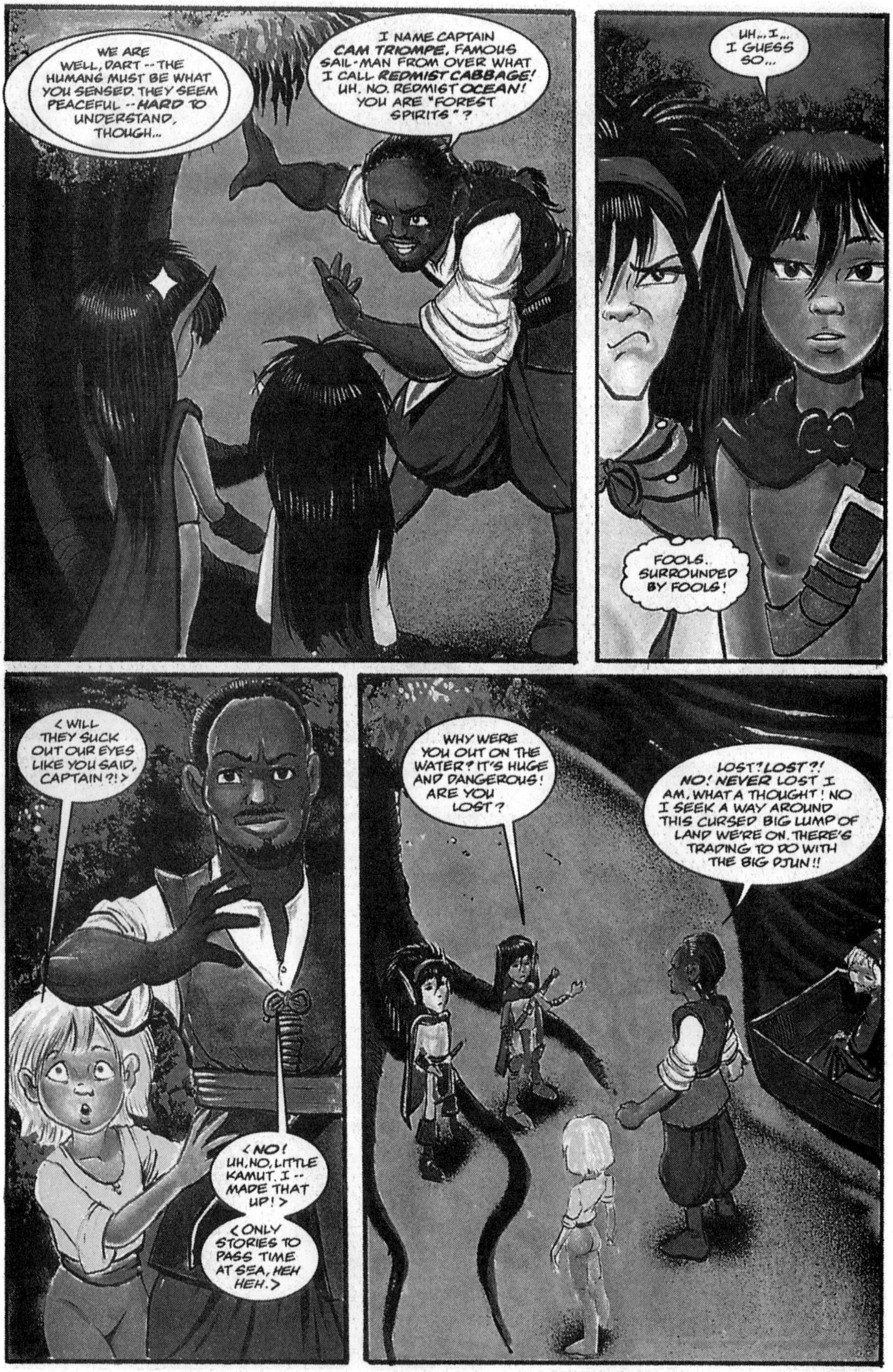
WE ARE WELL, DART -- THE HUMANS MUST BE WHAT YOU SENSED. THEY SEEM PEACEFUL -- HARD TO UNDERSTAND, THOUGH...
I NAME CAPTAIN CAM TRIOMPE, FAMOUS SAIL-MAN FROM OVER WHAT I CALL REDMIST CABBAGE! UH. NO. REDMIST OCEAN! YOU ARE "FOREST SPIRITS"?
UH... I... I GUESS SO...
FOOLS. SURROUNDED BY FOOLS!
< WILL THEY SUCK OUT OUR EYES LIKE YOU SAID, CAPTAIN?! >
< NO! UH, NO, LITTLE KAMUT. I -- MADE THAT UP! >
< ONLY STORIES TO PASS TIME AT SEA, HEH HEH. >
WHY WERE YOU OUT ON THE WATER? IT'S HUGE AND DANGEROUS! ARE YOU LOST?
LOST? LOST?! NO! NEVER LOST I AM, WHAT A THOUGHT! NO I SEEK A WAY AROUND THIS CURSED BIG LUMP OF LAND WE'RE ON. THERE'S TRADING TO DO WITH THE BIG DJUN!!

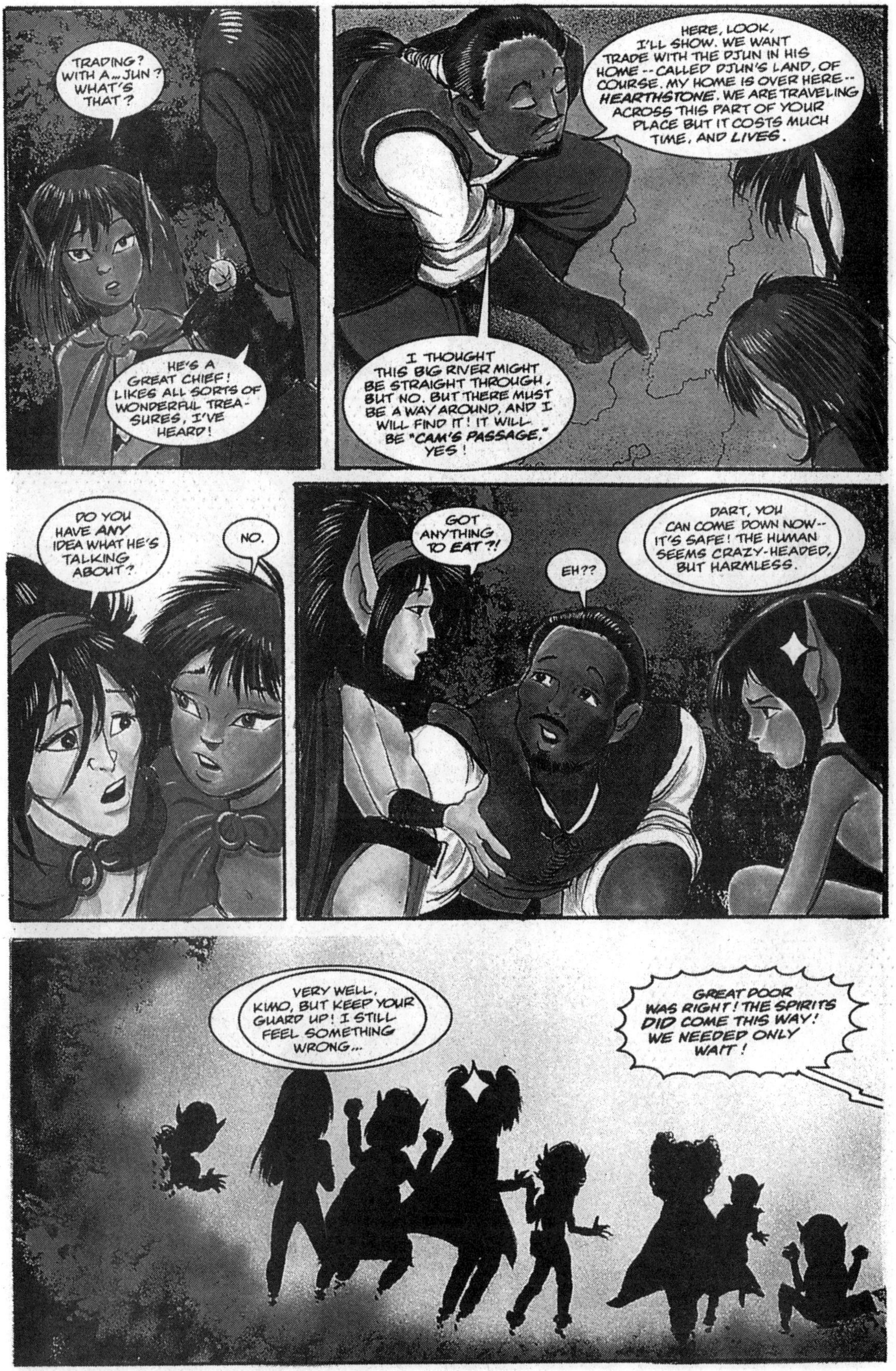
TRADING? WITH A...JUN? WHAT'S THAT?
HE'S A GREAT CHIEF! LIKES ALL SORTS OF WONDERFUL TREASURES, I'VE HEARD!
HERE, LOOK, I'LL SHOW. WE WANT TRADE WITH THE DJUN IN HIS HOME -- CALLED DJUN'S LAND, OF COURSE. MY HOME IS OVER HERE -- HEARTHSTONE. WE ARE TRAVELING ACROSS THIS PART OF YOUR PLACE BUT IT COSTS MUCH TIME, AND LIVES.
I THOUGHT THIS BIG RIVER MIGHT BE STRAIGHT THROUGH, BUT NO. BUT THERE MUST BE A WAY AROUND, AND I WILL FIND IT! IT WILL BE "CAM'S PASSAGE." YES!
DO YOU HAVE ANY IDEA WHAT HE'S TALKING ABOUT?
NO.
GOT ANYTHING TO EAT?!
EH??
DART, YOU CAN COME DOWN NOW -- IT'S SAFE! THE HUMAN SEEMS CRAZY-HEADED, BUT HARMLESS.
VERY WELL, KIMO, BUT KEEP YOUR GUARD UP! I STILL FEEL SOMETHING WRONG...
GREAT DOOR WAS RIGHT! THE SPIRITS DID COME THIS WAY! WE NEEDED ONLY WAIT!

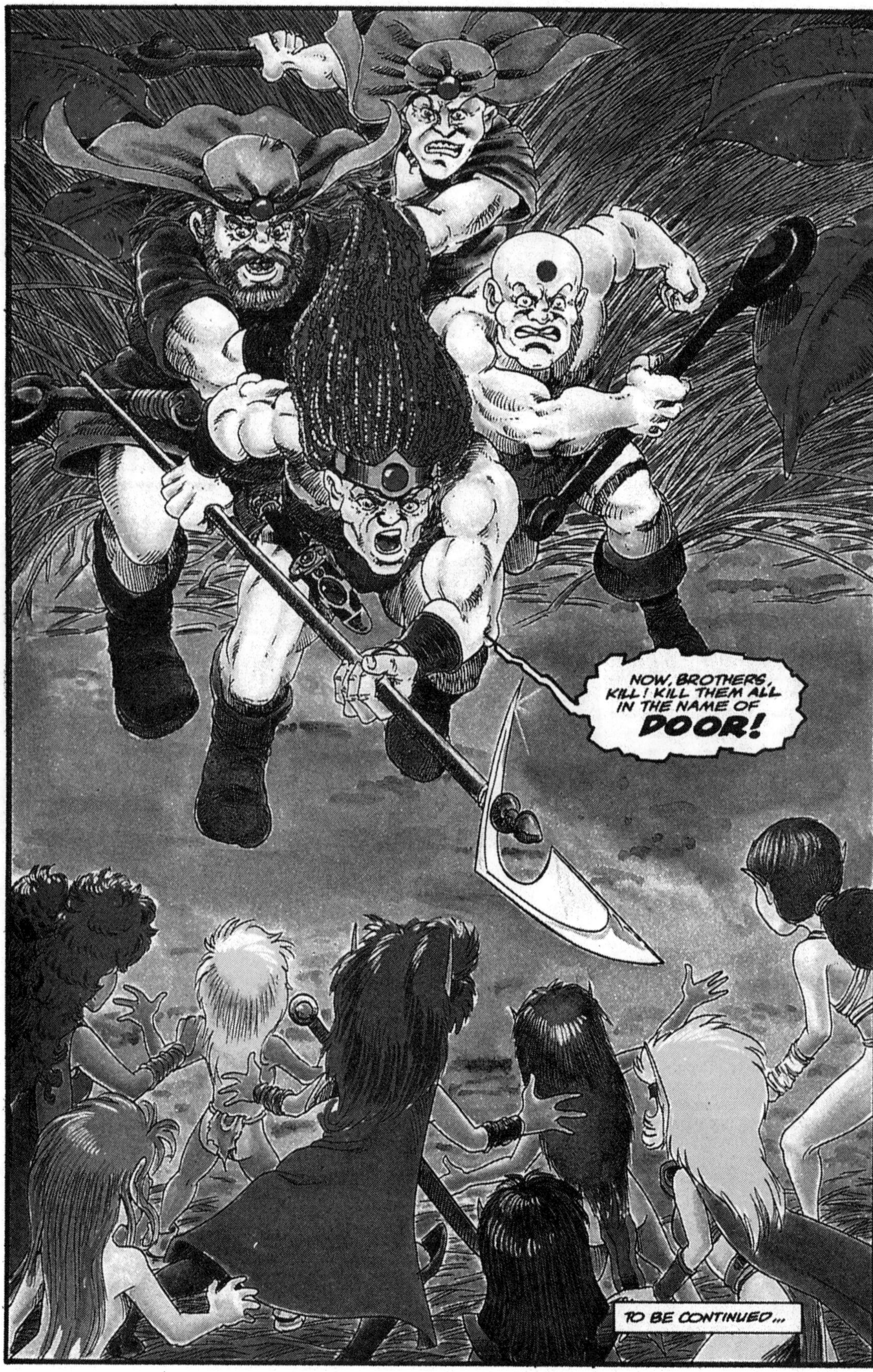
NOW, BROTHERS, KILL! KILL THEM ALL IN THE NAME OF DOOR!
TO BE CONTINUED...

The storm clouds
build on the horizon.
The players take their sides
in battles that no one can win.
Sorrow's End has fallen.
Will the Forevergreen be next?

The tale concludes in
volume 15b, "Phoenix."

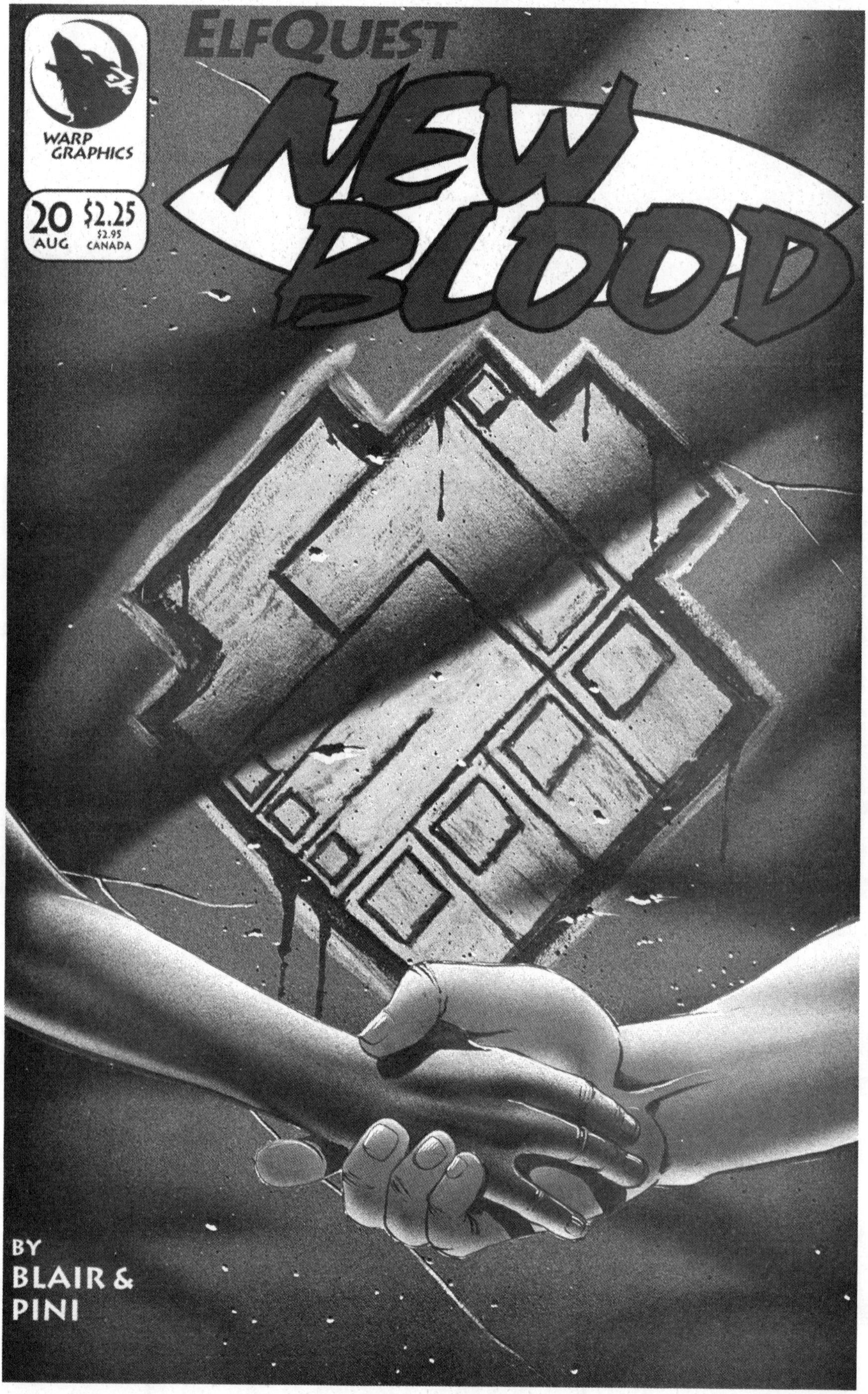
WARP GRAPHICS
ElfQuest
New Blood
20 AUG
$2.25
$2.95 CANADA
BY
BLAIR &
PINI

WARP GRAPHICS

ELFQUEST
NEW BLOOD

21 SEP
$2.25
$2.95 CANADA

BY
BLAIR &
PINI

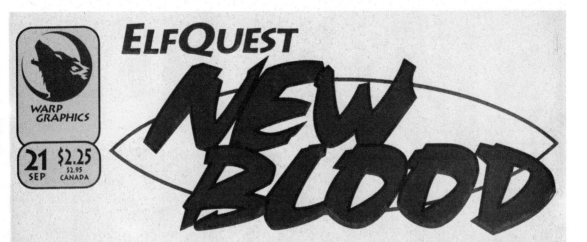

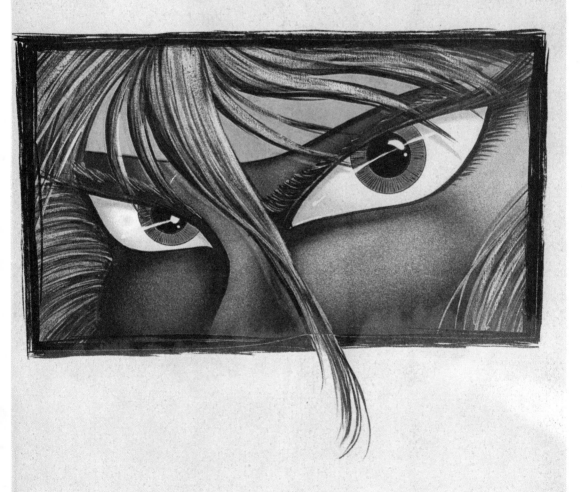

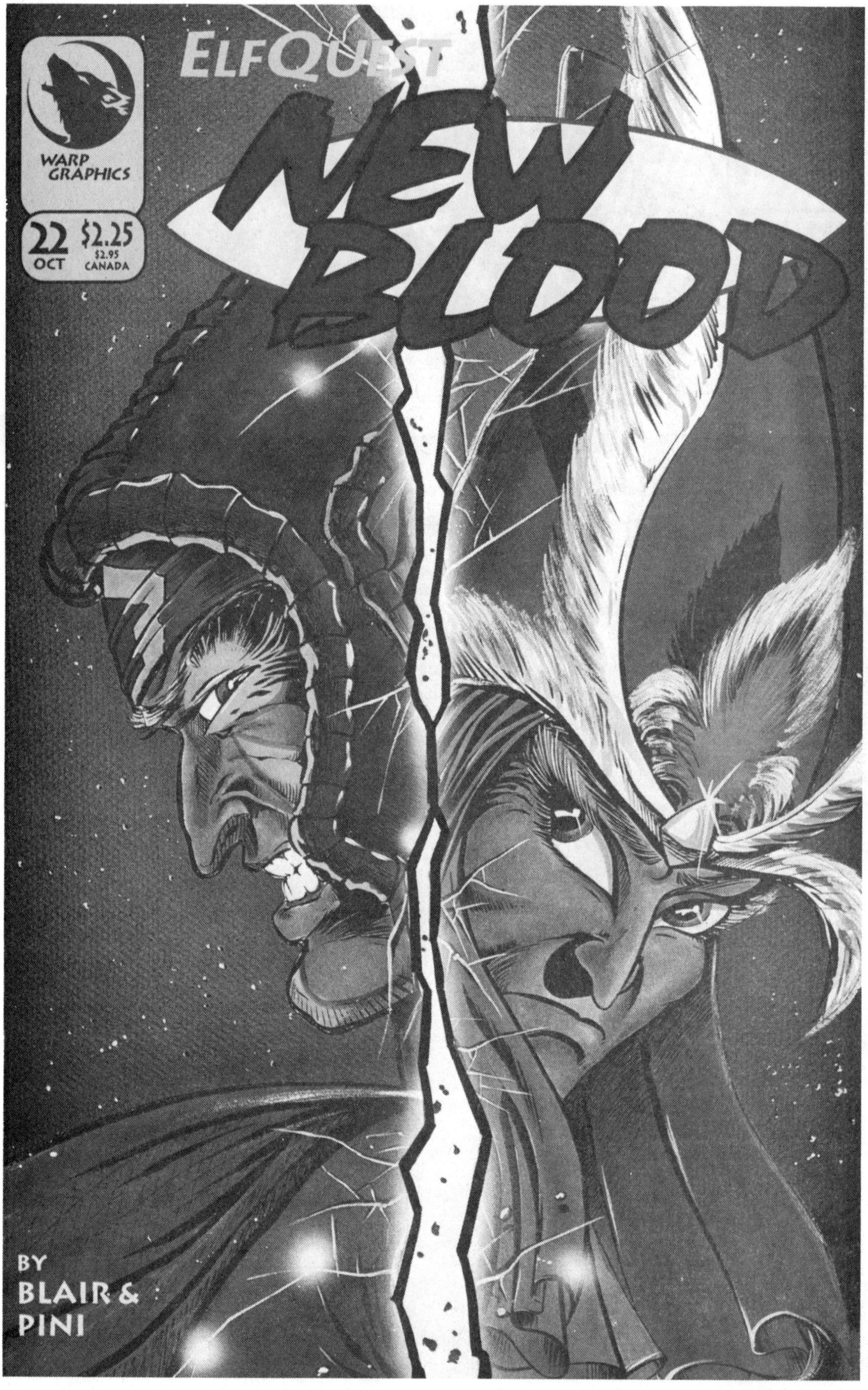
ElfQuest
WARP GRAPHICS
22
OCT
$2.25
$2.95 CANADA
NEW BLOOD
BY
BLAIR &
PINI

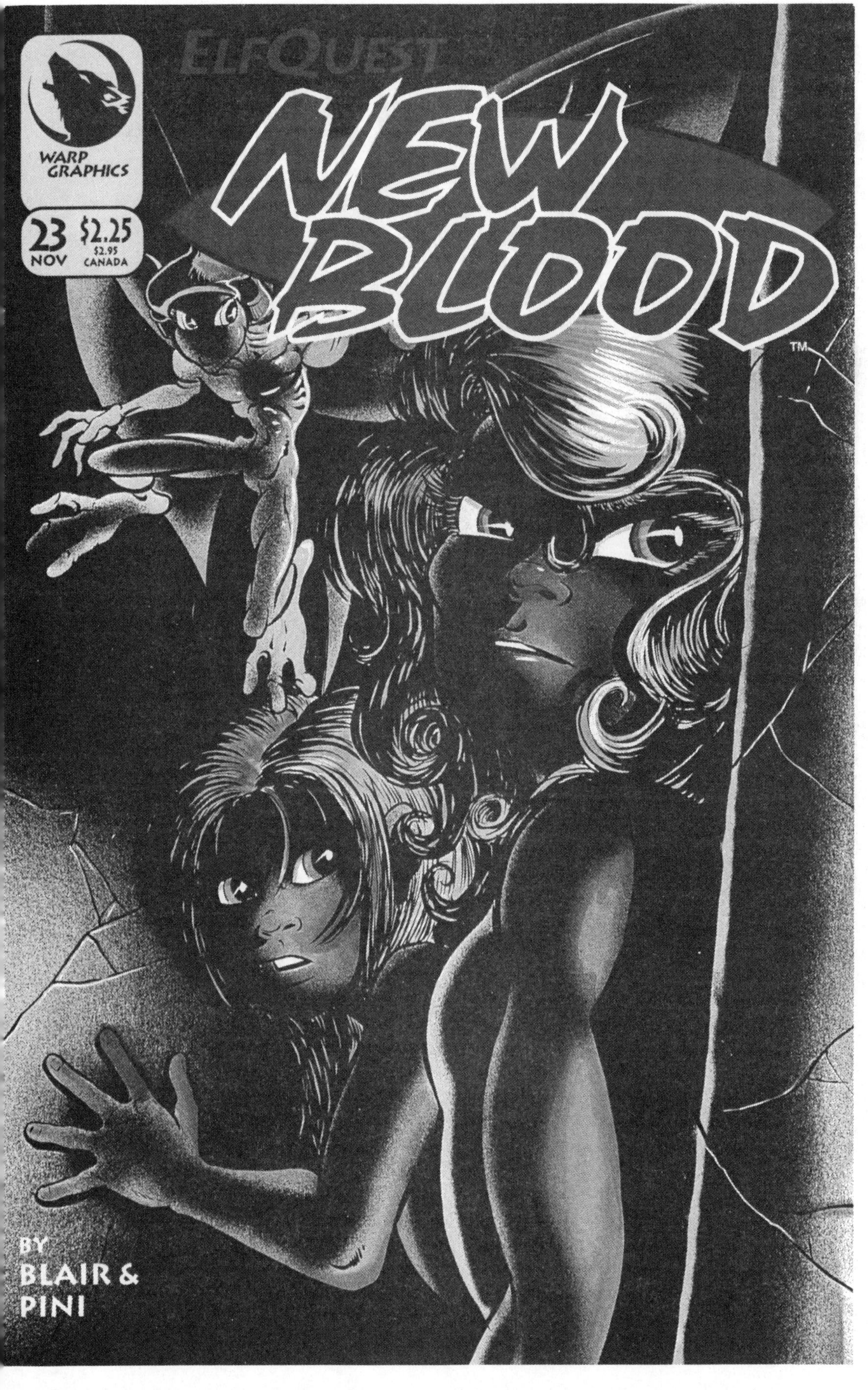

WARP GRAPHICS
ElfQuest
New Blood™
23 NOV
$2.25 $2.95 CANADA
BY BLAIR & PINI

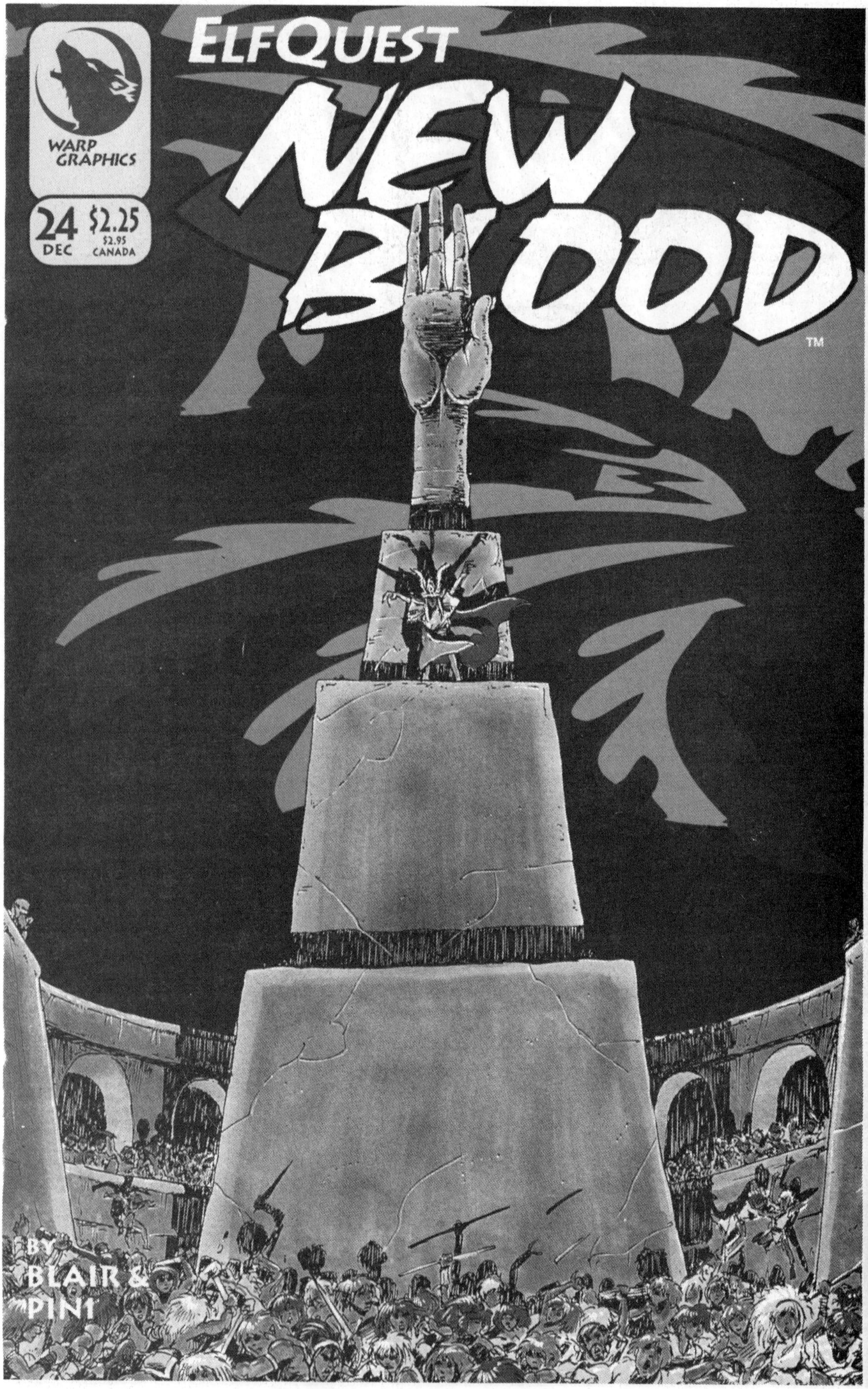

WARP GRAPHICS
24 DEC
$2.25
$2.95 CANADA
ElfQuest
NEW BLOOD
TM
BY BLAIR & PINI

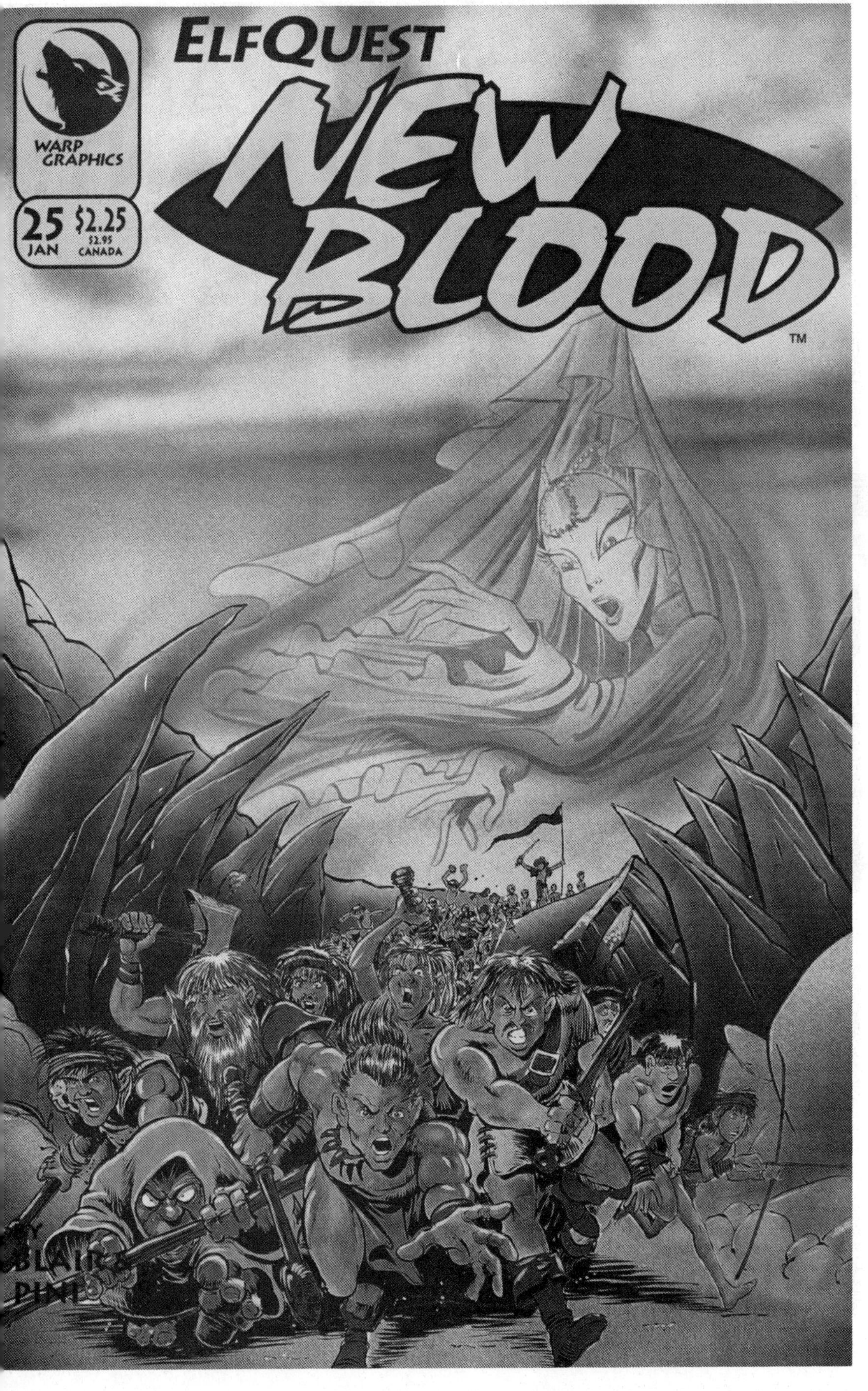
WARP GRAPHICS
25 JAN
$2.25
$2.95 CANADA
ELFQUEST
NEW BLOOD
TM
BLAIR
PINI

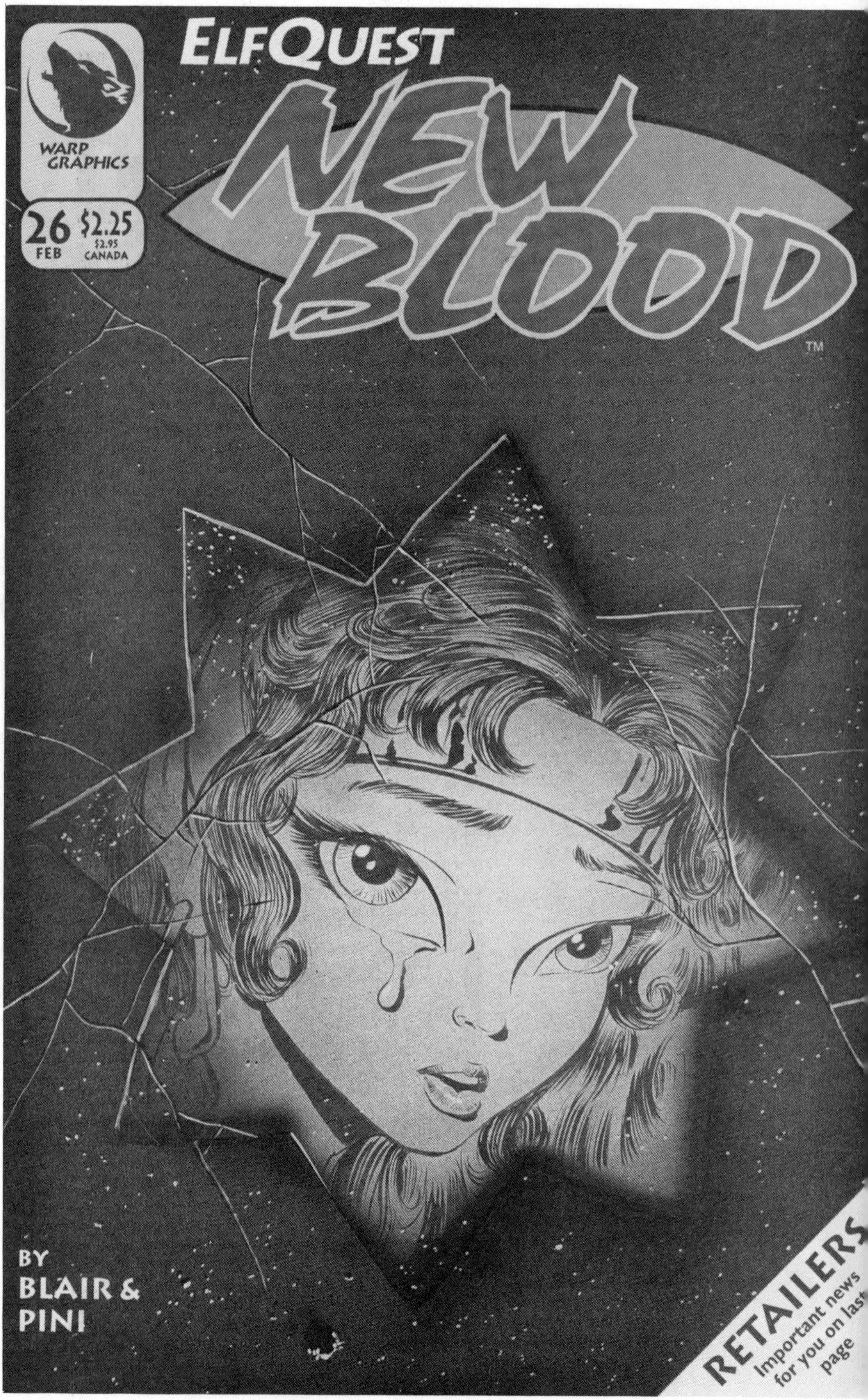
WARP GRAPHICS
26 FEB
$2.25
$2.95 CANADA
ElfQuest
NEW BLOOD
TM
BY BLAIR & PINI
RETAILERS
Important news for you on last page

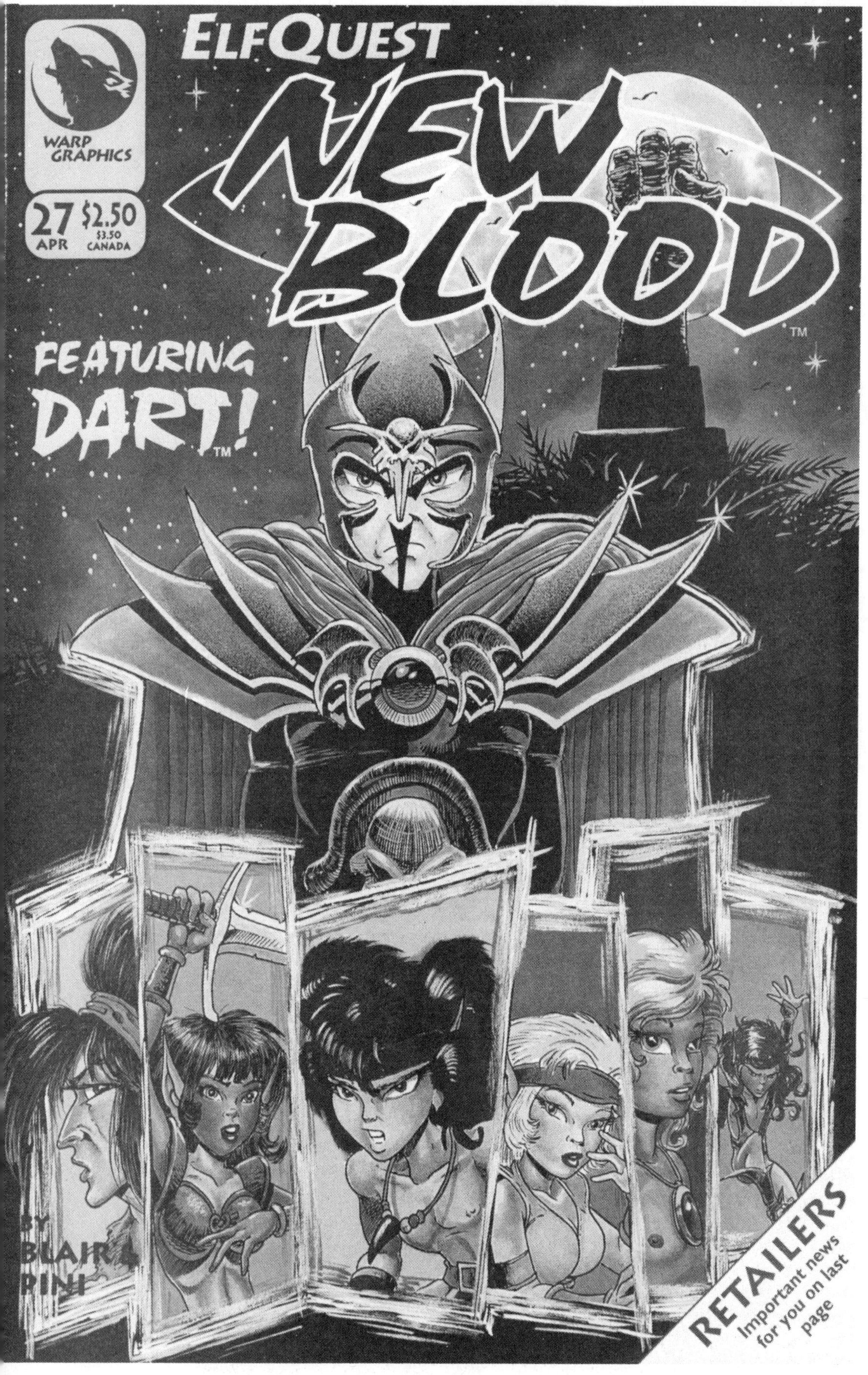

WARP GRAPHICS
27 APR
$2.50
$3.50 CANADA
ElfQuest
NEW BLOOD
™
FEATURING DART!
™
BY BLAIR & PINI
RETAILERS
Important news for you on last page